# PUBLICATIONS BY RICHARD PIPES

**WORKS:**

*Formation of the Soviet Union* (Harvard, 1954; revised ed., 1964)

*Karamzin's Memoir on Ancient and Modern Russia* (Harvard, 1959)

*Social Democracy and the Saint Petersburg Labor Movement* (Harvard, 1963)

*Europe Since 1815* (Harper & Row, 1970)

*Struve: Liberal on the Left, 1870–1905* (Harvard, 1970)

*Russia Under the Old Regime* (Scribners, 1974)

*Struve: Liberal on the Right, 1905–1944* (Harvard, 1980)

*U.S.-Soviet Relations in the Era of Détente* (Westview, 1981)

**WORKS EDITED:**

Giles Fletcher, *Of the Russe Commonwealth (1591)* (Harvard, 1966, with John Fine)

*The Russian Intelligentsia* (Columbia University Press, 1961)

*Revolutionary Russia* (Harvard, 1968)

*Collected Works in Fifteen Volumes* (P. B. Struve) (Ann Arbor, MI, 1970)

*Soviet Strategy in Europe* (Crane, Russak, 1976)

# SURVIVAL IS NOT ENOUGH

## Soviet Realities and America's Future

### Richard Pipes

SIMON AND SCHUSTER
NEW YORK

Copyright © 1984 by Richard Pipes
All rights reserved including the right of reproduction in whole or in part
in any form

Published by Simon and Schuster, A Division of Simon & Schuster, Inc.

Simon & Schuster Building
Rockefeller Center
1230 Avenue of the Americas
New York, New York 10020

SIMON AND SCHUSTER and colophon are registered trademarks of
Simon & Schuster, Inc.

Designed by Jennie Nichols/Levavi & Levavi

Manufactured in the United States of America

10  9  8  7  6  5  4  3  2  1

Library of Congress Cataloging in Publication Data

Pipes, Richard.
    Survival is not enough.

    Bibliography: p.
    Includes index.
    1. Soviet Union—Politics and government—1953–        .
2. Communism—Soviet Union.   3. Soviet Union—Economic
conditions—1975–        .   4. Soviet Union—Foreign
relations—United States.   5. United States—Foreign
relations—Soviet Union.   6. Peace.   I. Title.
DK274.P53   1984        327.73047        84-13848
ISBN 0-671-49535-6

The author is grateful for permission to use the following:

"Bargaining Chips"—copyright © 1983 by Herblock in *The Washington Post.*

"Comparison of Existing NATO/Warsaw Pact Land-Based Surface-to-Surface War-
    heads in Europe (Aggregate Yield in Approximate Megatons)" from USSI Report
    83-1, *The Nuclear "Balance" in Europe: Status, Trends and Implications,* by Donald
    Cotter et al. (Washington, D.C., United States Strategic Institute).

Cartoon by Steiger from *Frankfurter Allgemeine Zeitung* (May 22, 1981).

# ACKNOWLEDGMENTS

I would like to express my appreciation to Ambassador Edward Rowny, Professor Michael Voslensky and Professor Wolfgang Leonhard for the valuable advice they gave me on various parts of the book. They are not responsible, of course, for any opinion contained in it. My assistant, Ms. Nellie Hauke, has also earned my gratitude for her dedicated work.

# CONTENTS

FOREWORD                                                        11

_____ Chapter I _____
THE COMMUNIST SYSTEM    17

1. The historic background                                17
2. The *nomenklatura*                                     29
3. The Stalinist economic system                          33
4. Soviet imperialism                                     37
5. The psychology of the *nomenklatura*                   44

_____ Chapter II _____
THE SOVIET THREAT    49

1. Soviet Grand Strategy                                  51
2. Soviet political strategy                              60
3. Soviet military strategy                               83
4. Strategy in the Third World                           102

_____ Chapter III _____
THE ECONOMIC CRISIS    110

1. General remarks about the economic crisis             111
2. Agriculture                                           120

3. Living standards     127
4. Population trends     128
5. Foreign debts     132
6. Attempts at economic reform     136
7. The second economy     142

————————— Chapter IV —————————
## THE POLITICAL CRISIS   148

1. The corrupt Party     149
2. Intellectual dissent     158
    A. The Westernizing (democratic) opposition     163
    B. The nationalist opposition     169
3. Imperial problems     178
    A. The Soviet Union and its nationalities     179
    B. The colonies     186
    C. The dependencies     188
    D. Communist parties     193
    E. China     198
4. Can the Soviet Union reform?     199

————————— Chapter V —————————
## WHAT CAN WE DO?   209

1. Past patterns of U.S.-Soviet relations     211
    A. Containment     218
    B. Détente     220
2. Strategic opportunities for the United States     222
3. The military aspect     224
4. The political aspect     246
    A. Party politics     247
    B. The Alliance     248
5. The economic aspect     259
6. Who should be in charge of policy toward the USSR?     273
7. Concluding remarks     277

NOTES     283
INDEX     291

# FOREWORD

The subject matter of this book demands no justification: relations between the United States and the Soviet Union and the means of preventing their disagreements from erupting into nuclear war have an obvious significance. What does call for an explanation is the rationale for yet another work in a field which is crowded already and every aspect of which seems to have been subjected to exhaustive treatment.

My reason for writing derives from the conviction that the existing literature on U.S.-Soviet relations and the nuclear threat suffers from a serious flaw: it treats these subjects almost exclusively as problems confronting the United States, to be debated and decided upon by Americans. The Soviet regime, with its interests, ideology and political strategy, is regarded in this context as only tangentially involved. It manifests an extraordinary insularity as well as arrogance on the part of Americans to regard "the fate of the earth" as dependent on what they think and do, as if the other party to the equation were nothing but a passive agent, capable only of reacting.

The shelves are full of books on the Soviet Union which describe in vivid detail conditions in that country: the political and cultural oppression, the social inequalities and corruption, the all-pervasive drabness. This literature is designed to satisfy the curiosity of the Western public about daily life in a country which impinges on it in so many ways and yet falls very much outside the range of its experience. Even the best books of this genre, however, make no connection between the Soviet system and Soviet foreign policy. They are, fundamentally, accounts of travelers returned from journeys to an exotic land, fascinating as human documents but politically irrelevant. Even in the specialized, professional literature on the political and economic system of the USSR, the link between its internal order and its international conduct is rarely established. The issue is treated as if what a country is at home and what it does abroad were two separate and self-contained matters.

Now this cannot be. Historical evidence indicates that the foreign policy of every country is a function of its domestic conditions and an extension of its internal policies. The foreign conduct of a state may be strongly affected by the international environment in which it has to operate, but the impulses invariably come from within. Hence, the regime which Moscow maintains inside the Soviet Union and in other areas under its control should be for the West a matter not of mere curiosity but of the greatest and most immediate relevance. The manner in which a government treats its own citizens obviously has great bearing on the way it will treat other nations. A regime that does not respect legal norms inside its borders is not likely to show respect for them abroad. If it wages war against its own people, it can hardly be expected to live at peace with the rest of the world. That intimate connection between the internal order prevailing in Communist countries and their external behavior, which Western authors virtually ignore, is clearly understood by intellectuals who live in these countries. They plead with the West to grasp that how Communist governments treat their citizens constitutes not only a violation of human rights but a direct challenge to the West's own vital interests. "States with totalitarian political systems are a threat to world peace," a group of Polish intellectuals stated in a recent appeal to Western "peace" movements; "the necessity for aggressive expansion arises wherever authority is based on force and lies, wherever societies are deprived of the possibility of influencing government policy, wherever governments fear those over whom they rule and against whom they conduct wars . . . The sole ideology of the adherents of totalitarianism is the maintenance of power by any means. In the present crisis, even war can be considered an acceptable price for this aim."

The author subscribes to this interpretation, and this shapes the contents as well as the argument of his book. The bulk of its contents is devoted to the Soviet system: its structure, its political interests and strategy, its strengths and weaknesses. This feature alone distinguishes it from most of the existing works on the subject, which address themselves primarily to American policies and their options. The book opens with a discussion of the essential feature of the political system prevailing in the USSR and its colonies, which is absolute rule by an oligarchy of Party officials who not only monopolize political authority but literally own their countries and everything that lies within their boundaries. It is the author's contention that its internal position commits the Communist oligarchy to engage in militarism and expansionism, and that as long as it is able to maintain its present status, international tension, with all the risks it carries, is unavoidable, no matter what the Western powers do. The discussion then proceeds to the methods which the Communist oligarchy employs to expand its influence abroad. This is depicted in terms of a "Grand Strategy" whose principal objective is global hegemony and whose principal means is political attrition. The middle chapters of the book are devoted to the economic and political crises which Communist regimes presently experience and which inhibit their ambitions and even endanger their authority. These crises, which include declining rates of economic growth, the emergence of an uncontrolled "second" or free economy, widespread corruption, political dissent, and the demographic decline of Slavs, cannot be overcome by repressive measures: they confront these regimes with the necessity of thoroughgoing internal reforms. The author concludes from this evidence that a growing discrepancy is emerging between the global aspirations of the Communist elite and the means at its disposal, that this elite is finding it increasingly difficult to pursue its global ambitions and to maintain intact the Stalinist system. While the Soviet government is in no danger of imminent collapse, it cannot forever "muddle through" and will have to choose before long between reducing its aspirations to worldwide hegemony and transforming its internal regime, and perhaps even find it necessary to do the one and the other.

These premises determine the practical recommendations contained in the concluding section of the book. The principal point they make is that the West, in its own interest, ought to assist those economic and political forces which are at work inside the Communist Bloc undermining the system and pressuring its elites to turn their attention inward. Experience has shown time and again that attempts to restrain Soviet aggressiveness by a combination of rewards and punishments do not accomplish their purpose because they address the symptoms of the problem, namely aggression, instead of its cause, which is the system itself. This is a call not for subverting Communism but for letting Communism subvert itself. By neutralizing its military threat and, at the same time, withholding those political concessions and that economic assistance which enables the Soviet elite to maintain the status quo, the West may well, in time, help to force it to emulate the example set by the post-Mao leadership in China and alter its priorities. For this to happen, the Communist elites must be subjected to the maximal internal pressures which the system itself generates. It is a central thesis of this book that the Soviet regime will become less aggressive only as a result of failures and worries about its ability to govern effectively and not from a sense of enhanced security and confidence.

The whole set of issues connected with the danger of nuclear war is addressed here in the same context of Soviet politics. Western books on the "bomb" look upon it as if it were some new breed of deadly bacillus, instead of a manmade device. They concentrate on the disastrous consequences of a nuclear exchange, by now familiar to most people, and ignore the men who design them, deploy them, and formulate a strategy for their eventual use. The consequence of this abstract approach is that the danger appears to come not from enmity and lawlessness but from the building of bombs, which again confuses effect with cause. After all, the United States border with Canada has been peaceful for nearly two centuries not because it is disarmed; rather, it is disarmed because it has been peaceful. It has been one of the most spectacular accomplishments of Soviet diplomacy and propaganda to persuade much of the Western public that the threat to its survival and way of life stems not from Soviet intentions and actions but from inanimate objects. This stratagem has achieved two objectives. In the first place, it has concentrated everyone's attention on the West's efforts at rearmament while the much grander military programs of the USSR have been discreetly concealed. In the second place it has enabled Moscow to create in the public mind a spurious identity of interest between East and West that overshadows all the genuine differences in their values and aspirations.

In sum, the principal purpose of this book is to alter the nature of the discussion on East-West relations and the means of preventing nuclear war by shifting attention from internal American concerns and disagreements to Soviet realities.

Richard Pipes

*Where there is less fear,
there is generally
less danger.*

—*LIVY*

# CHAPTER

# I

# THE COMMUNIST SYSTEM

## 1 THE HISTORIC BACKGROUND

In its present form, the Communist system of the Soviet Union and its dependencies is the product of two factors: the Russian political tradition and the ideology of Marxism-Leninism. Neither of these factors, taken by themselves, can explain the structure and the behavior of Communist regimes. This hybrid has been produced by the grafting of a modern ideology on the ancient stock of Russian statehood.

The Russian state came into being early in the fourteenth century and developed under conditions very different from those familiar to Western readers.* Its home lay in the forest regions of northwestern Eurasia, a territory with an unlimited supply of land but poor soil and a climate unfavorable to agriculture. For many centuries the Russians carried on a semi-nomadic form of cultivation which involved ceaseless movement in search of virgin soil. Because of their mobility, they could not develop advanced forms

---

* A full account of the growth of the Russian state can be found in my book *Russia Under the Old Regime* (New York, 1974).

of social and political organization, which demand a sedentary population with territorial roots. Such social institutions as they did develop were of a rudimentary kind. State and society led separate existences; in medieval Russia, the former represented primarily a military force that protected the land from foreign assaults and went on the offensive to conquer new territories for settlement whenever it felt stronger than its neighbors. This background exerted strong influence on the character of the Russian monarchy, which developed in the fifteenth and sixteenth centuries with a capital in Moscow.

**1.** Russia had no feudalism which, in the West, enabled powerful lay and clerical figures to usurp monarchical authority; instead, it experienced a dispersion of authority among numerous independent princes. While in Western Europe the creation of the modern state required the kings to retrieve the authority that had been taken away from them, in Russia it called for conquest and absorption of independent principalities under a single ruler. Thus, from early times, territorial expansion became in Russia a hallmark of sovereignty.

**2.** The northwestern regions where the Russian state was formed were sparsely populated. They were subsequently colonized by the princes, who provided the settlers with protection and the means with which to transform wilderness into habitable land. Because of this role, Russian rulers came to regard their realms as private property. A regime in which sovereignty and property—that is, political authority and ownership—are fused is known as "patrimonial." Russia was a classic patrimonial regime until the middle of the eighteenth century, when, with the introduction of the concept of private property, it began to undergo a gradual evolution toward governmental forms of the Western type.

**3.** Russia adopted Christianity not from Rome, as did Western Europe, but from Byzantium. After Byzantium had fallen to the Turks in 1453, Russia was for all practical purposes the only state left in the world professing Orthodox Christianity. Separated from the heretical Latins and the infidel Muslims, who surrounded Russia in the west and east, its rulers, clergy and common people developed a sense of national-religious uniqueness rather than one of belonging to a broader, supranational community. This tended to produce in Russians a feeling of being isolated and under permanent siege, even though their relatively inaccessible location ensured them of a high degree of protection from foreign invasions.

From this historic legacy flow a number of consequences of great importance for the understanding of Russian political culture—a culture that greatly influences Russian political behavior, whatever the declared objectives of the government in power.

□ Until quite modern times (the end of the eighteenth century) Russia was unfamiliar with the distinction between political authority and the rights of private ownership, a distinction fundamental to the Western political tradition. Professor Charles McIlwain, in his survey of Western political thought, concluded that if he were asked to produce one maxim that best reflected the political thought of the West in the late Middle Ages, he would choose an aphorism of Seneca's: "To kings belongs authority over all; to private persons, property." [1] This crucial distinction has very shallow roots in Russian political thought and practice, which accounts for some of the greatest differences between the behavior of Russian and Western governments.

□ The lack of a feudal tradition meant, among other things, the absence in Russia of the concept of law as a force superior to human will, binding alike on rulers and subjects. Russian governments have always tended to regard law as a device for controlling the population—that is, as a tool of administration, rather than as a principle regulating relations between themselves and their people.

□ Because they viewed the population under their control as private property, Russian rulers of premodern times imposed on all their subjects ties of bondage. They required the landowning gentry to render the monarchy lifelong military or civil service and enserfed virtually all the commoners, compelling them to work either for the rulers or for their service class. Until the middle of the eighteenth century, there were in Russia, for all practical purposes, no freemen endowed with rights; there were only bondsmen endowed with duties who directly or indirectly served the Crown. As recently as the middle of the eighteenth century, in the central provinces of Russia, 85 percent of the population consisted of people bonded either to the state or to landlords; they enjoyed neither legal status nor rights of any kind.

The political culture of Russia is thus very short on the notions of private property, law and human rights, and long on everything that serves to enhance the might of the state. The state, for its part, tends to be expansionist and to feel no allegiance to any supranational community, such as was common among the peoples of Christian Europe or the Islamic world.

The evolution of Russia from the patrimonial tradition to the Western began in the late seventeenth century and accelerated after the accession of Peter the Great. The impetus toward Westernization came largely from the awareness that the West was richer and stronger, and that if Russia hoped to attain the rank of a first-rate European power it had to model itself on the West. The initial motive for Westernization was military—namely, the inability of Russian troops in the seventeenth century to stand up to the better organized and equipped forces of Sweden and Turkey. Awareness of this inferiority led Peter the Great to carry out major reforms. Subsequently, in an effort to keep up with Europe in other than military respects, still more fundamental changes were introduced. In 1762 the gentry were freed from compulsory state service, and ninety-nine years later serfdom was abolished. The principle of private property was introduced in the late eighteenth century; as the Russian economy developed, the traditional fusion of sovereignty and property began to break down. Legal codes, trials by jury, and other judiciary reforms, enacted in the middle of the nineteenth century, introduced into Russia the law as a force regulating relations among citizens (though not relations between the state and citizens, for the state continued to stand above the law).

Even while Westernizing, the Russian monarchy clung tenaciously to the monopoly on political power. It refused to share legislative authority with society long after the other European governments, including Turkey, had introduced constitutional and parliamentary institutions. Russia was governed by a bureaucracy responsible only to the tsar until October 1905, when humiliating defeats in a war with Japan and the nationwide civil disorders that followed compelled the monarchy to concede to the country a constitution and a legislative parliament. But old habits died hard, and in the few years that it had left before its collapse, the monarchy regularly contravened the constitution. The absence of political institutions effectively linking the Crown with its own people contributed greatly to the downfall of tsarism in 1917 and to the chaos that ensued.

Political culture, shaped by a nation's historic experience, enters the nation's bloodstream and changes as slowly and reluctantly as does language or customs. Revolutionary governments may attempt by means of decrees to reshape this culture to their liking, but in the end they are invariably defeated: the fate of revolutions everywhere indicates that instead of traditions changing to suit revolutions, revolutions sooner or later accommodate themselves to traditions. The fate of Marxism in Russia provides an excellent illustration of this rule.

Socialism, of which "Marxism-Leninism" is an offshoot, originated in the West. Formulated in France and Germany, it was imported into Russia in the middle of the nineteenth century and promptly attracted support among the country's educated, public-minded elite, the so-called intelligentsia. Because it is an ideology imported from abroad, many Russian conservatives, both before 1917 and since, have blamed it for Russia's revolutionary excesses. This argument enables them to ascribe to the West their country's misfortunes; this is the position taken by Dostoevsky one hundred years ago, and by Solzhenitsyn today. The position, however, is unconvincing, because the very same socialist ideology that in Russia has come to be identified with totalitarianism has had no such result in the West, which suggests that the decisive factors are not the ideas but the soil on which they happen to fall. In Western Europe, socialism quickly shed its authoritarian and revolutionary elements, transforming itself into a movement for social reform. Nowhere in the West has it led to totalitarianism. It is only in Russia and in Asian, African and Latin American countries— which, while receptive to European ideas, lack European traditions—that socialist ideology has given rise to extremely repressive forms of government.

In view of this evidence, the explanation for Soviet totalitarianism must be sought not in socialism but in the political culture which draws on socialist ideas to justify totalitarian practices. In the West, with its strong traditions of private property, law and human rights, socialism has evolved into a movement for social justice and a supplement to political democracy. Where such traditions are lacking and the state is viewed primarily as a means of enriching the ruling class, socialist theory is automatically harnessed in the interest of the government, allowing it to lay claim to the property and labor of its people. Thus it happened that, while in the West the ideology of socialism had the effect of broadening the concept of democracy by augmenting political democracy with the goal of social justice, elsewhere it provided a rationale for the destruction of customs and traditional institutions that in the past had restrained the power of the state.

Like their Western counterparts, Russian socialist intellectuals were committed to democratic ideals; they wanted their country to become a model of political freedom and social equality. It was an axiom among them that the Russian people had to emancipate themselves from oppression by their own efforts and that the role of intellectuals in this struggle would be confined to rendering them assistance. But they quickly learned that the "masses," mainly peasants, did not share either their political or their social idealism, and this caused them to wonder whether a revolution in

Russia had any chance of succeeding as a mass movement. In 1879 a small band of radicals who called themselves the "People's Will" launched a campaign of terror against the monarchy, which culminated in 1881 in the murder of the tsar. The People's Will was the parent organization of all subsequent terrorist organizations in Russia and in other parts of the world. It represented a perversion of the original ideal of democratic revolution, because its aim was the forceful overthrow of government for the purpose of enabling a small band of revolutionaries to seize power and carry out a revolution from above.

The so-called Marxists, or Social Democrats, who gained popularity in Russia in the late nineteenth century, opposed terror, counting on industrial development to produce a revolutionary proletariat. But they too experienced disappointment as factory workers showed no more revolutionary spirit than the peasants. As a result of this experience, in the early years of this century, a group of Social Democrats, led by V. I. Lenin, split off from the main body of the party to form a separate faction, which later became the Bolshevik Party. Observing the behavior of industrial workers at home and abroad, Lenin concluded that the working class was not at heart revolutionary and, if left to follow its own inclinations, would make an accommodation with capitalism. To counter this development (Lenin was interested mainly in revolution, not in improved conditions for workers), he formed a small conspiratorial party, whose members were to devote themselves full time to the revolutionary cause. Their task was to wait for an opportune moment to seize power and use the resources of the state to carry out a revolution from above. The masses were relegated to a subsidiary role—a genuine industrial worker obviously could not belong to a party that demanded of its members fulltime commitment. Lenin's Bolsheviks were from the outset an elitist body of middle-class intellectuals who appointed themselves to speak and act on behalf of the working class. In their internal organization, they followed a strictly authoritarian model; the Party's administration and theoretical authority were concentrated in the person of Lenin, the infallible *vozhd' (Führer)*, who claimed to embody the historic mission of the proletariat. This is Marxism-Leninism—that is, Marxism divested of its democratic component and adapted to Russian political conditions. It is the forerunner of all modern totalitarian, one-party movements whether of the left or of the right variety.

The penchant of Russian socialists for violence, conspiracy and undemocratic methods can be justified by the difficult conditions under which they had had to operate: an arbitrary regime and a population among whom survived strong traces of serf mentality. Unlike Western socialists, who were able to agitate in the open and participate in elections, they were harassed, imprisoned or exiled. This explanation, however, only serves to show that an undemocratic political culture twists democratic ideologies out of shape and that undemocratic environments breed antidemocratic socialists.

Until 1917, Lenin's party was a fringe phenomenon in Russia's political life. As soon, however, as tsarism collapsed and anarchy spread, its influence rose. In the Russia of 1917, the Bolsheviks constituted the only disciplined party willing and able to take power. Notwithstanding their small size—in February 1917 they had a mere 30,000 members in a country of some 160 million— they and they alone disposed of the personnel able to fill the administrative vacuum produced by the dissolution of the tsarist bureaucracy. The so-called October Revolution in Petrograd, which secured for them control of the central governmental machinery, was not a revolution at all but a classic *coup d'état*, carried out swiftly and almost bloodlessly.

Observing the birth of the Communist regime, the historian is struck by the ease with which Lenin and his lieutenants slipped into the role so recently vacated by the imperial sovereign. Lenin arrogated to himself not merely the powers of the constitutional monarchy of Nicholas II, nor even the semipatrimonial authority of nineteenth-century emperors, but those of patrimonial autocracy in all its seventeenth-century splendor. The violence of 1917– 1920 resulted in the wholesale destruction of the upper and middle classes, which happened to have been the principal Westernized groups in Russia. The disappearance of that relatively thin Westernized layer permitted the unregenerate Muscovite Russia, which had survived intact underneath the veneer of European influences, to float to the surface. Nationalizing, in the name of socialism, the means of production in land and industry had the effect of once again placing all the resources of the country at the disposal of the government; as in medieval Muscovy, sovereignty and ownership came to be fused. The introduction of the principle of compulsory labor for the state, the sole employer, rebonded the entire population of the country in the service of the state. Laws and courts were swept aside to be replaced by summary justice. Lenin himself assumed with perfect ease the role of a Muscovite autocrat, issuing on his personal authority ordinances and decrees, abolishing old institutions and introducing new ones, condemning people to death, without feeling the need either to obtain concurrence from representatives of the "masses" in whose name he claimed to rule, or to observe legal norms of any kind. The Bolsheviks acted in this high-handed manner not only because their situation as a minority party striving for dictatorial power called for rough-and-ready methods, but also because they believed that such were the wishes of the Russian people. When a few days after the Bolshevik power seizure, the Central Executive Committee of the Soviets, in whose name the Bolsheviks theoretically governed, protested Lenin's autocratic methods, Trotsky responded as follows:

> This whole bourgeois scum which presently is incapable of committing itself either to this or to that side will be with us when it learns that our authority is strong . . . The petty bourgeoisie looks for a power to which it must submit. He who does not understand this understands nothing in the world, and less in affairs of government.[2]

The fusion of traditional Russian autocracy and Marxism, adapted to Russian conditions and mentalities, produced a regime that was quite outside the experience of the West but that the West nevertheless has ever since sought to explain in Western categories. It pushed to the forefront in Russia those elements that had remained unaffected by Western culture. Here no sociological or other "scientific" theories are of much help. The Revolution threw Russia back to its pre-Western origins, to patrimonialism, to lawlessness, to human bondage, to the sense of uniqueness and isolation. In the words of the novelist Boris Pilniak:

> The Revolution pitted Russia against Europe. More than that: right after the first days of the Revolution, in its habits, morals, city life, Russia reverted to the seventeenth century.[3]

All Russian revolutionary movements and parties, the Bolsheviks included, pursued international objectives—that is to say, as Russians they dedicated themselves first and foremost to the overthrow of tsarism, but tsarism to them was an integral part of a worldwide regime of political and economic exploitation. "Socialism in one country" and "peaceful coexistence" between socialism and capitalism were to them unacceptable except as transitional phenomena, until such time as the forces of socialism had gathered enough strength to triumph all along the line. The historic advance of socialism could no more stop at national boundaries than could the changing seasons. When seizing power in Russia, Lenin and his associates believed that they were snapping the weakest link in the capitalist-imperialist chain, and that the revolution that they had unleashed would promptly set off similar upheavals in Europe, America, and their colonial possessions. Lenin and Trotsky affirmed on numerous occasions that the Russian Revolution was doomed to fail unless the upheaval in short time spread to the more advanced industrial countries. Trotsky wrote in 1918:

> Without direct political aid from the European proletariat the working class of Russia will not be able to retain its power and to turn its temporary supremacy into a permanent Socialist dictatorship.[4]

Lenin, referring to the recent past, said in 1921:

> It was clear to us that without the support of the international world revolution the victory of the proletarian revolution was impossible. Before the revolution, and even after it, we thought: either revolution breaks out in the other countries, in the capitalistically more developed countries, immediately, or at least very quickly, or we must perish.[5]

As long as they viewed their own Revolution as a prelude to a worldwide conflagration, the Bolsheviks felt no need to consider in any detail the manner in which Revolutionary Russia would be administered. Rough-and-ready methods of dealing with the "counterrevolution" and measures to raise production were all that the situation would require. Like socialists everywhere, the Bolsheviks were loath to work out the forms of their future government, and, in particular, to elaborate what the "dictatorship of the proletariat," which they intended to introduce, would be like. Their concern was almost exclusively with destroying the old order. Thus it happened that the leaders of what became the most centralized and pervasive governmental system in human experience gave hardly any thought to the subject of administration prior to taking power. In his *State and Revolution,* which he wrote in the summer of 1917, Lenin predicted that the socialist revolution would bring about the abolition of government; after it had annihilated the bourgeoisie, the new socialist regime would require no professional bureaucracy and would so simplify life that any "literate person" would be able to take care of the few administrative responsibilities that still required attention.

Such was the vision of the future, after the power of the bourgeoisie had been broken everywhere—that is, not only in Russia but also in the rest of the world. In the meantime, however, it was necessary to maintain the state as an instrument of class war.

Within days after taking power, Lenin applied himself with great energy to questions of administration. As might have been expected, the new government faced myriad problems that it had to solve in order to make good its claim to power—the cities had to be provided with food and fuel; the factories needed raw materials; civil servants had to be paid; railroads had to be kept running; the armed forces had to be rebuilt to protect the new state from a threatened German invasion and the White forces. Ignoring his previous assurances to the contrary, Lenin set about creating a Communist bureaucracy. Because a large majority of the civil service had rejected the Bolshevik claim to power and went on strike, Lenin issued decrees (very reminiscent of tsarist practices) ordering all functionaries of the deposed regime to stay on their jobs. The order was ignored. Determined to break such "sabotage," Lenin resorted to a combination of terror (e.g., the taking of hostages) and inducements (mainly in the form of allotments of food and fuel, which were in critical supply). By the summer of 1918, much of the civil and military personnel of the old regime was back at work, this time in the employ of the Communists. Some did so in order to survive; others had convinced themselves that they could protect the population from Communist excesses; still others had concluded that Lenin, after all, served Russian national interests. These converted bureaucrats and army officers carried with them attitudes and procedures which they had acquired under the old regime.

Thus, however revolutionary the proclaimed goals of the Bolsheviks, in the first years of their rule they had no choice but to rely heavily on personnel inherited from the conservative, nationalistic monarchy to implement them. Statistical surveys show how large a proportion of officials in the so-called "central apparatus" of the early Soviet government and its armed forces consisted of veterans of the old, "bourgeois" regime, which the Communists were determined to uproot. In the summer of 1918, more than 50 percent of high officials in the Soviet commissariats (or ministries) had a record of service in the Imperial and Provisional governments; in some, their share exceeded 80 percent. A scholar specializing in this subject has reached the surprising conclusion that the innovations in the central administrative apparatus of Russia after the Revolution were hardly revolutionary:

> The structural changes were scarcely greater than those sometimes accompanying changes of government in Western parliamentary systems. The personnel changes were greater, and could perhaps be compared with those occurring in Washington in the heyday of the "spoils system."[6]

The situation was similar in the armed forces. In 1920–21, when the Red Army stood at the peak of strength, between one third and one half of its 130,000 commissioned officers consisted of veterans of the imperial army. The proportion of such holdovers was higher still in the top command posts: over 80 percent of the commanders of the corps, divisions and regiments of the Red Army had received their commissions from the hands of a tsar.[7]

Given this massive influx of imperial bureaucrats and officers, it should cause no surprise that the new order adopted many of the habits of the old. As before, the civil and military personnel tended to look upon the state as the country's proprietor and upon itself as serving the state rather than society.

Lenin watched the penetration of the Soviet bureaucracy by personnel inherited from the old regime with an anxiety, which toward the end of his life turned to alarm. In January 1923, in what turned out to be one of his last writings, he complained:

> With the exception of the Commissariat of Foreign Affairs, our state apparatus is to a considerable extent a survival of the past and has undergone hardly any serious change. It has only been slightly touched up on the surface, but in all other respects it is a most typical relic of our old state machine.[8]

His colleagues, however, tended to dismiss these concerns. The anticipated revolutions in Europe had not broken out, and Soviet Russia had to settle for a long period of "socialism in one country." It was further felt that the Party apparatus could monitor and control the state bureaucracy, the military command, and the industrial managers. Each governmental bureau, each army unit, each factory was assigned a commissar whose task it was to ensure that the hired "bourgeois specialists"—presumed to be hostile to the new regime—would not engage in sabotage. And the Party itself, of course, was kept clean of "bourgeois" elements by rigid admission requirements and frequent purges. The device of commissars did, indeed, succeed in neutralizing potential opposition, but at the price of institutionalizing in Soviet Russia a cleavage between political authority and professional expertise, between those who enjoy the power to make the decisions and those who possess the knowledge on which intelligent decisions have to be based.

To make matters worse, the Party itself did not long escape corrupting "bourgeois" influences. The immense responsibilities which it assumed with its claim to direct every aspect of organized activity in the country required it to keep on expanding its ranks and, in so doing, to lower standards. Between February 1917 and

March 1921, the Party membership grew from 30,000 to over 700,000. Many of those who had joined after the Communists had established themselves in power were motivated by such personal considerations as preferred access to housing and ration cards and the many other rewards and privileges that in Russia have been traditionally associated with state service. This resurgence of "bourgeois" attitudes in the Party did not go unnoticed. In 1921–22, the Party carried out a purge to rid itself of the worst opportunists; this reduced its ranks to 500,000. At Party congresses held in the early 1920s, when it was still possible to discuss unpleasant matters with a certain degree of candor, delegates complained of the "Soviet bourgeoisie" that exploited official posts for personal benefit. Trade-union representatives accused Party functionaries of losing contact with workers. Party congresses passed all sorts of resolutions to deal with this danger and appointed commissions to investigate abuses, but to no avail. The Communists discovered that their claim to total control of society compelled them to create a monstrous bureaucracy, that in the natural course of events this bureaucracy attended more to its private affairs than to public ones, but that it could not be significantly reduced either in authority or in numbers without the whole system unraveling. Instead of reforming itself, therefore, the Party ejected its critics and a few years later got rid of them by the firing squad.

Trotsky would later argue passionately that this development represented a betrayal of the Revolution, but it had been implicit in the nature of Lenin's party, when it had made it practically impossible for workers to participate in its decisions. Once the premise had been tacitly accepted that workers were an unrevolutionary class which had to have a revolution made on their behalf by others, then those others sooner or later inevitably lost sight of their original mission and turned attention to their own affairs.

Among those who had foreseen the emergence of a self-seeking Communist bureaucracy was the leading anarchist critic of Marx, Michael Bakunin. He opposed Marx's notion of the "dictatorship of the proletariat" on the grounds that in such a dictatorship power would inevitably pass into the hands of a new class of exploiters, the revolutionary intellectuals:

> According to Mr. Marx, the people should not only not abolish the state, but, on the contrary, fortify and strengthen it, and in this form turn it over to the full disposal of their benefactors, guardians and teachers, the chiefs of the Communist party, in other words, to Mr. Marx and his friends, who will then proceed to liberate [them] in their

own fashion. They will concentrate all the reins of government in a strong hand, because the ignorant people is in need of strong guardianship. They will create a central state bank, which will concentrate in its hands all commercial-industrial, agricultural and even scientific production. They will divide the mass of the people into two armies, the industrial and the agricultural, under the direct command of state engineers, who will form the new privileged political-scientific class.[9]

# 2 THE NOMENKLATURA

The "state engineers" whose emergence under socialism Bakunin had predicted are known in the Soviet Union as the *nomenklatura*. It is this "privileged political-scientific class" that for the past sixty years has run the Soviet state: when one says "Soviet government" one actually means the *nomenklatura*, because it is not only the population at large that is excluded from the political process (except for ritualistic purposes) but also the rank and file of the Communist Party, presently some 18 million in number, who have been reduced to the status of executors of the *nomenklatura*'s will. The *nomenklatura* holds the Soviet Union in ownership. Its position can best be rendered in the words of Marx, who spoke of the post-1830 monarchy in France as a "company for the exploitation of French national wealth," of which the king was the director and whose dividends were distributed among the ministers, parliamentary deputies, and 240,000 enfranchised citizens.

The emergence of the *nomenklatura* as the supreme elite within the ordinary elite of the Communist Party is connected with the ascendancy of Stalin. This semieducated follower of Lenin realized much more quickly than his theoretically more sophisticated rivals that the new Communist bureaucracy had no interest either in worker emancipation or world revolution, but was vitally concerned with its own security, advancement and access to material goods. He formed his power base of this class of upstarts and opportunists, who had joined the Party when doing so no longer carried any risk, by placing them in important positions and making them dependent on himself. When the struggle for Lenin's succession got underway in earnest, Stalin held an invincible advantage by dint of having at his disposal private clients in many key party positions.

The secret of Stalin's success lay in cadre selection. When Lenin was still alive, Stalin had introduced formal procedures for scrutinizing the qualifications of party officials nominated to important posts; in practice, the only qualification which he required was loyalty to his own person. In 1922, as illness forced Lenin increasingly to withdraw from day-to-day administrative duties, Stalin already disposed of a private retinue of 15,000 officials. This group formed the nucleus of the *nomenklatura:* they alone were certified to fill the highest and most influential positions. Stalin kept on increasing the number of posts subject to cadre selection by the Central Committee and its Secretariat. The result was a two-tier party structure in which the top echelons, hand-picked by Stalin and his lieutenants, filled the senior offices and made decisions, while the rank and file of Party members carried them out. In his conflict with Stalin, Trotsky found that although his fame was greater than Stalin's and his popular following not insignificant, he was unable to translate these assets into political power because his rival had secured an iron hold on personnel selection. Stalin concurrently kept on flooding the Party with new members so as to have a large pool from which to draw his minions; between 1924 and 1928 the Party membership grew from 472,000 to 1,304,000 and then, in the five years that followed, to over 3,500,000 members and candidate members. At this juncture Stalin instituted gruesome "purges" to eliminate from the apparatus old Bolsheviks and all those of whose loyalty he could not be certain. By 1937, Party membership was reduced to two million. How thoroughly Stalin had succeeded in transforming the Party can be seen from the following statistic: at the Party Congress of 1934, on the eve of the purges, four fifths of the delegates had enrolled in the Party before 1920; in 1939, four fifths reported having joined it since 1924.

The group that today controls the Soviet Union consists in large majority of individuals who had made their careers in this selection process. Stalin's death freed them from the dread in which his unpredictable moods had always held them; in this sense, they welcomed the "de-Stalinization" campaign carried out by Khrushchev in the 1950s, which gave them, for the first time in their lives, a sense of personal security. But they have retained the Stalinist system in all its institutional essentials, because they owe to it membership in the *nomenklatura* with all the benefits and privileges that this status bestows. Since 1953, the Soviet Union has been run by a Stalinist elite acting as a collective body, a bureaucratic oligarchy originally created to serve the interests of a despot but emancipated from despotic whim and dedicated to the pursuit of its own interests instead.

In Soviet bureaucratic usage, *nomenklatura* has a double meaning: (1) a list of the most important Party offices, appointment to which requires approval by the Secretariat and the Central Committee; and (2) a roster of the personnel who either hold these positions or are eligible to hold them. The whole concept is an adaptation of practices introduced into Russia by Peter the Great in 1722, under which government posts were staffed exclusively with persons with an appropriate state service rank, or, as it was then known, *chin*. Information on the *nomenklatura* is difficult to obtain, because the Communist authorities treat all that concerns it as a state secret. It is only in recent years, thanks to data furnished by émigrés, that the structure and workings of this peculiar institution have become better known.

The principal organization associated with the *nomenklatura* is the Central Committee of the Communist Party, the true seat of Soviet government. The Central Committee is composed of two dozen or so departments, each of which has assigned to it an allotment of *nomenklatura* posts that it staffs with persons chosen from the pool of eligible officials. The best estimate (by M. Voslensky) gives the number of its personnel as 750,000 individuals; together with their families and other dependents, they may number 3 million persons, or less than 1.5 percent of the country's population. The *nomenklatura* network extends throughout the administrative machinery, but some branches have a higher proportion of such posts than others; thus, all KGB officials and diplomats, as well as top media specialists, come from its ranks. Membership in this elite group is for all practical purposes permanent. Neither demonstrated incompetence nor gross corruption—indeed, nothing short of treason—can cause a *nomenklatura* member to be expelled from its lists; his tenure ensures that at worst he will be shifted to a less desirable assignment. In common with other privileged classes, the *nomenklatura* has been acquiring characteristics of a hereditary caste, as sons of its members are given educational and other opportunities that make it easier for them to enroll in the elite corps.

The rewards to which *nomenklatura* members are entitled come in a variety of forms, the principal ones being access to scarce, high-quality goods and services reserved for their exclusive use, and tribute in cash and kind rendered to them by the population. The most privileged echelons, estimated at 100,000 and concentrated in Moscow and Leningrad, rely on privileges, although they are not averse to pocketing contributions from the populace; the provincial *nomenklatura* people are required more to fend for themselves.

*Nomenklatura* officials receive high salaries; these are treated as state secret and therefore not made public. Top functionaries on its lists are estimated to receive 2,000 rubles a month (compared to 164 paid to an average worker and 80 to a physician fresh out of medical school). This figure easily doubles as soon as the numerous perquisites that go with the status are taken into account. The most valuable of those is the right of entry into special retail facilities, open only to the privileged, which sell at reduced prices goods and services unavailable to the public at large. For the Moscow *nomenklatura*, this means first and foremost access to food stores and restaurants known by the euphemism "Kremlin Canteen" (*kremlëvskaia stolovaia*). This is a mammoth and luxurious catering service, located on Granovskii Street 2, which supplies those eligible with all their culinary wants, including imported foods. Whereas, according to recent surveys, the ordinary Soviet citizen has less than one chance in three of finding in a state food store such staples as potatoes or cabbage, the elite are assured at the *kremlëvka* of whatever their hearts desire; payment is made not in cash but in vouchers, which are purchased at a fraction of the price they would fetch on the open market. Officials who prefer their food in prepared form can indulge, on the same terms, at the Central Committee Buffet, at Nikitnikov Pereulok 5, near the Hotel Rossiia. In addition, scattered throughout Moscow and other cities are clothing and shoe stores, bookstores and theater agencies, admission to which is strictly limited.

Reserved for the exclusive use of the *nomenklatura* are also hospitals, pharmacies, sanatoriums and even cemeteries. Living quarters are allocated to this elite without regard to the skimpy norms applicable to ordinary mortals (16 square meters, or 172 square feet, per person); they are entitled to more spacious accommodations, usually in the better parts of town. The *nomenklatura* even enjoys the unique privilege of protection against nuclear war. The Moscow contingent, with its families, and an increasing proportion of its provincial counterparts, is assured of space in well-constructed nuclear shelters. In accord with Soviet civil defense plans, the remainder of the population must try to protect itself against nuclear blast and fallout as best it can, by evacuating cities and taking cover in improvised shelters. The *nomenklatura* thus treads the same ground and breathes the same air as the rest of the people but in every other respect it inhabits a world of its own.

So much for the benefits obtained in the form of ordinary perquisites. The irregular, quasi-legal bounties obtained by the *nomenklatura* at the expense of the population form a web of officially tolerated corruption, which will be discussed in Chapter Four.

The Soviet *nomenklatura* is predominantly Russian in composition; as a small "in" group, it feels uncomfortable with "ethnics," especially Jews, whom it regards as an "in" group of their own and virtually excludes from its ranks. Outside the Soviet Union, however, each Communist country has local clones of the Soviet elite. They enjoy many but not all the privileges of their Soviet counterparts and are closely linked to them by class status. On occasion, colonial elites are seized with outbursts of patriotic zeal that reunite them with the people and cause their ties to Moscow to be severed; this happened in Hungary in 1956 and in Czechoslovakia in 1968. But such occurrences are exceptional. As a rule, Communist elites feel connected by strong ties of interest. Something like the spirit of a *nomenklatura* international binds its diverse members, especially in moments of crisis. It was instructive to observe the tortured reaction of the Yugoslav and Chinese bureaucracies to the rise in Poland of an independent labor movement. On the face of it, both governments should have welcomed this development, since it had the effect of weakening Moscow's hold on one of its most important dependencies, thereby enhancing their own national security. Yet in the end both Belgrade and Peking reacted negatively to the emergence of Solidarity. It was as if the elites in these two capitals realized that although the pressure of democratic forces caused discomfort to the foreign power they feared the most, indirectly it also threatened their own privileged positions. Squabble as they might, the *nomenklatura*s of all Communist countries tend to come to one another's assistance whenever any of them confronts the mortal threat of genuine democracy.

## 3  THE STALINIST ECONOMIC SYSTEM

When the Bolsheviks seized power in 1917, they acted on two major expectations, both of which were disappointed. One of these has already been noted—the belief in the imminent spread of the revolution from Russia to the leading industrial countries in the West. Failure of this hope led to the establishment in Russia of a gigantic state and party bureaucracy.

The other expectation was that a socialized economy would prove more efficient than the market economy. This belief was shared by all socialist movements since their emergence in the second quarter of the nineteenth century. Socialist theoreticians of every school viewed capitalism as an irrational mode of production, wastefully competitive, afflicted with alternating phases of overproduction and idleness, booms and depressions. A common goal of socialist programs was centralized economic management, which would introduce into industry the most advanced scientific methods of production and in agriculture eliminate the inefficient small producer. The Bolsheviks shared this conventional socialist wisdom. Their faith in the advantages of central economic management was reinforced by the performance of Germany in World War I, which, owing to its centralized management, succeeded in waging war on two fronts notwithstanding shortages of raw materials and an enemy blockade. Once in power, the Bolsheviks intended to establish central control over all the economic resources, including capital and labor, introduce national planning, and operate the economy in accord with the latest scientific methods. Shortly after the Revolution, Lenin declared his intention of transforming "the whole of the state economic mechanism into a single huge machine, into an economic organism that will work in such a way as to enable hundreds of millions of people to be guided by a single plan." [10] The enhanced productivity that was expected to result from such centralization was to provide the socialist state with the means to resist the anticipated onslaught of the international "bourgeoisie" and then to spread the revolution around the globe.

Such considerations lay behind the program of "War Communism" introduced by the Bolsheviks into parts of Russia under their control in the winter of 1917–18.[11] In the first half of 1918 they nationalized Russia's industries, trade, transport facilities, large estates, utilities and banks. They left, for the time being, the status of small landholding ambivalent, because they feared antagonizing the peasantry; but their ruthless expropriations of foodstuffs and the unprecedented prohibition on private trade in grain, left no doubt that they did not intend to respect the principle of private property in land. In December 1917, two months after seizing power, the Communist government formed a Supreme Council of National Economy "to regulate the economic life of the country," with broad coercive powers.

In 1921 the plans to centralize the national economy had to be temporarily shelved, because the country was approaching the brink of economic collapse. Industrial productivity, which had declined precipitately after the February 1917 revolution, continued to drop still further under Communist rule. In 1921 the gross output of Soviet industry fell to one third of what it had been in 1913; agricultural production barely reached 60 percent of its prewar level. A combination of poor weather and shortage of seed caused by forced expropriations brought about in the principal graingrowing regions of Russia in 1920–21 a famine of dimensions exceeding anything previously known in the history of Europe. These economic disasters coincided with growing political unrest. Responding to the crisis, Lenin decided in March 1921 on concessions to the "petty bourgeoisie." The New Economic Policy, which he inaugurated at this time, permitted peasants once again to sell their produce on the open market and authorized private entrepreneurs to carry on industrial production, mainly of consumer goods. Lenin thought of the NEP as a breathing spell that would allow the country, ravaged by seven years of bloodshed and social experimentation, to regain its strength. The government jealously guarded control over what it called the "commanding heights" of the economy, such as heavy industry, transport, banking and foreign trade. It could hardly have been otherwise: the Soviet regime had come to depend on its bureaucracy, and the bureaucracy, for its part, served mainly to enrich itself at the nation's expense. Thus, state ownership and management of the means of production, inefficient as they were, provided an indispensable political base of the new regime, as has been the case ever since.

By 1927, thanks to the private initiative unleashed by the NEP, the indices of industrial and agricultural productivity regained their pre-1914 levels. At this time, Stalin decided to resume the economic and social revolution. The ensuing upheaval, which lasted several years, affected every branch of the national economy. Because it required the abolition of private property in agriculture, it resulted in harrowing violence as the regime resorted to military action, deportations, and even artificial famines to reduce the resistance of the peasantry.

Just as was the case with the political regime that Lenin established in 1917–22 and Stalin subsequently perfected, so the economic regime that Stalin set in place in 1927–32 constitutes to this day the foundation of the Soviet system. The Stalinist economy is essentially an arrangement that permits the rapid mobilization of national resources for military purposes, such as democratic societies can achieve only in wartime. Ideal as it may be for crash programs, it is not well suited either for the promotion of high production or the advancement of technical innovation. Because the Stalinist economic system is at the bottom of the economic difficulties encountered by the current Soviet leadership, its main features deserve a brief summary.

**1.** Stalin introduced, and his successors have preserved, central economic planning; the state planning agency, Gosplan, determines allocations of capital, equipment and resources, setting production targets for the economy as a whole and for its separate branches. Essentially, the Soviet Union is run as if it were one vast conglomerate; decision making is extremely centralized throughout.

**2.** Soviet planning operates with quantitative production norms; quality is not a major consideration. Wages are pegged to fulfillment of norms. Workers and managers thus have no interest in improving quality, because, as a rule, it brings them no benefits. Furthermore, they have a positive disinterest in producing more than their norms require, because this only results in these norms being raised in the next plan. Thus there exists a dearth of meaningful economic incentives.

**3.** As the country's only legitimate employer, the state assumes responsibility for the basic material needs of its population. It provides its citizens with heavily subsidized food staples, housing and transport. This arrangement recalls the one that was prevalent before the Revolution in some branches of Russian industry (e.g., the textile), which paid workers substandard wages, but added valuable side benefits, such as housing. This practice weighs heavily on the Soviet treasury.

**4.** Owing to a prodigious rate of population growth (before 1914, the highest in Europe) and limited economic opportunities, old-regime Russia suffered from chronic overpopulation. It is estimated that on the eve of the Revolution the country had a surplus of over twenty million working hands. This permanent excess has engendered a habit, perpetuated by the Soviet government, of relying on cheap, unskilled labor to compensate for shortages of capital and skills. The country that claims to be the second industrial power in the world, still has 40 percent of its industrial labor force engaged in manual work.[12] Such a method assumes an unlimited pool of available workers, an assumption that sharp declines in population growth have invalidated some time ago.

**5.** From its inception, the principal objective of Stalin's economic policy has been the enhancement of the country's military might. Its highest priority was, and continues to be, the construction of an industrial base capable of providing the Soviet Army with all it needs to wage modern war. In 1927, when the first Five Year Plan was inaugurated, ostensibly to lay the industrial foundation of "socialism in one country," Marshal Tukhachevskii made clear the intimate link between Soviet industrialization, the centralized management of the economy, and the capability to wage war. All things being equal, he said, the country that is most powerful industrially will acquire the greatest military power. Things, however, were not equal, because, according to him, the Soviet Union, owing to its centralized economic system, enjoyed a special advantage over capitalist countries, which, with all their wealth, lacked the ability to mobilize their societies:

We have this advantage that the entire heavy industry is concentrated in the hands of the government . . . This makes it possible to approach the question of mobilizing the country much more systematically and consistently. The industrialization of the [Soviet] Union opens up in this respect entirely new perspectives. Under conditions of our socialist construction it is much easier to achieve full conversion to warfare and to adapt for the conduct of war all our resources, human as well as industrial.[13]

The Red Army was the foremost beneficiary of the new Soviet industries; the flow of new hardware accomplished what some observers describe as a "technical revolution" in the Soviet armed forces and made them, in the middle 1930s, the most modern in Europe.[14] Ever since, the needs of the military have enjoyed the highest priority in Soviet economic planning.

# 4 SOVIET IMPERIALISM

One of the salient features of the Russian historical experience has been a propensity for imperialism. Russia, of course, has no monopoly on expansion. Most European states have gone through an imperialist phase. Germany, which in the twentieth century became a byword for aggressive militarism, in the eighteenth century had been regarded as a nation of poets and dreamers. Peaceful Sweden in the seventeenth century devastated Central Europe. Holland and Portugal in their day conquered great empires.

Even when this point is conceded, however, Russian imperialism displays certain unique features. One of these is its persistence. In the history of Russia, expansion is not a phase but a constant. Except for brief intervals when domestic difficulties have forced it to turn inward, the Russian state has been expanding since the early fourteenth century with extraordinary vigor; between the middle of the sixteenth century and the end of the seventeenth, it acquired every year the territorial equivalent of modern Holland for 150 years running. The second distinguishing quality of Russian imperialism is its military character: unlike Western colonial powers, which supplemented and reinforced their military activities with economic and cultural penetration, Russia has had to rely mainly on the force of arms. The third is colonization. Because until very recent times Russia's expansion had taken place along its frontier, the conquest of foreign lands was usually followed (and sometimes preceded) by the influx of Russian settlers. Once colonized, every conquered region turned into Russian "patrimony"—that is, inalienable state property, which was under no circumstances to be surrendered to anyone, including its previous owners.

Expansionism of such persistence and an imperialism that maintains such a tenacious hold on its conquests raises the question of causes.

One can dismiss the explanation most often offered by amateur Russian "experts" (although hardly ever by Russians themselves) that Russia expands because of anxieties aroused by relentless foreign invasions of its national territory by neighboring countries. Those who make this point usually have but the scantiest familiarity with Russian history. Their knowledge of Russia's external relations is confined to three or four invasions, made familiar by novels or moving pictures—the conquest of Russia in the thirteenth century by the Mongols (who are sometimes confused with the Chinese); Napoleon's invasion of 1812; the Allied "intervention" during the Russian Civil War; and the Nazi onslaught of 1941. With such light baggage one can readily conclude that, having been uniquely victimized, Russia strikes out to protect itself. Common sense, of course, might suggest even to those who lack knowledge of the facts that a country can no more become the world's most spacious as a result of suffering constant invasions than an individual can gain wealth from being repeatedly robbed. But common sense aside, there is the record of history. It shows that far from being the victim of recurrent acts of aggression, Russia has been engaged for the past three hundred years with single-minded determination in aggressive wars, and that if anyone has reason for paranoia it would have to be its neighbors. In the 1890s, the Russian General Staff carried out a comprehensive study of the history of Russian warfare since the foundations of the state. In the summary volume, the editor told his readers that they could take pride in their country's military record and face the future with confidence—between 1700 and 1870, Russia had spent 106 years fighting 38 military campaigns, of which 36 had been "offensive" and a mere 2 defensive.[15] This authoritative tabulation should dispose of the facile theory that Russian aggression is a defensive reflex.

More serious explanations of Russian expansionism take account of concrete economic, geographic and political factors.

Russia is naturally a poor country. Located far away from the main trade routes, it was unable to participate in international commerce. It is rich in natural resources, but these are difficult and costly to extract. Above all, neither its soil nor its climate is well suited for agriculture, which until the 1930s had been the main source of livelihood for eight or nine out of ten Russian inhabitants. Scientific estimates indicate that the soil of northern Russia, the homeland of the Russian state, cannot support more than 25 inhabitants per square kilometer; this figure compares with some 250 inhabitants per square kilometer for the climatically more favored Western nations. Population growth has made it necessary to acquire ever new land to accommodate the surplus peasantry, and this requirement, in turn, called for a large army, first to conquer territory and then to protect the settlers who colonized it. Thus, unlike the great European powers and Japan, whose imperialism represented an overflow of national wealth in search of profitable investment outlets or fresh markets, Russian imperialism was an escape from poverty. The whole situation had about it the quality of a vicious cycle—poverty necessitated expansion; expansion necessitated large military outlays; and large military outlays robbed the country of productive resources, perpetuating poverty.

The second factor is geographic. The same location that has such a negative effect on Russian agriculture affords Russia unique opportunities for aggression. Russia occupies and controls that region which geopoliticians have defined as the "heartland."[16] It is the only country in the world bordering on the regions that contain the bulk of the globe's population and natural resources: Europe, the Middle East and East Asia. Russian infantry can reach any part of the European, African and Asian continents without getting their feet wet (a short crossing of the man-made Suez Canal excepted). This geopolitical position affords Russia opportunities for conquest enjoyed by no other power. It can freely shift military forces inside its 67,000 kilometer (or 41,500 mile) frontier from the Baltic to the Black Sea, and from there to the Pacific, and back again, applying pressures and exploiting opportunities with speed and ease that are beyond the reach of any other power in the world. Opportunity has always offered fresh temptations to advance; and because economic conditions have always encouraged expansion, few Russian governments have been able to resist them.

The third factor is the quest for loot and luxuries with which to satisfy the elite. In the tsarist period that loot consisted of agricultural land that was lavishly distributed to the service nobility in the conquered territories. Today it consists mainly of consumer goods and comforts, for which the *nomenklatura* has an insatiable appetite. What this means concretely can be seen from a report sent recently by a Swedish correspondent stationed in Afghanistan, one of the world's more backward countries, where the Soviet elite has nevertheless managed to establish a style of colonial life of a brazenly exploitative nature:

The poor mountain nation has also been blessed with yet another un-welcome "novelty": the new upper class, consisting of what are pop-ularly called Soviet advisers and their families.

The new rulers live in their own well-protected residential areas in Kabul in prefabricated houses manufactured in a Russian-built factory in the city.

They shop in well-stocked shops at prices far below those considered normal at home in the Soviet Union. Their children go to special schools and since birds of a feather flock together they only have social contacts among themselves.

"The Russian upper class," as the advisers and their dependents are called in Kabul, have the advantage of living in something which can be likened to a free trade zone—and they make the maximum use of this.

Nearly all the products which we in the West have grown used to being able to buy, but which for the normal Russian are unattainable luxuries, are available in Afghanistan, both legally and on the flourish-ing black market.

The largest part of the entertainment electronics imported from Japan every year is to be found in Russian homes, and Afghanistan's famous furs are to be found hanging in every closet. . . .

The Russian advisers and their families live totally isolated from the people they have come to liberate. Their residential areas in Kabul are a good example. Every taxi driver, every illiterate, knows that the Russians live in so-called *microrayons*, a Russian word which has found its way into the local language.

They have simply cleared away the traditional slums in certain areas and erected Soviet minicondominiums where a few fortunate Afghan party functionaries are allowed to live.

Fortunate, because they now live in houses with running water, electricity (which is, however, subject to power cuts at regular inter-vals) and central heating, an enormous luxury in the run-down capital, where the shortage of fuel of all types always makes itself felt, espe-cially during the bitterly cold winter months.[17]

The fourth and most complex set of factors is political. One of these has been noted already—the tradition of making territorial acquisitions in the course of state building. The others have to do with the relationship between Russian governments and their sub-jects.

Russian governments have always felt the need to solidify their internal position by impressing on the population the awe which they inspired in other nations. There is a Russian proverb that says, "Beat your own people and others will fear you." The pro-verb is equally valid in reversed form, "Beat others and your own people will fear you." By inspiring respect in foreign govern-ments, by bullying neighbors, by undermining them and distributing their lands and riches among their own subjects, Russian governments have historically enhanced their claims to legitimacy and obedience. This close relationship between external expansion and internal authority has been noted by perceptive observers long before the Revolution. Among them was Friedrich Engels, who like his friend Marx devoted much attention to Russian affairs. In 1890, referring to the Russian diplomatic service, Engels wrote:

> It is this secret society, recruited originally from foreign adventurers, that has elevated the Russian empire to its present might. With iron perseverance, with eyes fixed on the goal, not shrinking from any breach of faith, any treachery, any assassination, any servility, lavishly dispersing bribes, never grown overconfident from victory, never discouraged by defeat, over the corpses of millions of soldiers and at least one tsar, it is this gang, as talented as it is without conscience, rather than all the Russian armies put together, that have contributed to the extension of Russia's borders. . . . [It is this gang] that has made Russia great, powerful and feared, and has opened up for it the way to world domination. In so doing, however, it has also strengthened the power of tsarism internally. For the vulgar patriotic public, the glory of victory, the conquests that follow one another, the might and splendor of tsardom fully outweigh all its sins, all its despotism, all its injustices and arbitrariness: the boastfulness of chauvinism fully compensates for all the kicks received[18]

The argument is emotional but deserving of attention. Governments of every kind seek every now and then to divert their citizens' attention from internal troubles by waging war. In the case of Russia, however, the phenomenon is not episodic. For Russian governments, foreign glory is not merely an escape from transient crises, but a feature of the very constitutional order; permanent conquests serve to justify the permanent subservience of Russian society. Because the bonds linking the Russian people with their government are so tenuous and the chasm separating them so wide, there exists always the danger that a Russian regime that is no longer feared at home and abroad (and the two phenomena are closely connected) will appear to have lost the mandate of heaven and fall apart. Psychologically speaking, the greater the awe in which a Russian government is held by foreigners, the stronger is its claim to rule and the more satisfying the compensation that it offers to its people for their debased status. The poet Lermontov expressed well this sentiment when he had a Russian tell a Muslim of the Caucasus, whose land the Russians were about to conquer, that he would soon be proud to say, "Yes, I am a slave, but a slave of the tsar of the universe."[19]

Communist ideology and the interests of the *nomenklatura* have reinforced these expansionist traditions, making Russian imperialism more aggressive and more persistent than ever before.

According to Marx, as interpreted by Lenin (see above, p. 25), the "dictatorship of the proletariat" is necessary as long—and only as long—as the class enemy, the bourgeoisie, survives to threaten the new socialist order; the "withering away of the state" can and indeed must begin the instant the class enemy has been eliminated. Theoretically speaking, the "bourgeoisie" was destroyed in Russia and its dependencies a long time ago, for which reason the survival of the state and the bureaucracy in Communist countries is an anomaly that can no longer be justified. The Communist state should by now have withered away completely. But, of course, the immense parasitic corps of the Party and state functionaries that had ensconced itself in power and privilege since the Revolution, has not the slightest interest in the state's disappearance. The state is the source of its livelihood; for the *nomenklatura* it provides a style of life that is not inferior to that of the Western middle class in a country where the vast majority of citizens subsist on a Third World standard. It needs to justify its power and privileges, and this justification it can find only in keeping alive the specter of the "bourgeoisie" and arguing that while the "bourgeoisie" has indeed been liquidated in Communist societies, it still survives and continues to threaten the socialist community, this time from the outside. Since the triumph of Communism in Russia, class war, which had once been internal, has been transferred onto the international arena; today, the "socialist community" champions the cause of the proletariat, while the "imperialist camp," led by the United States, stands for the cause of the bourgeoisie. In other words, the *nomenklatura* requires the foreign class enemy to legitimize its authority; without him, and without the threat that he allegedly poses, it has no excuse left for holding on to power. For this reason, international tension and the specter of war, in the form of an "imperialist" attack on the Soviet Union, are vital to the interests of the Communist elite. In a world genuinely at peace, its survival as a parasitic class would be in danger.

The best way to demonstrate the need for a powerful Communist state and military establishment is constantly to expand the Communist realm. Each encroachment on the "enemy" camp proves the justness of the cause and its inevitable ultimate triumph. It has been noted by many observers that Soviet aggrandizement and acts of repression abroad (e.g., against Czechoslovakia and Poland) enjoy popularity with the mass of Soviet citizens; it confirms to them that their own lot, with which, as a whole, they are not very happy, will also be that of the rest of mankind, that those foreigners who boast of freedom and prosperity will not be allowed to do so for long. The situation is, indeed, as Engels has described it in regard to tsarist expansionism: the glory of victory, the ceaseless conquests, the might and the splendor of the Soviet state—all compensate the ordinary people for the injustices, the arbitrariness, and the "kicks received." And for the *nomenklatura* they provide an indispensable rationale for practices that, in terms of its own ideology, have long lost any validity.

The greater its successes abroad, the heavier the blows meted out to the "imperialist" enemy, the greater the security of the *nomenklatura* and the vaster its power. A Russian émigré scholar, familiar with the mentality of this group, explains its intense imperialism in Marxist terms:

> [The] expansionist drive is the direct expression of the properties of the [Soviet] system, above all, of the class nature of Soviet authority. The politics of the Soviet Union are expansive because political power constitutes the sole basis of its ruling class. One can compare the *nomenklatura* with the class of Western entrepreneurs. . . . This class, too, is expansionist, but in the realm of economics. The class foundation of the bourgeois is property, and it is through property that he attains political influence. The class foundation of the *nomenklatura*, by contrast, is political power. It is through power that it attains to property and privilege.
>
> Every class seeks to expand its class basis. Thus, the bourgeois entrepreneur strives to gain maximum profit, and every enterprise expands on the world market according to its ability, with its goods and capital, wherever there open up gaps in the market. The *nomenklatura* also seeks openings in the market: Lenin described them as the "weakest links in the chain of imperialism."
>
> The psychological background of expansionism in the East and in the West may be similar, but for those concerned it makes a great deal of difference whether, through its expansion in Europe, a Japanese concern sells more watches, or the Moscow *nomenklatura* seeks to impose on Europe its political dominance.[20]

Thus, the negative consideration—the need to justify its authority—combines with the positive one—the desire to enhance this authority—to produce an imperialist drive that would be difficult to duplicate from the historical record.

The essential fact to bear in mind is that Soviet expansionism has little if anything to do with what is sometimes called "legitimate Soviet national interests." In the past, when the Russian peasantry pressed on their country's neighbors in search of new land to colonize, expansion might be said to have served in some ways the interests of the people. But this has long ago ceased to be the case. The Soviet Union presently suffers from rural under-population; it has more land than people able to cultivate it. Its aggression is carried out exclusively in the interest of the elite, and because of the immense resources that it absorbs and the risks that it entails, aggression is profoundly contrary to Russia's national interests. Western statesmen who hope to appease Soviet aggres-siveness by pledging to respect "legitimate Soviet national inter-ests" are dealing with a phantom. The only interests that count are those of the proprietors of Communist countries, and their interests require permanent international tension and ceaseless territorial aggrandizement. Only if and when the power of the *nomenklatura* will be substantially curtailed and the interests of the people allowed legitimate expression will one be able to speak of the national interests of countries presently in the *nomenklatura*'s iron grip. And that, of course, will require fundamental changes in the Soviet system, away from the Stalinism which constitutes its framework.

"Pragmatists" may consider such an expectation utopian. Time alone will tell. But the record of the past leaves no doubt that it is entirely utopian to expect Communist regimes to abandon aggres-sive behavior as long as they continue to be organized on the current model.

# 5 THE PSYCHOLOGY OF
# THE NOMENKLATURA

What kind of people run this awesome political conglomerate with its insatiable appetite for territorial acquisitions and mergers, an appetite that seemingly nothing short of control of the globe will ever appease?

One of their distinguishing characteristics is a penchant for se-crecy. They do not seek publicity either as a group or as individ-uals; indeed, they dread personal publicity, lest it appear as self-seeking and arouse the envy of their comrades. Such egos as they have, they seem to be able to satisfy within the anonymity of their circle. They differ in this respect greatly—and to their advantage —from functionaries in Washington, whose status is much less secure and many of whom are tempted to establish their creden-tials as persons of influence by parading such inside knowledge as they think they have and attracting the attention of the media. The *nomenklatura* is faceless and silent. We know nothing but the barest essentials about the Politbureau with its Central Committee and Secretariat—that is, about a government that rules one sixth of the globe and by common consent commands the world's second-greatest economy and a military establishment second to none. The private lives of the members of the *nomenklatura* are a closely guarded state secret—their families, their residences, their salaries, their amusements.

The world has come to accept this secrecy as normal; it is said to be the "Russian way." But is it not a fantastic situation? We know more about the structure and functioning of the Senate of ancient Rome than about the Politbureau of the present-day Soviet Union. We are better informed about the background and personality of Genghis Khan than we are about those of Yurii Andropov, who recently headed a modern "superpower" and served as chairman of a committee that has it within its power to unleash on the world thousands of nuclear warheads. This kind of obsessive secrecy and the uncertainty that it engenders, both assiduously fostered by Communist governments, should arouse the deepest suspicions. Commendable as modesty may be, such morbid fear of exposure is more appropriate to the underworld than to political authority.

The Soviet official is a cynic who ascribes to human beings only the basest of motives. His entire outlook on life and people has been shaped by personal experiences in an environment where dog-eat-dog is the rule. He views people as driven exclusively by self-interest, and self-interest as consisting of the desire to survive and accumulate material benefits (such as power, goods, physical pleasures). Any other motive he dismisses as humbug. If he happens, nevertheless, to encounter instances of apparently sincere idealism, as in the case of democratic or religious dissenters in the USSR, he ascribes such behavior to mental derangement. The authorities who commit unregenerate dissidents to psychiatric hospitals seem genuinely to believe that they are dealing with lunatics in need of medical care. Foreign visitors who demonstrate emotions other than fear or greed throw the *nomenklatura* into confusion. When prominent figures from the West—publicity-hungry millionaires, earnest pacifists, "concerned" scientists, and the like —journey to Moscow to discuss with them the need for universal disarmament and peaceful coexistence, or, worse yet, with the aid of Soviet propagandistic slogans, condemn their own governments, the *nomenklatura* is perplexed. It is easy enough to understand such talk when it is linked to commercial or other self-interest. The *nomenklatura's* system of values adequately accounts for the motives of a foreigner who echoes Soviet propaganda preliminary to a request for contracts to sell the Soviet Union soft drinks or pipeline equipment or to gain access to archives, or to be given an opportunity to be photographed peacably chatting with the Soviet leader, for the benefit of the voters back home. But how is one to interpret the visitor's intentions when no personal interest is apparent? For the Soviet elite, with its peasant background, the ability and willingness to defend one's own interests is the primary test of intelligence. It finds it difficult to conceive, therefore, that a foreigner whom the Soviet bureaucrat instinctively treats as his counterpart, a member of the bourgeois *nomenklatura*, got to where he is if he is really as simple-minded as he appears to be. The suspicion therefore arises that the foreign visitor is a cunning deceiver who, with his silly chatter, is trying to insinuate himself into the confidence of the Soviet leadership in order to extract from it some political advantage or to lull it into a false sense of security. The *nomenklatura* vacillates when confronted with "liberal" Westerners whom it neither understands nor trusts. It uses them, of course, for its own purposes, but it much prefers "class enemies" in their pure, unadulterated form: in its eyes, they are more honorable, because they leave no doubt as to where they stand.

Its misanthropic outlook severely limits the *nomenklatura*'s understanding of human behavior. It knows how to intimidate and manipulate people, but not how to govern them, inasmuch as government always entails some measure of persuasion and consent. Democratic societies are entirely beyond the pale of its comprehension. In the end, with their thousands of "American experts," free to travel in the United States and communicate with its elite, with access to more information about the West than they can possibly assimilate, the Soviet authorities probably have less of a grasp of the spirit and operations of the open American political process than even the intellectually indolent, psychologically isolationist ordinary American has of their complicated and secretive system. Little wonder. Churchill's famous saying that Russia is "a riddle inside a mystery wrapped in an enigma" misstates the case. For all its novel and idiosyncratic aspects, the Soviet regime is of a type familiar from the past in the sense that it rules by coercion. The real mystery and the real innovation is government based on consent—how millions of people can individually pursue their private interests and yet voluntarily sacrifice enough of them to maintain public order and, when threatened, be capable of putting their very lives at stake. This is the truly inexplicable enigma and an exception in the course of world history; one cannot blame the Soviet elite for being unable to comprehend it.

A foreigner cannot hope to penetrate the mental recesses of

people joined in a secret order, in a culture so much removed from his own. For this reason it is useful to cite a description of the *nomenklatura* by an insider. Here is his sketch of a typical specimen:

He sits behind his desk, clad in a decent but not overly fashionable suit. He is carefully shaven. His hair is properly cut, but in a style that is not too modern. There is here neither anarchic slovenliness nor bourgeois foppishness: everything is "bureaucratic semi-modern." At one time, he—or his predecessor—had posed as a "representative of the proletariat," behaving in a demonstrably uncultured manner, rude and overflowing with energy. Later on, he turned silent and strong, a bloc of steely will. Nowadays he is sociable: he inquires about [his visitor's] health, and instead of bellowing rudely, "Get going, get this done!," or issuing a firm order, "This must be done!" he says in a friendly manner, "What do you think, Ivan Ivanovich, would it not be better to do it this way?" But the meaning is the same: it is a command.

And this is just what he enjoys. He issues commands and everyone is obliged to carry them out. Let anyone try to disobey! He has the deadly grip of a bulldog, and can bring the insubordinate into line in such a way that the others, too, will lose any temptation to ignore his instructions.

He is a fanatic of power. This is not to say that he is indifferent to everything else. By nature he is anything but an ascetic. He likes to drink, in quantity, preferably expensive Armenian cognac. He eats well too—caviar, sturgeon, salmon—items which can be obtained at the Kremlin Canteen or at the buffet of the Central Committee. He enjoys a mandatory hobby, whatever happens to be "in" in his circles: once it had been soccer and hockey, later it was fishing, nowadays it is hunting. He goes to the trouble of obtaining for his new apartment furniture from Finland, and, through the book department of the Central Committee, works unavailable on the open market—of course, only the kind that adhere to the party line.

But the joy of his life lies not there. His joy, his only passion, is to sit at the table on which stands the official telephone. To clear drafts of Central Committee resolutions which in a few days will become law; leisurely to decide the fate of others; to say over the phone, in a friendly voice: "Think it over, but it seems to me that it would be better to proceed in this way"—and then to lean back in his chair, aware that he had issued an order and that his order will be carried out. Or to make an appearance at affairs organized by his subordinates—famous scholars, popular artists or authors. It is agreeable modestly to take one's place in a corner and to observe with concealed satisfaction as the famous and the popular rush up with requests for instructions.

To taste these supreme pleasures of his life, he would be prepared to give up all else: the Finnish furniture, even the Armenian cognac. After he had fallen from power, Khrushchev said that one can have enough of everything—food, women, even vodka—but never of power. Djilas, who had moved in these circles himself, called power "the pleasure of pleasures."

For the *nomenklatura* this pleasure, considerable at the urban, regional, or district level, expands into infinity once it extends over a country that stretches from Sweden to Japan. Its member is still more thrilled when his amicable commands can be conveyed to friendly countries, which one remembers from school days as remote, foreign lands: Warsaw, Budapest, Berlin, Sofia, Prague, Kabul, the fabulously remote Havana and Hanoi. During an interview held in his office with the correspondent of *Stern*, Brezhnev could not resist showing him a telephone with red buttons which one only had to press to obtain direct connections with the First Secretaries of the Communist parties of socialist countries. One presses the button, inquires about the state of health, asks best wishes to be conveyed to the family—and offers "advice." And then one leans back in the leather chair, to ponder with profound satisfaction how they will now scurry in that foreign capital to carry out the "advice."

The leading figures of the Soviet *nomenklatura* travel from one capital to another and everywhere deliver their smooth, as if lubricated, speeches: about peaceful coexistence, about the inviolability of frontiers, about the impossibility of "exporting revolution." But before their eyes temptingly loom rich lands, splendid cities, bearing names known from childhood, which it would be marvellous to have at one's disposal. And new buttons. Ever new buttons.[21]

# CHAPTER

# II

# THE SOVIET
# THREAT

For reasons presented in the previous chapter, the Soviet Union and countries that copy its system tend to be expansionist. This observation gives rise to the following questions: What is the objective of Soviet and Soviet-type expansionism, and by what means is it pursued?

As concerns the objective, no one familiar with Communist theory can entertain much doubt. It is the elimination, worldwide, of private ownership of the means of production and the "bourgeois" order which rests upon it, and its replacement with what Lenin called a "worldwide republic of soviets." This theme has been restated with monotonous regularity in Communist speeches and publications from 1917 to the present. The following example is representative. It comes from an article in a leading Soviet theoretical journal devoted to the legacy of Lenin's last writings. At the very head of the list of Lenin's injunctions to his followers stands the goal of Soviet imperialism:

> The development of the world revolutionary process, including the awakening of the eastern nations oppressed by imperialism and, in this connection, prospects for the development of world revolution and the final victory of socialism.[1]

**49**

These objectives, it needs stressing, are not a distant, unfocused hope, as is the case with the synthetic "national goals" that issue from time to time from committees of distinguished Americans appointed for the purpose, but a concrete expectation and an operative principle. In Communist societies it is drummed into the head of every school child and memorized by every university student. By virtue of constant reiteration, this idea turns into a psychological reality that even many opponents of the regime learn unconsciously to accept. It is critical to the survival of the *nomenklatura*. Ultimately, it is the prospect that some day the whole world will be like the Soviet Union and its dependencies that makes resistance appear futile and instills in their citizens the spirit of acquiescence. But it also bolsters the *nomenklatura*'s own morale; this parasitic elite will feel completely secure only on the day when there no longer will be any alternative to its authority and system of government.

People who react with skepticism to the proposition that the Soviet Union seriously expects to transform the world into its own image assume that the "final victory of socialism" must mean the physical occupation of the world by Soviet forces; and since they rightly consider such an occupation to be impractical, they dismiss the whole idea of a "worldwide republic of soviets" as empty rhetoric. However, there is no reason why the domination of the globe must assume the form of physical control: For that purpose, hegemony is sufficient. The concept of hegemony, which was introduced in ancient Greece to describe the preeminence on the Hellenic peninsula of one city-state (such as Macedon), is very relevant in this context. In a world from which the United States has been eliminated as a power of the first rank, the Soviet Union would enjoy such overwhelming economic and military preponderance that opposition to its wishes on the part of any other "socialist republic"—which is all that would remain—would be inconceivable. Moreover, with each "socialist republic" administered by a native *nomenklatura* put in power and kept in power by the Soviet Union, the chances of defiance would be reduced still further. How long such an arrangement would last, if it ever came to be, is another question. The important thing is that the Communist concept of a postcapitalist world is not visionary and must not be dismissed on the grounds that realistic men, such as the Soviet leaders, cannot possibly seriously entertain it. A regime built on utopian expectations and driven by utopian aspirations may be coldly realistic in its choice of means and, indeed, use utopia to buttress very mundane interests. As one cynic put it, what are ends for if not to justify the means?

Global hegemony as an ideal requires unconventional methods, all the more so because under modern conditions classic military conquest of infinite spaces, such as attempted by Alexander the Great or Napoleon, is no longer feasible; for that to happen, the Soviet Union would have to dispose of the kind of overwhelming technical superiority that Europe enjoyed from the fifteenth to the early twentieth centuries, and with the help of which it subjugated most of the world. In an age when science and technology know no frontiers, such preponderance is no longer available to any country, except fleetingly. In modern times, successful imperialism demands a combination of means—diplomatic, psychological, ideological and economic, as well as military—for the purpose of eroding the opponent's ability and will to resist. The accepted term for politics of combined operations of this kind is *Grand Strategy*. Democratic governments find it difficult to conduct a grand strategy except in wartime, because normally they control neither the productive wealth of their countries, nor the labor of their citizens, nor the organs of opinion, as they must in order to carry out coordinated campaigns. Totalitarian regimes, by contrast, find grand strategy a natural way of conducting foreign relations, since all the instruments which it requires are in their hands to begin with. The purpose of this chapter is to describe Soviet Grand Strategy in both its principles and its applications.

# 1 SOVIET GRAND STRATEGY

Soviet leaders claim, with unconcealed pride, that they approach every problem that confronts them in a scientific manner. By this they mean that they act neither on emotional impulses nor out of moral considerations, but always seek to determine dispassionately, first the laws that govern the business at hand, then the "objective factors" of the situation, and finally, where pertinent, the "correlation of forces" between the contending parties. In their dealings with foreign powers, they try to initiate actions or respond to the actions of others in accordance with a systematic assessment of the correlation of forces. Whether politics in fact lends itself to such scientific management is questionable; at any rate, frequent Soviet foreign-policy failures suggest that the appropriate methodology has not yet been discovered. Nevertheless, it is true that the individuals who make foreign policy in Communist societies analyze and weigh more carefully the factors likely to influence the outcome of political or military initiatives than is the case with their democratic counterparts. This habit the Communists first acquired in the revolutionary underground. Experience taught them long ago that, when engaging a superior opponent (and until they triumph, revolutionaries are by definition weaker than the governments they seek to overthrow), one must always act with utmost caution, paying close attention to the correlation of forces and underestimating rather than overestimating one's own strength. Inasmuch as the trend of history is on the side of Communism anyway, there is no point in precipitating events when circumstances appear unfavorable; one merely has to wait for the correlation of forces to shift to one's advantage.

We have no knowledge how the Soviet leadership assesses its strengths and weaknesses in the global correlation of forces. A hypothetical balance sheet, however, might look as follows:

### SOVIET STRENGTHS:

□ A unique geopolitical situation that assures the USSR of relative immunity from conquest by hostile powers and yet allows it to probe for and exploit such opportunities for expansion as develop on the other side of its immensely long frontier with Europe and Asia;

□ Virtually complete control of its population and resources, unconstrained by constitution, representative bodies, or overt public opinion, with the resulting ability to coordinate political, military, economic and ideological instrumentalities in a Grand Strategy;

□ The opportunity to exploit to the fullest the internal differences in democratic societies without fear of being subjected to the same treatment; greater unity within its imperial bloc than is the case with the opponents' loose alliance of sovereign and democratic states.

### SOVIET WEAKNESSES:

□ An economy that, owing to the country's inherent poverty and an inefficient, heavily politicized method of organization, cannot adequately support the regime's global ambitions;

□ A political system that for all its outward solidity is ill-suited to cope with emergencies, such as political succession or foreign failures; because its domestic authority rests largely on the population's belief that it is invincible, the regime always faces the risk that humiliation abroad will subvert its power at home;

□ The danger that military involvement abroad may lead to a conflict with the United States and unleash nuclear war;

□ The unpopularity of Soviet-style Communism among the

world's masses and the absence of an attractive culture or life style.

This particular combination of strengths and weaknesses shapes Soviet Grand Strategy. Its relatively weak economy and its unappealing culture do not permit the Soviet Union to seek the kind of financial, commercial and cultural influence that greatly contributed to the successes of British imperialism. At the same time, fear of the political consequences of defeat on the field of battle, reinforced by the desire to avoid nuclear war with the United States, keep the Soviet Union from resorting to military force in the brash manner of twentieth-century Germany and Japan. The Soviet regime has had to develop a special kind of imperialism, adapted to its own strengths. These, in the ultimate reckoning, are political in nature and consist in *the unique ability of Communist regimes to impose tight control over their own domain while destabilizing the enemy's.* Given these realities, it is understandable that Communist leaders should rely most heavily on political means (which, in their thinking, include military power used for purposes of intimidation) and prefer to commit to military operations by proxy forces rather than their own. This kind of imperialism calls for a protracted, patient and prudent but unremitting *war of political attrition.* Its purpose is to undermine the authority of hostile governments and the will of their citizens to resist, while maintaining their own base solid, impregnable, and in a permanent state of mobilization.

Political attrition can be accomplished in a variety of ways: by exploiting the "contradictions" in the enemy's camp; by playing on his fears, especially those of nuclear destruction; by redefining the political vocabulary and bending the rules of international conduct to one's own advantage; by isolating enemy countries from one another and from their sources of raw materials. It is the sum of these diverse measures that constitutes Soviet Grand Strategy.

The term *politics* is used in Communist societies in a sense very different from that common in democracies. In the West, politics means civic activity—that is, the practice of administration or, more broadly, the art of governing. Communist theoreticians, however, have militarized politics and view it exclusively as a form of class warfare. This is how the subject is taught in Soviet school textbooks:

> In working out the strategic [or political] line of the Party under conditions of capitalism it is important, first of all, to define the *principal aim* of the working class at this stage and the *principal class enemy,* against whom it is essential at this point to concentrate class hatred and the striking force of all the workers in order to break his resistance.[2]

Noteworthy in this passage is the assumption that the objective of politics is "to break the resistance" of the opponent; this is essentially a military concept, and as such, it differs fundamentally from the view of politics prevalent in the West since the days of Aristotle, which sees its essence not in destruction but in cooperation.

Is it possible for a country with so many divergent interests, in a world so full of the unexpected, to conduct the kind of purposeful, long-term foreign policy that the concept Grand Strategy implies? Many deny this possibility. Men of the world, including practicing politicians, for whom history is a succession of emergencies to be disposed of as they come up, reject the whole notion as unworthy of serious consideration. To them, the foreign policy of the Soviet Union qualitatively in no way differs from that of any other great power—whatever its declared objectives, Moscow pursues its national interest. The latter is defined to consist, first and foremost, of ensuring the country's physical security, and secondly, of seizing advantage of such opportunities as the course of events offers to enhance its power and influence. In short, foreign policy is everywhere and at all times the same, even if some allowance must be made for local peculiarities, which in the case of the USSR are a non-Western past and the revolutionary background of its ruling class. Soviet talk of the "strategic line," of "breaking the enemy's will," of the "final victory of socialism" is treated by these people as rhetorical drivel, the Communist equivalent of democratic campaign oratory. Soviet foreign-affairs specialists assiduously encourage this "pragmatic" outlook in their Western counterparts.

The trouble with this pragmatic approach, which prevails in the foreign-policy establishments of all the Western countries, is that every attempt made since 1917 to treat the Soviet Union as another great power concerned exclusively with safeguarding its national security and increasing its international influence has ended in failure. One need only recall the Yalta accords. At Yalta, the United States went out of its way to satisfy what President Roosevelt considered Russia's legitimate national interests. Eastern Europe was acknowledged as Soviet sphere of influence. To ensure its entrance in the war against Japan—which probably nothing short of a United States threat to use atomic bombs could have prevented in any event—the Soviet Union was awarded territories belonging to China and Japan. The Ukraine and Belorussia, constituent units of the USSR, received double representation in the United Nations General Assembly. None of these extravagant concessions brought about the desired results; their immediate outcome was unprecedented Soviet expansionism and the Cold

War. State Department specialists on the Sovet Union, confronted with the breakdown of the Yalta accords and the ruin of their assumptions about that country, consoled themselves for a while with the fantastic notion that perhaps Stalin had come under attack from his colleagues on the Politbureau for having conceded too much to the Allies.[3] This experience, however, has taught the "pragmatists" nothing. A quarter of a century later, President Nixon decided to base détente on the very same principle that had served President Roosevelt so badly at Yalta. Early in his administration he informed his associates that United States-Soviet relations were to rest on mutual respect of the parties' "vital interests."[4] Disappointments with détente notwithstanding, the theme resounded again in the speeches of President Carter, who asked the Soviet Union rhetorically whether it was prepared to "promote a more stable international environment in which its own legitimate, peaceful concerns can be pursued."[5] The point, of course, is that the *nomenklatura* is concerned not with national interests but only its own, which are profoundly antinational, and that it does not even accept the notion of "legitimate" concerns in a "stable international order," inasmuch as it regards this whole order as thoroughly illegitimate and meriting overthrow. To be sure, the *nomenklatura* is pragmatic, but its pragmatism happens to require a strong commitment to what Western "pragmatists" dismiss as ideology.

To properly understand Grand Strategy one must not make it into a straw man. This concept has nothing in common with global "master plans" or "timetables." No country has ever produced anything of the sort: Even Hitler, who had a clear view how and in what stages he would secure control over Europe, had to adapt himself to unexpected events that sometimes promoted his plans (e.g., Chamberlain's surrender at Munich and Stalin's offer of a nonaggression pact) and sometimes disrupted them (e.g., his defeat in the Battle of Britain and Mussolini's unsuccessful invasion of Greece). There is no contradiction, whether in warfare or in politics, between the pursuit of strategic objectives and the exploitation of tactical opportunities; the one subsumes the other. Strategy is not getting what one wants but knowing what one wants and what it takes to get it. No great imperial power has ever come into existence either by mindless seizure of every opportunity that came its way or by a single-minded advance toward the ultimate objective without regard to opportunities. The dichotomy between Grand Strategy and opportunism is, therefore, a false one.

The growth of the British Empire demonstrates this contention. John Seeley coined the celebrated phrase that Britain had "con-

quered and peopled half the world in a fit of absence of mind."
On closer inspection, however, the manner in which Britain had
accomplished this task turns out to have been much less haphaz-
ard. It is true that British archives have yielded no documents with
comprehensive schemes of imperial strategy. Nevertheless, in the
words of an authoritative study of the subject, while "subjectively
and consciously [English statesmen] may have had no permanent
policy for the advancement of the State, but only a number of
expedients, temporary and shifting: yet, objectively and in practical effect, a policy [was] there." [6] This claim can be corroborated
by a glance at the historical atlas. It surely was no accident that
Britain concentrated its colonial acquisitions in two regions of the
world, namely North America and the lands bordering on the
Indian Ocean. Nor could it have been fortuitous that Britain seized
almost all of East Africa but largely ignored Africa's Atlantic coast;
that it took Gibraltar from Spain but returned to it the Balearic
Islands; that it inspired the United States to proclaim the Monroe
Doctrine which opened up Latin America to its commerce without
requiring it to establish costly political and military control over
the region.

Recent scholarship has shown that at the time it entered World
War I, Imperial Germany had developed a grand scheme of recon-
structing Europe after victory, which, had it won, would have
given it hegemony over the Continent and made it a true global
power.

The record of Imperial Russia indicates that it too undertook
major expansionist moves in the context of long-term political objectives. Its assault early in the eighteenth century on Sweden's
Baltic possessions and its interventions in the second half of that
century in Poland, which led to that country's destruction, were
inspired by conscious geopolitical considerations. They were not
mere seizures of opportunities but also creations of opportunities
for the purpose of advancing the government's principal foreign-
policy objective, which at the time was the introduction of Russia
as a permanent member into the European community. Later,
Russia's expansion into China, which in 1904 led to a war with
Japan, was undertaken in fulfillment of strategic plans for the political and economic domination of the Far East worked out by the
Minister of Finance, Serge Witte.

Now, if such planning on a global scale held true of conventional imperial powers, how much more must it be true of a regime
that by its very nature thinks globally and approaches politics in a
"scientific" manner. Soviet sources since 1917, especially from the
early years when Soviet leaders, confident of imminent victory,

spoke of their plans frankly and openly, provide ample evidence to this effect. The minutes of congresses of the Party and the Communist International, as well as internal communications from the immediate postrevolutionary years, are filled with discussions of Grand Strategic plans in which the globe is treated as if it were a giant chessboard. The following are two examples drawn from a large body of evidence.

In 1920 the Communist International held its second Congress, at which the strategy for the worldwide revolutionary struggle was formulated. One of its resolutions called for expanding the struggle against the "bourgeoisie" in geographic breadth in order to compel the class enemy to dissipate his forces:

> In the period of the Communist Revolution, the Communist Party in its essence turns into a party of the offensive, of pressure on capitalist society. . . . It is obligated to do everything in order directly to lead the working masses in this offensive, everywhere where the conditions for it are ripe . . . These conditions consist, first and foremost, in *exacerbating the struggle in the camp of the bourgeoisie itself on the national and international scale.* When the struggle in the camp of the bourgeoisie assumes dimensions which open perspectives that the working class will deal with enemy forces in a condition of dispersal, then the party must take into its hands the initiative, so that, after careful political and, insofar as feasible, organizational preparation, it can lead the masses into combat. . . .
>
> The experience of the revolution indicates that the broader the field of combat, the greater the hope for victory.[7]

We find a similar habit of global strategic thinking in Trotsky's analysis of the world situation outlined in his letter to the Central Committee of August 1919:

> There is no doubt at all that our Red Army constitutes an incomparably more powerful force in the Asian terrain of world politics than in the European terrain. Here there opens up before us an undoubted possibility . . . of conducting activity in the Asian field. The road to India may prove at the given moment to be more readily passable and shorter for us than the road to Soviet Hungary. The sort of army, which at the moment can be of no great significance in the European scales, can upset the unstable balance of Asian relationships, of colonial dependence, give a direct push to an uprising on the part of the oppressed masses and assure the triumph of such a rising in Asia. . . .
>
> One authoritative military official already some months ago put up a plan for creating a cavalry corps (30,000–40,000 riders) with the idea of launching it against India.
>
> It stands to reason that a plan of this sort requires careful prepara-

tion, both material and political. We have up to now devoted too little attention to agitation in Asia. However, the international situation is evidently shaping in such a way that the road to Paris and London lies via the towns of Afghanistan, the Punjab and Bengal . . .[8]

Trotsky's analysis has reached us by accident; the resolutions of the contemporary equivalents of the dissolved Communist International are much less explicit. Even so, there is no shortage of material to show that the present-day Soviet leadership thinks and plans much as its predecessors had done.

The Soviet penetration into the Middle East, which began in 1954–55 with the signing of military accords between the Communist Bloc and Cairo, is commonly depicted as a defensive move in reaction to the Baghdad Pact with which John Foster Dulles had attempted to bar the Soviet Union from penetrating the Middle East. In the interpretation of the "pragmatic" school of thought, this was a Soviet reaction to an American initiative and, as such, perfectly consonant with conventional great-power politics. But we happen to have it on good authority that the Egyptian accords had for the Soviet Union broader and more aggressive ramifications—that they were, in fact, a strategic move whose target was not the Middle East but Western Europe. Here is what Andrei Sakharov remembers from the days when he was still a trusted member of the Soviet Establishment:

I often recall a talk given in 1955 by a high official of the USSR Council of Ministers to a group of scientists assembled at the Kremlin. He said that at that time . . . the principles of the new Soviet policy in the Middle East were being discussed in the Presidium. And he observed that the long-range goal of that policy, as it had been formulated, was to exploit Arab nationalism in order to create difficulties for the European countries in obtaining crude oil, and thereby to gain influence over them.[9]

To think of oil as an instrument of political leverage and of the Middle East as a backdoor to Europe is the very essence of Grand Strategy.

In open Soviet publications, many of which are translated into English for the benefit of radical intellectuals in the Third World, Soviet Grand Strategy is outlined in thinly veiled language. Thus, in 1973 appeared a book, edited by V. V. Zagladin, whose very title would evoke condescending smiles in NATO's foreign offices were it written by a Western author—*The World Communist Move-*

*ment: Outline of Strategy and Tactics.* The book contains theoretical directives from the Soviet Central Committee to Communist parties in "capitalist" countries. In it appears the following passage:

> The present stage of the revolutionary movement in the capitalist countries cannot as yet be regarded as a period of revolutionary assaults against the citadels of capitalism. It is primarily a period in which the way is paved for the socialist revolution, and the political army of revolution is formed. The workers' revolutionary movement in these countries is developing and acquiring political maturity. Even in the conditions of the so-called "calm" development of capitalism, the working class, by extending anti-monopoly action, is ever more undermining the foundations of capitalism from within. The leading role of the working class and its revolutionary vanguard in the broad anti-monopoly movement of the people . . . is enhancing the revolutionary consciousness of the masses. Thus, the material and socio-political conditions are ever more maturing for a revolutionary replacement of capitalism by a new social system. . . .[10]

To understand the above message, the reader only has to decipher a few code words, substituting for "workers' revolutionary movement" and "revolutionary vanguard" Communist parties. Thus decoded, the statement says that as of 1973 (when it was made), the time was not yet ripe for a direct assault on Western democratic societies ("citadels of capitalism") but was better employed for organizing one's forces for a future assault. As explained in another part of the book, the "broad anti-monopoly movement of the people" meant exerting pressures on capitalist systems to nationalize private enterprises and bring workers (read: Communist trade-union leaders) into corporate management. Once such changes in the capitalist economy have been carried out, the result will be clashes "between the working people and the state . . . in the course of which the question of the nature of state power is bound to arise sooner or later." The end result will be a "revolutionary replacement of capitalism" by socialism.[11] In plain language, a Soviet political theorist exhorts Communists in Western countries to work for the expropriation in their countries of private property and the transfer of corporate management to Communist trade-union leaders as a means of securing a base from which, at the appropriate time, to launch an assault on the "capitalist" state.

These passages have been cited to illustrate a mode of thinking characteristic of the revolutionary mind, whether the revolutionary in question is in the underground, battling to seize power, or sits comfortably ensconced by his multi-buttoned phone in the Central Committee's headquarters on Moscow's Staraia Ploshchad', planning the "class struggle" on the international scale. It takes for granted the inevitability of unremitting global social conflicts until ultimate victory; it sets the schedule of action in the context of a sober assessment of the correlation of forces; it subordinates everything to political objectives.

This manner of thinking is quite alien to Western societies, especially to the diplomats, lawyers, businessmen and professional politicians who set the tone of East-West relations. These people are unprepared by either education or experience to believe that there is anything in the world worth doing or possessing that does not lend itself to "deals." Confronted with "nonnegotiable" demands, they take them to be negotiating ploys. Whenever they do succeed in striking a bargain on some particular issue with a power like the Soviet Union (or Nazi Germany, for that matter) that has the reputation of being engaged in an uncompromising pursuit of Grand Strategy, they feel not only pleased but vindicated. It never occurs to them that for the other party the deal is not an end to the dispute but one move in a larger game, and that this or that concession that they may have succeeded in extracting from it will be lost once the stakes are raised further, as they invariably are.

## 2 SOVIET POLITICAL STRATEGY

As previously mentioned, the logic of the situation—its particular blend of strengths and weaknesses—compels the Soviet Union to rely heavily in its Grand Strategy on political means. Political strategy, in turn, means first and foremost promoting and exploiting divisions in the enemy camp: driving wedges between citizens of democratic societies and their elected officials, aggravating relations among social classes as well as ethnic and religious groups, and sowing discord among Allies. This classic *divide et impera* policy, which forms the essence of Soviet political strategy, was formulated as early as the 1920 Congress of the Communist International as "exacerbating the struggle in the camp of the bourgeoisie itself on the national and international scale."[12] Lenin often stressed the supreme importance of this technique. In a tract written in 1920 against the advocates of a "direct" assault on capitalism, he expressed his views in a particularly blunt manner:

> [The] entire history of Bolshevism, both before and after the October Revolution, is *full* of instances of changes of tack, conciliatory tactics and compromises with other parties, including bourgeois parties!

To carry on a war for the overthrow of the international bourgeoisie . . . and to renounce in advance any change of tack, or any utilization of a conflict of interests (even if temporary) among one's enemies, or any conciliation or compromise with possible allies . . . is that not ridiculous in the extreme? . . .

After the first socialist revolution of the proletariat, and the overthrow of the bourgeoisie in some country, the proletariat of that country remains *for a long time weaker* than the [international] bourgeoisie . . . The more powerful enemy can be vanquished only by exerting the utmost effort, and by the most thorough, careful, attentive, skillful and *obligatory* use of any, even the smallest, rift between the enemies, any conflict of interests among the bourgeoisie of the various countries . . . and also by taking advantage of any, even the smallest, opportunity of winning a mass ally, even though this ally is temporary, vacillating, unstable, unreliable, and conditional . . .[13]

This strategy is designed to exploit clashes of opinion and of interest, which are the essence of democracy, to the advantage of a regime that tolerates neither—in other words, to turn constructive competition into self-destruction. That this technique must be employed by any power bent on conquering a Western country was noted with remarkable prescience a century and a half ago by the father of modern strategic doctrine, Karl von Clausewitz—"It is impossible," he wrote, "to obtain possession of a great country with European civilization otherwise than by aid of internal division."[14]

The *divide et impera* policy strives to sow discord among the allies as well as within each allied country by inflaming antagonisms and arousing mutual suspicions, using for this purpose political, military and economic inducements or punishments, as the situation requires. The following are some examples of this tactic as applied by the Soviet Union toward NATO countries:

◻ In signing business contracts for projects in the USSR and Eastern Europe, preference is given to countries which pursue an accommodating policy toward Moscow and are prepared to "decouple" commercial relations from political ones; countries which are deemed unfriendly or (because of their resort to sanctions and embargoes) "unreliable" are penalized. Such contracts encourage political accommodation, but they also create a dependence of the countries concerned on the Communist client. In Germany alone, some 300,000 jobs are said to be directly or indirectly linked to business with the Soviet Union and Eastern Europe. Since many of these jobs are in so-called "sunset," or declining, industries, liable to go under without the benefit of sales to Communist countries, aggravating unemployment, an economic dependence is created that no German government, regardless of its political preferences, can ignore.

□ The Soviet Union has persuaded much of the United States business community that if Washington conducted a more "friendly" policy—that is, reconciled itself to its aggressive actions —they would receive lush export orders. The lure of these orders has transformed United States business leaders into the most vociferous neutralist lobby in the country.

□ In countries with powerful Communist trade unions, such as Italy and France, the Soviet Union takes advantage of their presence to threaten industrial unrest to firms that hesitate to enter with it into commercial agreements.

□ The Soviet Union has for years exploited the yearning of West Germans for personal contacts with their families in East Germany to extract from Bonn an accommodating stance; it has used, to the same end, West Germany's desire for the eventual unification of its divided nation.

□ France's fear of the supremacy of the "Anglo-Saxons" as well as of the Germans on the Continent is played upon to incite Paris to conduct an "independent" foreign policy.

□ The Soviet Union interferes in democratic elections abroad by bestowing its blessing on candidates whose stand on international issues happens to suit its interests. They and their parties are depicted as forces for "peace," whose election will lead to the improvement of relations with Moscow and lower the risk of war (e.g., Richard Nixon in 1972; Giscard d'Estaing in 1973 and 1981; and the German Social Democratic Party in 1983).

□ The USSR pressures the West to enter with it into "mutual security" accords, the most comprehensive of which was signed in Helsinki in 1975; these create the illusion that it shares with the United States responsibility for safeguarding the peace and integrity of the Continent as a whole, thereby undermining NATO and pushing Western Europe toward neutralism.

□ Moscow increases or diminishes the flow of Jewish émigrés in accord with the status of over-all United States–Soviet Union relations as a device for pressuring the American Jewish community to influence its government toward accommodation.

□ The USSR offers support to terrorists of every political hue, right-wing as well as left-wing, sometimes both concurrently, in order to destroy in foreign countries the basis of law and order and thus either make them vulnerable to a Communist-power seizure or else drive them into the arms of a right-wing dictatorship, which enables native Communists to assume leadership of the "united democratic front"; this practice by the Soviet client, Bulgaria, has caused civil unrest to break out in Turkey a few years ago and nearly resulted in that country's political collapse.

Such instances of the application of the principle of *divide et impera* can be multiplied without difficulty from the experience of Europe and other regions; they implement Lenin's call for exploiting the "rifts" in the enemy camp. It is a devastating strategy when applied against democracies, because democracies cannot remain true to themselves unless they tolerate dissent among their citizens and disagreements within their alliances. Such dissent and such disagreements, however, offer Moscow infinite opportunities to interfere in their affairs by throwing its not inconsiderable weight to support now this, now that contending party. Confronted with another totalitarian state, such as Nazi Germany or Communist China, the Soviet leadership, unable to resort to this strategy, finds itself severely handicapped—prevented by the hostile regime's tight grip on its population from reaching over its head to the diverse social and political groups, it tends toward accommodation. Thus, after signing the nonaggression pact with Hitler in 1939, Stalin scrupulously refrained from interfering in internal German affairs. When in January 1940 Mussolini berated his ally for being too friendly with Moscow, Hitler responded that a basis had been created for an "acceptable" relationship with the USSR—"We no longer have cause [to complain] that any Russian department attempts to exert influence in internal German affairs."*[15] It goes without saying that the vulnerability of democratic societies to internal interference causes Moscow to favor the broadest kind of democracy for countries that it has an interest in weakening, in accord with the adage, "When I am the weaker, I demand from you liberty, because this is your principle; when I am the stronger, I deprive you of it, because this is my principle."

So much for political tactics. Above them stands the "general line" that determines the application of Grand Strategy to given

---

* The Soviet government, indeed, showed a tolerance toward Nazism that it has never displayed toward the democracies. In a speech which he delivered on October 31, 1939, in the midst of furious attacks on England and France for waging war on Hitler, V. M. Molotov, Soviet Commissar of Foreign Affairs, declared preference for National-Socialism to be a question of taste: "The ideology of Hitlerism, as any ideological system, can be accepted or rejected: this is a matter of political opinion" (*Pravda*, Nov. 1, 1939, 1).

historic circumstances. In Lenin's day, the general line focused on two targets: in the industrial countries, aggravating social strife and the competition for markets; in the colonial areas, inciting movements for national independence. This approach largely lost its utility after World War II. The extraordinary economic progress of Western societies under "Pax Americana" and the movements of social reform that accompanied it have in all Western countries reduced class consciousness as well as social strife. The modern Western working class can by no stretch of the imagination be treated as *proletariat* in the classic Marxist sense. This concept, which derives from the Latin *proles* ("offspring," defining a class in ancient Rome whose whole wealth consisted of children), lost meaning in the advanced industrial countries as labor merged into the lower-middle class. Surveys conducted since the Second World War indicate that only a small minority of German workers think of themselves as workers, and many of them do not even know what the word *proletarian* means. In addition, everywhere in industrial countries the proportion of manually occupied employees steadily declines as white-collar and service employees take the place of blue-collar workers. Any Communist political strategist worth his salt would have to conclude that the objective trends of modern economies point toward an irreversible decline of labor as an isolated and aggrieved class and, consequently, that a strategy based on the exploitation of differences between the haves and have-nots in advanced industrial countries offers little scope. The same holds true of expectation of conflicts among "capitalist" countries for markets and sources of raw materials. In the 1920s Trotsky could still fantasize that economic rivalries will lead the United States and Great Britain to war. But nothing of the kind has ever occurred or even came close to occurring. The emergence after the war of multinational corporations has further smoothed competition among states over markets and resources. Those economic differences that continue to divide democratic societies—as, for instance, over tariffs or subsidies—are resolved peacefully through high-level negotiation; they hardly lend themselves to political exploitation by Moscow.

The old general line is no more appropriate to conditions in the postwar Third World. Since 1945, all the non-Communist colonies have been emancipated, making agitation for "national liberation" irrelevant. Here and there it is still possible to stoke the fires of anti-Westernism (e.g., among the Palestinians and in Namibia) but these areas offer limited opportunity. Here too, therefore, new strategies had to be devised. We will discuss these changed policies later in this chapter, and now turn to the central theme of the current Soviet general line toward the West, which revolves around the related subjects of "peace" and "the bomb."

The slogan of peace has served the Communists well in the past. In 1917, their readiness to come out for an immediate and unconditional end to the war (they were the only party in Russia to adopt this policy) contributed substantially to their ability to take power. The call for peace enabled them to transform Russian armies into mutinous mobs and to gain majorities in the soviets of the principal cities filled with fresh recruits. Although today the peace slogan does not have the same relevance that it had in Russia of 1917, since the world is at least formally at peace, in some respects it reverberates in the human consciousness even more powerfully than in the past, because of the appearance of nuclear weapons, which not only threaten unprecedented casualties but are believed by many to place at risk the very survival of the human race.

In its most rudimentary sense, *peace* means the absence of hostilities. Such a negative definition, however, is not very meaningful; by its criterion, an efficient prison or a regime of military occupation creates conditions of peace, whereas, in reality, both merely institutionalize violence. The preferred usage is positive in emphasis, defining peace not as the absence of hostilities but as the existence of accord. Its distinguishing feature is law, which provides a mechanism for resolving disputes on the basis of objective principles, acknowledged as binding on them by the parties involved. Formal "peace," imposed by the application or the threat of force, produces at best a truce; its rationale is the realization by the weaker party that resistance is futile. It is thus by its very nature precarious, being liable to be upset whenever the imbalance of forces that has made it possible in the first place is rectified. The true antithesis of war, therefore, is not the absence of overt hostilities, or war in the dictionary sense, but the rule of law.

This is not, of course, how the *nomenklatura* defines and exploits this concept, so charged with emotion. Its definition is the most formalistic imaginable: peace means nothing more nor less than a condition in which sovereign states do not shoot at each other. Any other manifestation of hostility is said to be quite compatible with peace—"ideological warfare," for example, which incites to hatred; or "class war," which pits one social group against another; or "wars of national liberation," which encourage racial conflict in the Third World. Such a definition is well calculated to serve Soviet interests, which are to avoid general war with the "imperialist camp" while inciting and exacerbating every possible conflict within it. A Russian joke has it that Moscow will never start a war but that it will wage peace so vigorously that not one stone shall be left upon another.

The Soviet government exploits the peace theme in a variety of ways. Of these, two deserve particular attention: defining peace to mean acquiescence to Soviet demands; and creating a false sense of identity between East and West by making weapons rather than the people behind the weapons appear the main threat to peace. Moscow dominates the international discussion about nuclear weapons, because it is able to counter the babble of contentious and emotional Western voices with a single, steadfast voice of its own. The commissioning of its nuclear weapons is surrounded with such a thick veil of secrecy that even high Soviet officials are kept in the dark. This contrasts with comprehensive debates in Congress and the media in the United States about appropriations for every proposed new nuclear system and, in Western Europe, about their deployment. While in the West strategies for waging nuclear war are discussed openly in bloodcurdling detail—"limited nuclear war," civilian versus military targeting, weapons that destroy people but spare inanimate objects, and so on—in the Soviet Union these matters are left exclusively to the discretion of a small body of military experts. As a result of the imposition of near-total secrecy on its own nuclear deployments and strategies, Moscow is able to create the impression that it does not even consider such matters and builds weapons solely to protect itself from "nuclear maniacs."

It is in the interest of the Soviet Union to depict the nuclear weapon, however employed, as capable of destroying life on earth —regardless of whether this is objectively true or not. In order to keep this threat clearly in front of the Western public, it insists that not only can there be no limited use of nuclear weapons, as postulated by NATO's theory of "flexible response," but that any resort to these weapons will inevitably unleash a nuclear holocaust. This is not a strategic doctrine, since Soviet nuclear deployments clearly indicate that Moscow entertains a variety of its own "flexible responses"; it is, rather, a psychological device, a means of behavioral manipulation. It helps to establish the principle which is at the heart of the current Soviet political strategy toward the West, that good relations with the Soviet Union must become the supreme objective of Western policy. This principle is conveyed by a series of half-truths linked by a pseudo logic, the appeal of which is not to the mind but to the heart. It is designed to translate the natural dread that most people have of war in general and nuclear war in particular into an overwhelming anxiety that paralyzes thought and will. The chain of casuistic reasoning runs approximately as follows: (1) nuclear war would destroy life on earth; (2) since life is the highest good, anything is preferable to nuclear war; (3) nuclear war can be avoided only if the interests of the Soviet Union and its Bloc are respected; (4) the interests of the Soviet Union and its Bloc are determined by the Soviet government; (5) any challenge to the wishes of the Soviet government, therefore, threatens nuclear war and extinction of life on this planet. From this sequence of reasoning, whose connections are anything but logical, it follows that every Soviet action, no matter how aggressive and immoral, need not be condoned but must be acquiesced to for the sake of the supreme objective, preservation of good relations with the Soviet Union, which alone makes it possible to preserve peace, which in turn ensures the survival of mankind.

The Soviet Union has achieved remarkable success with this specious argument. One can often hear Western intellectuals and politicians echo it with a conviction worthy of a better cause. Thus, Congressman Jonathan Bingham of New York has expressed the following sentiment:

> *Above all,* we must remember that the Soviet Union remains the world's only other superpower—the only country in the world capable of destroying us. Maintaining good relations with the Soviet Union must be our *paramount* objective.[16]

On the face of it, the statement appears unexceptionally trite. But what is it really saying? That objectives of life other than physical survival, objectives which enabled our ancestors to bequeath to us the benefits of the civilization—among them, personal freedom, the rule of law, and human rights—must in our age take second place to "good relations with the Soviet Union"? That should other powers also acquire the capacity to destroy us, "good relations" with them will also have to become our "paramount objective"? That we must give the Soviet government carte blanche to perpetrate inside its country and abroad any barbarity as long as it refrains from firing nuclear weapons at us? It is doubtful that Congressman Bingham had thought through the implications of his words, they seemed such a reassuring string of clichés, but whether he knew it or not, he had adopted the Soviet definition of peace.

Another example of this mentality, in some respects even more appalling, comes from Carl-Friedrich von Weizsäcker. The author is a distinguished scientist who has close connections with the leadership of the German Social-Democratic Party. He felt no compunction in saying, in what appears to be oblique criticism of President Reagan:

> A policy which divides the world into the good and the evil, and which views the greatest power alongside which it is our destiny to live as the center of evil is not a policy of peace *even if its moral judgments are correct.*[17]

What Mr. Weizsäcker seems to be saying is that in relations with a nuclear power of the first magnitude, moral judgments have to be suspended or at least not voiced. Morality itself is subordinated to the cause of "peace," in the sense of getting along with "the greatest power"—that is, the Soviet Union. Inconsistently, Mr. Weizsäcker does not condemn Soviet leaders for abusing the United States in incomparably more offensive terms; for some reason he does not consider abusive pronouncements when they emanate from Moscow as a disservice to the cause of peace. Such are the inconsistencies and immoralities one is driven into when one adopts the principle that survival is the supreme goal of individuals and nations.

Once the principle has been established that irritating or standing up to the Soviet Union must be avoided at all costs, no matter how grave the provocation, an important psychological battle has been lost. In this atmosphere, the Soviet Union is able to set the rules for the conduct of international relations in a manner that gives it license to perpetrate any outrage short of launching nuclear weapons without having to worry about reactions other than opprobrium; and, if Herr von Weizsäcker has this way, even opprobrium will be silenced. Should this view prevail, the driving force behind the foreign policy of Western powers will no longer be the commitment to protect national interest or the values of Western civilization, but the naked terror of the caveman. Terror-driven fear, however, lends itself to political exploitation. The subject has not attracted much attention from scholars; among the few to have considered it is the Swiss writer Urs Schwarz. Mr. Schwarz draws a useful distinction between fear proper *(Furcht)*, which he defines as a healthy response to an identifiable threat that produces a defensive reaction, and anxiety *(Angst)* which is a generalized condition of fear, focused on no particular threat, and, as such, liable to feed on itself and to paralyze the will. Referring to nuclear weapons, he says:

> That the danger in the technical sense is real and that the accumulated forces of destruction are monstrous requires neither emphasis nor

proof. One knows them and has every reason to be deeply concerned. But the attitude of the majority of the people toward these facts is not one of fear or of concern but of pronounced anxiety . . . It is precisely in this connection that the distinction between fear and anxiety assumes great significance . . . While fear . . . is an entirely desirable reaction to the threat of nuclear weapons, because it makes possible the reaction of deterrence and thereby prevents war, anxiety can produce the contrary effect.[18]

Andrei Sakharov has warned the West of the dangers of accepting the Soviet "rules of the game" in international relations. But as with much else that concerns this wise and brave man, he is praised and his counsel ignored. Manipulation of the international rules of conduct to its exclusive benefit, against a general climate of nuclear terror, is one of the most effective and least noted tools of Soviet foreign policy. Of the rules skewed in favor of the Communist Bloc the following may serve as examples:

□ The so-called Brezhnev Doctrine, which insists that any country that has crossed the line separating "feudalism" or "capitalism" from Communism must under no conditions revert to its previous status, whereas all non-Communist social and political systems are subject to change of ownership at all times. This principle of one-way change, tacitly accepted by the West, ensures that the East-West competition over spheres of influence takes place exclusively at the expense of the West or third parties.

□ In any region where they come under attack from Communist guerrillas, non-Communist governments (e.g., in El Salvador) are subjected to international pressure to negotiate with their armed opponents; when the same situation arises in countries under Communist control (e.g., Nicaragua, Afghanistan, Angola) such pressures are absent.

□ The Soviet Union claims that its interests extend to every region of the globe—in the words of Andrei Gromyko, "today [1971] there is no question of any significance that can be decided without the Soviet Union or in opposition to it."[19] This claim allows Moscow to demand a voice in the solution of regional crises in any part of the world. At the same time, the Soviet Union denies other countries, the United States included, a comparable right; in high-level negotiation between the two countries, Soviet representatives insist that the agenda remain strictly confined to bilateral issues, which, in practice, means arms control.

□ The Soviet Union claims the prerogative of engaging in unrestrained "ideological warfare" even under conditions of détente.

This concept embraces hate campaigns against the United States, official pronouncements linking it with Nazi Germany, and predictions of the inevitable doom of the "capitalist" order. When, however, a Western statesman, such as President Reagan, refers to Communism as a historic failure or the "focus of evil," outraged voices in the Soviet Establishment and in the West complain of bellicosity and dangerous interference in the internal affairs of another "superpower."

□ The Soviet Union demands and receives the right to present its views on international affairs in Western media; no comparable right is accorded to Western spokesmen in Soviet media.

□ The Soviet Union is suffered to manufacture and deploy nuclear missiles with an unmistakable first-strike capability; when the United States commissions similar weapons, it is accused of "destabilizing" the nuclear balance and provoking war. The same applies to missile defenses.

This double standard cannot be defended on grounds of either logic or equity; it is nevertheless widely accepted and rationalized by left-of-center opinion in Western countries. The Brezhnev Doctrine goes unchallenged in the name of "realism." It would be "unrealistic," the argument runs, to try to alter the map of Eastern Europe or to remove Castro, even though these Communist regimes are admittedly unpopular and maintain themselves in power by the force of arms. (Oddly enough, the principle of realism is not invoked in regard to Israel's presence on the West Bank or South Africa's in Namibia.) Communist guerrillas are said to embody irresistible forces of social progress, whereas their anti-Communist counterparts stand for reaction. The one-sided Soviet access to Western media is defended as proof of democracy's superiority.

Soviet strategy has had much success in enforcing the principle that the West must present it with no proposal concerning East-West relations that Moscow has declared in advance to be unacceptable to it. As a consequence, East-West negotiations often take place within the Western camp, the contending parties arguing among themselves over the best terms that may reasonably be offered to Moscow. Proposals considered unacceptable to Moscow are rejected *a priori*, without a discussion of their intrinsic merits. An instance of such self-regulation occurred in the summer of 1983. During testimony before the Senate Foreign Relations Committee, the new director of the Arms Control and Disarmament Agency, Kenneth Adelman, came under pressure to define what weapons the Russians would have to give up to make it possible to cancel the MX program. Mr. Adelman objected that this question could not be meaningfully answered; but as the questioners would not relent, he volunteered that a dismantling of the Soviet SS-17, SS-18 and SS-19 systems would allow the United States to dispense with its new ICBM system.

How seriously Mr. Adelman meant this answer to be taken need not detain us. What matters is that the discussion that ensued centered not on the question whether the proposal was sensible and fair, but whether it would be acceptable to the Soviet Union. Senator Charles Mathias reacted at once negatively: he said that the Administration "has made impossible demands" on Moscow. Deputy Secretary of State Kenneth Dam, testifying in Congress, expressed the opinion that "to talk about eliminating an entire weapons system would go far beyond anything . . . the Soviets are willing to talk about."[20] By contrast, when the United States government made it known that it found entirely unacceptable Soviet proposals for a "nuclear freeze," no clamor was raised on either side of the Atlantic for the Soviet Union to give it up on the grounds of its "unacceptability" to the United States. In this case, whatever discussion took place concentrated on the merits of the Soviet proposal.


The impressive successes of the Soviet strategy of political divisiveness are in good measure explicable by the cooperation that it receives from witting and witless elements in the West.

Moscow has few reliable followers in NATO countries. In most of them, Communist parties enjoy little influence; in the few where they do dispose of a significant following, the local leaders often openly take issue with Soviet policies. Here and there, Communists manage to penetrate and capture the leadership of trade unions, church organizations, and other public bodies; they establish or support institutes that turn out pseudo-academic publications supportive of Soviet interests; they muster temporary alliances of "progressives" to oppose United States involvement in some Central American country or to pressure the United States to adopt a more "flexible" response to a Soviet arms proposal. If, however, the Soviet Union had to rely exclusively on these elements to advance its political strategy, it would scarcely be able to achieve much.

Of incomparably greater value to it are individuals and groups that have sympathy neither for Communism nor for the Soviet Union, but who, for reasons of their own, often unconnected with security considerations, find themselves supporting Soviet causes and abetting Soviet political strategy. They are the "useful idiots" whom Lenin had long ago taught his followers to exploit.

Democratic societies are oriented toward the satisfaction of private interests; the public sector exists for, and justifies itself by, its ability to create optimal conditions for the pursuit of such interests. Ideally, it should have no interests of its own; the democratic state is meant to be a service organization. Under any circumstances short of armed conflict, the democratic state finds its citizenry loath to sacrifice private interests to those of national security. This makes it possible for the most bizarre informal alliances to be formed between Western groups and Moscow. An American businessman, who receives orders from the USSR but cannot fill them because he is unable to obtain an export license looks upon Moscow as a friendly customer and upon Washington as a foe. An American politician who wants public money to fund "social" programs (an activity not unconnected with the garnering of votes) finds himself at one with Moscow in opposing increased United States defense expenditures. Rivals of the party in office derive malicious satisfaction from its foreign-policy failures, since these vindicate their opposition and bring the time nearer when they may come to power. As long as East-West competition remains at an acceptable—that is, nonviolent—level, major private interests in the West find it to their advantage to stress alleged similarities between East and West and to minimize the Soviet threat. In so doing, they are, in effect, making common cause with Moscow.

Weapon manufacturers apart, it is difficult to think of a group in the West that has a vested interest in bad relations with the Communist Bloc. And the production of military hardware is neither a significant nor a particularly profitable sector of Western economies, notwithstanding the mythology that surrounds the subject. The list of the four hundred wealthiest Americans, published annually by *Forbes* magazine, carries no names of arms manufacturers; it indicates that the road to riches leads by way of oil, real estate, computers or cosmetics, not national defense. The so-called hard-line trend in United States foreign policy is almost exclusively ideological in motivation: it brings little, if any, profit. It is in the "soft-line" end of the spectrum that one can identify a wide range of self-interest. This interest can assume various forms, material and other.

To begin with the academic community. In the 1930s, university circles showed a great deal of sympathy for Communism, but of this little remains. Western specialists on the Soviet Union in particular are, with few exceptions, highly critical of that country and regard sojourn there as hardship duty. Professional considerations, however, compel most of them to keep their opinions to themselves. A "sovietologist" feels that he must be able to travel to the USSR from time to time to consort with specialists there and to carry out research in libraries and archives. Since public criticism of the Soviet system or its actions may result in visa denials, the typical expert will not speak out on East-West relations other than in a most circumspect manner, balancing criticism of the one side with condemnation of the other. He will also strongly endorse cultural and scientific exchanges, even when these can be shown to be inequitable, because he is eager to ensure for himself access to the countries in which he specializes.

In broader intellectual and academic circles an interesting ambivalence prevails in regard to this subject. Most Western writers, scholars and scientists look upon the Soviet regime and its clients with unconcealed distaste. They are disgusted with the suppression of freedom there and the persecution of their friends and colleagues. They readily sign letters and petitions protesting such uncivilized behavior; some even go to the lengths of boycotting conferences held in Communist countries. But there is always present, especially among self-styled social scientists frustrated in their ambition to gain the prestige accorded to genuine scientists, an undercurrent of resentment against their own societies for not treating them with the proper respect, and, related to it, envy of their counterparts in the East. Although they entertain no illusions about the price which the Communist authorities exact, they begrudge the distinctions and privileges that faithful service to the *nomenklatura* brings with it, and of which they feel unjustly deprived. Such sentiments are quite common among Western academicians, although they are rarely expressed with the candor that the British historian A. J. P. Taylor displayed in his report on a visit to Hungary: "The treatment of [Hungarian] historians and other scholars fills me with envy," he confessed on his return—

> The Institute of Historical Research in Budapest has extensive quarters on Castle Hill and over sixty paid researchers on its staff. The comparable English Institute in London has modest quarters in the Senate House and no paid researchers. The Hungarian Academy has a palace all to itself just across from the Parliament House: colonnaded entrance and marble staircase. The Academy also owns country cottages, on Lake Balaton and in the mountains, which members of the Academy can use for free during the summer. The British Academy occupies a few rooms in Burlington House and possesses no country cottages.

Professor Taylor cannot be ignorant that the colonnaded entrances, marble staircases, and country cottages that have aroused such envy in him must be paid for in directed research, censorship, and other forms of intellectual humiliation. Even so, he resents society for denying him the rewards he considers rightfully his; and he does so despite the evidence that he himself adduces that the Hungarian academics themselves do not seem aware "how well off they are," for it appears that during his visit most of them were out of the country on sabbaticals in England, the United States and Finland.[21]

Allowance must also be made for public groups and their patrons in the federal and state governments who draw on money raised through taxes (or paid for with deficits) to subsidize their programs and pay their salaries. The powerful associations of teachers and health-care personnel, for example, have a vested interest in keeping the defense budget as small as possible, since that budget is in direct competition with their own for public funds. To keep defense budgets small, they minimize the Soviet threat, and represent the real danger to United States security as coming from inadequately financed social services. It helps to assess the quality of this argument by imagining how it would have sounded in the 1930s, when the Nazis were arming for war, had it been said of Poland, Britain or France that they were threatened not by the Wehrmacht, but by inadequately funded schools and hospitals. Self-serving and specious as this argument is, it has persuasive force, because it involves immense sums of money and affects the welfare of millions of voters.

The most unabashed voice in the West favoring accommodation with the Soviet Union, however, belongs to the business community. On the face of it, pro-Soviet sympathies on the part of a group that the Soviet Union is committed to destroying may seem absurd, but it is a fact that only serves to emphasize the elitist character of the Soviet leadership and the affinities that elites feel for each other, notwithstanding ideological or national differences. The workers of all countries have never united as effectively as have their ruling elites, which constitute the only true international. In United States elections, as a rule, the most "liberal" candidates fare best in precincts with educated and affluent voters, whereas conservative ones draw their support from the poorer classes. This trend runs contrary to historical experience: conservatism has traditionally been the ideology of the privileged who have a vested interest in the *status quo* and oppose change. The Soviet *nomenklatura*, which is a rigidly conservative body, conforms to this pattern. Public-opinion polls further indicate that in the United States, the desire for accommodation with the Soviet Union is strongest among the educated upper-income groups, and declines as one moves down the educational and social scale, yielding among the lower strata to belligerent anti-Communism. It surely is astonishing that Soviet emissaries are received with open arms by the National Association of Manufacturers and the Chamber of Commerce, but dare not set foot in the headquarters of American trade-union organizations.*

This unnatural good will for the Soviet Union of those who stand to lose the most should it attain its ultimate objectives is most readily explained by commercial interests. The United States business community has always believed that the Soviet Union constitutes a vast potential market for its capital and goods. Its representatives beat a path to Lenin's Moscow as soon as the last shots of the Civil War had died down, in search of profitable concessions and contracts.[22] Experience has never borne out these expectations. Because the Soviet government is chronically short of both capital and goods to sell in industrial countries, its hope for extensive trade with the West rests on receipt of loans, either issued or guaranteed by Western governments.

The United States government has not adopted the practice of European states in this respect; indeed, in the early 1970s it imposed stringent limits on the amount of credits the Import-Export Bank could extend to the Soviet Union. As a consequence, United States–Soviet trade has never come near the levels that its advocates in both countries had hoped for. In the 1970s, during the era of détente, the total nonagricultural trade between the two countries (imports and exports combined) hovered around one billion dollars a year. United States nonagricultural exports to the USSR between 1971 and 1981 averaged annually slightly over $500 million; even in the second half of the decade, when the USSR had begun to make large-scale agricultural purchases, exports barely reached $2 billion. Total United States imports from the USSR remained through this decade in the low hundreds of millions.[23]

---

* The first (and, so far, last) occasion when a Soviet dignitary met with U.S. labor leaders occurred in January 1959, when Deputy Prime Minister Anastas Mikoyan paid a visit to the AFL-CIO. In the spirit of bourgeois good will, *The New York Times* (Jan. 7, 1959) reported that "although some embarrassing questions [were] raised there had been no heated exchanges," conveying the impression that the guest and hosts parted amicably. In reality, as is known from an eyewitness (John Herling in the *New Leader*, Feb. 2, 1959, 3–6), the encounter turned highly acrimonious as U.S. labor leaders pressed Mikoyan about Soviet policies and practices. After heated exchanges, Mikoyan said: "The American trade-union leaders were more antagonistic to the Soviet Union than were the American capitalists whom I have met." This has always been the case.

United States imports from the Soviet Union even before the Afghanistan embargoes (1979) were one half those from Trinidad and Tobago. In spite of this disappointing record, United States corporations continue to look toward significant expansion in trade with the USSR, once political relations are improved. Leading business executives stand in the forefront of organizations dedicated to promoting better relations between the two countries; they vigorously oppose punitive sanctions and embargoes; and they are the most vociferous champions of arms control and summit meetings. The *nomenklatura*, which realizes these facts very well, courts the business community with great zeal, not only because it hopes to reap economic benefits from this quarter, but also and above all because it regards "capitalist" businessmen as their most effective lever in Washington. In Western Europe, whose commercial relations with Moscow are much more extensive, the business and banking communities play a critical role in promoting the spirit of détente and pressuring for NATO's decoupling of commercial dealings from political relations with the Soviet Bloc.

Still, the number of business enterprises actually or even potentially involved in United States–Soviet trade is too small and their turnover too low to explain the commitment of the United States business elite to friendly relations with the Soviet Union regardless of the outrages which that country perpetrates or its hostile actions against the United States. The deeper causes for this phenomenon must be sought in social and cultural factors.

The modern corporate officer bears little resemblance to the classic bourgeois entrepreneur; he lacks the latter's spirit of individualism, his belief in himself and in his contribution to society, and his ethical values. He is a bureaucrat to whom stands open the path to potentially unlimited rewards, but whose personal status, as that of any salaried employee, is insecure. The corporation is his world; there is little connection between his personal morals and his work ethic. In these respects he has a great deal of affinity with a functionary of the *nomenklatura* with that difference that while he strives for higher profits, his Soviet counterpart strives for higher productivity. An American business executive instinctively understands a Soviet industrial manager, for, like him, he wants above all to get things done; like him, he views workers' demands as an impediment to higher production and profits, and intellectuals who talk of human rights as impractical dreamers. Today, the classic bourgeois can be found mainly in the younger branches of the economy, where risk taking and private ownership continue to predominate. This type of businessman tends to be conservative in his politics. Executives of large, established and public corporations incline toward unideological pragmatism.

The other factor, even more imponderable, is snobbery. In the drawing rooms of New York's East Side, Georgetown, Cambridge or Beverly Hills, one is unlikely to meet with pro-Soviet sympathies; this sort of thing has long gone out of fashion. The occasional Communist who turns up in these circles is treated as an eccentric, rather endearing if he happens to be rich—a millionaire Communist is, after all, not unlike a missionary who champions cannibalism. But anti-Communism is taboo. It is regarded as vulgar and low class, conjuring images of Senator McCarthy, the Moral Majority, and other unspeakable subjects. In contemporary America and Britain, anti-anti-Communism has become an important indicator of social status. Such use of ideas as a device for separating the right from the wrong persons cannot be new, since three quarters of a century ago Arnold Bennett had a character in one of his plays say that "it isn't views that are disreputable, it's the people who hold them."

That anti-anti-Communism should have become a hallmark of superior social standing has probably a great deal to do with the shifting standards by which such standing is defined. As Hilton Kramer has pointed out, the diffusion of affluence and the democratization of life styles which it has made possible have debased, one by one, the tokens with the help of which the upper classes have traditionally distinguished themselves from their inferiors: art, sexual freedom, travel and good food are now accessible to the multitude and are, therefore, useless as status indicators. Politics is virtually the last reliable social indicator left. "There, as nowhere else, the appeals of snobbery remain sharply defined. Nothing else nowadays gives people of a certain taste such a confident sense of the chasm that divides 'us' from 'them.' "[24] Since the common man, to judge by labor unions and mass-circulation newspapers, is patriotic and anti-Communist, patriotism and anti-Communism have become unacceptable to anyone with social aspirations. To adapt the terminology devised by the linguist Alan Ross to distinguish the upper ("U") from the lower ("non-U") vocabulary current in modern England, anti-Communism can be confidently relegated to "non-U" usage, a kind of intellectual equivalent of chewing tobacco.*

---

* In the United States and England, that is. In France, attitudes have radically changed during the past decade and anti-Communism has become fashionable, but either this information has not yet reached status-seekers in the English-speaking countries or Paris no longer sets the tone in these matters.

We have identified a number of factors in Western societies which create an atmosphere favorable to Moscow's strategy of political divisiveness. The resentment of intellectuals and academics of what they consider shabby treatment at the hands of their societies; the desire of businessmen to trade without political interference; the need of politicians and special-interest groups for funds from the defense budget; the quest of climbers for social symbols in a world where these have become scarce—all these combine to make influential segments of democratic society unwilling to face the threat to their country's security and prone to minimize it or even deny that it exists.

The power of these groups is much magnified by the influence they exert over the media. That the media, especially the prestige organs, are dominated by people given to anti-anti-Communist views, people for whom the main danger to the United States comes from internal failures rather than from external threats, can be in some measure statistically demonstrated. In a 1979–80 survey, 240 editors and reporters of the most influential newspapers, magazines and television networks in the United States indicated that in the preceding two decades four out of five of them had voted for Democratic candidates; in 1972, 81 percent had cast ballots for George McGovern, a Presidential candidate rejected by the voters in forty-nine of the fifty states.[25] The situation is similar in Europe: in West Germany, for instance, three quarters of the journalists employed in television are described as left of center.[26] Among members of the self-designated public-interest groups in the United States (e.g., consumer and environmental-protection societies) the prevalence of such sentiments is higher still—96 percent of the persons polled from such groups stated that they had voted for McGovern; they further expressed preference for Fidel Castro over Ronald Reagan by a margin of nearly seven to one.[27]

To derive maximal benefit from their convergence of interest with the inward-oriented, isolationist liberal establishment in the United States, Soviet foreign-policy specialists have concocted an artificial language of international communication. Its purpose is to create the illusion that the totalitarian East and the democratic West not only have no quarrel but share a common destiny. The threat to democratic societies, this synthetic jargon says, comes not from Communist regimes and their aggressive actions, but from nuclear weapons, the arms race and, above all, anti-Sovietism, which the two sides have an equal interest in liquidating. Once this language becomes assimilated by non-Communist societies, the communality of language conveys the sense of a communality of interest. Much of the terminology currently employed

in the West for East-West relations has either been coined by Soviet specialists or extracted by them from Western liberal sources,
assigned the desired meaning, and frozen into mandatory clichés.

A veritable treasury of cant deployed for this specific purpose
can be found in a recent book of interviews with Mr. Georgi Arbatov. The best-known (if not necessarily the most influential)
Soviet expert on the United States, Mr. Arbatov has paid many
visits to this country, in the course of which he established close
contacts with liberal intellectuals and détente-prone businessmen.
His fluency in English and mastery of the American liberal patois
have earned him among his American admirers the reputation of
a man who speaks with the authentic voice of the Russian people.
In *The Soviet Viewpoint* he draws on the whole gamut of newspeak
to assure his readers that the United States and the Soviet Union
have one common enemy, the "hard-liners" in Washington:

> The eerie thing about *The Soviet Viewpoint*, written in the form of several
> long interviews . . . conducted by Dutch journalist Willem Oltmans, is
> that Georgi Arbatov seems to be impersonating Cyrus Vance.
>
> What the book stunningly reveals is Arbatov's sophistication about
> American liberalism. He knows its peculiar gullibility, and he speaks
> its idiom with near-perfect nuance. No "running dogs" or "Wall Street
> lackeys" or "capitalist bloodsuckers" here; Arbatov utters the Leninist
> vision in terms that might have been lifted from *Foreign Affairs*.
>
> Soviet-American relations have need of *reciprocity*. We must seek
> *mutually acceptable solutions*. Let us avoid *confrontation*, but instead con-
> front *new realities*, eschewing the while any *mood of nostalgia* that might
> lead to a *new cold war* (much as such a development might please *hard-
> liners in Washington*, who are fond of *saber-rattling*).
>
> This is a time for *international cooperation*. We face *global problems*, such
> as the *depletion of natural resources*, which can't be dealt with through
> *old perceptions inherited from the cold war*.
>
> *Whether one likes it or not, we are chained together on this planet*. We dare
> not treat the situation as a *zero-sum game*, or *continue to squander our
> resources through the arms race*. Not *if we are to avoid doomsday*. It is imper-
> ative that we pursue the *possibility of lessening tensions*, of *lowering the
> level of military confrontation*.
>
> Despite our *different social systems*, there are *overriding common inter-
> ests, that call for cooperation. We are talking of human survival on this planet*,
> *of today's increasingly complex, fragile, and interdependent world*.
>
> The real issue is the *quality of life*. If we are serious about *building a
> new society*, we must combine a genuine commitment to *social spending*
> with *a new, broader approach to human rights*.
>
> Remember, *the Vietnam War torpedoed the Great Society*, and in a nu-
> clear war, *there will be no winners*. Think of the *human cost!* Not only of
> *the war threatening humanity*, but of any *new massive military buildup*.
>
> Any *significant improvement* in the *infrastructure* must be *viewed in the*

*context* of the phenomena of *wide-spread alienation* and *social atomization* stemming from *McCarthyist witch-hunts,* and the *long-term trends* that culminated in *Watergate* with all its attendant *pressures for change* in the *military-industrial complex* whose *macho* posturing has thus far precluded *meaningful redistribution . . . social expenditures . . . purely internal Afghan development. . . .*

"There's hardly a sentence in this book," the author of the review concludes, "that couldn't have been picked up on the narrow frequency band between *The New York Times* and the Institute for Policy Studies."[28]

On the face of it, such abuse of language may appear harmless — what, indeed, is linguistic pollution against the danger of nuclear war? But language does shape the framework within which people think and communicate; he who controls the vocabulary exerts powerful influence on the content of thought and speech. Thus, the absence from their authorized vocabulary of such terms as *Holocaust* and *Gulag* makes it difficult for citizens of the Soviet Union to discuss these phenomena in public. Oliver Wendell Holmes rightly classified "verbicide" as a major crime.

From the Communist point of view, the principle of what M. Alain Besançon has called *logocracy,* or "rule of words," is correct and deserving of rigorous application. In the interwar period, the Italian Communist Antonio Gramsci constructed a whole political strategy on the premise that ideas are not a superstructure set on an economic base, as orthodox Marxism holds, but a force in their own right. In this theory, mastery of human consciousness becomes a paramount political objective. Although the Soviet establishment rejects Gramsci's views, it quietly puts them into practice. Adam Michnik, a leading theoretician of Polish Solidarity, defines control of consciousness as the principal aim of Communism—"The fundamental characteristic of the regime under which I live," he writes, "is the striving for mastery over the human mind."[29] Such mastery is secured, in the first place, by control of the organs of information. Censorship, however, is far less effective than its advocates like to believe, because information can be readily obtained from observation, hearsay, radio broadcasts and various other means difficult to regulate; it has ways of seeping through the tightest of barriers. It is more effective to control thought at the source—that is, in the mind that absorbs and processes the information—and the best way of accomplishing this is by shaping words and phrases in the desired manner.

From the instant they seized power in Russia, the Bolsheviks began to address their subjects in a canonical language deliberately detached from living reality. Its object was to contrive a complete make-believe reality that conformed to their slogans and to them only. "Dictatorship of the proletariat" for a system of government that is a dictatorship over the proletariat is a good example of such usage; "agrarian cooperatives" for state farms imposed by force is another. As the gap between Communist "reality" and the reality of life under Communism widened, a kind of linguistic schizophrenia developed in the Soviet Union; from there, it spread to other countries with Communist regimes. In time, every Communist society learned to speak two distinct languages. One is the language of communication among ordinary people, the language they employ when discussing private affairs, that is, things that actually exist; it is rich in slang and adapts its vocabulary to changing conditions. The other is the official language, a dead, abstract idiom used between the authorities and the people they rule, which the latter are required to employ in public. This language reflects not life but the regime's notions of what life ought to be; it is shaped by the rulers' will, rather than by observation and reflection. In the words of one observer, the official language introduced by Stalin and still in use "is no longer a means of communication but of domination . . . The Stalinist speaks not to address others —he speaks to assert, in the very act of pronouncing the word, his monopolistic power to proffer the 'truth' in accord with the requirements of the moment." [30] George Orwell, who had familiarized himself with the language of Western Stalinists, noted its catastrophic effects on thought:

> As soon as certain topics are raised, the concrete melts into the abstract and no one seems able to think of turns of speech that are not hackneyed: prose consists less and less of *words* chosen for the sake of their meaning, and more and more of *phrases* tacked together like the sections of a prefabricated hen-house . . . It consists of gumming together long strips of words which have already been set in order by someone else, and making the results presentable by sheer humbug. [31]

Such abuse of language in the service of domination instead of communication has dangers also for its perpetrators. In some respects, perhaps, its main victims are even not the ordinary people, who adapt themselves to a regime of bilingualism, but their masters, who grow so accustomed to thinking in the artificial language they have invented that they ultimately lose touch with life. Khrushchev told a Yugoslav diplomat that "in the final years of his life Stalin learned about Russia and the world from films which were made specially for him, and he ruled the country in the belief that everything in the Soviet Union was prospering." [32] This is a *reductio ad absurdum* of manipulating reality.

Until the middle 1950s, linguistic regimentation was confined to the Soviet Union and foreign Communist parties. Stalin did not attempt to impose his terminology on anyone outside his political control. Things have changed since his death. The appearance of the "bomb" made it possible for Soviet propagandists to argue that humanity shares one destiny, that it is "chained together," in Mr. Arbatov's phrase: coexistence of this sort calls for a common language. Over the past thirty years, a Soviet-type jargon has been spreading over the world; it pervades discussion of everything that touches on East-West relations and increasingly replicates the situation which prevails inside Communist societies.

> By calling "autonomous" that which is powerless, "federated" that which is unitary, "democratic" that which is autocratic, "united" that which is schismatic, "popular" that which is imposed by terror, "peaceful" that which incites war—in brief, by systematically corrupting language to obscure reality—the Communists have made inroads into our sense of political reality. Language is, after all, the only medium in which we can think. It is exceedingly difficult to eliminate all the traditional connotations of words—to associate words like "For a lasting peace and a People's Democracy" with neither peace nor popular movements nor democracy. [33]

To disparage the United States–Chinese *rapprochement*, Soviet propagandists have put into circulation the condescending term "China card," and to denigrate United States use of satellites to verify arms-control agreements they dub them "spies in the sky." Sometimes, Soviet language manipulation goes to ridiculous lengths, as when censors insist that Soviet publications refer to the army that is ravaging Afghanistan as "the limited contingent of Soviet troops in Afghanistan" and never in another way.

By formulating and consistently using terms applicable to international relations in the desired mode, Moscow accords them legitimacy even when they bear no relationship to anything real—terms such as "peaceful coexistence," "Zionist racism," or "Polish counterrevolution." The vocabulary of East-West relations, shared by Western liberals and the Soviet apparatus, serves the same purpose as the official jargon inside the Soviet Union. It focuses the discussion on matters that are desired but may or may not exist, and places out of bounds subjects that emphatically do exist but are deemed best unmentioned. It perverts one's perception of phenomena by attaching to them pejorative words when they are considered inimical, and positive ones when they are useful. Thus, the countries of Eastern Europe under the occupation of the Soviet Army are labeled "People's Democracies." Such usage is not only deceptive but absurdly tautological: since "democracy" means "people's rule," a "people's democracy" is "people's rule by the people." Because "Communism" evokes negative images in the West, it has been gradually supplanted with "socialism." For some time now, Moscow has been calling its bloc the "socialist camp," and this usage too has spread to Western media. The title General Secretary suggests a bureaucratic dictator, so for purposes of foreign dealings it has been replaced with that of President, which, in the Soviet context, is meaningless. How much easier it is, however, to meet and shake hands with the "President" of a "socialist country" than with the dictator of a Communist one!

Liberal journalists not only have assimilated much of this vocabulary but also introduced refinements of their own, which are promptly borrowed by Moscow. They routinely call someone critical of the Soviet Union a "hard-line anti-Communist," but never refer to anyone as a "soft-line pro-Communist," even though every adjective demands its opposite. "Extremist," when applied to a person's views on the Soviet Union, invariably means anti-Communist, a pro-Soviet "extremist" being unknown to journalism—the latter is a "moderate."

Linguistic manipulation leads to intellectual confusion, and as such it is dangerous. It enables Soviet political strategists to dominate the intellectual climate of East-West relations and to insinuate themselves into Western political discussions. It allows them to project false identities of interest between the two systems and to incite internecine conflicts of opinion as well as of interest within the Western community. It blurs the line between fiction and reality. If this is allowed to go on, the day may well come when Western citizens, like Stalin in his waning years, will be regaled with specially prepared films that show the world basking in peace, while "limited contingents of Soviet troops" are shooting their way into their homes.

## 3 SOVIET MILITARY STRATEGY

Marxism-Leninism is a militant doctrine that regards conflict as a natural state of affairs and violence as the ultimate regulator of human relations. Peace is for it a remote ideal which will come about only after private property in the means of production has been universally abolished. Ceaseless struggle between classes tears apart every non-Communist society; capitalist nations fight each other; and over all hovers the great historic contest between the "bourgeois" and "proletarian" camps. Within the Communist camp, conflicts are by definition impossible; such conflicts as do occasionally erupt—as, for instance, in Poland—are ascribed to the machinations of foreign intelligence services. When they pit Communist countries—as, for instance, the Soviet Union and China—each of the contestants charges the other with having abandoned the socialist community and turned bourgeois or even fascist. The outlook of this movement has been molded by Social Darwinism, from which it has adopted such notions as "struggle for survival" and "survival of the fittest." The notion that war is a deviation from man's natural state is entirely alien to Marxism both in its original form and in its Leninist revision. It was precisely because of the adherence of early socialists to social pacifism, their desire to bring together the diverse classes to cooperate for the common good, that Marx dismissed them as "utopians."

Lenin often delivered himself on the subject of war and peace, and he did so with complete consistency. He said that war must not be viewed from the "sentimentally democratic standpoint," that numerous wars had been waged, which, "despite all the horrors, atrocities, distress, and suffering," proved "progressive," that war "is not only a continuation of politics, it is the epitome of politics," that the "struggle must consist . . . not simply in replacing war by peace but in replacing capitalism by socialism," and that peace was merely a "respite" for war.[34] He had no patience with the notion that capitalism and communism could either coexist or resolve their differences by peaceful means:

> it is inconceivable for the Soviet Republic to exist alongside of the imperialist states for any length of time. One or the other must triumph in the end. And before that end comes there will have to be a series of frightful collisions between the Soviet Republic and the bourgeois states.[35]

It is sometimes said that the ideals of Communism are noble but that man, unfortunately, has proven unequal to them. One may say more plausibly that, fortunately for himself, man's common sense has prevented such "ideals" from becoming reality.

For pacifism, Lenin had nothing but contempt; it was bourgeois prattle, fit only for export, a weapon to confuse and divide the class enemy by playing on his delusions. This attitude is revealed with stark cynicism in a recently published letter from Lenin to his Commissar of Foreign Affairs, G. V. Chicherin. The occasion was the forthcoming conference at Genoa, the first international gathering to which the Soviet government had received an invitation.

Lenin had instructed Chicherin to present to the foreign delegations at Genoa a "comprehensive pacifist program." When Chicherin, who was in some respects an honest, old-fashioned intellectual, objected that pacifism was a "petty bourgeois illusion," Lenin wrote back:

> Comrade Chicherin: You are too nervous . . . You and I have fought pacifism as a program of the revolutionary proletarian party. This is clear. But who, where, when has ever denied this party [the right to] utilize the pacifists for the purpose of disintegrating the enemy, the bourgeoisie?[36]

When evidence of this kind is presented, Soviet spokesmen usually retort that such ideas on war, peace and pacifism have been rendered obsolete by the appearance of nuclear weapons. These weapons, it is said, have invalidated the Clausewitzian view of war as the pursuit of politics by other means. But this view of the effect of nuclear weapons on warfare is of Western origin and has been adopted by Soviet political experts exclusively for the purpose of "disintegrating the enemy." As we shall show below, this is not at all what the Soviet political and military say on this subject when communicating with each other within their own circles. They not only consider the Clausewitzian dictum on war to be a scientific law, immune to advances in weaponry, but treat nuclear weapons, properly used, as a shortcut to decisive victory. Accordingly, the Leninist view of pacifism remains permanently valid. A recent volume of the Soviet *Military Encyclopedia,* published by the Ministry of Defense, reaffirms the "necessity of *using* pacifism as a means of strengthening the position of the Republic of Soviets and preventing imperialist aggression"—that is, as a political weapon.[37]*

---

* A book recently published in East Germany by two military experts minces no words in rejecting "bourgeois" views of nuclear war. Called *Just and Unjust Wars in Our Time,* it takes issue with the theory that nuclear weapons have rendered meaningless the traditional distinction between the two types of armed conflict: "The danger of total destruction of both sides leads to the conclusion that it has become impossible for one of the parties to wage a just war." According to the Communist authors, this is a "theoretical error of bourgeois thinking." The error consists in "proceeding exclusively from the consequences of war without analyzing the social causes that lead to the presumed consequences and making them the decisive criterion in the assessment of the justness or unjustness of nuclear war." Wolfgang Scheler and Gottfried Kiessling, *Gerechte und Ungerechte Kriege in unserer Zeit* (East Berlin, Military Publishing House of the German Democratic Republic, 1981) as reported in *Frankfurter Allgemeine Zeitung,* October 30, 1981.

Such ideas are inculcated in Soviet citizens of all ages. They create a climate of opinion bewildering to the ordinary Soviet citizen who hears his government assert peaceful intentions and yet in the same breath tell him that clashes between the two systems are all but unavoidable.

Having militarized everything within reach—politics, social relations, economics, ideas—the Soviet regime no longer treats the armed forces as the exclusive instrument of warfare. When they speak of the correlation of forces, Soviet strategists have in mind something much more comprehensive than the balance of military forces; among the other factors that enter into their calculation are the productive capacity of a country, its technological level, the quality of its political leadership, its public morale and social cohesiveness. The concept thus embraces everything that experience has shown to contribute to victory in a modern, industrial war. The Soviet military are taught to think of the balance of power in this comprehensive manner. Soviet sources define "military science" as the discipline that studies the progress and outcome of war in dependence on "politics, economics, [and] the correlation of the moral-political, scientific-technical and military potential of the combatants."[38] For all the importance they assign to military power, Soviet strategists do not detach it from the rest of the instruments of Grand Strategy. They profess to being perplexed by the narrow technical manner with which their American counterparts approach security issues, by concentrating on military forces to the exclusion of all else. In the prime of détente, some of them openly criticized the United States approach in what they must have considered a constructive manner:

> The "technical" approach to the problem of national security has led to serious changes in the military-strategic and—what is particularly dangerous—the political thinking of the United States. The efforts of American strategists have yielded a whole system of concepts which may be applicable and even useful in the analysis of the purely military correlations of forces but lead to unavoidable distortions when applied to politics and such political problems as international and national security. In this approach, the very question of war is, as it were, isolated from politics, from the analysis whether or not war can bring about the desired political objectives.[39]

If military power is to serve political ends, then it follows that politicians must control generals. In this regard, Soviet practice is consistent. While in terms of the resources it allocates to its armed forces and the martial spirit it inculcates in its citizenry the Soviet

Union qualifies as a militarized state, it is not a military state which allows generals to make other than strictly technical professional decisions. The Communist Party has insisted since the revolution on undivided control over its armed forces, at first because it mistrusted its predominantly old-regime commanding staff, and later, after its own cadres had taken charge, from fear of Bonapartism, that is, a military takeover. By a variety of safeguards the *nomenklatura* ensures that the men in uniform will not threaten its authority. The supreme body directing military affairs in the country, the Defense Council, is a subcommittee of the Politbureau. This Council, whose membership and operations are secret, is known to be headed by the General Secretary and is believed to include the Prime Minister, the Ministers of Defense and Foreign Affairs, and the Director of the KGB. The General Secretary and Minister of Defense, although usually lacking in military experience, often hold the rank of Marshal. Day-to-day political control over the armed forces is exercised by the Chief Political Directorate, an influential section of the Central Committee with the status of a department. Within its purview falls the indoctrination of the armed forces and of Soviet youth, as well as censorship over all military publications; the latter ensures that every public statement on military matters made in the USSR either expresses official opinion or is articulated with official approval "for purposes of discussion." The political officers whom the Directorate assigns to the armed forces to supervise and indoctrinate are responsible to it and the Central Committee, rather than to the military high command. Its current chief, General A. A. Epishev, who has held the post for over two decades, is a veteran of the KGB. In addition, there is the Third Department of the KGB, whose responsibility it is to prevent sedition in and by the armed forces; its agents penetrate military ranks at all levels, causing no little friction with professional officers, who resent its tutelage and spying. Should all these preventive measures, nevertheless, fail and the army stage a *coup d'état*, the *nomenklatura* has at its disposal a powerful military force of its own in the form of so-called "internal armies," controlled by the Ministry of the Interior, to suppress it. Numbering several hundred thousand men, these troops have the means to quell officer plots and soldier mutinies of the kind that in February 1917 had brought down tsarism. These elaborate preventive and repressive measures make a mockery of the arguments of Soviet disinformation specialists that the West must offer all kinds of concessions to Soviet "civilian" leaders lest hawkish generals take over.

In the USSR, warfare is treated as a science. It is a subject taught at institutions of higher learning, including a network of General Staff academies. The most important of those, named after K. E. Voroshilov, enrolls generals and admirals to study strategic matters. Another Academy, named after M. V. Frunze, deals with the art of operations and tactics. Others specialize in chemical warfare, and so on. As professionals, the officers are expected to carry out specific missions when called upon by the Party; they are not allowed to mix into politics, but, in return, the *nomenklatura* does not overly interfere with strictly military affairs. There is no reason to think that the Soviet Army is unhappy with this arrangement. Since they have neither an interest in running the country nor the competence to do it, the officers are content as long as they get the hardware and incipient peace movements in the country are firmly dealt with.

This said, it must be conceded that the military does exert strong and growing influence on Soviet political life. The main cause of this development is the sheer weight of responsibility that the *nomenklatura* imposes on the military, both in the matter of allocating economic resources and in executing imperial missions.

The gigantic Soviet military effort, which we will discuss in greater detail in the next chapter, makes excessive demands on the Soviet economy and affects adversely the production of consumer goods. This fact is widely known. To justify these unpopular policies, the *nomenklatura* has recourse to an unceasing campaign of vilification against "imperialism," which plays on the basest xenophobic instincts of the population—instincts whose roots reach back to the Middle Ages, when Orthodox Russia stood alone on the field of battle championing true Christianity against Latins and Muslims. To make this claim more persuasive, the regime goes to great lengths to keep alive the memory of World War II. A connection is incessantly drawn between the genocidal "Fascists" who invaded the Soviet Union in 1941, and NATO, for the purpose of implanting in the mind of Soviet citizens a sense of continuity between the enemies of yesterday and those of today. By arming itself at heavy cost, the Soviet regime tells its people, it is protecting them from the evil designs of the contemporary imperialists, who are direct descendants of the Fascists.* The fact

* Soviet authorities always refer to the Nazis as "Fascists"; the correct term "National Socialists" is not allowed, presumably because it might create undesirable associations between Communist and Hitlerite "socialisms." Such usage also facilitates pinning the label on governments which it would strain the credulity of even Soviet citizens to identify with Hitler's Germany.

that from 1939 to 1941 the USSR had actively collaborated with Nazi Germany, supplying its war industries with raw materials for use against Britain and France, goes, of course, unmentioned, as does the fact that, once Germany had attacked Russia, Britain and the United States promptly came to its aid.

The party line requires that the anxieties of the Soviet population be kept at a high pitch by constant reminders that the bloodbath of yesterday may be repeated.

Thus, in May 1983, on the occasion of the thirty-eighth anniversary of the "Soviet victory over Fascist Germany" (the contribution of the Allies to this victory being virtually glossed over), Marshal Ustinov, the Soviet Minister of Defense, delivered an address in which he reaffirmed this proposition. His purpose was to warn Soviet citizens that the war which they had waged with such immense sacrifices in 1941–45 had really never terminated:

> The past war was not only a battle of armies but also a clash of two social systems, two ideologies, two ways of life. It was a battle of the people against the shock detachments of international imperialism. . . . The war revealed the true culprit of aggression—international imperialism—and raised, in all its acuteness, the question of the struggle against its militaristic strivings [and] for the restraining of its aggressive forces. Unfortunately, the crushing of Fascist Germany and its satellites has taught the reactionary circles little. Justifying themselves with utterly false myths about the "Soviet military threat," "Soviet military superiority," they once again place reliance on politics conducted "from a position of strength," unleash an unrestrained arms race, prepare for a new World War. The course of the imperialist reaction, headed by the ruling circles of the United States, has become particularly aggressive at the beginning of the 1980s.[40]

These charges, made by a person who, at the time he made them, was perhaps the second-most-powerful figure in the Soviet Union, merit close scrutiny: in Communist practice, it is such formal declarations, and not private confidences, that enunciate policy. Ustinov's message, partly explicit, partly implicit, is that the "Great Patriotic War" was merely one battle in a war that is still in progress; that Russia's real enemy at that time was not "Fascist" Germany but "international imperialism," which the Wehrmacht's murderous troops had served as "shock detachments"; and that the North Atlantic Treaty Organization, headed by the United States, is the heir to this legacy. These accusations are more than slander. They are a signal delivered in simple code, readily deciphered by every Soviet citizen, that World War III, the war that will end in the worldwide triumph of "socialism," may be inevitable because the "imperialists" have failed to draw the correct lessons from the defeat of Nazi Germany. Anyone who accuses the Reagan Administration of inflammatory rhetoric will do well to keep in mind what rhetoric it is forced to respond to.

The extravagant commitment of Soviet economic resources to the military unavoidably involves the Soviet military in every phase of economic planning and production. As early as 1928–29, when the first Five Year Plan was initiated, the Party established a Military-Economic Department in the State Planning Commission (Gosplan) to ensure that the armed forces were properly serviced. This Department has ever since enjoyed a powerful voice in economic planning. Staffed by officers, it has first claim on resources; these claims must be satisfied before the other branches of the economy receive their share. It also has extensive authority to interfere with nonmilitary appropriations in order to ensure that they meet the needs of wartime mobilization. Furthermore, many industrial establishments have attached to them military representatives who supervise procurements and have powers to divert to the Armed Forces resources assigned to the civilian sector. It is true, of course, that the military do not get everything that they want and are often overruled. Nonetheless, the fact that they are not mere passive recipients of such bounty as the *nomenklatura* is willing to bestow upon them, but active participants in the drafting of economic plans as well as in their implementation, assures them of unique influence over the national economy. It blurs to the point of meaninglessness the distinction between the "military" and "civilian" sectors, which exists in democratic societies and is all too often projected by them onto Communist ones.

The other cause of the growing political influence of the military is the accelerated pace of Soviet imperial expansion—which, as noted, relies much less on economic and cultural means than on the force of arms. During Stalin's lifetime, the Soviet military were confined to areas under Communist political control. Today, the situation is very different. Over 100,000 Soviet troops are fighting in Afghanistan. Elsewhere, in thirty Third World countries, there are stationed an estimated 20,000 Soviet and East European and 40,000 Cuban troops. In Ethiopia, Angola, Vietnam, South Yemen, they help local governments conduct military operations. Soviet personnel man Syrian antiaircraft batteries and Nicaraguan communication centers. In each instance, it is the political establishment that has made the decision to dispatch the troops abroad; but once operations have gotten under way and run into the usual difficulties, it is the military's turn to tell the politicians what must be done to carry the enterprise to a successful conclusion.

Their growing influence has given the generals power to affect the selection of General Secretaries. Since Stalin's death, no one has been able to gain this post without the support of the armed forces, and such support can only be purchased at the price of generous commitments to them. This development makes it dubious whether, as long as the present political system remains in place, it will be possible significantly to reduce the frenetic pace of Soviet armaments.

As stated, Soviet military power is meant to serve political ends, and the principal Soviet political objective is to undermine by means of internal divisions the will and ability of foreign governments to resist Red expansion. In this Grand Strategy, the Soviet army performs a dual task—a political one, to intimidate; and a military one, to win, should intimidation fail and hostilities break out.

Napoleon has said that "the conqueror is a friend of peace." In this sense, the Red Army is indeed an instrument of peace, since its primary function is so to cow the enemy that he is incapable of defending himself. It is, in the first place, a shield that protects the USSR and its clients from Western and Chinese retribution for encroachments on foreign territories. It guarantees that no hostile power will be able to compel the USSR once again to retreat under the nuclear threat, as it had to do in 1946 in Northern Iran, in 1953 in Korea, and in 1962 in Cuba.

In this scheme, nuclear weapons have come to render an invaluable service. Without them, Soviet imperial ventures would have run into incomparably greater obstacles. Missiles enable Moscow to threaten universal destruction for resistance to its demands; they give the *nomenklatura* the means to terrorize humanity outside areas of its political control much as totalitarian controls allow it to do inside its domain.

In Soviet doctrine, nuclear weapons do not serve primarily deterrent purposes; they are the principal instrument of modern war. They constitute the pivot around which the three branches of the armed services revolve. Should general war break out, they are expected to determine the outcome. Outrageous, inhuman, and possibly even unrealistic as these propositions may appear to the Western reader, a sober assessment of both the theoretical writings and deployments of Soviet armed forces leaves little doubt that such, indeed, are the views of its political leaders and military commanders.

As the first country to detonate nuclear weapons, the United States pioneered the formulation of nuclear strategy. The prevalent American doctrine, first developed by American scholars and scientists within months after the destruction of Hiroshima and Nagasaki, may be summarized as follows: Nuclear weapons are unlike any weapons ever devised, not only because of their unique destructive properties but also because they cannot be defended against. They have rendered war irrational; the Clausewitzian view of war as the pursuit of politics by other means has lost its validity. Nuclear war is unwinnable; its only conceivable outcome is mutual suicide for the combatants and much of the rest of humanity. The sole utility of these weapons is to deter someone else from using them.

An influential treatise on the subject, under the title *The Absolute Weapon*, brought out in 1946 by the Yale University Press, enunciated on the basis of these assumptions the principles of what was later to become the official United States doctrine of "mutual deterrence." The contributors to *Absolute Weapon* must have believed themselves to be the beneficiaries of a unique opportunity to formulate a radically new strategic doctrine; inspired by this prospect, they advanced some startling ideas. The mission of the armed forces in modern times was no longer to be victory. "Thus far the chief purpose of our military establishments has been to win wars," wrote Mr. Bernard Brodie, the editor of the book, "From now on its chief purpose must be to avert them. It can have almost no other useful purpose." While Mr. Brodie did not go so far as to recommend that the Department of Defense be abolished and its functions taken over by the Department of State, the implication that diplomacy had replaced warfare was certainly there. Another contributor, Mr. Arnold Wolfers, went one better with a claim that must be without precedent in the entire history of strategic thinking. He argued that, to enjoy genuine security, the United States had to make certain that its potential enemy, the Soviet Union, possessed the capability of inflicting on the United States total destruction. The argument supporting this eccentric proposition was that as long as the United States retained a monopoly on nuclear weapons and hence the ability to destroy the USSR with impunity, the latter would feel threatened and behave aggressively. The novelist Ivan Turgenev called statements of this type "reverse commonplaces." Scientists, when speculating on matters in which they lack professional experience—and these include virtually the entire realm of human relations—have a propensity for them, especially if the reward promises to be a place in history books.

The United States government did not immediately adopt these views. Under President Eisenhower, the United States doctrine called for "massive retaliation," which threatened the use of atomic weapons to stop Soviet aggression. When, however, the Soviet Union, having tested both nuclear fission and fusion weapons, demonstrated in 1957 its ability to launch intercontinental missiles, the whole strategy of "massive retaliation" collapsed in a heap. At this point, the doctrine formulated by the scientists took over. In the early 1960s, Secretary of Defense McNamara committed this country to an ambitious program of nuclear deterrence. His basic premise was that if the United States had an indestructible retaliatory force strong enough to respond with devastating power to a Soviet preemptive strike, it would need fear no attack. When fully deployed, the "triad" of ICBMs, bombers and submarines was to be capable of inflicting on the aggressor "unacceptable damage," arbitrarily set as a certain proportion of his population and industrial capacity.

The scientists who in the late 1940s formulated the United States strategy, and the engineers, analysts and accountants in the defense community who in the 1960s implemented it, seem to have taken it for granted that objects possess an inherent logic that determines their "rational" use. In this view, there no more could be two nuclear strategies than two kinds of nuclear physics. But, as Frederick Hayek has demonstrated, the use to which people put objects is determined not only by the latter's objective properties but also by the subjective ends which man has in mind for them: thus, a match, properly struck, always produces fire, but fire can be used to cook a meal or to burn books. Scientists have neither the training nor the experience which would prepare them to make allowance for such subjective complications:

> What men know or think about the external world or about themselves, their concepts and even the subjective qualities of their sense perception are to Science never ultimate reality, data to be accepted. *Its concern is not what men think about the world and how they consequently behave, but what they ought to think.*[41]

Afflicted by such *déformation professionelle*, American strategists ignored that the "rationality" of anything can be determined only in the context of objectives, which themselves need not be rational; and consequently, since weapons do not use themselves but are used by people, if one wished to know how they are going to be employed one had to know the people in question—their past, their culture, their special interests. Western scientists never doubted (and many still do not doubt today) that sooner or later the Russians would have to adopt the same strategy for nuclear weapons as the one they themselves advocated.

A few objected to this simplistic view, among them experienced diplomats like George Kennan, who well understood the mentality of the Soviet elite and passionately warned against sharing nuclear secrets with it, as some scientists, thinking along the lines developed by Mr. Wolfers, believed desirable. In a dispatch sent to the Secretary of State from Moscow one month after Hiroshima, Mr. Kennan wrote:

> I have no hesitation in saying quite categorically, in the light of some eleven years experience with Russian matters, that it would be highly dangerous to our security if the Russians were to develop the use of atomic energy, or any other radical and far-reaching means of destruction, along lines of which we were unaware and against which we might be defenseless if taken by surprise. There is nothing—I repeat nothing—in the history of the Soviet regime which could justify us in assuming that the men who are now in power in Russia, or even those who have chances of assuming power in the foreseeable future, would hesitate for a moment to apply this power against us if by doing so they thought that they might materially improve their own power position in the world. This holds true regardless of the process by which the Soviet Government might obtain the knowledge of the use of such forces; i.e., whether by its own scientific and inventive efforts, by espionage, or by such knowledge being imparted to them as a gesture of good-will and confidence. To assume that Soviet leaders would be restrained by scruples of gratitude or humanitarianism would be to fly in the face of overwhelming contrary evidence on a matter vital to the future of our country.[42]

One year later, Mr. Kennan followed this appeal with an urgent call for the United States to promote the development of both atomic and biological weapons. It was important, he wrote, that "the country be *prepared* to use them if need be, for the mere fact of such preparedness may prove to be the only deterrent to Russian aggressive actions and in this sense the only sure guarantee of peace."[43]

The community of political scientists and political-minded physicists rejected this counsel. In the 1960s the doctrine which triumphed in Washington assumed an identity of interests in regard to nuclear weapons by the two "superpowers." Neither the then Secretary of Defense, Mr. McNamara, nor his advisers thought it worthwhile to consult Soviet views on the subject. According to one of his associates, Mr. McNamara looked into the recently published Soviet strategic manual by Marshal V. D. Sokolovskii, which reaffirmed the Soviet view that technology had no effect on the science of war, and put it aside unimpressed, because the book lacked "a sophisticated analysis of nuclear war."[44] For their part, the leading United States nuclear theoreticians, in voluminous studies on the subject, scaled ever new peaks of sophistication, developing an abstract strategy for the nuclear age, without bothering to take into account the thinking of those from whom these weapons were meant to defend. Thus, in his influential treatise *Strategy in the Missile Age* (Princeton, 1959), Bernard Brodie saw it fit to make only a couple of offhand references to Soviet doctrine, as if it were a matter of marginal interest.

Caught up in this mentality, the Central Intelligence Agency consistently misinterpreted its data on Soviet deployments. In the 1960s it explained the massive Soviet nuclear program then underway as a quest for parity with the United States. When, around 1969, the Soviet Union had attained this parity and yet continued to enhance its nuclear forces, the explanation provided was that it now needed to protect itself against a new enemy, China. And when Moscow had accumulated enough to take care of both NATO and China and yet still kept on testing and deploying new systems, it was said that Russians have been conditioned by their history to require overinsurance. CIA analysts hardly bothered to take into account Soviet theoretical writings, even though they disposed of classified material that made Soviet intentions unmistakably clear. As a result, CIA projections persistently underestimated the momentum of the Soviet nuclear buildup.[45] Such misinterpretations were responsible for the absence of a vigorous United States response to Soviet nuclear programs in the 1970s, which kept on adding to the Soviet arsenal one new strategic system each year.

It is true that Soviet writings on nuclear matters are unsophisticated—indeed, crude. But where serious matters are concerned, sophistication is not necessarily an advantage. Historically, this word has always carried a pejorative meaning. It is derived from the Sophists, an early Greek philosophical school distinguished by oversubtle, devious reasoning. According to the *Oxford English Dictionary*, *sophisticated* conveyed such negative connotations as "investing with specious fallacies" and "disingenuous alteration or perversion." The word was assigned a favorable sense only early in this century by social and intellectual *arrivistes*, whom everything simple makes uneasy; they would rather be wrong than appear common. For them to say that Russian generals had no "sophisticated analysis of nuclear war" was equivalent to saying that they were vulgar and, as such, undeserving of serious attention. Now the *nomenklatura* is, in truth, unsophisticated; the

Russian language lacks even a word to convey this concept. But the relevant fact is that these same Russian generals and their party leaders, simple, crude and primitive as they may be, unable to sparkle at seminars and hopeless at dinner parties, did crush the Nazi Wehrmacht, which had swept before them the French and British forces led by politicians and commanders of undeniable sophistication. Soviet generals reasoned plainly: preventing war was the job of politicians; theirs was to win them, and any means to this end was good. If nuclear weapons had an incomparably greater destructive capacity than any hitherto known, so much the better; this meant that they deserved the place of honor in the armed forces and in military strategy. The notion that a technical innovation could upset validated laws of the "science of war" struck them as no less absurd than the idea that some invention contradicted the laws of nature.

As long as they lacked dependable means of delivering nuclear warheads against the continental United States, Soviet leaders made light of these weapons, at least in public. Their official line maintained that wars were governed by Stalin's "five constant principles," which assigned pride of place to the "stability of the home front," followed by the "morale of the armed forces"; "military equipment" came fourth. They rejected the concept of an "absolute weapon" as unscientific, as well as the claim that the new weapons were impervious to defense. All this time, Soviet scientists and engineers were feverishly at work to design and produce intercontinental missiles. While this work was in progress, the authorities, now headed by Stalin's successors, initiated professional discussions to determine the effect of nuclear weapons on the art of war. (In Soviet usage, the "science of war" furnishes immutable principles, while the "art of war" deals with their application under changing circumstances.) One school of thought followed American thinking that nuclear war was unwinnable and nuclear weapons had no military utility other than deterrence. Another took the contrary view that these weapons had become the decisive instruments of modern warfare and demanded a thorough revision of military doctrine and organization. The proponents of this latter view argued that the revolutionary contribution of nuclear weapons lay in their ability to reverse the traditional relationship between strategy and tactics. Whereas in conventional warfare, the strategic objective—the disarming of the enemy—is attained by an accumulation of tactical gains, nuclear weapons made it possible to achieve the strategic objective at once, in the first hours of war, with the result that the role of tactics is reduced to securing the fruits of victory.[46]

While, of course, the other side too could avail itself of these assets, in the view of Soviet strategists their country enjoyed special political and geopolitical advantages over the enemy in this respect:

> The socialist countries possess objectively more favorable conditions for utilizing such possibilities in the interest of defeating the enemy. They can assure a more effective transformation of the economic, scientific [and] moral potential into the military factor. In addition, the socialist camp enjoys an advantage over the imperialist camp in respect to territory and population. From the western borders of the German Democratic Republic and Czechoslovakia to the Pacific Ocean it constitutes a single mass. By contrast, the countries of the imperialist bloc form a chain of states occupying a narrow coastal rim of Europe and Asia, while their principal economic base—the United States—lies beyond the ocean. As a result, the lines of communication connecting these countries . . . are extremely extended and vulnerable. In time of war, such communications can be readily disrupted by nuclear missile weapons.*

By the end of the 1950s these arguments carried the day. At this point the discussion was terminated and the proponents of the "American" view were reduced to silence. From then on, all talk of the "suicidal" nature of nuclear war was banned from the internal literature, although it continued to be bandied about at Pugwash, Dartmouth, and similar semiofficial meetings held with Western scientists to discuss joint efforts to preserve "peace." †

---

* General Major N. Ia. Sushko and Colonel S. A. Tiushkevich, *Marksizm-Leninizm o voine i armii;* 4th ed. (Moscow: The Military Publishing House of the Ministry of Defense of the USSR, 1965, 90–91). It is worth noting that this revealing passage was omitted from the English translation of this book, published in Moscow in 1972 under the title *Marxism-Leninism on War and Army.*

† Soviet propagandists have been lately telling Western audiences that their military no longer believe in the possibility of winning a nuclear war—see, for example, the statements to this effect by Lieutenant General Mikhail A. Milshtein in *The New York Times,* Aug. 25, 1980. For proof of this contention, General Milshtein refers the reader to the writings of the current chief of the Soviet General Staff, Marshal N. V. Ogarkov. However, Marshal Ogarkov happens to confirm that the advantages possessed by the Communist camp "give it objective possibilities of winning victory [in a nuclear war]." (*Sovetskaia voennaia entsiklopediia [Soviet Military Encyclopedia],* VII, Moscow, 1979, 564). It is true, however, that having realized the political damage that open talk of their military about winning a nuclear war had caused them abroad, the authorities have lately clamped down on it.

The practical result of these decisions was the creation, in the winter of 1959–60, of the Soviet Strategic Rocket Forces as a separate, fourth branch of the armed services. Its command was placed in charge of all missiles with ranges in excess of 1,000 kilometers —that is, weapons which in United States terminology qualify as both of strategic and intermediate range. The Rocket Forces became the preeminent service, while the army, navy and air force assumed auxiliary roles. The new doctrine and the mission of the Strategic Rocket Forces in implementing it were discussed with surprising frankness in the open literature published in the 1960s and 1970s under the auspices of the Ministry of Defense for the purpose of instructing military personnel. Soviet generals apparently took it for granted—correctly, as it turned out—that United States strategists, wrapped up in their own theories, would either ignore this material or shrug it off.

The following passage from one such publication articulates the Soviet position in a manner that for clarity of exposition and emphasis, leaves nothing to be desired. Having described the nuclear monopoly of the United States in the 1940s the authors go on to explain that the Communist Party decided to develop its own nuclear arsenal:

> Realizing this task, the Party pursued the goal of attaining such *superiority* over the bloc of imperialist powers which would enable [it] to prevent an annihilating war, to preserve and strengthen the global socialist system, and, in the event the imperialists nevertheless initiated a war, *to destroy the aggressor in short time with the smallest losses for the socialist countries.* . . .
> The content of the military-technical policy of the Party reduced itself to realizing the following basic tasks:
>
> □ organizing the mass production of nuclear weapons as *the main weapons of destruction* as well as the mass production of rockets of diverse missions as the principal means of delivery of nuclear charges to the objects to be destroyed;
> □ equipping the army and navy with nuclear-tipped rockets and fundamentally reorganizing the Soviet Armed Forces as a consequence of the introduction of the new weapons;
> □ formulating a modern Soviet military doctrine, military strategy, [and] art of operations and tactics appropriate to the nature and requirements of nuclear rocket war. . . .

The book goes on to explain that the Party accomplished all these objectives in the belief that "under contemporary conditions, the defensive capability of a country [and] the combat capability of the army depend *decisively* on nuclear weapons and their means of delivery to the target. It was decided that *the basis of the entire system of modern armament consists in nuclear charges, rockets and military radioelectronic devices.*" In consequence of these decisions being implemented,

> *the Strategic Rocket Forces have become the principal branch of the [Soviet] Armed Forces.* They are assigned the task of carrying out the most important missions that issue from the nature of contemporary war. They are charged with annihilating in minimum time the enemy's troop concentrations, command centers [and] military-industrial potential, disorganizing his political and military administration, his means of nuclear attack, [and] the arsenals and enterprises manufacturing nuclear weapons.[47]

If a document containing these statements had been purloined from the vaults of the Soviet General Staff, its importance and implications would have been immediately understood and, very likely, acted upon. But being available on open library shelves it has been ignored, even though from what is known of Soviet practices, every word in pronouncements of such gravity must have the endorsement of the highest political instances. To this day one can find people in the West questioning whether Moscow "really" believes that nuclear weapons can be used for any purpose other than preventing war, accusing Westerners who take statements to this effect seriously of warmongering, and blaming Washington for even giving thought to survival in nuclear war.

Nowhere is the Soviet rejection of United States nuclear strategy more clearly in evidence than in the attention paid by the Soviet military to defensive preparations. In their internal discussions, Soviet generals go to great lengths to demonstrate that, in a nuclear conflict, defense is no less important to victory than offense. In accord with this thinking, the Soviet government has launched an ambitious and expensive defensive effort which is incompatible with the spirit of mutual deterrence. It has surrounded the country with a ring of antiaircraft defenses (such as the United States has all but dismantled); it has provided hardened shelters for the leadership and the cadres needed to reconstruct a war-ravaged country and has devised for the rest of the population civil-defense programs; it has ensured the security of its command, control and communication networks by making them highly resistant to enemy disruption as well as redundant; it has funded a major effort to develop antiballistic-missile defenses; and as early as the 1960s it initiated a program to produce antisatellite weapons capable of depriving the enemy of essential surveillance capabilities in the event of hostilities.

Nor do the Soviet military accept the view, which prevails in the United States, that there is such a thing as "sufficiency" in nuclear weapons. While the United States, consistently with this principle, has deployed in the decade 1972–82 only one new strategic system (the Trident submarine), the USSR has tested and deployed during this time no fewer than ten systems—three ICBM systems (the SS-17, SS-18 and SS-19); the Backfire bomber; and three models of the Delta submarine, armed with three different types of missiles. It has also significantly upgraded its force of medium-range missiles with the deployment of several hundred SS-20s, as well as shorter-range, tactical systems.* Recently, the USSR has tested two new, fifth-generation ICBMs.

To make matters worse still, the figures we have on Soviet nuclear forces are almost certainly incomplete—that is, while one can be confident of our estimates of their minimum size, one can have no precise notion of their actual size. The Soviet Union adamantly refuses to provide comprehensive data on its launchers and missiles, compelling the United States to rely on the so-called national means of verification, consisting of satellite and electronic surveillance. Satellites are able to distinguish launchers located in the open, but they cannot penetrate structures where spare missiles for these launchers may be stored. Because of this technical limitation, the unit of account adopted in arms-control negotiation from the outset consisted of launchers rather than missiles—in other words, guns instead of shells. It can be taken for granted that the USSR has more missiles than launchers if only because the mobile SS-20 is assigned more than one missile per launcher. As a consequence, the nuclear balance-of-power charts and graphs displayed for the enlightenment of the Western public render the true state of United States nuclear forces but only a portion of the Soviet ones. Even if the Soviet Union were to allow on-site inspection and furnish complete data on actual Soviet forces, it would still not be easy (though incomparably easier) to arrive at a meaningful view of the balance, because of the multiplicity of elements that have to be factored into it—besides the numbers of missiles, launchers and warheads, also the throw-weight of the missiles and

---

* Because of its estimated range of 5,000 kilometers, the SS-20 is not treated as a strategic weapon for purposes of arms negotiation; in fact, however, even if it cannot strike the continental U.S., it can readily destroy targets in Europe, Asia and Africa, which are continents in their own right.

their state of readiness; the yields and accuracies of the warheads; the noise levels of the submarines; the radar profile of the bombers; the ability of silos to withstand pressures generated by nearby explosions of nuclear charges; and many others. No one or two units of measurement taken in isolation as a standard can furnish a meaningful picture of the balance of nuclear forces. To count launchers or warheads and on this basis conclude that, because both sides have an approximately equal number of each, they are equally powerful is like saying that two individuals who carry the same quantity of banknotes in their wallets enjoy the same purchasing power. There is a certain amount of self-deception built into all assurances of parity; once allowance is made for the fact that we are ignorant of the full dimension of the Soviet missile arsenal, and that the units of comparison in use—launchers and warheads—are inadequate in any event, any sense of comfort one may derive from such statistics tends to vanish.

Unfortunately, the public is being continually confused about these matters by ill-informed and emotional journalists and politicians. Even if one concedes the difficulty of grasping all the elements involved in the nuclear competition, there is no excuse for the kind of nonsense that is routinely dispensed by opponents of United States nuclear rearmament. Thus, for example, Mr. Anthony Lewis, a columnist for *The New York Times*, assures his readers that the MX is unnecessary because, were the Soviet Union to launch a first strike on United States land-based missiles "[it] would leave the United States with a relatively greater advantage over Soviet missiles."[48] Mr. Lewis's justification for this bizarre claim is that in order to take out one United States ICBM the Soviet Union would have to expend two missiles of its own. In this instance, Mr. Lewis happens to confuse missiles with warheads; in reality, a single Soviet SS-18, with its ten warheads, has the potential of destroying five Minuteman silos (allowing two warheads per target). Thus it would take 200, not 2,000 Soviet rockets to disable the United States force of 1,000 Minutemen, leaving the USSR stronger, not weaker, as a result. *The New York Times* also in all earnestness has quoted Senator Gary Hart that the MX was a provocative weapon because it "was vulnerable to a 'first strike' by the Soviet Union and therefore would be viewed by the Russians as an offensive rather than a deterrent weapon."[49] The contorted reasoning behind this claim is that a weapon vulnerable to a Soviet first strike can be seen as intended to be fired first, before it could be destroyed. By this kind of logic one could argue that the failure of the United States to develop air defenses or to deploy an antiballistic missile system or to take seriously civil defenses are indicative of an intention to attack the Soviet Union. When reading such statements, one understands what Oscar Wilde may have had in mind when he said that, its failings notwithstanding, there is much to be said in favor of journalism in that "by giving us the opinion of the uneducated, it keeps us in touch with the ignorance of the community."

In recent years, scientists have raised serious doubts whether major nuclear war can be waged without causing universal destruction. The validity of this proposition ultimately cannot be tested except under combat conditions, which, one hopes, will never occur. However, the issue at stake is not the objective reality, such as it may be, but the perception of that reality by those who make the political and military decisions. Throughout history, nations have gone to war in pursuit of goals that could have been demonstrated beforehand to be beyond their reach. Alexander the Great had not the means to conquer the world, nor Germany those to defeat its vastly superior neighbors in a *Blitzkrieg*, and yet both chose to try. The unceasing efforts of the USSR to upgrade both its offensive and defensive nuclear forces at all levels, far beyond any conceivable deterrent needs, strongly suggest that its leaders believe in their doctrine that nuclear weapons are the means of quick and decisive victory. In view of this overwhelming evidence, the burden of proof falls on those who are of a different opinion.

# 4 STRATEGY IN THE THIRD WORLD

The ultimate object of Soviet Grand Strategy has been defined above as the establishment of Soviet hegemony in the world through the transformation of the international state system into an aggregation of clients, each patterned on the Soviet model. To attain this end, the USSR must reduce the United States to the status of a power of minor rank; until this has been done, Soviet endeavors abroad will run into insurmountable difficulties. A British student of Soviet global strategy explains the Soviet predicament as follows:

> . . . since the day, in 1946 or 1947, when Stalin decided that the United States had entered the lists against Soviet expansion and the spread of Communism in Europe and Asia, the United States could, in some form, be discerned behind almost every failure of a Soviet strategical or tactical plan. When such a plan succeeded or some event developed successfully for the Soviet Union it was usually because America was absent or disinterested.[50]

The United States is formally committed to come to the defense of Europe and Japan, and protects other strategic regions that Moscow desires; it provides military and economic assistance to Third World countries threatened with Communist takeover; its navies rule the seas, its air force commands the skies, and it is on its way to placing outer space under its domination as well; its broadcasts inform and, by informing, subvert the populations under Communist rule. In view of these facts, it is hardly surprising that Soviet foreign policy concentrates with single-minded attention on the United States: "The Soviet leaders know that the existing world power of the United States of America must be removed or drastically reduced before the world can be brought to Communism."[51] Nasser learned from dealing with his Soviet patrons how overwhelming the United States looms in their thinking. He told one of his associates that Moscow was "obsessed" with the United States to the point that "the American element affects every decision, even those decisions which apparently have no connection with the United States."[52] If the fashionable term "zero-sum game" has any application, none better can be found than United States-Soviet relations as seen from Moscow.

Given the existing correlations of forces, United States power cannot be reduced by direct assault: this much has been conceded by Mr. Zagladin (above, pp. 58–59). For the time being, anti-American operations must be confined to political, psychological and economic attrition which will sap the enemy's strength and resolve, but will not alarm him and prod him into a violent reaction. Such territorial encroachments on the "imperialist camp" as can be safely undertaken must, in the meantime, take the form of flanking operations, which put at risk the enemy's vital military and economic interests in regions not covered by NATO and specific United States guarantees. This means essentially the Third World, exclusive of China, whose political system, modeled on the Soviet, renders it virtually impervious to *divide et impera* tactics. The Third World consists mostly of states that either have obtained their independence since World War II or else, while formally independent for a long time, have not been able to translate political sovereignty into economic independence. They are torn by social, ethnic and religious strife; they are politically unstable; and they are unaligned, in the sense that they belong to no international system that carries with it automatic pledges of foreign assistance. A Soviet Union hemmed in on the West by NATO and in the East by China, prefers to expand into this region of least resistance—the Middle East, Africa, Southeast Asia, Central and South America.

It is one of the cardinal tenets of Marxism-Leninism that once "capitalism" has entered its terminal phase—which is said to have occurred at the end of the nineteenth century—it is subject to convulsions of mounting severity. As industrial and financial power is concentrated in ever fewer hands, monopolies, cartels and trusts divide among themselves the world's resources and markets. Capitalist industry turns out more goods than it can sell; with the decline of opportunities for expanding markets and profitable investments, capitalist countries desperately struggle to survive. The struggle expresses itself mainly in competition for colonies which serve as sources of raw materials and as markets for finished goods. This is the final epoch of capitalism, the stage of "imperialism." Lenin developed this thesis in his *Imperialism, the Highest Stage of Capitalism* (1916–17) with due acknowledgment to its originator, the English liberal economist, John Hobson (*Imperialism*, 1902). Like Hobson, Lenin was impressed by the frenetic scramble for colonies which took place at the end of the nineteenth century. He was convinced that the world was witnessing the last gasps of a dying system.

Proceeding on this assumption, the Communist International from the moment of its founding in 1919 attached crucial importance to subverting Western colonial empires. Trotsky's notion that the road to Paris and London lay through Afghanistan and India (pp. 57–58 above) is a good example of Bolshevik thinking of that time. The Second Congress of the Communist International, held in 1920, laid great stress on the need to incite colonial rebellions, on the grounds that colonies provided the last available source of life support for dying capitalism. Its resolutions stated:

> European capitalism draws its strength primarily not from the industrial European countries but from its colonial possessions. For its existence it requires control over extensive colonial markets and a broad field of exploitation. England, the bulwark of imperialism, has been suffering already for a century from overproduction. Without extensive colonial possessions, indispensable for the marketing of goods and, at the same time, for the acquisition of raw materials, the capitalist regime of England would have long ago collapsed under its own weight . . . The surplus value extracted from the colonies is the principal source of the means of contemporary capitalism . . . By exploiting the colonial population, European imperialism is able to offer a quantity of compensatory gratuities to the labor aristocracy in Europe . . . The separation of the colonies and the proletarian revolution at home will overthrow the capitalist order in Europe . . . For the full success of the world revolution, it is necessary for the two forces [the proletariat and the colonial peoples] to work together.[53]

These ideas turned out to have little relation to reality, and Stalin abandoned them soon after coming to power. Under conditions of the 1920s, revolutionary activity in underdeveloped countries required the Communists, who were very weak, to collaborate with elements that the Party defined as "bourgeois-nationalist." In practice it turned out that the bourgeois-nationalists, whose primary objective was national independence, not Communism, took whatever help they could get from their Soviet and Communist allies and then, once in power, turned their backs on them. This pattern occurred in China. Moscow extended generous support to Chiang Kai-shek's Kuomintang and forced the small Chinese Communist Party to follow suit. Chiang Kai-shek freely availed himself of this support to create a political power base. As soon as the latter was reasonably secure (1927), he broke with his Communist allies and in some cases savagely repressed them. The fiasco of a policy on which they had placed great expectations cured Stalin and his adherents of such illusions as they may have entertained of manipulating bourgeois-nationalists in the colonies for the Soviet Union's own purposes. Henceforth, Stalin trusted only forces under his direct control. He supported anticolonial movements after World War II, because these contributed to weakening the strategic position of his "imperialist" opponents, but he was careful to avoid close associations with the emergent nationalist leaders.

Stalin's policy was abandoned by his successors, who reverted to the practices of Lenin and the Communist International. In the second half of the 1950s, Moscow once again began vigorously to support "bourgeois-nationalist" leaders in the Third World, in order to exploit their anti-Western and anticapitalist sentiments. Since most of the regions once dominated by the imperial powers had by then received their independence, the old slogans ceased to be relevant: Moscow could not very usefully agitate for sovereignty of countries that were sovereign already. The Party's theoreticians went to work and came up with a solution to this problem. Around 1960, they advanced the argument that classic colonialism had been replaced by "neocolonialism"—that is to say, that the onetime possessions of the "imperialist" powers had been granted sham sovereignty in the shape of formal political independence, while continuing to remain economically dependent on their onetime colonial masters. Communist strategy henceforth called for a completion of the process of emancipation by urging the former colonies to nationalize their economies and sever their links to "imperialist" industries and banks. Third World countries which in many cases had not even entered the "feudal" stage were given dispensation to proceed directly toward "socialism" by way of a transitional order, called "National Democracy." A National Democracy bypassed capitalism and laid the foundations of socialism on a primitive, precapitalist base. Soviet experts believed that such a hybrid system provided the Communists with a favorable environment in countries where the economic prerequisites for socialist revolution in the Marxist sense were absent. Boris Ponomarev, the director of the Central Committee's International Department, gave the following explanation of the new strategy for the Third World:

> Experience with the development of states which had recently freed themselves from imperialist slavery shows that the nationalization of foreign banks and of the property of monopolies, and the subsequent creation of state enterprises, banks, and so on, leads to the emergence of a more progressive form of property than the private one, namely, state property of the means of production. State property is a major force. Its development and consolidation under a government of National Democracy make it possible to squeeze large private capital [and] give progressive forces an opportunity to occupy ever more important positions in production and to enhance their political influence.[54]

If one substitutes "Communist parties" for "progressive forces," the meaning of Ponomarev's remarks becomes clear: he is saying that the nationalization of industrial and financial institutions in Third World countries will give native Communists the opportunity to gain control of the local economies to use as a power base on which to build a full-blown Communist state.

What this involves in practice is described by Professor Wolfgang Leonhard:

> [Skipping the capitalist stage of development] among other things . . . entails the nationalization of the key industrial sectors of the nation concerned, the enactment of a far-reaching land-reform program, drastic limitation of the influence of large landowners and private capitalist economic circles, the introduction of state planning, and the creation of political conditions that involves a convergence with the Soviet type of system. Especially important is a dependence upon the Soviet Union in foreign-policy matters, and a corresponding clearcut dissociation from the Western nations.
>
> Those nations that from the Soviet perspective follow the "noncapitalist path of development" particularly successfully are classified as "socialist-oriented nations"; as of 1982–83 the nations included in this category [were] Ethiopia, Mozambique and Angola in Africa, and the People's Republic of Yemen in the Arab world.

These patently abstract conceptions revolve in reality around the decisive question as to whether the Third World nations, after achieving their independence, follow a "Japanese path," and develop into modern industrial states of the parliamentary-democratic type, or pursue a "Cuban path," which leads to a system of the Soviet type. The strong commitment of the Soviet Union testifies to its fear as well as its hope: if most of the nations of the Third World follow the "Japanese path," the Western system will maintain and even extend its preponderance. If on the other hand the Kremlin succeeds in pushing developments in the Third World increasingly in the direction of the "Cuban path," a Soviet preponderance in the world will gradually be achieved.[55]

This strategy has run into frustrating obstacles, which will be discussed in Chapter Four. Here suffice it to say that the Soviet Union has proven to lack the economic resources needed to help Third World countries willing to take the path of "National Democracy" and left them no alternative but to continue and in some instances even to expand their relationship with the "imperialist camp." These difficulties, in turn, have forced Moscow to assume a more direct role in Third World activities—that is, to rely less on drawn-out processes of economic and political change and more on military intervention with its own or proxy forces. Nonetheless, the general policy adopted in the early 1960s remains in effect: the USSR attaches critical importance to expelling Western influence from the Third World in the belief that this undermines the "imperialist camp" and helps to shift the global correlation of forces in its favor.

Four geographic regions are of particular importance to this strategy: the Middle East (Persian Gulf), sub-Saharan Africa, Central America and Southeast Asia. Each of these regions either contains raw materials or controls access to raw materials considered essential to the economies of the West. Their loss to the West would, indeed, have a dramatic effect on the global balance of power.

Soviet interest in the Middle East dates back to the late eighteenth century, when Russia first laid claim to the Straits and stirred up the Christian subjects of the Sultan. Throughout the nineteenth century, Russia sought to partition the Ottoman Empire and to raise its flag over Constantinople. After the development, early in the twentieth century, of Middle Eastern oil resources, Russian interest in this region extended eastward, toward the Persian Gulf, which, together with the Straits, has come to constitute the focal point of Moscow's strategic interests in the Third World. This became clear during the Nazi-Soviet negotiations in late 1940, when Stalin and Hitler were dividing the spoils

of what appeared to be an expiring British Empire. Hitler offered
Stalin a sphere of influence extending "south of the Soviet Union
in the direction of the Indian Ocean." This offer did not satisfy
Stalin, who demanded areas lying "in the general direction of the
Persian Gulf" as well as military control of the Turkish Straits.[56]
Moscow's strategic interest in this region has not abated to this
day, and the reason for it is transparent: Western Europe draws
one half and Japan almost two thirds of their oil supplies from the
Gulf. Should Moscow dominate the Gulf or even only the approaches to it, it would be in a position to engage in very effective
blackmail against America's principal allies. As we have seen
(p. 58 above), the desire to obtain leverage over West European oil
supplies was the rationale given to the Soviet establishment as
early as 1955 for an alliance with the Arabs. The most persistently
aggressive Soviet moves in the past thirty years have occurred in
this region: the lavish support of Egypt, the military assistance,
first to Somalia, then to Ethiopia, military aid to Syria, and the
virtual occupation of South Yemen have provided the USSR with
powerful political and military influence over the western approaches to the Gulf. The occupation of Afghanistan has cut in
half the distance that Soviet troops and rockets need to cover in
order to reach the Gulf. The Soviet shadow over this area looms
so large that many Muslim regimes cannot find the courage to
challenge it; the more savagely the Russians deal with the Afghan
resistance, the greater the dread which they strike into the heart
of other Muslim countries.

The importance of sub-Saharan Africa to Western economies is
a less familiar subject. If oil is excepted, the Republic of South
Africa ranks as the world's fourth-largest producer of minerals
(following the United States, the Soviet Union and Canada). In the
middle 1970s it was the world's leading producer of gold, platinum, vanadium and antimony, the second-largest producer of
chrome and manganese ores, and the third-largest producer of
diamonds, uranium and asbestos. Three quarters of its mineral
output (exclusive of gold) is shipped to Western Europe and
Japan, which, unlike the United States and the USSR, cannot meet
most of their needs from domestic resources. Were South Africa
to fall under Communist control, not only would America's allies
become dependent for their supply of these raw materials on the
good will of Moscow, but the latter would secure a near-monopoly
of the world's known reserves of platinum, vanadium, manganese
and chrome.[57] In addition, South Africa's Cape of Good Hope
adjoins the world's busiest waterway for transporting oil, because
modern supertankers, too large to use the Suez Canal, sail this

route when traveling between the Near Eastern oil centers and the Atlantic.

The third strategic area in which the Soviet Union has shown an active interest is Central America. For a long time Moscow had stayed away from this region out of deference to the Monroe Doctrine. The Kennedy-Khrushchev accords of 1962 put an end to this restraint. Moscow interpreted President Kennedy's pledges to respect the sovereignty of Communist Cuba in exchange for the removal of Soviet missiles from that island to mean the renunciation of the Monroe Doctrine. From then on it began to intervene in this region with growing boldness by dispatching army, navy and air units to Cuba and using Cuban mercenaries in Africa. For Moscow, this region holds interest for three reasons:

**1.** It is an area of very active maritime trade, through which transits a high proportion of United States imports of oil and other strategic materials. Soviet specialists call attention to the fact that between 40 and 100 percent of the strategic materials which the United States imports from abroad originate in South America.[58] Since these are shipped mainly by way of the Caribbean and the Gulf of Mexico, Moscow's ability to intervene militarily in this region in case of war is of considerable strategic importance.

**2.** The Panama Canal is here; despite its inability to accommodate supertankers, this Canal remains of major importance to Western economies.

**3.** Turbulence in this region, so close to the continental United States, is likely to divert United States attention from other areas of the world, allowing Soviet and pro-Soviet forces greater freedom for action in the Middle East, Africa, and perhaps even Europe.

The fourth and least important region of strategic interest to the USSR is Southeast Asia—that is, Vietnam, Laos and Cambodia. This region provides, first and foremost, a base from which to threaten China's southern flank; secondly, it offers opportunities for choking off the Straits of Malacca through which pass large volumes of Japanese imports and exports.

In each of these four regions, Communists put together Third World coalitions bound together by incitement to hatred of hostile minorities or countries—Israel and the Jews in the Middle East; the white inhabitants in sub-Saharan Africa; the United States in Central America; and the Chinese in Southeast Asia.

# THE
# ECONOMIC CRISIS

We have discussed, so far, the sources of the Soviet *nomenklatura*'s imperialism and the nature of its Grand Strategy. These subjects lie in the realm of motives and intentions. What of capabilities? Does the Soviet regime have the means to carry out its ambitious designs? More precisely, can its economy and political system sustain militarism and expansionism of such extravagant proportions? Outwardly, Soviet leaders exude assurance: they appear confident that the political strategy that they have adopted will prevail and bring them the desired results without resort to arms. Should general war, nevertheless, break out, they feel that geopolitical advantages, superior ability to mobilize their population and resources, and meticulous peacetime preparations for war, will bring them victory. They find great comfort in the fact that the major wars of this century have helped the spread of Communism. World War I enabled Communists to take over Russia, while World War II allowed them to extend their system to many countries of Europe and the Third World. In the light of this record, the *nomenklatura* thinks it reasonable to assume that should worst come to worst and the West provoke World War III by its futile efforts to turn back the tide of history, such a war will prove the "grave of capitalism" all over the world.[1]

**110**

A more detached appraisal of the realities, however, indicates that Soviet prospects in this regard are considerably less promising. Soviet imperialism is unique in that its primary purpose is to protect the political power and privilege of a small, self-perpetuating elite; the peculiar consequence is that instead of bringing wealth to the imperial power, as imperialism is meant to do, it severely drains its resources. "In the past," observes an Italian writer, "imperial powers had come into existence for the purpose of enriching the metropolitan areas and making them more powerful, as well as pushing ever farther outward their security borders. In the case of the Soviet Union, by contrast, its worldwide influence makes it ever poorer, because the USSR is not able to keep up with its numerous strategic and economic commitments."[2]

This chapter and the next will discuss the economic and political strains afflicting the Soviet system and aggravated by its imperial ambitions. Emphasis will be placed on those phenomena that make it increasingly difficult for the Soviet regime to maintain intact the Stalinist system and, at the same time, engage in a quest for worldwide political and military hegemony that this system was not designed to support. It is the author's conviction that Soviet intentions and capabilities are at odds with each other. This does not mean that the Soviet empire is about to collapse; it does mean that internal pressures are bringing the day nearer when the *nomenklatura* will have to choose between moderating its ambitions and altering its economic and political regime or, indeed, when it may be forced to do both.

# 1 GENERAL REMARKS ABOUT THE ECONOMIC CRISIS

That the Communist economies are inefficient and unproductive is known to every reader of the daily press. It is a commonplace that they can neither provide their citizens with a living standard expected of industrial nations nor manufacture goods that anyone who has a choice in the matter will buy. It further is common knowledge that these economies are in decline, as indicated by the downward trend of the rate of growth of their estimated Gross National Product (GNP).

| TABLE 1 | |
|---|---|
| AVERAGE ANNUAL RATES OF GROWTH OF SOVIET GNP | |
| Years | Percent |
| 1951–1960 | 5.8 |
| 1961–1970 | 5.1 |
| 1971–1975 | 3.8 |
| 1976–1980 | 2.8 |

The CIA believes that the rate of growth of the Soviet GNP will hover around 2 percent a year for the rest of the decade. The situation in the countries of Eastern Europe is more dismal yet:

| TABLE 2 | |
|---|---|
| AVERAGE ANNUAL RATES OF GROWTH OF EAST EUROPEAN GNP | |
| Years | Percent |
| 1971–75 | 4.8 |
| 1976–78 | 3.7 |
| 1979 | 1.7 |
| 1980 | 0.5 |

Even if allowance is made for the fact that GNP statistics, under the best of circumstances, are imperfect, there is little disagreement among experts that a decline in the rate of growth of Communist economies has been occurring for some time and that a reversal of the trend is not in sight.

A steady diminution of economic growth does not augur catastrophe; no serious observer holds this expectation. If Albania can survive economically, so, surely, can the Soviet Union. These statistics carry different implications. They place in question the ability of the Soviet economy to meet its three principal commitments: expansion of the industrial and technological base; preservation and perhaps even improvement of living standards; and support of the armed forces and the country's imperial commitments. That the *nomenklatura* is well aware of the relevance of declining rates of growth to its ability to maneuver is evident from the pronouncements of Soviet political leaders and economists. "Only by raising the economy's efficiency," Brezhnev stated a year before his death,

is it possible to find sufficient means and resources to ensure simultaneously a substantial growth in the well-being of the working people, possibilites for the rapid development of economy in the future, and requirements for maintaining the country's defense capability at the appropriate level.[3]

Western experts agree with Brezhnev that inefficiency, that is, low productivity, is at the root of the trouble with the Soviet economy. Raising output per worker and per unit of production is the obsessive theme of all the economic discussions held in the Communist Bloc. Countries obliged to commit ever more capital to turn out the same quantity of goods—in the USSR, these so-called capital-output ratios have doubled between 1960 and 1980—afford their rulers ever less freedom of action.

Many Americans believe that the failures of the Soviet economy derive from the lack of "know-how"; some people even seriously propose that as a contribution to world peace, the United States share its productive skills with the Russians. Such suggestions are naïve in the extreme. The high productivity of the United States economy and the affluence that flows from it are due not to unique skills but to unique advantages: the natural affluence of the country; the peace the United States has enjoyed through most of its history; and a political system designed to facilitate the creation and accumulation of wealth. Russia lacks these particular advantages. It is inherently poor; being poor it finds it more attractive to appropriate the wealth of others than to create its own; and, most damaging of all, it is burdened with a political regime that—whatever its other uses—virtually guarantees economic underperformance.

In every Communist country, the economy serves first and foremost political ends. Its principal task is to ensure the security of the *nomenklatura* by giving it control over the means of livelihood of its subjects; its second task is to furnish the military power needed to intimidate neighbors and conquer new territory. All else is subordinate. The Party is undoubtedly sincere in its desire to improve productivity; yet, whenever the needs of productivity come into conflict with those of internal or external power—which happens repeatedly—it is productivity that must give way. Here lies the crux of the problem. Every Russian with a high-school education knows what is wrong with his country's economy and what it would take to set it right. The difficulty is that every reform that will lead to significant improvements in economic performance will inevitably weaken the *nomenklatura*'s grip on the levers of power; and since the *nomenklatura* is not eager to place its power at risk, it talks about changing the system, putters with it, rearranges it, but never really comes close to reforming it. Political interests in this instance are starkly at odds with the requirements of the productive forces, which creates a strange predicament for a regime that claims to adhere to the principles of Marxism.

The faltering performance of Communist economies can be laid to the account of three specific causes: administrative overcentralization; the absence of meaningful incentives; and the excessive burden of militarism. The first two of these handicaps may be called systemic in the sense that they are built into the structure of the regime and cannot be removed without far-reaching reorganization. The third seems capable of being more readily taken care of, because it depends on political decisions that can be taken without affecting the system; however, militarism is so deeply imbedded in the mentality of the *nomenklatura* that it is probably as difficult to be rid of it as it is to change the system of which it is the product.

The Soviet economy is absurdly overcentralized. It is a mammoth conglomerate that owns and manages all of industry, all of agriculture, and the full range of services. It runs giant automobile plants and two-men barbershops, the country's national airline and secondhand bookstores, the world's largest merchant marine and village groceries. This overcentralization has several reasons, and it is difficult to decide which is the most important. One, of course, is Marxist dogma, which demands that the liberated "proletariat" abolish private ownership of the means of production. The second has to do with the conviction that size equals efficiency. The Bolshevik leaders who put into place the economic system subsequently adopted by the other Communist countries had little practical experience in economic affairs—if one sets aside what they had learned from robbing banks and extorting money for their Party's treasury. Observing trends in advanced industrial countries immediately before and during World War I, they concluded that large-scale production led to efficient and low-cost outputs. From this correct observation they concluded incorrectly that the larger the unit of production, the greater its efficiency. The centralization of the Russian national economy, first attempted in 1918–20 but completed only a decade later, was expected to unleash productive forces to an extent unimaginable in the dispersed and wastefully competitive market economies.

But behind the determination to centralize the economy there always lay concealed a third consideration, one that had to do with the security of the Bolshevik Party. It is, of course, one of the fundamental tenets of Marxism that political power grows out of the ownership of the means of production. From this premise it follows that if one desires a monopoly on political power one must secure a monopoly on the means of production. This proposition is difficult to refute either in theory or in practice. Where no independent wealth exists, there can be no independent political parties and therefore no organized opposition, but there the masters of public wealth have at their disposal the means with which to reward political loyalty and to exact general obedience. The proven ability of Communist governments to regiment their subjects is only partly explainable by their ubiquitous security services. After all, the police cannot be everywhere and even Communist prisons and camps have finite capacities. An even more effective instrument of political control is the monopoly that Communist regimes have on employment and material rewards. With the government the sole employer, every citizen who needs a regular income to support himself and his family has no choice but to work for the government, and this compels him to conform to the regime's standards of loyalty. In all Communist societies there exist individuals who manage to make a living outside this rigid system—such as artists who sell their works privately and illegal entrepreneurs or middlemen of all sorts—but viewed from the standpoint of economics, they play a marginal role. The theory has been—and, as we shall see, it is now being increasingly violated—that the entire gainfully employed population has a single paymaster, the government. The other side of the coin is that its monopoly on the country's wealth enables the *nomenklatura* to reward itself with a style of life that compares favorably with that enjoyed by elites in much more affluent societies. For reasons of political control alone, therefore, one cannot conceive a Communist regime being willing, except under duress and then only as a temporary concession, for a significant part of the productive forces to slip from its hands. Whenever it has had to acquiesce to such a situation, as for instance in Poland, where three fourths of agriculture has been left in private hands, the result has been an imperfect dictatorship and no end of political trouble.

The price that the *nomenklatura* has had to pay for owning and managing the economy, however, has not been insignificant; it has vitiated the benefits that had been expected to accrue from placing the entire national economy under a single roof. A gigantic central bureaucracy had to be created to supervise factories, farms and retail facilities, to allocate capital and raw materials, to direct the labor force, to borrow capital and purchase equipment abroad, and to engage in the myriad other activities that the economy of a large country entails. No single organization can possibly assimilate the mass of data that an economy with a GNP of over one trillion dollars (in the case of the USSR) disgorges every hour of the day, nor come up with rational solutions to the problems that arise from them. The predicament which confronts the economic managers of Communist countries is not unlike that which Western conglomerates experience once they grow too large, and which they resolve by either administrative decentralization or divestiture. Where neither of these solutions is politically acceptable, the result is stupendous mismanagement. Some Soviet economists go so far as to admit privately that no one in the country really knows what goes on in the economy.[4] The Five Year Plans, which Gosplan compiles and then solemnly proclaims to the world, are discounted before they even go into effect. The investment projections are perhaps realistic enough, but the production that is supposed to ensue falls at once behind schedule and rarely attains its stated objectives. Life goes on, of course, but not according to plan, which has turned into a grand fiction of ritualistic utility to a regime whom its own standards require to appear at all times omniscient and omnipotent, fully "in charge." Making allowance for these facts, all reform projects in the Soviet Union call for a certain degree of administrative decentralization and the sharing of authority between Party officials and managers. Although proposals to this effect have been cropping up in the Soviet Union with monotonous regularity since Stalin's death, no attempt has ever been made to put them into practice. The *nomenklatura* evidently fears that such innovations will weaken its power base and undermine its security. Moscow has tolerated and even encouraged reforms in Western Europe, notably Hungary (of which more later) but it has not had the courage to introduce them at home.

The second major flaw of central planning as practiced in the Soviet Union is the shortage of incentives that would give managers and workers an interest in increasing production. Indeed, the system is so absurdly designed that those responsible for production may be said to have a vested interest in preventing it from improving. Instead of allowing costs and profits to determine what is produced and in what quantities, the government sets arbitrary production quotas for each branch of the economy. Underperformance is sometimes penalized, but overproduction is rarely rewarded; should an industrial enterprise or a collective farm turn out more than its plan calls for, as a rule its bonus will be not a share of the resulting profits but a higher production target in the next plan. Under such circumstances, Soviet managers, workers and farmers find it to their advantage not to exceed the required minimum and to seek additional income from moonlighting or stealing state property. The same reason explains their resistance to the introduction of procedures and equipment capable of improving productivity. Under the existing system, enterprises benefit from having more working hands than they need—that is, in effect, from maintaining a low *per capita* output. According to one Soviet publication,

> [it is] more advantageous even in economic terms for an enterprise to have a surplus than a shortage of manpower. The enterprise's category is determined by numbers [of employees]. The more people there are, the bigger the wage fund as well as the bonus allocations. The salary scales of the leaders are directly dependent on the number of personnel and not on the efficiency with which the personnel is utilized.[5]

Low productivity is thus imbedded in the existing planning system, and it is futile to exhort managers, engineers and workers to produce more, as long as doing so runs against their own basic interests. This reality is known to the leadership, as the following remarks of Andropov indicate:

> An economic planner who would take a "risk" and introduce into the enterprise new technology, who would put to use or invent new equipment, would often turn out to be the loser, whereas he who stays clear of innovation loses nothing. To work out such a system of organizational, economic and moral measures which would create an interest among managers, workers and, of course, scientists and designers in modernization—this is the task.[6]

This, indeed, is the task, but it is not organizational or technical in nature: it is political in the fullest sense of this word.

In addition to overcentralization and the absence of incentives, the Soviet economy is burdened by excessive expenditures on its armed forces and imperial dependencies.

The funds allocated by the Soviet authorities for military purposes have long been a subject of controversy among specialists. There is agreement that the figures shown in the official Soviet budget are meaningless and that the bulk of military expenditures is concealed under various nonmilitary rubrics. Using elaborate estimating techniques, the Central Intelligence Agency has concluded that Soviet military expenditures represent between 12 and 14 percent of the country's Gross National Product. (This figure compares with 6–7 percent of the United States GNP spent for this purpose in the budgets of President Reagan.) The CIA is confident of its estimate, but its confidence would be more contagious if until May 1976 it had not placed this figure, with equal assurance, at 6–8 percent, only to double it overnight on the basis of fresh evidence that had come into its possession. Some independent specialists estimate the share of Soviet military appropriations as high as 18 and even 20 percent of the Soviet GNP.[7]

The problems in assessing Soviet military expenditures are many. For one, the civilian and defense sectors are intertwined to such an extent that it is doubtful whether the Soviet leadership itself could give an accurate accounting of how much it allocates to the one and how much to the other. There is also the equivocal nature of the concept Gross National Product, further complicated by the fact that Soviet economists do not employ this standard. How to translate ruble costs into their dollar equivalents—if one can do it at all—is a subject of continuing dispute. Then there are whole categories of military expenditures that do not lend themselves to quantification. For instance, in all their investment allocations to the consumer sector, Soviet authorities always bear in mind how adaptable a given facility is for purposes of war mobilization. It gives priority to those branches of industry that lend themselves to being readily converted to the manufacture of instruments of war; it further makes a point of placing them in locations where they are less vulnerable to enemy attack, which may or may not be rational from the economic point of view. The USSR has been willing for years to overproduce television sets, because plants that manufacture TV's can be rapidly converted to produce electronic equipment for the armed forces. Similarly, in trying to overcome low agricultural yields it has consistently given preference to the manufacture of tractors over chemical fertilizers, because a plant that turns out tractors can be made to turn out tanks. Furthermore, most of the cost of military training is borne by the educational system, which provides such training to students in the final two years of secondary schooling.[8] How does one calculate the cost of such investment decisions and activities to the national economy? And need one try? Given the inherently speculative nature of computations of this kind and their controversial results, one wonders what utility they have other than helping persuade legislators of democratic societies to increase defense appropriations. Inside the Soviet Union, among people worried about the immense burdens which military costs impose on the economy, the various estimates that circulate privately indicate more meaningfully just how oppressive these are. A prominent Soviet economist is reported to have told his colleagues in 1965 that of the 100 million citizens employed in the country, between 30 and 40 million were working for military industry. Andrei Sakharov calculates that some 40 percent of Soviet national income is spent on defense, broadly defined, while some Soviet economists privately place the figure at between 41 and 51 percent.[9] The latter estimates would imply that the Soviet Union, from an economic standpoint, is on a wartime footing.

The extent to which commitments to the military retard both the development of productive forces and improvements in general living standards is conveyed by trends in Soviet investment figures. For purposes of planning, industrial production in the Soviet Union is divided into two sectors. Sector A turns out producers' goods, that is, plant, equipment, transport and all else that goes into the creation of additional means of production. Sector B is the consumer sector. Not acknowledged officially but immensely important, of course, is the military sector, which in practice forms a distinct part of Sector A. Since Brezhnev assumed office, approximately three quarters of Soviet output has come from Sector A. It has been Soviet practice to maintain a roughly equal rate of growth in all three of these sectors, but in the face of declining rates of over-all growth it has become increasingly difficult to do so. Unwilling to slight the military and afraid to slight the consumer, the authorities have had no choice but to cut into that part of Sector A on which economic growth over the long term depends. In the Ninth Five Year Plan (1970–75), investments for capital goods were still kept at an impressive 41 percent above the previous plan. In the Tenth Plan (1975–80) they were reduced to allow for a growth rate of 24–26 percent. When time came to draft the Eleventh Plan for 1981–85, the authorities cut back capital investments still further, initially to 12–15 percent, and finally to 10.4 percent, which is the lowest growth figure for this sector since World War II. Significantly, in the Tenth and Eleventh Plans the growth rate of the consumer sector was only slightly affected, while military allocations remained untouched.

The Soviet government justifies its change in investment practices with the argument that the time has come to make better use of the existing plant. For years, it argues, immense resources have been poured into capital goods, and now the country has the right to expect these investments to produce results; extensive growth, paid for with manpower and money, must give way to intensive growth. The argument is not without merit, but it is a cold fact that, instead of rising, productive growth is falling. If henceforth ever fewer funds will be committed for the purchase of equipment, the industrial plant will inevitably grow obsolete and more shopworn. (Under ordinary circumstances, Soviet industry uses machinery twice as long as is the practice in market economies.) The expectation, therefore, is that production will be still more adversely affected in the years to come. As someone has observed,

Reprinted with permission from *Frankfurter Allgemeine Zeitung*

the choice before the Soviet leadership is not one between guns and butter—that would be an easy one to make (in fact, it has been made a long time ago)—but between guns and factories.

Can the Soviet Union muddle through with an economy in which nearly all productive indices are on a falling curve? The answer, assuredly, is Yes. Can it remain, under these circumstances, a great imperial power with aspirations to global hegemony? The answer is, probably not—unless, that is, the West comes to its assistance.

We shall now turn to several specific problems afflicting the Soviet economy that bear on its capacity to sustain military and imperial efforts at their recent pace.

## 2 AGRICULTURE

Nature has not intended the territory occupied by the Soviet Union to be used for growing food. Its extremely northern location makes for a short agricultural season, which, in turn, demands highly concentrated labor in the spring and fall accompanied by long periods of forced inactivity. In the northern half of Russia, the rainfall is abundant, but the soil, which tends to be sandy or clayey, lacks adequate organic matter. In the south, where the soil is fertile, rain happens to be both sparse and unreliable. Distances are great, and roads are difficult to maintain. As a consequence of these adverse factors, Russia was never able to produce the kind of food surpluses that experience shows to be necessary for a high level of civilization. Even so, except for occasional crop failures caused by a succession of poor weather, the Russian peasant over the centuries has managed to feed himself and the country's small nonagricultural population. In the second half of the nineteenth century, Russia was even able to export grain to the industrial countries; in the five years preceding the outbreak of World War I (1909–13), it sold abroad an average of 11 million metric tons of grains a year, which represented nearly one third of the international grain trade. Most of this excess food came from large, privately owned farms which were subsequently expropriated in the Revolution.

The Marxists regarded agriculture as a primitive form of economic activity and the peasant, with his acquisitiveness, superstitious nature and anarchism, as an incorrigible petty bourgeois. Marx expected the individual peasant holding to go the way of household industry; and although the statistical evidence that accumulated in the late nineteenth century proved this particular forecast of Marx's, as so many of the others, to be groundless, the Social Democrats clung to it through thick and thin.[10] Living in a country three quarters of whose inhabitants supported themselves from the land, the Russian Social Democrats regarded the peasant as material ill suited for the new society, a class enemy of the proletariat; his only useful contribution to the revolutionary cause, they held, was to throw the countryside into chaos and thus make it easier for the industrial workers to seize power in the cities. This role the Russian peasant performed admirably well. As soon as he had learned of the tsar's abdication, he went on a rampage, seizing and merging into communes properties of private owners, large and small, landlord and peasant. Lenin encouraged this rural rebellion, which played no small part in the collapse of the Provisional Government that had struggled to establish in Russia democratic institutions.

As soon as power was in their hands, the Bolsheviks introduced a policy of exacting food from the village on behalf of the city, where their own power base lay. They dispatched gangs of armed thugs to the countryside to appropriate, in the guise of collecting a "tax in kind," the peasants' grain and whatever else they could lay their hands on. Decrees that had no precedent in Russian history forbade the peasant to sell his produce on the open market and forced him to turn his surplus over to the state at absurdly low prices. The bewildered peasant fought back as best he could;

but, skilled as he was in circumventing governmental orders, he had no experience in the class war unleashed by intellectuals who treated him as expendable raw material. In 1920, after two years of expropriations and other punishments, the tormented Russian village was struck by adverse weather; it recurred the following year. The result of man-made and natural disasters was a famine unlike any that Russia had ever known—25 million peasants experienced hunger and (according to contemporary Soviet statistical accounts), 5.2 million of them perished from malnutrition and the typhoid fever that accompanied it. Were it not for the American Relief Administration, organized by Herbert Hoover and assisted by European relief missions, the toll would have been much heavier.

In 1921, faced with general economic collapse, Lenin reversed his policies. The New Economic Policy, which he introduced in the spring of that year, restored to the peasant most of his traditional rights, including that of marketing his produce. The resilience of the Russian peasant is so great that in a few seasons he managed to bring agriculture back to the relatively prosperous condition of the immediate prewar years. This was one of the happiest periods in the history of the Russian and Ukrainian village. But soon a second, more terrible tragedy struck. In 1927, Stalin decided on a revolutionary program of forced industrialization. Capital, which was in very short supply, was to come mainly from the village. The village was to be harnessed in the service of industry; since nearly the entire effort of the Five Year Plan was to go into the production of capital goods and military equipment (Sector A), consumer and light industrial goods, which the peasant demanded in exchange for food, would become virtually unavailable. Under these conditions, the peasant was certain to withhold his grain.

To ensure food for the cities and industrial centers for years to come, a more efficient system of exaction than seasonal requisitioning had to be devised. The solution was nationalization of agricultural land and all that was required for its cultivation. Between 1929 and 1931, the Soviet peasant was deprived of all his property—land, livestock, implements, crop. The land and livestock went into a collective pool, administered by Party officials, whose orders henceforth were law, very much as the landlord's had been in the days of serfdom. Tractors and other equipment came under the control of special units administered by the Party's Central Committee. The peasant was transformed into a rural proletarian paid a pittance for hard and compulsory work. Under the new arrangement, the collective was required first to meet state quotas for grain. The government purchased this grain at ridiculously low prices and resold it to consumers at an immense profit, sometimes as high as 1,000 percent. What remained after the state quotas had been met went for seed and village consumption. If the village produced no surplus, it starved. The only silver lining in this odious arrangement was the right granted to collective-farm peasants to keep a small plot (1 acre maximum) on which to grow fruits and vegetable for their own use and for sale at negotiated prices in state-supervised collective-farm markets. As under serfdom, the peasant was tied to the land and forbidden to leave the village, either permanently or temporarily, without authorization.

The peasant fiercely resisted these measures. Entire villages that rebelled had to be reduced into submission by units of the Red Army. Up to ten million well-to-do and industrious peasants, misnamed *kulaks* (the term traditionally applied to village moneylenders) were deported, for the purpose of "liquidation," to forced labor camps. A famine engineered in the Ukraine in the early 1930s claimed up to nine million lives, which is the greatest number of hunger victims in recorded history, surpassing even the appalling casualties in the Indian famines of the nineteenth century. In the end, Stalin won his battle: the villages submitted. But the price proved staggering and not only for those who had paid it with their lives. Collectivization of agriculture broke the spirit of the Russian and Ukrainian peasantry, transforming it into a class of sullen helots, engaged in permanent passive resistance, forever scheming how to evade its obligations and escape to the better-supplied city.

The industrial surge of the Soviet Union was thus built on capital pitilessly extracted from the villages in the form of lives and virtually gratuitous labor. In 1935, the average rural family in the Soviet Union earned in cash for one year's work on the collective farm, 247 rubles, which was just enough for the purchase of one pair of shoes. In 1940, only one village in twenty-five had any electricity.[11] Running water and sewers were all but unknown.[12] The food that the peasant produced was more readily available in the cities than in the villages. Confronted with such insufferable conditions, the peasantry retreated within itself. An unprecedented situation was created in which a country, 60 percent of whose inhabitants worked on the land, could not provide itself with foodstuffs above the bare subsistence level.

Immediately after his death, Stalin's successors took steps to improve the conditions in agriculture. They lacked, however, the courage to tackle the problem at its root, which is collectivization, that is, state ownership and management of agriculture. All the rural reforms introduced since 1953 have been of a palliative nature.

The *nomenklatura*'s reluctance to solve the problem that causes it so much difficulty is due to at least two considerations. One is political. The *nomenklatura* fears that if it returned ownership of the arable land to its cultivators, lifting Party control over the village, it would give rise to a dangerous class enemy. Food is so scarce and precious that a peasantry free to dispose of its entire surplus at market prices would promptly accumulate a great deal of capital and, along with it, political power. Tension between city and village is endemic to the Soviet Union. The peasants regard the party and state officials who run their lives much as they had once regarded the less meddlesome tsarist landlords and officials —namely, as outsiders and parasites. They would like nothing better than to "smoke them out" of the land. Under the existing arrangement, the city dominates the village, exacting from it tribute; under privatized agriculture, the village could turn the tables and dominate the city, which happens to be the seat of the *nomenklatura*.

A related consideration is economic. For the past fifty years the Soviet government has kept a tight leash on the consumer sector and poured the bulk of its investments into capital goods and military hardware. Such practices, which have enabled the USSR to attain the status of a global power, require that food be extracted from the producer at below-market prices. Should the peasant be in a position to charge for his product whatever the market will bear, prices will soar. Currently, free-market prices for food are from two and one half to three times those charged in the poorly stocked state stores; but farmers' markets do not usually sell grain, and they supply only a portion (about one third) of the meat, vegetables and dairy consumed in the USSR. The liquidation or severe reduction of state outlets selling subsidized foodstuffs would result in inflation, at least initially, until supply rose to satisfy demand, making it difficult for the urban inhabitants, who account for two thirds of the country's population, to make ends meet. These prospects are so unpalatable to the *nomenklatura* that they muddle through with the system inherited from Stalin, despite its calamitous costs, rather than venture on the road to genuine reform.

These costs can be measured in several ways. There is the drain on the national budget. In 1965, the Party increased investments in agriculture in the hope of raising output. In the ten years that followed, it allocated twice as much money to agriculture as in the preceding thirty-eight. By 1980, 27 percent of capital investments in the USSR went into this sector, mainly for the purchase of agricultural equipment. In addition, the government has been forced to spend great sums to keep down the price of bread; thanks to these subsidies, bread today costs no more than it did twenty-five years ago. In fact, it is so cheap—in state stores, where it is the only item always available, a loaf of bread costs less than a single egg on the open market—that some peasants feed it to cattle.

The results of these measures have not met expectations; agricultural productivity has experienced declining rates of growth and, in the early 1970s, even showed a negative rate. In the middle 1970s the Soviet government found itself in the embarrassing situation of having to place large grain orders abroad. Such imports have become a permanent feature of the Soviet economy and, in the opinion of experts, are likely to continue for the remainder of this century. In 1981, they absorbed 40.6 percent of the hard currency spent on imports.

Even with the massive infusions of capital begun in 1965, Soviet agriculture remains undercapitalized. The U.S. Department of Agriculture estimates that in the Soviet Union the value of assets per farmer is one half those allocated per industrial worker, whereas in the United States it is nearly 60 percent higher.[13] Moreover, most of the capital invested in Soviet agriculture goes for equipment; the rural infrastructure continues to be badly neglected, as are the amenities that would make village life more appealing. Roads are in a state of permanent disrepair, machines break down from overuse and lack of service, fertilizer is always in short supply, and last but not least, storage facilities are very inadequate. Soviet specialists estimate that each year some 20 percent of the grain and vegetable crop is lost in harvest, transit, storage or processing.[14] The grain wasted in this manner, amounting to between 30 and 40 million tons, corresponds to that imported at heavy expense from abroad.

When all is said and done, however, the basic problem with Soviet agriculture is neither technical nor financial, but human— namely, the absence of incentives that would motivate the peasant to exert himself on behalf of the collective farm. He can earn twice as much from cultivating his minuscule private plot as from putting in a "work-day" on the farm. As we shall note below, the productivity of the private sector in Soviet agriculture is several times that of the state sector.

Because living conditions in the countryside are so miserable and agricultural wages so low, the younger population flees from the countryside in a ceaseless stream. In theory, it is next to impossible for a peasant to move permanently into the city; Soviet security organs, mindful of how, in the closing decades of the old regime, millions of peasants milling about the cities in search of work turned into revolutionary mobs, closely monitor rural migration into the urban areas, especially Moscow and Leningrad, requiring work permits and other documents. Even so, the rural population keeps on deserting the collective farms. Upon completing their military service, many peasants find jobs in the cities and settle there. Temporary permits to visit cities are extended to become permanent. Marriage to an urban inhabitant is another way of changing residence. In such ways, the Soviet city population is steadily growing from the influx of peasants in search of better-paying jobs, more consumer goods, and such amenities as Soviet cities have to offer. As recently as 1926, 82 percent of the Soviet population resided in the countryside, which was approximately the same proportion as before the Revolution; in 1939, as a result of the depredations of collectivization, this figure fell to 67 percent; by 1959 it declined further to 52 percent; and in 1971, to 43 percent. In 1981 it stood at 37 percent. In the early 1980's, the net outflow from village to city has been estimated at 1.6 million people a year.

Urbanization is commonly regarded as a "progressive" trend in that it marks the transition from a lower to a higher stage of production and material culture. It also helps to absorb the excess rural population. But in the USSR it is not an excess rural population that is moving into the cities: it is the very core of the agricultural labor force, indispensable to the efficient production of food. In a mere eleven years, between the censuses of 1959 and 1970, the share of men aged twenty to twenty-four in the Soviet rural population fell by one half. Those who had departed had done so not because they were unable to find work in the village or were lured by factory work, but because rural conditions are execrable even by Soviet standards: in 1966 the Soviet peasant earned only one half as much as an urban inhabitant.[15] This exodus leaves mostly women and older men to carry the burden of feeding the country. To overcome the shortages of agricultural labor, the government has had for years now to resort to compulsory levies of students and other urban inhabitants to help out with the harvest.

The failures of state agriculture have led to the burgeoning of private agriculture, which supplies the population with a high proportion of foodstuffs. We shall discuss the phenomenon of the "second economy" in food later on. Here suffice it to say that the capital, effort and time that go into the production of food in the Soviet Union are entirely out of proportion to the results obtained. Next to defense, agriculture represents probably the heaviest burden on the Soviet economy.

## 3 LIVING STANDARDS

In the West, some fantastic statistics circulate about the Soviet standard of living. A contributor to a recent Congressional study, for example, claims that the *per capita* consumption by the Soviet population in the late 1970s was one third that of the United States and less than one half that of West Germany and France.[16] Such conclusions undoubtedly rest on very professional analysis of official Soviet statistics, but they fly in the face of common sense as well as data obtained from other sources, especially those that have the benefit of personal contact with Soviet reality. One good indicator of living standard is the proportion of income spent on food—the higher a country's living standard, the smaller the share of the family budget that is devoted to food purchases. In the United States, this figure stands at 23 percent for a family with an intermediate income; a high proportion of that money goes for proteins, vegetables and fruits. In the USSR, according to recent figures, 54.4 percent of the average family's income is spent on food (much of it starches), which represents a higher proportion than is devoted to this purpose in Greece and Portugal, and even slightly exceeds that which a Russian family had spent on feeding itself in 1900.

The sheer difficulty of obtaining food in the Soviet Union, which is, after all, the most basic indicator of living standard, makes mockery of comparisons with the United States or Western Europe. In 1982, the research staff of Radio Liberty conducted interviews with 698 Soviet citizens who had recently emigrated to the West. They were asked to estimate from their personal experience the availability and cost of foodstuffs in state stores and on the open market in the one hundred or so cities whence they came. The summary results of the inquiry are shown in Table 3.

Availability of food is only one of the hurdles facing the Soviet consumer; the other is prices. Except for bread, which is so heavily subsidized by the state as to be virtually given away, the Soviet citizen is dependent on the collective-farm market, where peasants sell produce grown on their private plots. Prices here, reflecting real demand, are between two-and-a-half and three times those charged in state stores; vegetables are nearly six times more expensive. What this allows the Soviet manual or white-collar worker to purchase can be calculated with some precision. In 1979, the average Soviet worker earned 164 rubles a month. Assuming both husband and wife to be employed and earning the same wage, a worker family would have at its disposal 328 rubles a month. Of this sum, 54.4 percent or 178 rubles is known to be spent on food. It is further known that approximately one third of the food budget goes for vodka and tobacco, leaving 119 rubles a month per family for meat, dairy products, vegetables and fruits (bread is so cheap that it can be left out of account). On the farmer's market, where it is available on only one shopping trip out of three, meat in 1982 cost from 6.42 rubles a kilogram for pork to 8.91 rubles a kilogram for poultry, with beef fetching 6.77 rubles. Thus, the purchase of one kilogram of beef on the open market would absorb four days' allowance for all foodstuffs of an average family composed of two wage earners.* In the light of these facts, unreflected in official Soviet statistics which deal with abstract state-store prices, it seems entirely unrealistic to speak of the Soviet living standard as between one third and one half of the Western. Its true base of comparison would have to be with the Third World.

TABLE 3
AVAILABILITY OF SELECTED FOODS IN SOVIET CITIES
(expressed as a percentage of the time that products are available)
*December 1981–July 1982* [17]

|  | Available in state stores | Available on collective farm markets |
|---|---|---|
| Meat | 12% | 36% |
| Dairy | 13% | 32% |
| Vegetables and fruits | 29% | 56% |

# 4 POPULATION TRENDS

No country in Europe has been as lavish with human lives as Russia; but then no European country has been as rich in this particular form of capital and so deficient in all the others. In the nineteenth and early twentieth centuries, Russia had the highest

* It must be noted, however, that in Communist countries it is not uncommon for people to hold two jobs, the other one being in the free or "second" economy; it is this additional income that makes it possible for many families to do more than survive.

rate of population growth in Europe. It had many more people than it could employ—around 1900, there were over 20 million inhabitants, or one sixth of the population, who could find neither land to till nor jobs in industry. The casual manner in which the new rulers of Russia after 1917 expended human lives on various "class" wars and the equanimity with which they viewed millions of their people dying from starvation stemmed in no small measure from the belief that the country had an inexhaustible supply of humanity; that, indeed, by "liquidating" a million here and a million there, one was reducing the burden that the masses of unemployed and unemployable imposed on the economy.

But the traumas which the population of the Soviet Union, and especially its Slavic component (Russians, Ukrainians and Belorussians), has suffered since 1917 have produced a biological reaction. Apart from the Asian, mostly Muslim, minorities, the population of the USSR has dramatically cut back on its reproduction rate. For the first time since the seventeenth century, Russia is experiencing a shortage of labor; the prospects are that this situation will not appreciably improve in the next two or three decades. This fact has a variety of important implications: it means, among other things, that the country will no longer be able to rely for its economic growth on inexhaustible reserves of cheap, unskilled, undercapitalized labor that makes up in numbers what it fails to achieve in productivity and which allows itself to be managed in total disregard of its wishes. As labor becomes scarcer, and therefore more precious, greater attention will have to be paid to its wants. Reports from Soviet industry indicate that even today skilled Soviet workers guilty of such offenses as absenteeism or drunkenness are all but immune from being discharged because they cannot be readily replaced.

The basic demographic facts are these: The natural rate of population increase—that is, the excess of births over deaths—in Imperial Russia and the Soviet Union kept on rising until the time of collectivization, attaining a peak of 18.1 persons per 1,000 in 1928. At that time, the demographic curve turned downward; in 1972, it stood at about one half of its 1928 figure (9.4 per 1,000). But these all-Union figures reflect only a part of the demographic reality. Low as it is, the Soviet reproduction rate stands where it does owing to the high fertility of the Muslim population. *The Slavs no longer replace themselves; more Russians and Ukrainians die each year than are born.*[18] Given that the Slavs are the dominant ethnic group in the country and make up the overwhelming majority of the *nomenklatura* as well as of the professional officer corps, this dry statistic reveals a fact of capital importance for the future of the

Soviet Union: The Slavic metropolis is being inundated by its colonial subjects. These trends so disturb the Soviet authorities that
in the official reports on the most recent (1980) census they have
quietly dropped figures that break down the nationalities by age
category, because these would indicate a most worrisome decline
of Russians and other Slavs among the country's youth.

The slowing of the population growth can be attributed to several causes:

▢ The staggering human losses inflicted by the regime's economic policies and purges as well as by World War II. Since 1917
the country may have suffered as many as 60 million casualties, of
this number up to 40 million victims of the Revolution and 20
million of the war. These losses have had a devastating effect on
the population's age structure by reducing the number of adult
males. The losses in young men in World War II have cut into the
demographic pyramid; they continue to reverberate to this day by
producing a "demographic echo" at twenty-year anniversaries of
the war (1960s, 1980s and so on).

▢ The shift of the population from the countryside to the cities.
As noted above, the share of inhabitants living in rural areas has
declined between 1926 and 1981 by more than one half. Urbanization everywhere in the world results in lower birth rates because
children, who are an economic asset in the country, in the city
become an economic liability. In the Soviet Union, this phenomenon, however, is aggravated by such factors as housing shortages
and difficulties in obtaining food and clothing. In fact, the Soviet
reproduction rate in the countryside is even at present two thirds
higher than in the cities. Since contraceptives are difficult to obtain, the common way of exercising birth control is through abortion, which is cheap and available on demand. Some
demographers estimate that the average Soviet woman undergoes
during her lifetime between six and eight abortions (the corresponding figure for the United States is 0.5). But since abortion is
virtually unknown among the country's Asian citizens, the ratio
among Russians and other Slavs is in fact higher than this figure;
some authorities place the incidence of abortions among Russian
women as high as ten.

▢ Health problems which afflict most severely males in the
prime of life. There is widespread alcoholism, despite exorbitant
prices charged for vodka (one liter of vodka retails for 11 rubles, a
sum equivalent to two days' wages of the average Soviet worker).
The peasantry, which cannot afford to buy at official prices, distills
oceans of moonshine. Those unable to quench their thirst either
with state vodka or moonshine resort to industrial liquids, a prac-

tice that results in an estimated 40,000 Soviet citizens, most of them able-bodied Slav males, being carried off each year with acute alcohol poisoning. (The corresponding figure for the United States is 400.)[19] A recent French book carries the facetious title, *Is Communism Soluble in Alcohol?* But for anyone concerned with the well-being of the Russian or Ukrainian people, such massive flight to alcohol is not a subject for amusement.

□ Alcoholism combined with primitive medical care and a poor diet have a detrimental effect on the nation's health and life expectancy. The Soviet Union must be the only industrial country in the world where life expectancy is declining: for Soviet males, life expectancy at birth is estimated by Western demographers to have dropped between 1965 and 1982 from 66 to 62–63 years.[20]

□ Infant mortality. For reasons that are not clear but are probably partly related to declining funds spent on medical care, infant mortality in the Soviet Union in recent years has shown alarming increases. In 1975, the Soviet statistical bureau reported that during the preceding five years, infant mortality had gone up by one third; after that year, in accord with the time-honored Soviet practice of not upsetting the public with disagreeable facts, the bureau ceased to release the relevant data. Some Western experts estimate that the rate of infant mortality in the USSR is currently 40 per 1,000 births. This figure is three times that prevalent in the West.[21]

Declining rates of population growth will be felt most immediately in the labor supply. In the 1970s, twenty million young people entered the labor force; in the 1980s, this figure will diminish by one half, due to the "demographic echo" of wartime casualties. By the 1990s the labor situation should improve again, but then fresh problems will arise. Because the population of the Asian borderlands is more heavily rural and does not practice abortion, it multiplies much faster—at present, three times as fast—than the Slavic population. This disparity in ethnic reproduction rate has all manner of political consequences, which will be discussed in the appropriate place. The economic consequences, however, are serious in themselves. The bulk of Soviet industry and agriculture is located in regions populated by Slavs. Therefore, even if the over-all figures for personnel entering the labor force in the 1990s should prove satisfactory, a disproportionate number of the potential new workers and farmers will reside in areas where they are least needed. Since Muslims live mainly in the south and neither like to move north nor have any financial inducements to do so, the Soviet regime can expect to face labor shortages for the rest of the century and beyond.

## 5 FOREIGN DEBTS

In the West, it is incorrectly believed that the Soviet economy is self-sufficient and free to choose whether or not to engage in trade with "capitalist" countries. This misconception benefits Moscow, because it allows it to call for a separation ("decoupling") of economic relations from political ones and to claim that Western embargoes and sanctions cannot hurt it. As shall be shown in Chapter Five, these claims are incorrect: the Soviet Union has been dependent in varying degrees on trade with the West almost from its inception. And because it generally shows a deficit in foreign trade with the West, in order to import the equipment required by its industries and armed forces, it must resort to loans.

In the 1920s, foreign banks would not lend to the USSR as punishment for its expropriation of Western investments and default on the country's international debts. Then, in the 1930s, when the memory of these confiscations and defaults began to fade, the world experienced severe shortages of liquid capital. To earn hard currency, Stalin exported everything he could lay his hands on, including grains and dairy products needed for his own starving population. By these means he raised some foreign cash and credit.

A major impetus for the policy of "peaceful coexistence" inaugurated by Moscow in the middle 1950s, when it had decided that the Cold War was no longer effective, was the need for Western credits with which to modernize the Soviet economy. Things went slowly at first, but in the early 1950s two events happened more or less concurrently that led to a surge in Communist Bloc trade with the West. They were inflation and détente.

The Soviet Union is rich in such raw materials as petroleum, natural gas, diamonds and lumber, which it can export to earn money. (The only manufactured goods that it can sell abroad in any quantity are military hardware, but this product finds customers mostly in the Third World and for obvious reasons cannot be marketed in Western Europe and Japan, where the capital is.) Until 1970 or so, Soviet raw materials did not bring much hard currency, because of low commodity prices prevailing on world markets. Among the commodities of which limited quantities could be disposed of abroad, was energy. The Soviet Union is the world's leading producer of petroleum (a position of leadership that Russia already once attained in 1900, when it produced nearly two fifths of the world supply). Following the sharp increases in petroleum prices imposed by OPEC in the 1970s, Moscow began to reap handsome returns from this source. Sales abroad of petroleum and natural gas, which had brought the Soviet Union only $414 million in 1970, fetched $14 billion in 1980; these two export items accounted for nearly two thirds of all Soviet hard-currency earnings. Gold and diamonds also appreciated greatly in price in the 1970s. It was largely owing to the rise in the international price of these commodities that the USSR was able, in a single decade, to increase its exports to hard-currency countries tenfold (from $2.4 billion in 1970 to $23.6 billion in 1980).

With this money, the USSR was for the first time in a position to purchase quantities of industrial goods from abroad. Its appetite for imports, however, still exceeded its ability to pay for them, with the result that throughout the 1970s the USSR ran a deficit in its trade with the free-market countries. In the first half of the 1970s, this deficit stayed within modest bounds; but in 1975 there occurred the first of several disastrous harvests, which compelled the *nomenklatura* for several years running to spend two fifths of its hard-currency earnings on imports of foodstuffs. The imbalance between exports and imports increased, producing an annual deficit of $3 to $4 billion. This deficit was made up by Western credits.

It is questionable how much money Western governments and banks would have been willing to lend to the USSR and its dependencies were it not for détente. It was a basic tenet of détente that increased commercial ties between East and West would bring positive political results in the form of "moderating" Soviet conduct. "In a crisis," writes Henry Kissinger, then Secretary of State, "we thought that the fear of losing markets and access to raw materials, Western technological innovations or bank credits, would produce Soviet caution." [22] This Western version of Lenin's theory of Imperialism became in the early 1970s the operative doctrine of Western statesmen. To facilitate East-West trade, Western governments either lent money directly to Communist governments, or else encouraged (some say, pressured) private financial institutions to do so, usually sweetening the arrangement with state guarantees against default. Détente was also in some measure responsible for the so-called "umbrella theory" adopted by Western bankers, which held that the Soviet Union had a political if not a legal obligation to bail out its East European dependencies, should these find themselves unable to service their debts. This reasoning assumed that if Moscow allowed any of its clients to default it would jeopardize its own carefully nurtured international credit standing, as well as endanger détente. The umbrella theory turned into a consensus among Western bankers despite repeated warnings from Moscow that it assumed responsibility for no debts other than its own. In this connection it may be said that it is a sound rule in private life as well as in politics to mistrust promises, but always to take threats at face value.

Spurred by their governments, persuading themselves that they were contributing to peace, and, last but not least, conscious that they stood much to profit and nothing to lose, Western bankers generously lent to the USSR and the countries of East Europe the petrodollars with which their coffers overflowed. Their best customer was Poland, which borrowed with utter recklessness left and right in the hope of staving off social upheaval. Precise figures on the indebtedness of the Communist Bloc are hard to come by, in part because of the secrecy with which international banking is carried on, and in part because these loans are being constantly rescheduled as they reach maturity and fail to be repaid. A reasonably reliable set of figures comes from the Swiss Creditanstalt: they show that at the end of 1981 the Bloc owed abroad a grand total of $81.4 billion, 70 percent of this sum to private banks and the rest to Western governments. (In reality, however, the share of debts owed Western governments is considerably greater than that, since they have guaranteed private banks a large proportion of the money lent to the Bloc.) The growth of indebtedness, by country, is as follows:

TABLE 4
COMMUNIST BLOC HARD CURRENCY INDEBTEDNESS*
(in billions of U.S. dollars)

| Country | 1971 | 1981 | Percentage Growth, 1971–1981 |
|---|---|---|---|
| Bulgaria | 0.7 | 2.3 | +229 |
| Czechoslovakia | 0.2 | 3.6 | +1,700 |
| East Germany | 1.2 | 11.4 | +850 |
| Hungary | 0.8 | 7.4 | +825 |
| Poland | 0.8 | 23.0 | +2,775 |
| Romania | 1.2 | 10.0 | +733 |
| Soviet Union | 1.1 | 23.7 | +2,055 |

Economically as well as politically this whole experiment in dollar diplomacy brought to the West nothing but disappointment.

* From *Frankfurter Allgemeine Zeitung*, April 22, 1982. The figure for East Germany is, in fact, higher than here reported, because one must add to it debts incurred in intra-German trade, which are not made public. When this is done, its indebtedness *per capita* is said to be even greater than Poland's.

The umbrella theory turned out to be wishful thinking once the Soviet umbrella failed to open in the hour of need. When Poland defaulted in its payments of both principal and interest, the Soviet Union refused to come to its rescue—at any rate, openly. (Apparently in early 1982, in a desperate attempt to keep open Poland's access to international money markets, Moscow did help it meet some of its most pressing financial obligations.) It would probably be realistic to assume that many of these loans, especially those extended to Poland, will never be made good. In the end, it is the Western taxpayer who will have to pay the bill, because nearly all those uncollectable loans are guaranteed with public funds.

Nor have the political rewards met expectations. Had the architects of détente familiarized themselves with the record of history, they would have known that the creditor nation is often more dependent on its debtor than the debtor on the creditor. Plutarch tells of a secretary of Alexander the Great, Eumenes, who must have known this: he made it a practice to borrow money from those "who most hated him, to make them at once confide in him and forbear all violence to him for fear of losing their money." In effect, the vast sums loaned to the East have made Western financial interests beholden to their debtors and, as such, tacit accomplices in their repressive policies. When in December 1981 the Polish military imposed martial law on the country to restore "discipline," the sigh of relief emitted by the international banking community was almost audible. The bankers hoped that repression would improve productivity in Poland and, by increasing exports, enable that country to repay some of its debts.

But the Communist Bloc has also suffered from the collapse of confidence in its creditworthiness. The flow of loans to the Bloc has all but dried up. Even the Soviet Union, which has a low debt ratio relative to its national assets, finds it difficult to obtain new loans; Eastern Europe has little hope in this regard. For some East European countries this portends serious problems. Poland in particular is heavily dependent on imports of equipment and spare parts from hard-currency countries to operate the industrial complexes which it built in the 1970s with Western help. To make matters worse, the prices on Soviet export commodities have declined in the early 1980s, as the result of a glut of oil on world markets and decreased demand for gold and diamonds. The opportunities for continuing purchases of technology from the West are thus smaller than they have been for some time.

# 6 ATTEMPTS AT ECONOMIC REFORM

The need for restructuring the Stalinist economy is self-evident, but so are its political risks. In the 1960s, the Czech economic reformers discovered that the only way to achieve significant improvements in productivity was to remove the Party from economic management. This procedure carries obvious dangers for the Party; and the recollection of how rapidly economic reform in Czechoslovakia led to the unraveling there of the whole Communist system is never absent from the collective memory of the Soviet leadership. Unable to let the system stand and yet afraid to change it, the *nomenklatura* has so far confined itself to tinkering. The results have been most unimpressive, because every time that even such modest changes cause production to spurt, the Party officials who supervise the economy recoil from fear of losing control and force a return to the traditional ways. Nevertheless, these half-hearted experiments in economic reform are instructive, because they indicate how powerful are the dormant productive forces and how quickly they awaken when given half a chance.

We have indicated three causes principally responsible for the poor performance of the Soviet economy: overcentralization of management, absence of adequate incentives, and excessive military expenditures. The last-named, as previously noted, can be altered without structural changes in the system; it is a matter for political decision. Almost all reform proposals drafted by Soviet and foreign experts focus on decentralization of decision making and improvements in the method of rewarding performance.

Decentralization in essence means transferring much of the authority to make economic decisions from the Party and its various economic branches to the professional managers. Talk on this subject never ceases. In April 1983, for instance, the principal Soviet institutions involved in economic planning held a closed seminar to discuss, once again, the country's economic troubles. One of the reports presented at this meeting was leaked to Western correspondents.[23] The author took as her point of departure the premise that the Soviet economy "has long passed the point where it was possible to regulate it efficiently from a single center." She went on to say that the system did not operate efficiently because supervising the implementation of plans drafted by the central bureau required the Party constantly to create new supervisory institutions that interposed themselves between planner and producer in ever thicker layers. Such institutions added "to the 'nonproductive' pool of labor" and reduced "the economic effectiveness" of enterprises. The report further asserted that orders issued in Moscow often ignored local conditions. In sum, central planning, introduced by Stalin, had been beneficial in its day but it no longer suited present-day conditions. The author recommended that the "administrative" system of management give way to an "economic" one—that is, that political criteria yield to those of efficient productivity. She also took notice of the difficulty of implementing such proposals—namely, vested interests of those who profited from the *status quo* and would lose their lucrative jobs if the qualification for holding them were based on professional rather than political criteria.

In July 1983, the Soviet government announced some cautious steps—on an "experimental" basis—toward administrative decentralization in a few selected branches of the economy. Under this scheme, the chosen enterprises were given greater freedom in rewarding efficient workers and providing inducements for the introduction of labor-saving devices by authorizing them to retain part of the profits. For all their moderation, these reforms will assuredly run into the same difficulties that have frustrated such attempts in the past. The bureaucratic establishment, pressured to do something to enhance productivity, would rather improve the central planning system than dismantle it. An American scholar who had recently visited Soviet planning institutes was shown elaborate schemes for reforming central planning with the aid of "computer-based modeling techniques." An article in the same vein in the journal *Kommunist* under the suggestive title "On the Political Approach to Economics" propounded the thesis that the USSR needed more, not less, economic centralization.[24] The planning bureaucracy is fighting tooth and nail against any reduction of its authority, and it solicits in this endeavor the assistance of anxious Party politicians.

The Soviet authorities have been somewhat more willing to experiment with incentives, since changes in this field are easier to reconcile with Party controls. As previously indicated, under the prevailing arrangement, workers and farmers are paid for meeting their production norms; inducements in the form of bonuses for exceeding these norms are at best minimal and sometimes negative. The problem facing the authorities is how to motivate wage-earners to exert themselves without resorting to forms of capitalist entrepreneurship that could create centers of economic independence and potential political opposition.

The various efforts in this direction during the past two decades bear striking resemblance to the traditional Russian cooperative association, known before the Revolution as *artel*. The *artel* was a voluntary association of craftsmen or agricultural workers, sometimes permanent, sometimes seasonal. It typically chose one member as a foreman to negotiate a contract with the employer on its behalf; earnings were distributed equally among the members. The combination of voluntary teamwork, collective responsibility for fulfillment of the contract, and equal participation in the rewards seems to be especially well suited to the Russian national temperament. The term *artel* is no longer in use, but the "normless brigades" and "links" currently experimented with are the same thing under a different name.

An early attempt to introduce the *artel*-type labor brigade in industry was made in 1967 at the Shchekino Chemical Combine near Tula. The workers at this plant were allowed to organize cooperatives which contracted with the management to deliver, by a certain date, a set quantity of products in return for an agreed-upon remuneration. The work time that the workers had to spend to fulfill their contract was disregarded. The experiment proved successful: the Shchekino Combine cut its labor force by 15 percent and still doubled productivity. This stellar performance, however, put the rest of Soviet industry in a bad light and so alarmed the officials in charge that, instead of honoring their promise to turn over to the Combine a share of the profits, they appropriated them for distribution to other, less efficient enterprises.[25] A similar arrangement was tried a few years later at the Kaluga Turbine Works. Here too, production soared, and workers' earnings doubled. The Kaluga system was adopted by other engineering plants, but its further spread has been prevented by the Party bureaucracy, which fears fueling the population's acquisitive instincts.

The successful application of the *artel* principle in certain branches of industry has provided a model for agriculture. The Soviet peasant is in one respect better off than the otherwise privileged industrial worker in that he can put his free time more readily to profitable use. An industrial worker cannot legally divert factory material and equipment to his personal profit; he can only loaf on the job. But the peasant has his private plot of land and livestock, which feed his household and the surplus of which he is free to sell. Given this opportunity, it is even more difficult to make the farmer apply himself to his regular job than it is the industrial laborer. So far, the only successful device discovered to increase production on collective and state farms has been the application of the *artel* principle.

The rural cooperative is known by several names, of which the most prevalent is "link" (*zveno*). This is a team of volunteers who sign a contract with the farm to cultivate a parcel of land set aside for their use. The "link" averages 15 to 20 peasants. In the spring, at the beginning of the agricultural season, it receives an advance, which it divides in equal shares among the members. To ensure good performance the link exercises strict internal discipline by relying on social rather than administrative forms of punishment: members who fail to do their share of the work are expelled. When the season is over, the link receives the rest of its compensation, the amount of which is determined by the size of the harvest it has gathered. Partly because the link functions as a voluntary unit, partly because it is rewarded not for the time spent on the job but for the results obtained, its motivation is high and its productivity significantly exceeds that of the "brigades" which ordinarily cultivate Soviet farms. The Secretary of the Central Committee responsible for agriculture, M. Gorbachev, has stated that contractual work improved agricultural productivity by 15 to 20 percent.[26]

The Party leadership is on record as favoring cultivation by links. Brezhnev more than once called for their adoption nationwide. A 15 to 20 percent improvement in agricultural productivity would free the Soviet Union from the need to import food. Nevertheless, the Party and state bureaucracies firmly oppose such "voluntarism" and do all in their power to discourage it. Soviet newspapers carry many complaints from peasants about local officials who sabotage efforts to improve production. For example:

> [The] orchard yielded no harvest, incurring losses. Ten diligent workers were selected to form a link based on the contractual-bonus system of compensation. When time came to reap the harvest, it turned out to be three times greater than stipulated in the plan. Of course, the link earned good pay.
>
> The following year, the regional administration amended [the plan]: on its own, it raised the norms and lowered the rates. The link agreed to the new terms. It obtained a still higher yield and suffered no reduction in pay. The administration then asked for new amendments. When, in violation of the statutes of the collective farm, this happened the third time, the entire link marched into the chairman's office and announced: "Take back your orchard, work it yourself." And so the orchard stands and, as in the past, brings nothing but losses.[27]

Owing to such bureaucratic opposition, links have been adopted by a mere 8 or 9 percent of Soviet farms. They are more common only in those few localities—among them the Leningrad region and the Uzbek Republic—where the Party authorities happen to be more supportive.

It is a question of great importance whether the Soviet government is prepared to become serious about major economic reforms and, if so, whether it has the power to break the resistance of groups interested in preserving the *status quo*. The answer to the first question is a tentative Yes: there are many indications that the highest echelons of the leadership have become persuaded that the Stalinist economic system has outlived its usefulness and that its perpetuation could bring disaster. The second question is much more difficult to answer because it hinges on such imponderables as the personalities in charge and their political will.

Should the Soviet authorities become serious about economic reform, they have a ready model in Hungary. Here, over the past fifteen years, fairly bold experiments have been carried out in the management of the economy. The Hungarian "New Economic Mechanism" was introduced in 1968 with Moscow's blessing as a low-risk effort that could be copied by other Communist regimes if successful and aborted if not. In the early 1970s, Moscow seems to have developed doubts and pressured Hungary to restrain its reformist zeal. But in 1978 it changed its mind once again and approved still more far-reaching structural and procedural changes. Moscow's willingness to countenance economic reforms in Hungary derives from a desire not only to improve conditions there, but also to test, in a practical way, whether economic reform is compatible with political stability. Hungary has thus become a kind of laboratory where experiments are carried out for possible application to the other colonies and perhaps even the Soviet metropolis itself.

The New Economic Mechanism combines over-all Party control of the national economy with a considerable degree of entrepreneurial autonomy and private initiative. Under this arrangement, the central planning authorities set general objectives and production norms, but allow the individual enterprises much leeway in their implementation. Instead of being required to meet prescribed production quotas, as is the practice in Stalinist economies, Hungarian enterprises must show a profit. To enable them to do so, managers are given wide latitude to fix pay scales and even to discharge workers. Prices for goods are set so as to reflect actual production costs. A good part of the profit realized from cost-efficient production is retained by the enterprises, partly for reinvestment, partly for distribution among the staff.

Recently, even bolder innovations have been carried out. Gigantic Hungarian enterprises, of the kind favored by Stalinists, are being broken up into smaller, more manageable units. State firms are allowed to buy shares in one another's assets and to issue interest-bearing bonds for purchase by other state-owned firms. In 1982, the government passed a law that allows individual citizens to form small private partnerships to provide services to the citizens.

The New Economic Mechanism, which began as a cautious experiment, has gathered momentum and seems to be pushing the country toward a mixed economy resembling Lenin's New Economic Policy. It balances the interests of the Hungarian *nomenklatura* with the advantages of decentralization and incentives. The usual resistance of entrenched bureaucratic interests and the absence of competition among enterprises have prevented "goulash Communism" from significantly improving Hungary's over-all economic performance. (At least on paper; some Western economists believe that Hungary is being penalized for releasing more honest statistics than its Communist neighbors.) But there is unanimous agreement that it has had a most salutary effect on the country's prosperity and social stability. Hungarian living standards are the highest in the Communist Bloc; food is available in abundance (there is even a surplus that goes for export), and so are consumer goods. One result has been a mood of political complacency among Hungarians that the *nomenklatura* finds very attractive. By means of economic reforms, the Hungarian authorities have managed to neutralize political dissent, once so ripe in their country and still very close to the surface in other parts of the Communist Bloc. Essentially, they have bought off the population with material rewards. Their relative prosperity has given Hungarians a sense of superiority over other, less placid Communist subjects; when in 1980–81 Poland was seething with unrest, they treated the volatile Poles with open condescension. All this is duly noted in Moscow. Soviet observers speak with an admiration tinged with envy of the public spirit animating Hungary, of the sense of trust between the Party, economic managers and ordinary people, and of the "enormous reserve of creative energy, enterprise, and initiative" that the reform has released.[28]

The fact that Bulgaria, Moscow's most servile client, has in recent years committed itself (at least nominally) to adopt the New Economic Mechanism and that similar steps are being discussed in Czechoslovakia and East Germany suggests that the Soviet *nomenklatura* approves. Why then has it refused so far to follow this model in its own country?

On the most rudimentary level the answer is that, as the guardian of Communist orthodoxy, the Soviet Union is better able to tolerate freedoms in its colonial dependencies than at home. This is not new in Russian history. Imperial Russia granted some of its possessions (Finland, the Baltic areas and, for a while, Poland) constitutional rights that it did not dare to give its own, Russian, subjects. The Russian bureaucracy has always held its own people in very low esteem as entirely unprepared for the responsibilities of citizenship; it believes that Russians lack the discipline to cope with the freedom that the New Economic Mechanism brings with it. Besides, if things got out of hand in one of the "People's Democracies," Moscow could always send in tanks to set things straight, but who would perform this service for the Soviet Union?

There is another, profounder and less apparent reason as well. Each "People's Democracy" is an occupied country administered by a government placed in power by the Soviet Union. Each of these countries experiences the tensions between rulers and ruled endemic to Communist regimes. Yet, at the same time, each enjoys a certain degree of internal cohesion in that the ruling elite and the people share an interest in resisting the occupying power. Much as the majority of Czechs may despise Husak or the East Germans Honecker, Husak and Honecker are all that stands between them and Moscow. The result is a degree of national unity that does not and cannot exist in the Soviet Union, the imperial metropolis. The USSR is neither nationally homogeneous nor under foreign occupation. It is a multinational empire and it has no external domination to resist; consequently, it lacks that bond that in some respects unites rulers and ruled in the Soviet colonies. Should Communist authority in the USSR break down, as has happened in Hungary, Czechoslovakia and Poland, there would be nothing to hold the country together—neither a sense of common national destiny nor the fear of outside intervention. For this reason, Moscow is today, as it has always been in the past, exceedingly reluctant to tamper with any of its own institutions or practices, lest such actions loosen the political fabric of the country. The Russian leadership has always preferred to resort to repression than to experiment with liberty. And so it watches with dismay the steady decline of productive growth, laments the untapped productive forces, realizes what economic decline portends for its security, and talks of changes; but every time it approaches the brink of reform, it draws back, terrified of leaping into the unknown.

# 7 THE SECOND ECONOMY

Life, however, will not await official decision; it proceeds to reform itself. One of the most fascinating developments occurring in the Soviet Union in the past two decades has been the development of a dynamic private sector, commonly referred to as the "second economy." This is not "controlled freedom" supervised by the state to increase productivity in its own economy, as envisaged under the New Economic Mechanism; it is economic activity free of government supervision, which emerges alongside the state sector to satisfy consumer demands. In the second economy the producer bypasses the state bureaucracy to deal directly with the consumer.

No one can form even an approximate notion of the size of the second economy in the Soviet Union, because it consists of myriad individual transactions completed every hour of the day throughout a vast empire, unobserved and unrecorded. It encompasses barter of goods and services; moonlighting by state employees; the use of government equipment and material for personal profit; construction work; and, above all, the production and marketing of food. The state, unable to satisfy the growing needs of consumers, is compelled to tolerate this unwelcome development, even though the practice challenges its claim to a monopoly on economic resources.

The only aspect of the second economy on which information is reasonably satisfactory is agriculture. Here it assumes two forms: production of food by peasants on their private plots, and auxiliary food production by industrial workers and others not normally engaged in agriculture. In official publications both are covered by the euphemism "subsidiary agriculture"; their output is usually included with that of the state sector, although they clearly lie outside of it.

The Soviet Union simply cannot feed itself without resort to private initiative. This fact was acknowledged by Stalin, who left the collectivized peasants a plot of land and a few domestic animals. Private plots have always played an indispensable role in supplying peasants and urban inhabitants with staples. The rural population derives most of its food from this source; and it is difficult to see how the nonrural population could feed itself without access to the farmers' markets.

At latest reckoning, the USSR had 33 million private plots, averaging one quarter of a hectare (0.6 acre). Their main product is meat, followed by vegetables and dairy products. The output of the private sector is remarkable, especially when one considers the adverse conditions under which it has to operate. To raise livestock and to grow food, the peasants are dependent on the good will of the collective-farm officials who control fodder, fertilizer, and all else that they require; and since these bureaucrats are not, as a rule, sympathetic to private initiative and assist it only because Moscow makes them do so, this good will is rarely forthcoming.

The area set aside for private cultivation in the USSR comprises a mere 1.5 percent of the country's cultivated land, and yet furnishes it with nearly one third of its foodstuffs. In 1979, peasants supplied the Soviet Union from their minuscule plots (somewhat augmented by access to collective-farm pastures) with 30 percent of the meat, 30 percent of the vegetables and milk, 33 percent of the eggs, and 59 percent of the potatoes.[29] Information from some regions indicates that as much as one half of the food consumed there is purchased at farm markets.[30]

Private agriculture has in the Soviet Union many supporters who see in it advantages other than compensating for shortages in food supplies. Russian nationalists view the peasant as the soul of Russia; to them, collectivization was a tragedy that all but destroyed the people's national spirit. Soviet journals and newspapers are filled with articles lamenting the Russian peasant's loss of love for the land and his flight from the countryside. The authorities have a less sentimental attitude. When harvests are poor, they do everything in their power to stimulate and assist the private sector; when harvests improve, they take it all back. In recent years, because of an unprecedented sequence of poor harvests, things have been looking up for the private sector. Since experience has shown that farmers can raise livestock using one third of the fodder required for the purpose by the collective, Moscow has authorized collective managers to lease livestock to peasant households on a contractual basis. Under this arrangement, the collective retains title to the cattle, but shares with the peasant the profits earned from its sale to the state. Another measure introduced in August 1982, apparently in response to an acute food shortage, allows peasants to bring their produce to the market even before their collective has met its obligatory state quotas. Yet another recent directive permits collectives to dispose of one tenth of their grain harvest directly to the consumer.

Unfortunately for the Soviet government, the prospects for the private sector in agriculture do not appear promising, so that even if it should decide to give it greater scope, the response may not be forthcoming. Indications are that in the past decade the output of private plots has remained static and even fallen. The over-all share of the private sector in the production of foodstuffs is declining, and there is evidence that peasants are not as eager to grow food and raise cattle as they once were. The main explanation for this development is the exodus of rural inhabitants to the cities, which leaves in the villages ever fewer people who have the time and energy to meet their responsibilities to the collective and still attend to their private plots. Able-bodied males who have the energy and the initiative to do both prefer to take up life in the city. Those who remain are discouraged by the attitude of the collective-farm bureaucracy.

As the contribution from private plots fails to meet the demands of the market, the gap is filled by "subsidiary farming." This is an extraordinary phenomenon possible only in Communist countries. In many industrial societies it is common for urban inhabitants to cultivate small plots of unused land (e.g., along railroad lines) to grow for their personal use flowers, vegetables and fruits. This is encouraged in the Soviet Union, too. What, however, is unique to the Soviet Union is the widespread and growing practice of industrial enterprises providing their workers with food grown on factory farms. Many industrial managers have discovered that to keep workers on the job they must ensure their food supply. This means in practice that they either develop their own, factory-linked subsidiary farms, or else enter with nearby collective farms into bartering arrangements to exchange scarce industrial materials for produce. Thus, the Soviet Union's equivalent of the Boeing Corporation, the country's largest aviation plant at Kuibyshev, has introduced, as an integral part of the enterprise, a poultry farm that raises for its employees hundreds of thousands of chickens. The manager of this department, boasting that the plant produces two types of "wings," announced that it will soon branch out into the production of honey.[31] An even more grotesque development has been recently noted in the Soviet armed forces, which in certain regions have resorted to growing their food.

> An analysis of the materials published in the central press shows that large and small enterprises in various branches of the national economy—metallurgical industries, construction materials, the aircraft, timber and oil and gas industries, instrument making, the railways, shipping, construction organizations, etc.—are switching to supplying their own food products. . . . *In principle, this whole sphere of the economy exists outside centralized state control, planning, subsidies, and material supply.* It began to develop spontaneously in the country, breaking through official bureaucratic barriers and utilizing more and more of the labor and material resources of society. The regime is now merely joining the current, attempting to regulate and direct its course, soberly conscious of its inevitability.[32]

This development, of course, represents a throwback to more primitive conditions. It has highly negative economic and political connotations. By compelling skilled industrial labor to occupy itself with raising food, it inhibits industrial productivity.

Another branch of the economy where free enterprise and contractual arrangements flourish is in the construction industry. Construction brigades now operating throughout the Soviet Union are virtually indistinguishable from pre-Revolutionary *arteli* and for all practical purposes engage in private enterprise. Members of construction associations are known as *shabashniki,* that is, "sabbath workers," or moonlighters; they are workers who have quit government employment to join groups that hire themselves out, on contract, to state enterprises, especially collective farms. Conditional on the enterprise providing them with the necessary materials, they undertake to complete by a fixed date a construction task for an agreed upon price. *Shabashniki* work as much as fifteen hours a day, seven days a week. They have acquired an enviable reputation for reliability and are said to earn four or five times as much as comparable workers in state enterprises. Because the work they perform is essential and because they are not confined to a steady place of employment where local Party officials can keep close watch on them, *shabashniki* have become something of an indispensable institution. In 1980, 38 percent of the construction work completed in the USSR was carried out by such freelance workers. In the Republic of Georgia, one seventh of the entire labor force is said to earn a living in this manner.

This brief survey of a subject of great complexity, made more complex by the deliberate concealment of data, should indicate how superficial and beside the point are the observations of those who reduce the whole issue to the question whether or not its economic difficulties will cause the Soviet regime to collapse. In reality, the problem is much broader and more fundamental. Economic failures lie at the very heart of the crisis presently experienced by Communist regimes because all their interests and ambitions depend for their realization on high economic performance. Without it, the second economy will continue expanding and threaten the *nomenklatura*'s control of the population. Without it, too, the forces of the Warsaw Pact will not be able to field arms in a quantity and quality necessary to give them superiority. Nor, as we shall see in the chapter that follows, will the USSR have at its disposal the material means it needs to keep in line its colonies and increase its influence in the Third World. A declining economy spells the doom of Soviet Grand Strategy, and, to the extent that this strategy serves the interests of the *nomenklatura,* it places in question its very future.

The ultimate tragedy, from the *nomenklatura*'s point of view, is that the economic difficulties that so perplex it are neither technical nor structural in nature and hence cannot be resolved by technical or bureaucratic means. They are human in the broadest sense of the word. As one Soviet writer has recently put it, "contemporary developments clearly elevate the 'human factor,' the principal link in improving the productivity of labor, into first place."[33] This human factor can be accommodated only by a thorough reorientation of the regime, and the replacement of a tutelary relationship toward the citizenry with a participatory one. Experience indicates beyond the shadow of a doubt that the worker and peasant under Communism will exert himself to produce more only if allowed to enter into a contract that guarantees him a set payment for completing a job by a certain date, rewarding him for the results achieved regardless of the time spent working. But the introduction of contractual relationships between state and citizen, even if confined initially to the economic sphere, represents a veritable revolution, because it establishes the principle of equality between the signatories. Over a century ago, the English legal historian Sir Henry Maine pointed to the "movement from status to contract" as a central feature of human progress. Once this principle has been introduced it can hardly stay confined to terms of employment in factories and farms, but is likely to spread to other spheres of public life. In other words, if the Soviet regime wishes to realize its global ambitions, it must move toward the adoption of economic and social institutions that will ultimately subvert it. This is a genuine dilemma, which for many years has been holding the Soviet leadership spellbound, distracting its mind and paralyzing its will.

# THE POLITICAL CRISIS

The Communist Bloc is in a political crisis in the sense that its ruling elites no longer are able satisfactorily to carry out the extremely broad responsibilities that they have taken upon themselves. The Party is growing increasingly ossified and corrupt, self-serving and out of touch with the population, among whom doubts are spreading about its ability to rule. The Soviet Communist Party is under attack from conservative and democratic dissenters, who, for their own and different reasons, regard it as inimical to the interests of the Russian people. The non-Russian inhabitants of the Empire, though outwardly quiet, show no inclination to shed their national identity and assimilate. Soviet client states and parties press demands which the Soviet *nomenklatura* cannot meet, displaying a degree of independence that puts in question Moscow's imperial aspirations.

The *nomenklatura* is highly competent in dealing with overt challenges to its authority; indeed, this may be the only political skill that it has mastered to perfection. Its abilities are much less impressive when the challenge comes not from identifiable individuals or groups but from faceless forces and processes that the KGB and its tanks cannot disperse or arrest. Declines in productivity and fertility, cynicism and indifference among the country's young, nationalism among the subjugated peoples and foreign Communist parties—all these are phenomena immune to repression. The same applies to the pervasive corruption among the ruling apparatus. How much such adverse processes can erode the authority of the Party was demonstrated recently in Poland. There, in less than two years, the Communist Party was compelled to surrender power, first to the trade unions, and then to the armed forces. This catastrophe occurred under the pressure of spontaneous movements, whose leaders deliberately avoided violence. They did not take the Party by assault—they made it irrelevant. Whether the Polish revolution occurred because the local Communists were too rigid or not rigid enough is a question that deeply divides the Soviet *nomenklatura*, because it has fundamental bearing on its own future.

In the meantime, as problems accumulate and nothing is done to resolve them, a sense of malaise spreads across the Soviet Union. The Russian people can suffer almost any kind of deprivation except weak leadership: the whole constitution of the Communist state postulates firm authority, and this has been missing for some time. The citizenry, unable to express its discontent actively, resorts to passive resistance on a grand scale that creates a very dangerous situation for the elite and propels it toward decisions which it desperately wishes to avoid.

# 1 THE CORRUPT PARTY

As conceived by Lenin, the Bolshevik Party was to have been a highly motivated and disciplined instrument of revolutionary action. Its totally committed membership was to pay for the privilege of power with self-abnegation, of which Lenin, with his modest personal habits, set an example. Workers had to be kept out of its leading positions (in fact, if not in theory) because, as Lenin had concluded early in his revolutionary career, real workers (rather than the idealized ones of socialist doctrine) were not committed revolutionaries but accomplices of capitalism. Even so, the Party was to maintain intimate and uninterrupted contact with the "proletariat," since without its support no revolution was possible. The Party was to penetrate every fiber of Russian life, directing affairs from above in accord with the "science" of Marxism, but be ever responsive to impulses from below. Its intended function can perhaps best be conveyed in the words of Mussolini, who, like Lenin, had traveled the road from socialism to totalitarianism and built his party on the Bolshevik model. The Fascist Party, Mussolini

said, was to be the "capillary organization" of the country, penetrating every cell of the social organism as blood vessels spread
through living tissue.

Unfortunately for Lenin, arteriosclerosis set in early. He was still
alive when the Bolshevik Party began to separate itself into a caste
with claims to special privileges and increasingly out of touch with
the people. This process accelerated with the rise of Stalin, who
detached from the main body of the Party an elite which became
the *nomenklatura*. But even if in Stalin's time the elite neither responded to the impulses from below, nor pretended to share the
life of the common people, it was still a service class that reacted
with alacrity to commands from above. For all its privileges, it
lacked any rights and lived in permanent terror. It was an instrument of someone else's will, without anything to claim as its own.

All this has drastically changed since Stalin's death. During the
thirty years that followed, the Soviet *nomenklatura* has succeeded
in emancipating itself from subservience to higher authority; indeed, it no longer acknowledges any authority over itself. It also
serves no one and fears no one; it has become master of a house
which it had entered as a menial domestic. It now picks its own
nominal leaders, making certain that these men know to whom
they owe their jobs and whose interests they are to promote. The
transformation of the Soviet *nomenklatura* from a grubby service
corps into a smug elite recalls a similar process that occurred in
imperial Russia during the eighteenth century, when the *dvorian-
stvo*, originally a menial service class, turned into an elite endowed
with every conceivable privilege and subject to no obligations.
Then, as today, this parasitic class favored weak rulers and conservative policies. One of the consequences of this development is
that each General Secretary chosen since Stalin's death is weaker
than his predecessor, which imposes great strains on a political
system built on the command principle and requiring firm leadership.

The post-Stalinist Communist Party departs in two important
respects from the Leninist ideal: it is estranged from the population which it rules, and it is thoroughly corrupt.

Over the years, the Party has succeeded in clogging one after
another avenue of communication linking it to the populace. True,
it encourages citizens to voice their complaints in the press and
provides them with some other legitimate outlets for expressing
discontent, but these are safety valves, which allow the *nomenklatura* to place the blame for whatever citizens are unahppy about
on an abstract "bureaucracy," while it keeps itself free of any taint.
Genuine public opinion, therefore, is either silent, or else flows

into dissenting channels which the authorities do not control. The only instruments available to the Party to ascertain the views and the mood of the population are the security organs whose spies and informants penetrate everywhere. The KGB undoubtedly is the best-informed institution in the USSR, and its staff has a very realistic view of the situation. But this was also the case with its prerevolutionary counterparts, the Imperial Department of the Police and the Okhrana. These security organs accumulated very accurate information on the mood of the country, on the basis of which, in late 1916, they warned their superiors of the possibility of imminent revolution. No one listened then, and one wonders whether the reports of the KGB are heeded today. The pronouncements of high security officials, from its onetime director Andropov down, indicate that they are very disturbed by the mood of Soviet society, where they find widespread apathy and cynicism, especially among the young, combined with passivity and self-indulgence. Since it cannot explain these phenomena in the categories of Marxism-Leninism, the KGB puts the blame for them, as for many other adverse developments, on foreign intelligence services. Thus, the First Deputy Chairman of the KGB, shortly before committing suicide in connection with a corruption scandal involving Brezhnev's daughter, wrote that the West supports no fewer than 400 centers and organizations, including "Zionist" ones, supposedly dedicated to the task of subverting Soviet society.[1] The information at their disposal moves KGB officials to urge the Party to intensify its ideological work. Immense importance is attached to this task. In a major policy address which he delivered in the spring of 1983, Andropov spoke of improvement in the nation's ideological standards as the first of the problems confronting the Party. Such exhortations, however, fall on deaf ears, because the bulk of the *nomenklatura* prefers to believe that all is well.

That the *nomenklatura* would rather not know what its subjects think is demonstrated by the fate of public-opinion research in the Soviet Union. Since they carry no obligations, surveys of public opinion represent an ideal solution for a regime that denies its people institutional outlets for the expression of their views and yet cannot rule effectively without knowing what bothers them. With such considerations in mind, and with the encouragement of Konstantin Chernenko, the Soviet Academy of Sciences in the 1960s founded an Institute for Concrete Sociological Research, to carry out systematic opinion surveys. This organization immediately came under attack from Party conservatives, led by the late Mikhail Suslov, who must have feared that empirical opinion research could challenge Marxist-Leninism, which has always held itself impervious to factual validation and other expressions of "bourgeois objectivism." A few years after its founding, the Institute was purged of its best experts and reduced to analyzing, on the basis of confidential research, the effectiveness of domestic propaganda.

Even more destructive to the Communist parties in the Bloc than the absence of two-way channels of communication with their citizenry is the corruption of the Party apparatus. If the former robs it of the knowledge essential to effective administration, the latter deprives it of the moral authority which it needs for the purpose of mobilizing the population.

The incidence and forms of public corruption are everywhere influenced by national traditions, which determine whether a society treats office primarily as a source of distinction and status or of personal enrichment. In most of the world, it is the latter tradition that prevails. In most societies, public officials expect at the very least tips for performing services on behalf of citizens; in many cases, they draw only nominal salaries and derive the lion's share of their income from such payments. Russia's tradition falls into the latter category. From the earliest period of their history, Russian governments, unable to pay their functionaries adequate salaries, allowed them to live off the land by means of a practice known as "feedings" (*kormleniia*). As long as they accurately delivered to the tsarist treasury such taxes and other dues as were imposed in the region in their charge, they could keep for themselves whatever else they squeezed out of the population. In tsarist Russia, provincial officials demanded from citizens payment for the rendering of routine services and for the granting of all kinds of favors. This practice was so well entrenched that in the seventeenth century Moscow set formal tariffs on the loot that governors could bring home upon retirement, confiscating any excess. Even in the Imperial period, after the civil service had been modernized and put on a regular (if far from sufficient) salary, bribery was universal. Excessively corrupt officials, especially if they enriched themselves at the Crown's expense, suffered the punishment of being transferred to lesser posts or premature retirement, but almost never faced trial. In pre-Revolutionary Russia, a servant of the Emperor could not be tried without the permission of his superior, which was almost never forthcoming, because officials were considered to be extensions of the Imperial person, whose conviction would tarnish the Emperor's image.

While national traditions play their part, no less important in influencing corrupt practices is the proportion of political power and national wealth placed in public hands. Corruption can be defined as the betrayal of trust by persons charged with responsibility for guarding something that belongs to others, be it authority or property, in return for money or some other personal reward. No one, obviously, can betray himself (except in a metaphorical sense), from which it follows that in a society without public authority and nothing but private property, corruption cannot exist. By the same token, where public authority is subject to no formal constraints and disposes of all the wealth, the opportunities for corruption are, theoretically, unlimited. In most societies, a balance is struck between the public and private sectors, so that corruption stays within tolerable limits. Democratic controls over the administration, furthermore, ensure that bribery and other forms of corruption run the risk of being exposed and punished. As a rule, however, the growth of the public sphere, whether in administration or in the disposal of national wealth, creates a climate favorable to corruption.

Communist regimes represent an instance of public authority that owns all the nation's wealth and invades every sphere of its life. And since they provide no external checks on those who wield this authority, they inexorably become corrupted from top to bottom.

Corruption in Communist states assumes a great variety of forms. We have alluded already to one of them, namely, access of high Party officials to exclusive consumer facilities. Strictly speaking, these privileges do not constitute corruption, since they are carried out with the government's connivance and involve no betrayal of trust. Nevertheless, they certainly contribute a great deal to the elite's moral degeneration. The right to purchase, at artificially deflated prices, goods and services which the rest of the population cannot obtain at any price, isolates the Party elite from the mass of ordinary citizens. It inculcates in it an arrogance and willfulness entirely out of keeping with the regime's egalitarian professions. To enjoy such rights is to participate in a regime of apartheid no less odious because its victims happen to be white instead of black.

Revelations by onetime Soviet officials and jurists indicate that in the Soviet Union any post, whether in the Party, the state or the economic apparatus, entitles the incumbent to extort money and services from those who depend on his good will—that, indeed, for many officials, the reason for aspiring to office is to be able to engage in extortion. Because of this feature, a cash value attaches itself to every post, proportionate to its potential for enriching the official who holds it. In the Asian republics of the USSR, there is a regular traffic in offices in the form of closed auctions.

As in tsarist Russia, officials in charge of the Soviet provinces elevate their life style above the modest level to which their salaries entitle them, by extracting tribute from subordinates; these subordinates, in turn, exact payments from workers, peasants and other ordinary citizens. It seems that virtually every official position affords opportunities for bribe taking. Because experience makes it possible to calculate in advance the income that a given office will yield, the price is approximately known; as soon as a post falls vacant, the bidding begins. Mr. Ilia Zemtsov, who had served as a sociological expert on the Central Committee of the Communist Party of Azerbaijan (admittedly, the most notorious republic in the Soviet Union), in his book *A Party or a Mafia?* provides a price list, in rubles, for offices traded there in the years 1969–72.[2]

| | |
|---|---|
| Minister of Trade | 250,000 |
| First Secretary of the Party's Regional Committee | 200,000 |
| Rector, institution of higher learning | up to 200,000 |
| Minister of Communal Economy | 150,000 |
| Minister of Social Security | 120,000 |
| Deputy 1st Secretary of Party Regional Committee | 100,000 |
| Factory Director | 10,000–100,000 |
| Chairman of State Farm (*sovkhoz*) | 80,000 |
| Chairman of collective farm (*kolkhoz*) | 50,000 |
| Head of the Militia | 50,000 |
| Academician | 50,000 |
| Regional Public Prosecutor | 30,000 |
| Director of a Theater or Opera | 10,000–30,000 |

Authority to dispense these lucrative jobs belongs to "patrons" in charge of the respective *nomenklatura* lists. They are expected to share the proceeds with colleagues, including high officials in Moscow who act on their recommendations.

One's imagination sets the only limit on the variety of incomes that officeholding in Communist countries can provide. For instance, the high fees charged in some republics for appointment to the rectorship of an institution of higher learning are due to the fact that admission to such institutions normally calls for stiff bribes. Mr. Zemtsov estimates that in Azerbaijan in 1972 acceptance by the Medical School cost 30,000 rubles; by the university, between 20,000 and 25,000; and by the School of Foreign Languages, 10,000. The economic posts, of course, afford especially lucrative opportunities for bribe taking, since material is always in short supply and the officials in charge often release it only upon payment of a bribe; if this is not forthcoming, they can always divert it to the black market. Party officials, such as Secretaries of Regional Committees, are like satraps and for years now have enjoyed virtual tenure; in this capacity, like tsarist *voevodas* and governors, they amass huge fortunes. Lesser fry augment their salaries by demanding compulsory deliveries of produce from collective farms under their authority, or free personal services (such as house or car repairs) from industrial establishments.

Gaidar Aliev, now a member of the Politbureau, carried out in the 1970s, on behalf of the KGB, a major drive against corrupt officials in Azerbaijan. From an interview which he gave to a Russian paper, it transpires that an important motive behind corruption, besides simple greed, is a sense of insecurity. Speaking of officials who try to accumulate some capital—an activity he calls hoarding—he said as follows:

> I am interested in the psychology of the hoarders. Sometimes they give honest answers. Akhmedov, the ex-chairman of the Shaumian regional Executive Committee in Baku, who was caught buying up gold coins, said at the meeting of the Bureau of the Party's Central Committee: "for a rainy day." They begin to fear for their "rainy day" the moment they assume a post to which they are not entitled. The feeling of insecurity, instability, of inevitable downfall haunts these unfortunates at all times. And when one looks into their past, then, as a rule, one runs into . . . a bribe that got them enrolled in an institution of higher learning, that bought them the diploma, the dissertation, the "profitable" job.[3]

This is a devastating concession from the highest circles, that it is possible in the Soviet Union to buy one's way to a university degree and an official post. And if Azerbaijan and neighboring Georgia are, perhaps, especially corrupt, they are not unique.

The system is ubiquitous and interlocked. It is impossible to have dealings with individual officials without involving their patrons as well as their clients. Every now and then anticorruption drives are undertaken of the kind that Aliev has carried out in Azerbaijan. On such occasions scores of officials are removed and transferred (they are rarely tried), and virtue is proclaimed triumphant.* Then the dust settles, and everything returns to normal.

---

* As in Imperial Russia, responsible officials—in the present case, members of the Communist Party—are above the law in the sense that they cannot be tried while in office. This calls for expulsion from the Party prior to judiciary proceedings.

The Soviet government is understandably reticent about the extent of corruption within its borders. But we happen to have official data from Poland, a Communist country that there is no reason to suspect of being worse in this respect. Under pressure from Solidarity, the Polish government in 1981 carried out mass arrests of high Party and state functionaries accused of appropriating state property. Beginning with the country's highest dignitary, First Secretary Eduard Gierek, the list of those arrested included 18 former ministers, 7 deputy prime ministers, 56 deputy ministers, and 3,500 others.[4] The fact that none of the accused has been brought to trial, while many of their accusers languish in jail, illustrates how entwined are the bonds of corruption that hold the *nomenklatura* together and how intractable the problem.

Official corruption, which has spread like a cancer since Stalin's death, especially under Brezhnev, has a most detrimental effect on the morale of Communist societies. A would-be Sparta cannot keep its population in austerity while its ruling elite wallows in Oriental self-indulgence. Lycurgus, the founder of Sparta, realized this elementary fact when he forbade citizens of his state, under severe penalty, to accumulate money. Mass mobilization, that particular strength of Communist regimes, is rendered very difficult by venality. For, while it is true that most citizens of Communist countries have learned to accept corruption as a fact of life, and in the Soviet Union they are said even to admire particularly audacious bribe takers, the result is that they turn deaf when appeals are made to their public spirit. Aliev, an expert in this matter, has assessed quite correctly the debilitating effect of this state of affairs on Soviet society:

> In an atmosphere of abuse of official positions, of corruption, whitewash, in an atmosphere of contempt for honest labor, the initiative of the masses [cannot] but diminish, moral indignation [cannot] fail but reign, giving way, among many social strata, to a state of despondency and indifference.[5]

In Poland, detailed revelations of corruption in Party ranks caused total revulsion against the Party among the citizenry. As reported in the government press, a poll conducted there in mid-1981 showed that, in response to the question in which of fourteen listed national institutions they had the greatest confidence, the Poles gave pride of place to the Church, followed by Solidarity; then came eleven more institutions; the Party ended up in fourteenth and last place.[6]

Perhaps the most tragic aspect of this whole phenomenon is

that citizens of Communist societies are all but driven by the system to engage in bribe-taking and bribe-giving as well as the stealing of state property. The system virtually compels honest people to turn criminal and thus to live under permanent threat of exposure and punishment. Analyses of family budgets in the USSR indicate that the average household cannot make ends meet on its salary because this is calculated on the premise of goods and services being purchased at official prices, whereas in reality shortages force everyone to resort a good part of the time to the much higher-priced second economy. Ordinary workers, peasants, and white-collar workers have no alternative but to augment their incomes with illegal earnings. In his *Corrupt Society*, Konstantin Simis, an émigré with long legal experience in the Soviet Union, depicts, from his personal practice, an all-pervasive and interconnected universe of corruption. He shows, for instance, that factory or collective-farm managers cannot hope to meet their production norms, as they must in order to retain their jobs, without bribing ministry officials to release to them the needed materials and equipment; and that the managers in turn, must dock workers' or peasants' earnings to raise the cash for such bribes. He further shows that a Soviet citizen accused of an ordinary—that is, non-political—crime, must slip hush money to officials of the judiciary if he hopes to obtain the semblance of a fair trial. In the early 1960s, a purge carried out among the Moscow judiciary resulted in the arrest, on charges of bribe-taking, of three hundred investigators, prosecutors, and judges.[7] What can one say of a regime that requires citizens who wish merely to do their job, to take and give bribes and engage in other illegal activities? Where lawlessness is not a deviation from norm but the very motor that drives society? Can the people who have devised such a system have any realistic hope of world hegemony?

Communist corruption is a progressive disease. For Mr. Simis, under Brezhnev the Soviet Union turned into a "land of corrupt rulers, ruling over a corrupted people." He believes that corruption has eaten so deeply into the Soviet system as to have become ineradicable: it cannot be eliminated for the simple reason that any serious purification would result in the elimination of the entire ruling apparatus[8]—as, indeed, has happened in Poland, where the military had to take over from the discredited Party personnel. To root out future corruption, it would be necessary also to provide more outlets for legitimate entrepreneurship as well as to rationalize the entire system of economic management, neither of which can be done without turning the whole system topsy-turvy.

It is a striking paradox that by attempting to abolish private interest and forcing everyone to work exclusively for the good of all, the Communists have merely succeeded in destroying all vestiges of public spirit and unleashing a frenzied pursuit of personal gain. This is what Hegel must have had in mind when he spoke of the World Spirit amusing itself at the vanity of human desires and playing games with those who presumed to direct its steps.

## 2 INTELLECTUAL DISSENT

Intellectual dissent as a movement of social protest is a relatively modern phenomenon whose origins date to the eighteenth century. A byproduct of science and the scientific spirit, it takes as its starting point the notion that human affairs are subject to laws like those that govern nature and, as such, are capable of being grasped and rationally managed. Since human affairs are not in fact anywhere managed in accord with scientific and rational principles, intellectual dissenters object to the existing order and demand that society be thoroughly reorganized. The spread of the scientific spirit has always assumed particular intensity in Russia, the first non-Western country exposed to its revolutionary influence. It is not accidental that a widely used term for active intellectual dissenters, *intelligentsia*, though not of Russian origin, has entered the English vocabulary by way of Russian.

The persistence of intellectual dissent in Russia is the result of inconsistent policies pursued by all its governments since the accession of Peter the Great three hundred years ago. To realize his ambition of making Russia a great European power, Peter needed an educated class—men capable of commanding artillery batteries and warships, of running modern tax offices, of managing manufactures and mines. Since such a class did not exist, he forced his landowning class to undergo compulsory education. He wanted no less—but also no more—than servitors skilled in whatever techniques were required to run a modern state. It quickly transpired, however, that education could not be confined to techniques. Landed gentry forced to study mathematics, navigation or mining acquired habits of reasoning that they occasionally applied to political and social issues; and this was even truer of their descendants. The authorities firmly forbade this. In effect, the Russian monarchy taught its upper class to think, and at the same time it imposed strict limits on the uses to which their thinking could be put. The paternalistic regime that governed Russia until October 1905 forbade its citizens, among them internationally acclaimed writers and scientists, to raise in public the most elementary questions about the manner in which Russian society was organized and governed. Russians were supposed to be modern Europeans in everything except where affairs of state were concerned, at which point they were to display the docility of children. Alexander Herzen, a Russian dissenter of the nineteenth century, complained eloquently of this contradiction: "They give us a comprehensive education," he wrote, "they inculcate in us the desires, the strivings, the sufferings of the contemporary world, and then they cry, 'Stay slaves, dumb and passive, or else you will perish.' "[9]

This contradiction has become more pronounced than ever since the Communists seized power. The Soviet regime, from the same motive of great power aspiration that had moved Peter the Great, has introduced education on a national scale and, at the same time, set the strictest constraints imaginable on the uses that the beneficiaries of this education are allowed to make of it. To any objective observer such practice is doomed to failure. The Soviet Union has nearly ten million citizens with completed higher education. Granted that the education these people have received is, by Western standards, often shoddy, yet even at its shoddiest it cannot help but inculcate in them habits of rational thinking—that is, thinking based on the rules of logic and a detached analysis of the empirical evidence. A Soviet geologist, exploring for oil in Siberia, uses reasoning that is no different from that of his counterpart in Alaska. A Soviet engineer designing an airplane or a dam has no "dialectical logic" to guide him, as distinct from "bourgeois logic." The entire material culture of the Soviet Union and the other Communist countries rests on principles of science that have universal validity and cut across national as well as ideological boundaries. Yet the very same geologists and engineers, when facing questions that concern man and society, are expected to suspend their scientific habits and revert to primitive modes of thinking where authority, not evidence and logic, has the decisive say.

The theoreticians of Marxism-Leninism claim theirs to be the most advanced explanation of social processes in existence, a doctrine whose "laws" are as solidly grounded as any known to the natural sciences. But this claim is sham, mere homage paid to the scientific spirit of the age. Lenin, its founder and authority of last resort, never permitted factual evidence to correct any of Marx's tenets, which he treated not as a set of hypotheses but as a finished, eternally validated system of scientific laws, on the order of Newtonian mechanics. Whenever evidence accumulated that one or another of Marx's "laws" or predictions ran contrary to facts,

Lenin brushed the facts aside, accusing those who called attention to them of "revisionism" and "bourgeois objectivism." This habit is solidly entrenched among his successors. The scientific element in Communist theory is confined to vocabulary and style of presentation. Communist thinking has nothing in common with the fundamental feature of scientific method, which calls for a detached, unprejudiced examination of the evidence and the willingness at all times to change opinions to conform to it. The Soviet government trains millions of its citizens to think in a genuinely scientific manner about natural phenomena and turns out some excellent scientists; at the same time, it insists that they and the rest of the population instantly switch to prescientific, medieval modes of thought whenever the subject is man and his works.

The term medieval here is not used casually. Medieval thinking was concerned more with the "spirit" of phenomena, their "essence," than with their observable manifestations. One of the consequences of this attitude was that in the Middle Ages forgeries of historic documents were perpetrated on an unprecedented scale. The churchmen and others who engaged in these forgeries believed themselves to be scrupulously honest when doctoring old documents to make them reflect not what had actually happened but what by definition ought to have happened. Referring to this phenomenon, so puzzling to the modern mind, a historian of the Middle Ages writes, "What in the scientific perspective appears as the 'falsification' of a name, a date, a document, for a different conception of history may be a naïve restoration of harmony between the event and the 'true' order." [10] This type of thinking proceeded from principle to fact rather than the other way around, and determined the veracity of an event from its conformity or lack of conformity to a higher "truth."

This prescientific approach is characteristic of Marxism-Leninism. One illustration must suffice. A Communist state, according to this theory, is a worker state in the sense that it embodies the interests and aspirations of its working class. In this conception, a conflict between workers and the Communist state is inconceivable since this would constitute a contradiction in terms. If, nevertheless, such a conflict does occur, as has happened recently in Poland with the rise of Solidarity, the explanation given is not that the accepted concept of the Communist state may be wrong, or else that faulty policies have caused it no longer to be seen by workers as serving their interests; rather, it is to declare Solidarity a counterrevolutionary organization, inimical to the interests of the working class. Never mind that nearly the entire class of industrial workers in Poland had joined Solidarity; to present this as evidence is to be guilty of "bourgeois objectivism." Even if every single worker were to turn against it, the Communist state would still be said to express the will of the working class since, by definition, it cannot be anything else.*

The liberties that Communist authorities take with evidence and require their subjects to tolerate put educated citizens, regardless of political convictions, in a quandary. Most of them adjust, conforming outwardly and pretending to accept the absurd as reality while driving their private thoughts deep inside. They end up like the Czech citizen in the anecdote about a poll conducted by the Party in Prague after its occupation by Soviet troops in 1968. "What do you think of the foreign policy of the Soviet government?" he is asked. "I concur with it wholeheartedly." "What about the policies of the Czech Communist Party?" "I am also in full accord." "Have you any ideas of your own on the subject?" "I do, but I am in complete disagreement with them," he responds. In practice, the result is intellectual schizophrenia. For some, however, such schizophrenia is unbearable and at some point they break with the system so as to bring their inner voice into harmony with the spoken voice—as Anatolii Shcharanskii put it, "closing the gap between thought and word." This is achieved at considerable cost to their material well-being and often their very liberty. But the reward is an inner serenity of which most Communist citizens have no inkling. In the Soviet Union, where the pressure for outward conformity is much greater than in Eastern Europe, it is easy to identify an overt dissident because instead of looking surly and wrapped up in his concerns, such a person is likely to appear at peace with himself and the world.

Because the Soviet government demands only external conformity and does not much care what its citizens really think, and because most people, if forced to choose, prefer intellectual schizophrenia to the painful break with the society in which they live, the prevalence of intellectual dissent is far greater than appears on the surface. Identifiable, overt dissenters, between 3,000 and

---

* Lest anyone conclude that such primitive reasoning is confined to Communist societies, it must be noted that some Western scholars and publicists are not to be outdone. Thus the English historian, Timothy W. Mason, confronted with what was to him a highly unpalatable fact, that in the early 1930s many German workers had voted for Hitler, neatly solved his problem by redefining the term "worker" to mean an industrial employee who did *not* vote for Hitler: "The working class cannot be defined otherwise than in its struggle against the ruling classes." (*Sozialpolitik im Dritten Reich*, Opladen, 1977, 9)

10,000 of whom are estimated to be imprisoned or exiled, are merely the visible peaks of a vast continent of dissent that lies submerged under the waters of conformity.

Present-day intellectual dissent in the Soviet Union bears close resemblance to pre-Revolutionary dissent and is best understood in this historical context. Now, as then, the movement is divided into two branches, a nationalist-conservative one and a Western-democratic one. Now, as then, the authorities restrain the nationalist opposition, but they do not actively persecute it and in some respects even make common cause with it, while reserving all their vengeful fury for the Westerners and democrats. Russian nationalists are not intellectual dissenters in the sense defined above in that they do not criticize their government from a scientific point of view. Their appeal is rather to the spirit of history. Their status as dissidents, under tsarism as under Communism, is determined by the fact that they are critical of all Russian regimes since Peter the Great for allegedly having abandoned the true course of Russian national development and forced the country to imitate the West, which, according to them, runs entirely contrary to Russian nature. As the pre-Revolutionary nationalists had placed the blame on Peter, so the Soviet ones place it, alternately, on Lenin, Stalin, or the "intelligentsia" in general. They want a return to the past; in the nineteenth century, that past was pre-Petrine Russia, today it is pre-1917, Imperial Russia. The psychology and the arguments used by the contemporary nationalists, for the major part, merely bring up to date attitudes and ideas found in the older literature. On the other hand, the modern Westerners, like their namesakes in the past, believe that the path of historical progress is the same for all mankind, that this path has been cleared by Western Europe, and that to the extent that Russia differs from the West it is due to its being backward and insufficiently Westernized. Russian nationalists have always tended to be apolitical and to lay stress on man's "inner," that is, spiritual freedom, whereas the Westerners have been and continue to be political-minded, favoring democratic forms of government, law and human rights. The barricades from behind which the two parties had battled each other for a hundred or so years before the Revolution and which Stalin's brutal repressions have leveled with the ground, seemingly without trace, have been reerected promptly after the despot's death, in the very same locations and with identical arguments.

## A. THE WESTERNIZING (DEMOCRATIC) OPPOSITION

Stalin persecuted the democratic and socialist intelligentsia with such single-minded savagery that there was every reason to believe he had destroyed it beyond any hope of resuscitation. But, as it turned out, he had only driven it out of sight. It raised its voice, cautiously, a few months after his death; and within a decade, having reforged links with the traditions of the pre-Revolutionary intelligentsia, it resumed its struggle.

The pro-Western, democratic opposition made itself heard first in literature. In the best Russian tradition, post-Stalinist writers reclaimed the right to tell the truth as they saw it, which usually was starkly at odds with the way the officialdom wanted it done. As in the nineteenth century, literary realism became a political statement. Khrushchev encouraged this tendency. His easing of censorship and revelations of Stalin's crimes against the *nomenklatura* were inspired by an effort to reanimate a society that Stalin's terror had left in a state of cataleptic shock.

Dissent, however, did not long remain within the approved boundaries. Taking advantage of certain legal measures that Stalin's successors had introduced, it spilled into other, more dangerous areas of public activity.

To restore to Soviet society a minimal sense of security, without which it seemed impossible to raise it from its spiritual stagnation, Stalin's successors dismantled the pseudolegal structure that he had created to provide sanction for his mass murders. This they did by sweeping changes in judiciary procedure. Immediately after Stalin's death, the dreaded Special Boards of the security police, which used to mete out, in secret session, summary justice to millions of political prisoners, were abolished. The powers of the police to carry out investigations were curtailed, and their right to pass sentences was taken away. The Criminal Codes of 1958 and 1960 thoroughly reformed criminal procedure. They introduced what for the Soviet Union was the revolutionary tenet that "only a person guilty of committing a crime . . . shall be subject to criminal responsibility and punishment." Crime was defined as a violation of existing law. Only courts were henceforth to dispense justice, even in political suits. Defendants acquired the right to counsel, and all trials were to be held in the open.[11]

Nothing illustrates better the difficulty of reforming a totalitarian regime in a piecemeal, controlled fashion, than the fate of these reforms. The Soviet authorities had reason to expect that the introduction of legal norms into a country accustomed since 1917 to institutionalized lawlessness would win them the sympathy of the citizens without weakening the authorities' hold on them. This expectation was disappointed. Once the government had committed itself to observing legal norms in criminal proceedings, it left itself open to charges of lawlessness in other, nonprocedural respects. Democratic dissenters realized that they could now challenge the authorities in the name of laws that the latter had issued but ignored. Beginning with the first open trial of dissenters, held in 1966 to try the writers Andrei Siniavskii and Iurii Daniel, friends of the accused appeared in court, testified on their behalf, and recorded the proceedings for distribution. All of a sudden, dissenting voices openly challenged, under the protection of the court, government practices that for decades no one had dreamed of questioning. Some dissenters appealed to clauses in the Soviet constitution guaranteeing citizens freedom of speech and religion. Others demanded that the government abide by the terms of international treaties that it had ratified, such as the Human Rights Charter of the United Nations, every provision of which it systematically violated. Later on, after the Soviet government had committed itself in the Helsinki Accords to a comprehensive code of human rights, private Helsinki "Monitoring Groups" sprung up in various parts of the USSR to verify compliance. The periodical *Chronicle of Human Events*, published illegally since 1968, carried reports of arrests and trials of Soviet dissidents and their subsequent fate.

The authorities were at first at a loss how to respond to this turn of events. Their problem was compounded by the fact that among the concessions they had made in détente, they granted considerable freedom to foreign correspondents accredited in the Soviet Union. Democratic dissidents availed themselves of this opportunity and through these journalists made their views and struggles known to the world outside; beamed back by Western radio stations, this information reached wide audiences in Communist countries, fueling more dissent. In time, the *nomenklatura* regained its composure and struck back. A vaguely worded omnibus clause was added to the Criminal Code following the trial of Siniavskii and Daniel, which made it a crime to engage in "anti-Soviet propaganda," even when evidence was lacking that the accused had intended to harm the regime. "Parasite courts" were introduced to deal with persons who had no visible means of support. Defense lawyers were intimidated, and those who proved too zealous were barred from legal practice. The police packed courtrooms with their agents to keep out friends of the defendants. Acting on the premise that anyone who took Soviet law seriously had to be out of his mind, from the late 1960s onward the authorities confined some of the bravest of the democratic and religious dissidents in psychiatric wards, subjecting them there to torture by drugs. In 1977, the KGB received authority to liquidate democratic dissent, and it proceeded to imprison or expel from the country the movement's leading spokesmen. A decree, quietly introduced in October 1983, shortly after the conclusion of the Madrid Conference at which human rights were a central subject of discussion, allows prison and camp authorities, without recourse to any legal procedures, to prolong sentences of prisoners guilty of "malicious disobedience" anywhere from three to five years.

By then the strategy of exploiting legal avenues to challenge the system had exhausted its possibilities. Indications are that recently some elements of the democratic opposition have gone underground with the intention of taking up the political struggle. If these reports are true, then the contemporary democratic-dissent movement will have retraced the route traveled by its nineteenth-century forerunners who had also begun with literature and ended with politics.

The outstanding feature of the democratic opposition in the Soviet Union is the stress on legality and human rights. So far, its adherents have refrained from openly challenging the regime's undemocratic structure and procedures, although in the long run these are obviously incompatible with legality and human rights. For the time being, they insist only that the government respect the laws of its own making. They regard the Soviet government as the heir of tsarism. They believe that their country needs, most of all, to be subjected to thoroughgoing Westernization. Andrei Sakharov, the most outstanding figure of this tendency and its acknowledged leader, is on record as saying that improvements in Russia are possible only as a result of Western influence. Sakharov has also spoken of the United States as the "historically determined leader of the movement toward a pluralist and free society, vital to mankind." [12]

A variant of the democratic movement is represented by the ideas of Roy Medvedev, who seems to form a party of one. Medvedev believes Marxism-Leninism to be a sound theory, which Lenin's successors have spoiled. He opposes collectivization and many of Stalin's other policies and favors a return to the New Economic Policy of Lenin. He rests his hopes on internal reform in the Communist Party, rejects Western pressures on behalf of human rights in the USSR as counterproductive, and endorses détente. His willingness to work within the framework of Marxism-Leninism and repudiation of Western interference in Soviet affairs have earned him the tolerance of the authorities. Although occasionally reprimanded, he is allowed to live in freedom and suffers no punishment for publishing abroad. This unusual treatment suggests that some highly placed members of the *nomenklatura* regard Medvedev as useful. His is the only tolerated wing of the opposition to the left of the Party. His Leninist ideas apparently constitute for the Establishment a fallback position should it ever decide to shift toward a slightly more liberal course.

The greatest difficulties that the democratic opposition encounters and the source of its worst frustrations lie in an inability to communicate its ideas to the Soviet population at large. The notions of law and universal human rights lack deep roots in the consciousness of the Russian people. A Westerner is prone to regard these concepts as innate to man and their absence as intolerable deprivation. In reality, they are the product of a unique cultural tradition that originated in Stoic philosophy and was transmitted to the West through Roman jurisprudence. They remain to this day confined to a small segment of humanity. In the course of its historical evolution, Russia failed to come within the orbit of classical influence; such legal traditions as it had managed to develop were imported by the Westernized monarchy and disappeared with it. The average Russian may have an instinctive sense of justice; he reacts strongly, even violently, when he feels that he has been wronged. But he lacks a consciousness of legality —that is, of an abstract system of universally binding conduct based on moral principles and the law of nature. Soviet society is fundamentally peasant by virtue of the fact that its elite is overwhelmingly descended from the rural population and has inherited its village culture. Students of the Russian peasantry before and immediately after the Revolution were virtually unanimous in emphasizing its inability to comprehend law as a universal and permanent set of norms. Nor did the Russian peasant or his Soviet descendant see himself as a human being endowed, by the mere fact of his humanity, with inherent rights, independent of social or political status; to the extent that he enjoys any rights, the Russian tends to see them as accouterments of the authority vested in him by those in power and, as such, revocable at any time. A Russian who is not a member of the Establishment is unlikely to think of himself as possessing any rights whatsoever. These attitudes, acquired from long historic experience, facilitate the task of the authorities in containing the challenge from the democratic opposition.

This thesis can be demonstrated on the example of the labor movement in the Soviet Union. In Poland, worker discontent assumed ideological forms under the influence of intellectuals who transformed spontaneous protests against increases in food prices into an organized movement of political resistance with an ambitious program of national reform. Solidarity was not satisfied to force a lowering of food prices: it demanded and obtained country-wide guarantees of workers' rights. Its own charter and the agreements which it compelled the government to sign laid the groundwork for the protection of the interests of Polish workers and provided legitimate outlets for the expression of their thoughts and grievances. This turn of events was possible because Poland enjoys a heritage of law and human rights that reaches back to the Middle Ages; it is so deeply impressed on the consciousness of Poles that forty years of German and Soviet occupation were not able to erase it. In Hungary in 1956 and in Czechoslovakia in 1968 similar trends were at work and for the same historic reasons.

In the Soviet Union such an evolution has not taken place. The country has experienced much strike activity, most of which goes unreported in the West because it tends to occur in the provinces from which foreign journalists are barred. Typically, these strikes are inspired by economic grievances such as reductions in wages, poor or unsafe working conditions and, most often, shortages of food. They usually take the form of leaderless and programless, spontaneous rebellions, reminiscent of peasant mutinies (*bunty*) under the old regime. The Soviet authorities deal with them in one of two ways. If the strikers are violent, they make a strong show of force and then proceed to arrest the most visible troublemakers. If they are peaceful, the authorities satisfy their demands. As a rule, these procedures quickly restore peace and things go back to normal.[13]

These patterns were evident in recent strikes. In 1981, strikes broke out in the Soviet Union's two largest automobile plants, at Gorkii and Togliatti. In both instances, the strikers protested food shortages. The authorities rushed in fresh food supplies; as soon as these had been distributed, work resumed. Later that year, exployees at the Kiev Motorcycle Works laid down their tools to protest cuts in wages and bonuses; when their pay was restored, they too called off the strike. Once in a while, industrial action takes a violent turn. The bloodiest incident of this kind occurred in 1962. The government that year raised prices for meat and dairy products and lowered piece rates, following which demonstrations broke out throughout the country, the most turbulent of them in Novocherkassk. A strike that began in a locomotive plant spread to other industrial establishments in the city; the women workers from a local textile plant displayed particular aggressiveness. On June 2, the security forces (personally directed, according to one account, by two members of the Politbureau) opened machine-gun fire on the demonstrators, killing seventy or more persons.[14]

These occurrences indicate that, contrary to a prevalent view in the West, there exist limits to the privations that ordinary Soviet citizens will bear and, therefore, that limits also exist on the government's ability to ignore the needs of consumers. What, unfortunately, they do not indicate is that the Russian worker senses any connection between his personal grievances and the system under which he lives, that he realizes that the injustices, against which he every now and then rebels, are but instances of a pervasive regime of lawlessness. It is true that in recent years organizations have been formed in the Soviet Union to uphold the basic rights of workers; but even these groups, prior to being destroyed by the KGB, have refrained from raising broader demands, preferring to confine themselves to forming genuine trade unions. It is depressing to learn from informal polls of Russian workers that most of them have a negative attitude toward Solidarity, sympathy for which is confined largely to Russian intellectuals.

The KGB, whose responsibility it is to deal with sedition, has utter contempt for ideas and ideologies, especially those that appeal to public rather than private interests. It seems confident of its ability to nip in the bud any attempt of intellectuals to organize resistance. As for workers and peasants, it has learned from experience that they can be brought to heel by a combination of repression and material rewards. Its main concern is to keep the intellectuals away from the population at large so as to prevent a recurrence of the events in Poland, where intellectuals succeeded in politicizing workers. Like the tsarist police, the KGB views democratic dissent as by and large a Jewish phenomenon. It is common talk in the Soviet Union that two thirds of the fighters for law and human rights are either full Jews or half-Jews. This perception helps to explain the virulently anti-American and anti-Jewish ("anti-Zionist") tenor of Soviet propaganda; by attacking these foreign targets, which it treats as virtually indistinguishable, the regime deals an indirect blow to its democratic opposition. The same purpose is served by the government's insistence that democratic dissidents who leave the country to go abroad, whether voluntarily or under compulsion, do so on Israeli visas, even if they happen to be pure Slavs. By depicting the movement for law and human rights as "Western" and "Jewish"—that is, un-Russian and therefore treasonable—the KGB appeals to the basest xenophobic instincts of the population.

The KGB allows a certain amount of democratic dissent to air itself in the open, in the belief that in this manner it is easier to keep it under control. It has even established a kind of informal working arrangement with the internal enemy, not unlike that which the police in many places have with the underworld. It allows the dissidents to talk and argue with one another, to commit their thoughts to paper, to engage in limited distribution of typed manuscripts (*samizdat*), and to read and store émigré publications. It ruthlessly cracks down, however, the instant they attempt either to spread ideas outside their circle or to organize. As a consequence of this arrangement, there exists in the Soviet a surprising amount of informed political discussion; and because of the absence of legitimate outlets for free opinion, no consensus is established, let alone socially enforced. Everyone thinks as he pleases and, when given half a chance, speaks out. Russian intellectuals are far more open-minded and less easily shocked than their Western, especially American, counterparts. This diversity of opinion is extremely encouraging from the point of view of the country's intellectual life; what it augurs for its political future is more problematic, given that a certain consensus is essential to the proper functioning of every political and social body.

## B. THE NATIONALIST OPPOSITION

Dissent on the right is more difficult to describe, because it rests not so much on ideology as on emotions, which cannot be readily systematized. Dominant among these emotions is nostalgia for old, pre-Revolutionary Russia—the never-never land of the Firebird, of icons and holy fools, of pious tsars and Christ-loving peasants. The nostalgia is accompanied by loathing for the West and the Westernized intelligentsia who had allegedly ravaged this Holy Russia. The conservatives fear that if the Communist regime is allowed to pursue its course much longer it will not only destroy what is still left of the genuine Russia but put into question the very survival of the Russian people. They are not especially interested in political questions, believing that the important things are personal and spiritual. Their principal objection to Communism is not its tyrannical form of government but its destruction of the private sphere of life. Freedom to them is not a condition that results from a set of legal guarantees and political institutions but an inner state. Some of them are even prepared to let the Communist regime continue to rule, provided that it stops interfering with the private life of the people.

The nationalist movement, sometimes called "Russophile," to distinguish it from the nineteenth-century Slavophile tendency from which it descends, has two branches. One of these operates legally in the Soviet Union, under Party supervision; the other is in emigration. Both appear to be thoroughly penetrated by agents of the security police. They share the same basic philosophy, although for obvious reasons nationalists active in the USSR cannot express themselves with the same candor as those abroad.

At first sight it may appear surprising that the Soviet government should tolerate a conservative-nationalist movement that condemns everything it stands for and treats the October Revolution as a calamity. The rapprochement between Communism and nationalism, however, is neither new nor casual. Bolshevism had originally evolved from Social-Democracy, a movement that was unequivocally committed to an antinationalist, pro-Western position. Like his associates, Lenin viewed his country as populated by semi-Asiatic barbarians who had to be Westernized as rapidly as possible. Nevertheless, already by 1920 Lenin began to make tactical advances toward right-wing, nationalist groups active at home and abroad, His unerring political sense told him that the democratic, socialist and pro-Western forces in Russia were weak and shallowly rooted; this had been demonstrated by the ease with which in October 1917 the ramshackle forces at his and Trotsky's disposal had dispersed the democratic and socialist Provisional Government. Such effective resistance as the Bolsheviks had encountered in their bid for power came from conservative and nationalist forces, grouped around the White Armies, against which for three years they had to wage a murderous Civil War that at one point they came very close to losing. As the prospects of revolution breaking out in the industrial countries of the West receded, Lenin decided to court his defeated enemies. When the Civil War was over, he liquidated the socialist parties, which he had tolerated until then, and made overtures to Russian monarchists and nationalists. What to Lenin was a short-term, purely tactical device, Stalin made into a basic policy. Stalin never shared the internationalist illusions of his colleagues; he knew that the only sources of appeal to the Russian masses were either anarchism or nationalism. Since anarchism was for him out of the question, he resorted to nationalism, especially Russian nationalism. He identified himself with the imperialist traditions of tsarist Russia and with time freely resorted to chauvinism and xenophobia as instruments of mass politics. His gradual elimination of Jews from positions of authority in the Party was a manifestation of this trend; it was designed to neutralize very damaging accusations of nationalist circles (as well as of Nazis) that Bolshevism was imposed on Russia by international Jewry as part of a conspiracy to take over the world.

In consequence of these developments, the domestic branch of Russian nationalist dissent has been coopted by the Soviet regime and placed in the ambivalent status of a loyal opposition. The nationalists are given their own publications, which tend to specialize in young audiences whose lack of ideological commitment and fascination with things Western cause the authorities much anxiety. Its leading organs are *Pioneer Truth* (*Pionerskaia Pravda*), *Young Guard* (*Molodaia Gvardiia*) and *Our Contemporary* (*Nash Sovremennik*). These journals and their respective publishing houses stress peasant life, the glories of Russia's past, and the superiority of the Russian race.

The main tenets of the nationalist opposition can be summarized as follows:

**1.** Russia is both "different" and superior. Its past is filled with struggles and hardships that no other nation has experienced or would have been capable of withstanding. In coping with them, Russians have developed their own political culture, which sacrifices "selfish" human rights and freedoms in favor of "selfless" service to state and nation. Their tragic past has "purified" Russia, making it spiritually superior to Western nations, which have been poisoned by the arrogance of intellectualism and pursuit of material wealth. Historians of this school write popular works that depict Russia as a country that at every point in its long history had been abreast of and even in front of other civilizations. Thus, F. Nesterov claims that in the Middle Ages Russia was in every respect a peer of contemporary France and Germany, and A. N. Sakharov describes how proto-Russians had, already in the sixth century developed a high level of diplomatic activity.[15] Books containing such fantastic idealizations of Russia's past, distributed in editions of tens of thousands, are hardly distinguishable from the works of nineteenth-century apologists of tsarist absolutism.

**2.** The Revolution of 1917 was not a natural outcome of the country's historic evolution; quite the contrary, it was a tragic shock, a violent reversal of the trends of history. Its primary cause was ideological—namely, the spread among the alienated Russian intelligentsia of Western culture with its atheism, rationalism, and socialism. The Revolution had no domestic roots, whether of an economic, political or social kind. Even the February 1917 Revolution, which most Western historians regard as a spontaneous outburst, is represented by Soviet conservatives (as it had been by their monarchist forerunners) as the product of conspiracies by left-wing intellectuals, Jews and Freemasons. Russia did not produce Communism; it was conquered by it. Russia is Communism's oldest and most tormented victim.

**3.** The policies of the Soviet government have poisoned and continue to poison the wellsprings of Russian nationhood, which lie in the village and in the Orthodox faith. Collectivization has all but killed the peasants' love for the land and driven them into the city, where they disintegrate into an amorphous mass. The persecution of the Church has robbed Russians of the main source of their spiritual and moral strength. Thus demoralized, the Russian people drown their sorrows in vodka and destroy their offspring with abortions. The depredations have reached a point where for the first time in their history, Russians face the possibility of becoming extinct as a nation.

**4.** Russia must recover its "roots." It is not exactly clear what this injunction means. It seems to call for an end to forced industrialization, collective farms, militarism and support of political movements far away from home, with the attendant restitution to its rightful place of agriculture as the basis of the national economy. The political future of the country is not, as a rule, addressed, except in the vaguest of terms, suggestive of firm state authority that does not interfere with the life of the people. Sometimes writers of this tendency hint at the restoration of the monarchy; and, indeed, their whole ideology impels the nationalists in this direction, but they prefer not to spell this out. The return to religion is a *sine qua non*, however.

**5.** In its most extreme manifestations, which are increasingly tolerated and even encouraged by the authorities, the right-wing opposition comes disturbingly close to the ideology of National Socialism, or, more precisely, National-Bolshevism, which views Russians as a sort of master race and the Jews as the archenemy.[16] It is not uncommon for publications that speak for this tendency to echo the most obscurantist ideas of pre-Revolutionary monarchists. Thus *Our Contemporary* recently carried an article which applauded the notion, formulated by Dostoevsky a century ago, that while Russians may, indeed, be behind Western peoples in economic and scientific achievement they are "best capable, of all the peoples, of accommodating the idea of universal human unity."[17] Apart from inculcating in Russians a sense of superiority over other nations, this view provides a rationale for their moral right to lord it over the world. Spokesmen for this school of thought see "international Jewry," commonly referred to by the code name "Zionists," as engaged in an international conspiracy to dominate mankind. One of the more bizarre manifestations of such thinking has been the publication recently, with the approval of the censor, of a book by the Soviet Union's official anti-Semite, one Lev Korneev, *The Class Essence of Zionism*. The author of this scurrilous tract adopts the main thesis of the so-called *Protocols of the Elders of Zion*, a fabrication of the tsarist police, that Jews are conspiring to take over the world. He further accuses Jews of professing "double loyalty" and forming a fifth column in every country where they live. He makes them responsible for anti-Semitism and claims that they had helped Hitler to come to power and to organize the Holocaust.[18] The generally accepted figure of six million Jewish victims of Nazi persecution is questioned by these sources, just as it is by the neo-Nazis in Germany. Such anti-Semitism is ladled out generously to Soviet schoolchildren as well as to the personnel of the Red Army for the purpose of stiffening their ideological resolve. One observer from the Soviet Union remarks that Soviet anti-Semitic propaganda "sometimes appears as a deliberate spread of a political psychosis, a pre-war escalation of hatred, an ideological preliminary artillery barrage. It literally recalls the phraseology of the Third Reich before the beginning of the military expansion of the German fatherland."[19]

The philosophy of restoration—a return to the mythical Russia of happy peasants and pealing church bells—can hardly withstand scholarly criticism. After all, if things had been so good under tsarism, why the Revolution? And even if one concedes, for the sake of argument, that the Revolution was an act of foreign intervention, if the regime it has brought to power is really so alien to the Russian spirit, why has it been able to stay in power for so long? Why has there been no attempt made in Russia since Lenin, as there has been in virtually every Soviet-ruled country, under Soviet occupation, to overthrow it? These questions are not answered or even addressed. Just as the inspiration of nationalist dissent is largely emotional, so is its appeal, and these qualities make it impervious to argument. It exploits the xenophobia widespread among semieducated Russians, who want someone other than themselves to blame for their plight. The nationalist ideology exonerates them of any responsibility with the reassuring message that the culprit is the foreigner, whether labeled generically "the West" or, more pointedly, "international Jewry." To the country's young, who no longer believe in anything except getting the most out of life for themselves, it proffers a religion of national pride to compensate for their sense of inferiority and mood of indifference.

The other source of strength of the nationalist movement lies in the support that it receives from the *nomenklatura*. Obviously, the *nomenklatura* cannot let itself be declared antinational, and where it exercises control, such charges are forbidden. Nor can it tolerate criticism of its economic system and priorities; criticism of this kind, therefore, is also prohibited. It also feels uneasy when the Russian people are too explicitly identified as a "master race," for, although many members of the *nomenklatura* probably believe this proposition to be true, they realize that their rule over a multinational empire and their global ambitions require Communism to appear scrupulously internationalist. Whenever the loyal opposition on the right goes a bit too far, it is reprimanded on the pages of *Kommunist* or *Pravda*.*

But these drawbacks pale by comparison with the benefits that the *nomenklatura* derives from its tacit alliance with the nationalist opposition. In the first place, by appealing to their chauvinism, this compact allows it to rally to its side the Russian people, the most important ethnic group in the country. More important still, it enables the *nomenklatura* to present a broad national front against the ideals of democracy, law and human rights as "un-Russian." For the *nomenklatura*, the appeal to nationalism—national pride, national traditions, national continuity—has in recent years become an indispensable weapon in the struggle against Western influences as expressed in demands for freedom, rights and consumer goods. The *nomenklatura* also relishes the apoliticism of the right, its predilection for "inner" or "spiritual" freedom, since freedom of this kind costs it nothing. The regime feeds the utopian conservatism of the nationalists by allocating them funds for the restoration of old churches and monasteries, printing the collected works of Dostoevsky, and turning over to their indoctrination the youth of the country with which it no longer has a common language. And then it draws on their anti-intellectualism and anti-Westernism to help keep at bay the democratic opposition, whose victory would spell the *nomenklatura*'s doom.

A variant of the nationalist opposition is represented by the ideas of Alexander Solzhenitsyn, the titular leader of its émigré branch, and the most influential figure of the entire movement. Solzhenitsyn has never collaborated with the Soviet regime nor has he belonged to the loyal opposition. Rather, he has declared war on this regime, dedicating his belletristic and publicistic writings to the exposure of Communism and its barbarities. Even so, the thrust of his thought comes very close to the central beliefs of the nationalist movement inside the Soviet Union. Solzhenitsyn also believes in the historical uniqueness of Russia and regards the

---

* There exists also a small nationalist underground, which operates outside government controls; its more extremist spokesmen are occasionally arrested and confined to prison camps, and even psychiatric wards.

1917 Revolution as a denial of the country's spirit and traditions. He, too, blames the West for Russia's tragedy. He wants the policy of state-imposed industrialization to be given up so that the country can recover its rural roots. He opposes militarism and imperialism, preferring that Russia concentrate its energies and resources on healing the wounds that decades of alleged foreign-induced turmoil have inflicted upon it.

His attitude toward the critical issues of political freedom and human rights is contradictory in the extreme. He seems to believe that liberalism regards freedom as an end in itself rather than as a means to an end and, of course, has no difficulty in demolishing this straw man. "Can external freedom for its own sake be the goal of conscious living beings?" he asks, and replies:

> We are creatures born with inner freedom of will, freedom of choice—the most important part of freedom is a gift to us at birth. External, or social, freedom is very desirable for the sake of undistorted growth, but it is no more than a condition, a medium, and to regard it as the object of our existence is nonsense. *We can firmly assert our inner freedom even in external conditions of unfreedom.*[20]

Similarly with human rights. He denounces Soviet violations of these rights in most compelling fashion in his *Gulag Archipelago*, and yet elsewhere says:

> You cannot reduce all your philosophy and all your activities to: Give us rights! In other words: Free our tied hands! Suppose they did, or we tore loose—what then? Here the democratic movement shows its ignorance of modern Russian history. . . . Following the general theory of liberalism, they simply want to repeat the February Revolution—and that means ruin.[21]

In effect, Solzhenitsyn is saying that the Russian people are either constitutionally unsuited for a regime of liberties and rights or not yet ready for it. Fearing anarchy, he seems prepared to have the Communist Party stay in power, provided that it subjects itself to some unspecified form of control by the soviets and observes legal norms. His entire political philosophy echoes the ideas of old-regime conservatives; he takes no account of what has occurred since 1917 or what lessons the Soviet experience has taught. His outlook is profoundly illiberal and in its fundamentals indistinguishable from that of the most reactionary Russian thinkers of the late nineteenth century, individuals whose refusal to countenance gradual reforms had greatly contributed to the revolutionary events that Solzhenitsyn so deplores.

Although Solzhenitsyn never tires of exhorting the West to stand up to the Soviet Union, he also delivers himself of opinions that parallel Soviet anti-Western propaganda—as, for instance, when he charges Washington with planning a genocidal nuclear war against the Russian people or exhorts the Japanese not to rely for their security on the "powerless" United States.

These contradictions in Solzhenitsyn's thinking—due in part to a highly emotional approach and in part to ignorance of history and political theory—have not been spared from criticism by the democrats. Sakharov, in particular, has pointed out the many flaws and dangers inherent in Solzhenitsyn's ideas. He argues that Solzhenitsyn overestimates the role of ideology in Communist regimes and underestimates the historic continuity between pre- and post-revolutionary Russia as well as the sheer lust for power of Communist rulers. He questions the dichotomy, Russia–West, which is as central to Solzhenitsyn's thinking as it is to that of the rest of the nationalist opposition. Referring to Solzhenitsyn's political manifesto of 1974, his "Open Letter" to the Soviet leaders, Sakharov writes:

> The very division of ideas into Western and Russian is altogether incomprehensible to me. In my view, the scientific, rational approach to social and natural phenomena knows only the division of ideas and concepts into correct ones and fallacious ones. And where is this healthy Russian pattern of development? . . . The servile, slavish spirit which had existed in Russia for centuries, combined with contempt for people of other countries, other races, and other beliefs, was, in my opinion, the greatest of our misfortunes, not [the source of] our national health. Only under democratic conditions is it possible to develop a national character capable of rational existence in a world that is becoming increasingly complex.

Sakharov expresses admiration for Solzhenitsyn's courage and literary talent, but he says of his philosophy of "religious-patriarchal romanticism," that it is as indefensible on intellectual grounds as it is politically harmful:

> Solzhenitsyn addresses the leaders of the country not only rhetorically but also in a practical manner, hoping to obtain from them at least partial understanding. It is difficult to argue with such a desire. But do his propositions contain anything that the country's leaders will find new and, at the same time, acceptable? Great Russian nationalism, enthusiasm for the conquest of virgin soil—all this they have used and continue to use. The appeal to patriotism: this is already something quite out of the arsenal of official propaganda. One unwillingly com-

pares it to the military-patriotic education and struggle against "obei-
sance" [to the West] of the recent past. During the war and until his
very death, Stalin generously tolerated a submissive Orthodox Christianity. All such parallels with the propositions of Solzhenitsyn are not
only striking—they should serve as a warning.

It may be objected that Solzhenitsyn's nationalism is not aggressive,
that it has a gentle, defensive quality, that its objective is to save and
resuscitate one of the countries that has undergone the greatest suffering. History teaches, however, that "ideologues" have always been
gentler than the practical politicians who followed them. A considerable part of the Russian people and a part of the country's leadership
is in the grip of Great Russian nationalism which combines with the
fear of dependence on the West and the fear of democratic reforms.
Solzhenitsyn's fallacies, falling on such a favorable soil, may prove
dangerous.[22]

Because its ideology is so diffuse, emotional rather than
grounded in rational argument, it is difficult to say what influence
the nationalist opposition exerts on the Soviet regime. On balance,
its main effect seems to be to drive it toward conservatism, that is,
away from Westernism and reform, in the direction of chauvinism,
anti-Semitism and a National-Bolshevism that in its more extreme
manifestations differs little from Nazism. Since the *nomenklatura,*
for reasons stated, needs the support of the right, and since it
desperately fears being outflanked from that direction, it responds
to the goading of the nationalists by making itself appear more
Russian, more traditionalist, more immobile than its more perceptive members might perhaps desire. Solzhenitsyn and his friends
abroad, like the writers for *Young Guard* and *Our Contemporary*
inside the country, compete with the Soviet establishment for the
same constituency and therefore, by the force of circumstances,
find themselves traveling the same road even while bespattering
each other with mud.

The achievement of intellectual dissent in the Soviet Union cannot be measured by Western standards. Judged in terms of its
impact on the structure of the regime and its policies, it would
have to be pronounced a failure, since it has altered neither. But it
is not, in fact, a failure because its accomplishments lie elsewhere,
in realms peculiar to totalitarian regimes.

The dissenters of the democratic and nationalist persuasion alike
have, first of all, shattered the uniformity of public behavior which
the authorities demand. In the words of the late Andrei Amalrik,
"the dissidents [have] accomplished something that was simple to
the point of genius: in an unfree country, they behaved like free
men, thereby changing the moral atmosphere and the nation's

governing traditions."[23] This breach of accepted norms has helped to dispel something to which the Soviet regime since the early 1930's has always attached immense importance, namely, complete external conformity of its subjects. And even if the democratic dissenters have so far failed to change the system and its conduct, they have indicated what it is that requires change and, in so doing, set an agenda for the future.

No less important has been the dissidents' challenge of the regime's monopoly on the language of public discourse. By speaking the truth as they see it, they have deeply influenced society's way of looking on life, a way that for decades has been shaped by the officialdom. Just as the private initiative of ordinary people, with its "second economy," has broken the state's hold on the production and distribution of goods, so the courage of its intellectuals has given Russia a "second reality." This restoration to language of its proper function as a means of communication instead of domination is an act of revolutionary significance. In the words of Alain Besançon:

> The Communist regime was, in effect, inaugurated by the public (state's) appropriation of the means not of production but of communication. Well before the factories and fields were seized, it had been the newspapers, the printing establishments, the media . . . Much more directly fatal than the restoration of the market is the restoration of the human word, the privatization of the organs of speech, individual ownership of the throat . . . The writer breaks the compact of lies on which the entire equilibrium of ideological power rests. He gives words their meaning. He redresses the ideological inversion of language. He restores reality in its capacity as the unique reality and vaporizes surreality.[24]

Once the spell has been broken, the regime may never again be able to reassert its control over human perceptions and means of communication, a control that in some respects constitutes the irreducible essence of Communist power.

## 3 IMPERIAL PROBLEMS

The Soviet Union is the world's last empire. It has not only refused to grant its colonies independence, as all the other imperial powers have done, but as if to demonstrate how much out of step it is with the rest of humanity, it has been seizing every opportunity to expand its colonial domain. In the process, it is learning why the other powers have found it expedient to pull out of their colonies: that in modern times the spread of nationalism turns the once docile colonial subjects into rebels and that an industrial metropolis not only derives no economic profit from its colonies but ends up paying them heavy subsidies.

The Soviet Empire is a complex structure composed of three principal kinds of possession:

**1.** Territories inhabited by non-Russians which had been conquered by the tsarist regime (with some subsequent "rounding-out"); these constitute integral parts of the Union of Soviet Socialist Republics and are considered Russian patrimony.

**2.** Countries outside the USSR but under occupation by the Soviet Army; although they enjoy some internal autonomy, they are ultimately accountable to Moscow and in matters of foreign and military policy cannot deviate from its directives at all; they are subject to the so-called "Brezhnev Doctrine."

**3.** Countries and Communist parties abroad that are nominally sovereign but are able to survive only with Soviet political, economic or military assistance; at this point they are still regarded as expendable.

## A. THE SOVIET UNION AND ITS NATIONALITIES

Due to its unique Eurasian location, Russia has an ancient tradition of imperialism which differs from the Western one not only in respect to its persistence and reliance on military means. In the history of empires, as a rule, the imperial metropolis is separated from its colonial possessions chronologically as well as geographically. The great empires of antiquity, Persia and Rome, and those of the modern West alike, came into existence after their respective imperial powers had constructed strong national states; empire-building represented, as it were, an outflow of national energies that would no longer be confined within the existing boundaries. Furthermore, in the case of Europe, which is not a true continent but an appendage of Asia with no opportunity to expand on land, colonies were in all cases acquired far from home, across seas and oceans.

Russia's imperial development followed a different course. The Russian national state emerged in the midst of a boundless plain which had no natural barriers and was surrounded on all sides by peoples of different races and religions. This geographic peculiarity explains why in the case of Russia the processes of state building and empire building merged to the point of becoming virtually indistinguishable. Once Ivan the Terrible had destroyed the Tatar kingdoms on the Volga, in the middle of the sixteenth century, there was nothing to stop the Russians from conquering and colonizing the immense territories of Siberia and Inner Asia. The fact that the Russian people built their empire at the same time that they were laying the foundations of their national state and, in addition, that their colonies were contiguous to the national state rather than separated from it by bodies of water, has had the consequence of confusing in the mind of most Russians their sense of nationhood with their status as an imperial power. They seem unaware that they have built an empire and, therefore, find it difficult even to contemplate giving freedom to their non-Russian subjects, because doing so would strike at the very basis of their national identity. The tenacity with which the Soviet Union holds on to every inch of conquered territory, no matter what its usefulness, and the popularity which imperial expansion enjoys among the Russian people, certainly have much to do with the unusually close links that history and geography have forged between the Russian nation and its empire.

The pre-Revolutionary Russian Empire was of a traditional European type: while conceding its subject peoples little self-rule it also refrained from interfering with their cultural and economic activities. The Imperial civil service was open only to Christians, with the higher posts virtually monopolized by Russians and Russified minorities. From time to time, the tsarist government experimented with Russification, but on the whole it left its subjects alone, as long as they did not question its authority or challenge the primacy of Russians and their Church. Apart from the Poles and the Finns, who demanded independence, the non-Russian citizens did not cause the imperial government much trouble.

Lenin realized earlier than his socialist rivals the political potential of minority nationalism. As a Marxist, he considered nationalism a regressive movement. Marxists viewed nationalism as a tool which the bourgeoisie used to divert workers from the class struggle; they also had a marked preference for large states as economically more efficient than small ones. These ideas Lenin shared. At the same time, he wished to benefit from the support of the ethnic minorities of the Russian Empire in the event that, like the other national minorities in Europe, they would come to demand national rights.* To this end, he developed his own rather idosyncratic, theory of "national self-determination," which offered the

---

* Strictly speaking, in pre-Revolutionary Russia the Russians themselves were a minority: in the 1897 census they constituted only 44.3 percent of the population.

non-Russian subjects of his country the theoretical right to independent statehood. Lenin's generosity was due to his knowledge that few of them in fact desired independence and his conviction that capitalism, as it matured in Russia, would forge such strong economic ties among the various parts of the empire that the minorities could not separate themselves even if they wanted to do so. To those nationalities that did not wish to avail themselves of the right to separation—and he expected this category to include virtually all of them—Lenin offered only assimilation with the Russians; they were to have neither federal status nor autonomy. By offering them more than they wanted on a take-it-or-leave-it basis, he denied them realistic alternatives that lay somewhere between assimilation and separatism.

It was a clever ploy, but it failed to work. Contrary to Lenin's expectations, most of the ethnic minorities took advantage of the Revolution to demand statehood as a means of avoiding the turmoil that was sweeping Russia and escaping Bolshevik rule. Faced with these realities, Lenin made short shrift of the "right to national self-determination." Declaring "proletarian" (i.e., Bolshevik) self-determination to supersede all the others, he dispatched troops to reconquer one separated borderland area after another. Only the Western regions, inhabited by Poles, Finns and the three Baltic nationalities, eluded this fate for a while, because of the support given them by France and England. The others were incorporated into the Communist state which was cleansed of identification with Russia and Russians by being assigned an ethnically neutral name, "Soviet Union." To give them compensation for the incorporation Lenin offered the ethnic minorities a semblance of territorial and cultural autonomy. The Union was formally transformed into a "federation." Each major and many of the minor ethnic groups were formed into "Soviet" or "autonomous" republics, in the capitals of which hand-picked natives ensconced themselves in offices outfitted with all the appurtenances of statehood, including national emblems, stationery and rubber stamps. Their power was exceedingly limited by virtue of the fact that under the Communist constitution the state apparatus is entirely subordinated to the Party and must carry out its instructions. For its part, the Communist Party of the Soviet Union was never federalized along national lines; it has been all along a unitary organization for the entire country and all its ethnic branches, without distinction, centered in Moscow under a Russian and Russified leadership. It was an ingenious arrangement from the public-relations point of view; it impressed ignorant foreigners as a brilliant solution of the "colonial" and "national" questions, a model for the rest of the world, whereas in reality it represented a novel and uniquely oppressive form of imperial domination.

The Soviet authorities have been hoping, ever since, that some day, somehow, the "national question" will disappear from their country and the minorities will dissolve to form a new "Soviet" nation, on the model of the American. Soviet publications carry numerous articles on the need for the diverse ethnic groups of the Union to "draw together" as the first step to "merging" or "fusing," without spelling out how or when this is to occur. Their implicit analogy with the United States, however, cannot stand up to analysis. The population of the United States consists overwhelmingly of people and descendants of people who had voluntarily severed ties with their native countries and emigrated to America expecting to become members of a new nation. The ethnic minorities of the Soviet Union, by contrast, are composed of cohesive national groups, in most cases conquered and kept under Russian rule by force. They inhabit their ancestral lands, speak their own languages, and maintain their own traditions, often more ancient than those of Russia. There is no conceivable manner in which the United States could be partitioned along ethnic lines; doing so would be a comparatively easy exercise in the case of the Soviet Union, which already formally constitutes a federal union of republics formed on the ethnic principle.

There is no evidence of ethnic assimilation occurring in the Soviet Union. True, Russian has become the accepted language of communication among the educated, but it is nowhere displacing local languages and dialects in daily use. Census returns indicate no diminution of attachment on the part of the major groups to their native tongues, even among those individuals for whom Russian had become a second language. As the experience of the British in India and of the French in Algeria and Vietnam has demonstrated, bilingualism does not lead to assimilation. Quite the contrary: in these colonies, it was precisely the class of Western-educated and bilingual natives that led the struggle for independence.

Following the practice of imperial powers, the Soviet leadership applies the divide-and-rule principle to its nationalities by deliberately exaggerating their ethnic diversity. Officially, the USSR has over one hundred ethnic groups. Interesting as this figure may be to the ethnographer, it is without political significance. From the latter point of view, the Soviet Union counts only eight or ten ethnic groups that matter. They are, ranked by size, the Ukrainians and the Belorussians, the Turkic Muslims, the two Christian groups inhabiting the Caucasus (Georgians and Armenians), and the three Baltic nations (Lithuania, Latvia and Estonia). These eight ethnic groups make up 83 percent of the non-Russian population of the USSR.

The Ukrainians and Belorussians are Slavs of the Orthodox faith, related to the Russians by ethnic background and language but heirs to a different cultural tradition. Both these nationalities have lived for several hundred years under Polish rule, in the course of which they came under the influence of the Catholic church and Western law. Communal land ownership prevalent in Russia was almost unknown here. It is common for Ukrainians and Belorussians to intermarry with Russians, and they have no difficulty assimilating into the Russian community. Nevertheless, there is strong evidence of persistent nationalism among them, especially among the Ukrainians. With fifty million people, 86 percent of them (as of 1970) Ukrainian-speaking, the Ukraine is potentially a major European state. Its separation would not only deprive Russia of an important source of food and industrial products, but also cut it off from the Black Sea and the Balkans, for which reasons the *nomenklatura* persecutes all manifestations of Ukrainian nationalism with especial savagery.

The over forty million Muslims inhabiting the Soviet Union's southeastern and eastern regions are for the major part Sunnis speaking local dialects of Turkish; only two major groups—the Azeris in Transcaucasia and the Iranian Tajiks in Central Asia—belong to the Shiite sect. In the 1920s, worried about the spread of Panislamic and Panturkic movements, the Soviet government broke up its Muslim population into artificial nationalities to each of which it gave a separate "republic." Since that time, everything possible has been done to magnify and perpetuate differences among them. They were also forced to adopt modified forms of the Cyrillic (Russian) alphabet in place of the Arabic and Latin scripts as a device for cutting them off from their national heritage and from contact with Muslim communities outside the USSR. These assimilatory pressures appear to have borne little fruit, and the available evidence indicates continuing attachment of these peoples to their native religion and customs. Soviet Muslims, however, do not seem to feel much affinity for Muslims in neighboring Afghanistan, Iran and Turkey, looking upon these peoples as primitive Orientals whereas they like to think of themselves as Europeans. Though they cannot avoid mingling with Slavs in school and at work, in their private lives Soviet Muslims prefer to keep to themselves: intermarriage and social contacts with Slavs are rare. The Muslims do not display their feelings and give the impression of docility, but their resentment runs deep, accentuated as it is by unbridgeable cultural differences from the Slavs settled in their midst.

The Georgians and Armenians are Christians who had of their own will come under Russian rule two centuries ago in order to escape persecution by Turks and Persians. The Turks continue to be the main enemy of the Armenians; and inasmuch as the Soviet government normally pursues a policy unfriendly to Turkey, they do not present it with much of a problem. The Georgians are a different matter entirely. Their dislike of Russian domination goes so far that not a few of them glorify the Georgian Stalin for having lorded it over the Russians. They are probably the most openly nationalistic group in the Union.

The Baltic Republics had formed part of the Russian Empire from the eighteenth century to the Revolution; independent during the interwar period, they were reabsorbed by the Soviet Union in 1939–49 by virtue of Stalin's treaty with Hitler. They have suffered heavily under Communist rule due to massive deportations and the subsequent influx of Russian settlers. Russians like to move into this area, especially Latvia and Estonia, because of its higher living standards. Their share in the population of the two republics has been steadily rising; in the cities, they now constitute between one third and one half of the inhabitants.

Minority nationalism does not present an immediate security problem to the Soviet government. Reliable Russians, sandwiched in at all levels of the Party and state apparatus, closely supervise native officials to make certain that they engage in no anti-Russian activities; the security organs are ever alert to manifestations of local "chauvinism"; and the overwhelmingly Slavic KGB and border units are well placed to stifle any unrest. But no one should have any illusions about long-term prospects. Unless history is to make a unique exception for the Russian Empire, leaving it intact while all other European empires have fallen apart, its future cannot be bright. It is impossible to justify to the Ukrainians that Ireland, with three million inhabitants, should be a sovereign country, whereas they, with 50 million, have been condemned to remain forever a Soviet dependency, or to persuade the Muslim "republic" of Uzbekistan, with its fifteen million people, that it is never to enjoy international status while the Seychelles, with a mere 70,000, do.

At present, ethnic conflicts in the USSR assume the form of battles of wits. The republican ministries try to outsmart Moscow in the allocation of resources and the setting of school curricula. There is competition over jobs and living quarters, each ethnic group giving preference to its own. These, however, are only surface manifestations; underneath the skirmishing, there smolders resentment and, in some areas, hatred that can quickly explode into genocidal fury should the heavy hand of Russian authority weaken. The Russians like to run away from the harsh conditions in their homeland to the more favored borderlands: the Russian regimes usually show population deficits because of low birthrates and internal emigration. But the Russian migrants who settle in the borderlands live there, as the French had once lived in Algeria, at the sufferance of time.

Even those Russians who are not troubled by the prospect of a future breakup of their empire have cause to worry about demographic trends which are unmistakably adverse to them and the other Slavic groups. Because Soviet Slavs do not reproduce themselves adequately, in the coming decades the Russians will have difficulty in maintaining the kind of ethnic preponderance that they have always taken for granted. In the labor force and in the armed forces, their share is declining and will continue to decline, as the following statistics indicate:

_____ TABLE 5_____
### THE ETHNIC COMPOSITION OF 18-YEAR-OLDS IN THE SOVIET UNION.

| Year | Russian | Other Slavic | Muslim | Other |
|------|---------|--------------|--------|-------|
| 1970 | 56% | 18% | 10% | 16% |
| 1980 | 48% | 19% | 13% | 20% |
| 1990 | 43% | 18% | 20% | 19% |

The preponderance of non-Russian youths in this table is not fully reflected in the population as a whole. Even so, by the year 2000, the overall proportion of Russians in the country's population is expected to drop to 46–48 percent; in 1926 it was 53 percent. This trend will cause the Soviet government all kinds of problems: for example, Moscow will find it increasingly difficult to maintain its preferred ratio of 90 percent Slavs in the officer corps.

To reverse these trends, the government has resorted to inducements, such as offering special maternity bonuses to women in the Russian Republic. The results have been meager, and the prospect of ethnic contraction remains, producing among some Russian nationalists a mood of despair. The situation that Russians face in this respect resembles that of the German-speaking peoples of Austria-Hungary a century ago, when ethnic minorities, mainly

Slavs and Jews, whose natural growth was much higher, threatened the hegemony of Germans in Austria. This atmosphere of ethnic crisis contributed significantly to the spread among Austrian Germans of racial theories and the rise of Nazism.

## B. THE COLONIES

The second category of Soviet imperial possessions consists of areas that do not form part of the USSR but are under Soviet occupation of one form or another. They are five countries in Eastern Europe (Poland, East Germany, Czechoslovakia, Hungary and Bulgaria) and Mongolia in the Far East.

The situation in Eastern Europe is sufficiently familiar to make a detailed description superfluous. Few disinterested observers would deny that Soviet domination of this region rests mainly on the military power represented by thirty-two Soviet army divisions. The only other source of support for the *status quo* comes from the local *nomenklaturas* and officials of lower rank, whose loyalty to the Soviet Union derives from the knowledge that if the Communist regimes were to fall they would be out of work. The one exception is Bulgaria, which has no Soviet army contingent on its territory. Having gained its independence in the nineteenth century from the Turks with the help of the tsarist army, its leadership is so overcome with gratitude to Russia that its toadying seems voluntary and apparently sincere.

The history of Eastern Europe since the death of Stalin is one of steady erosion of Soviet power. Yugoslavia, whose powerful partisan force had saved it from occupation by the Red Army, emancipated itself from Soviet control while Stalin was still alive. Rumania, a member of the Warsaw Pact, refuses to allow forces of the Pact on its soil, out of fear that once there they will refuse to leave. Although it maintains an exceptionally odious regime, in some respects more oppressive than those of its neighbors, it is not a colony but an independent state. Even after the imposition of military rule in 1981, Moscow's hold on Poland remains insecure. Its nervousness about that country is demonstrated by the decision to run the gas pipeline from Siberia to Western Europe by way of Czechoslovakia instead of across Poland, which provides the most direct route.

For a long time, control of Eastern Europe had been profitable to the Soviet Union, because it was able systematically to loot its colonies by forcing them to supply it with raw materials and manufactured goods at less than world prices. Although such matters are difficult to quantify, the situation now seems to have taken a different turn and the occupation of Eastern Europe costs more than it brings. The greatest single expense is the supply of energy that otherwise could be disposed of for hard currency. The USSR sells Eastern Europe tens of millions of tons of petroleum and gas at the equivalent of one half of the world market price; it is estimated that the oil exported by Moscow to Eastern Europe in the form of cheap oil each year would earn it $18 billion in hard currency.[25] Yet there is no escape from this predicament, because if Soviet clients were to purchase energy on the open market they would have to pay for it in hard currency, which they could only earn from trading with hard-currency countries; this, in turn, would require them to reorient much of their business from the USSR to the West.*

Given its global ambitions, the Soviet Union, however, has no choice but to hold on to this area, regardless of the costs, because it is irreplaceable as a forward base for military operations against the West in time of war and the political intimidation of the West in time of peace.

The ideal way out of the difficulty would be for the "People's Republics" to be incorporated into the USSR. This solution would enable the Soviet *nomenklatura* to take direct charge of affairs in these countries, to draft their citizens into the Red Army, to draw on their labor force, and to end once and for all the danger that some day these countries may secede. In 1920, as Soviet troops were advancing on Warsaw, Stalin proposed to Lenin in regard to Poland and other European countries, about to become Sovietized, a "confederational" tie with Soviet Russia.[26] More recently, in the middle 1960s, Soviet leaders threatened the Czechs with outright incorporation. But it is doubtful that this extreme step will ever be taken. For one, Moscow can hardly wish to see the proportion of Russians in the Soviet Union diluted further by the addition of nearly 90 million East Europeans; should this happen, the Russian component in the population of the USSR would shrink at once

---

* A recent analysis by the Rand Corporation concludes that the costs to the Soviet Union of controlling areas which are here defined as colonies and dependencies has risen, in constant 1981 U.S. dollars, from about $18 billion in 1971 to $41 billion in 1980. In terms of the share of the Soviet GNP, as computed in rubles, this would represent an increase from 1.8 percent to 6.6 percent. The results of this study, directed by Mr. Charles Wolf, Jr., are summarized in *The Wall Street Journal* of January 30, 1984. Included in the calculations were expenses for trade subsidies, export credits, military and economic aid, operations in Afghanistan, and subversive activities in the Third World.

from the current 52 to 40 percent. Secondly, the nationalism and the Western orientation of the peoples of Eastern Europe would inject a destabilizing element into Soviet domestic politics and substantially strengthen the democratic opposition. Taking such factors into consideration, Moscow prefers to rule Eastern Europe indirectly, relying on the self-interest of the local elites to keep the area in the fold, while watching closely for signs of sedition or defection through the native armed forces and security organs, which are integrated with and subordinated to their Soviet counterparts. Should all fail, the Soviet occupation forces are well positioned to crush resistance. Experience shows that the countries of Western Europe acknowledge Eastern Europe as a Soviet sphere of influence and do not act whenever Moscow resorts to violence there. The United States, which has never reconciled itself to Soviet violations of the Yalta accords, responds differently, but it cannot do much without the support of its allies.

## C. THE DEPENDENCIES

The colonial possessions of the USSR are covered by the Brezhnev Doctrine—that is to say, their status is regarded by Moscow as irreversible. Whenever appropriate, Soviet and East European spokesmen emphasize that attempts to detach any of these areas from the Bloc or to alter its system of government will be met with force. This principle does not apply to those Third World countries which fall into the category of Soviet dependencies. Their status is ambivalent: they are protected by the Soviet Union, but they do not, as yet, form part either of Russian patrimony or of the Communist community and hence do not qualify for ironclad Soviet military guarantees. Even Cuba, which for all practical purposes is a member of the Soviet Bloc, has so far failed in its attempts to secure from Moscow unconditional pledges of support against foreign attack. The Soviet position on this issue is frankly stated:

> The path of non-capitalist development has been taken not only by countries which adjoin socialist states, but also by those which are many thousands of kilometers away. . . . Their considerable remoteness makes it difficult for socialist countries to render them military assistance in the event of imperialist aggression. Consequently, these countries must also be able themselves to defend their sovereignty. . . .[27]

As previously noted, it is an essential ingredient of Soviet Grand Strategy to isolate "imperialist" countries from the sources of raw materials and markets in the Third World and, at the same time, to assist the latter's passage to Communism. To this end, Soviet theoreticians have called for the creation in the Third World of regimes of a transitional type, defined either as "National Democratic" or (since the early 1970s) as "socialist-oriented." Regimes of this type are to sever relations with "capitalist" economies, nationalize their productive resources, and legitimize Communist parties. In the early 1960s, when they had developed this strategy, Soviet theoreticians believed that they had discovered a practical way of ensuring the transition of the Third World to a Soviet-type political and economic order and its eventual integration into the Communist Bloc.

This strategy, however, has proven a failure, as none of its expectations has been realized. Although it has not as yet been formally abandoned, recent Soviet actions suggest that in practice it is giving way to less theoretical, long-range, and more conventional forms of intervention.

The principal reason for the strategy's disappointing results has been economic—namely, the inability of the Soviet Union to provide those Third World countries ready to follow its advice with the assistance that they require. Unless they dispose of marketable commodities, these countries rely on aid from Western governments, banks and international financial institutions. Those that have something to sell depend heavily on trade with the West. When Moscow urges them to sever ties with the West, it implicitly assumes the obligation to compensate them for the resultant losses in credits, loans and income from commerce. This obligation the Soviet economy is unable to meet. It cannot come close to matching the capital for investments or outright grants that the West provides as a matter of course.

According to recent estimates, the total aid extended by the USSR to underdeveloped countries between 1976 and 1980 amounted to $8 billion, which is approximately what the United States alone gives to them in grants and credits in a single year. The combined assistance to the Third World by Eastern Europe is estimated to be less than that extended to them by Belgium.[28] The disparity between the capabilities of West and East is greater still in the field of trade. The Communist Bloc is unable to absorb a significant share of the exports of these countries, which consist mainly of raw materials. Thus, prepared as some of the Third World leaders might be to follow the Soviet blueprint, economic realities compel them to preserve and even expand economic ties with the "imperialist camp." This fact is acknowledged by some Soviet strategists:

The socialist countries lack as yet the ability fully to satisfy the needs of all the young countries for capital, credit, and technical assistance. In the total sum of foreign assistance extended to countries of a socialist orientation, credits and subsidies from the capitalist states still constitute between 20 and 70 percent. The situation is rather similar in the field of foreign trade . . . This circumstance makes it increasingly urgent for the countries of socialist orientation to be economically viable.[29]

There could be no clearer acknowledgment of the restraints that the weakness of its economy exerts on the Soviet Union's imperial ambitions.

The Soviet Union not only cannot replace the West as the principal source of aid and an export market for the Third World, it also cannot rescue its friends from the disasters that follow expropriations of capital and other socialist measures. It is an invariable consequence of the economic program which the USSR urges on the Third World that capital flees, and the middle class gives way to a parasitic bureaucracy. Productivity in all fields except paperwork declines, whereupon the Soviet Union is asked to step in and help. Most of the time it neither can nor wants to waste its resources on such a hopeless cause. Recently, authoritative Soviet journals have been cautioning Third World countries not to rush ahead with programs of forced industrialization, on the grounds that it "lowers the already very low living standard of the population, [and] undermines the political stability of society as well as faith in the advantages of the socialist orientation." They are further reminded not to ignore the limits on the ability of the Communist Bloc to render them assistance.[30]

Moscow not long ago demonstrated rather brutally that there are limits on its willingness to assist Third World countries out of the difficulties that they bring upon themselves by following the Soviet program, when it rejected Mozambique's application for membership in the Communist Bloc Economic Community. Mozambique is a member in good standing of the "socialist-oriented" camp, but it also happens to be terribly mismanaged as well as unable to cope with hostile guerrilla forces on its territory. This Soviet action, understandable as it may be, had the effect of pushing Mozambique toward a *rapprochement* with its archenemy South Africa, as well as with Portugal, its previous colonial master. Such a reaction certainly did not enter Moscow's plans.

As they survey the results of the strategy toward the Third World adopted twenty years ago and draw up a balance sheet of its accomplishments and failures, Soviet foreign-policy experts can have little cause to feel gratified. Although they like to boast that many millions of people in the Third World have joined the ranks of "socialist-oriented" nations, the political benefits that were expected from this process have failed to materialize. In most cases, Third World leaders, knowing where their self-interest lay, have refused to legitimize local Communist parties, and in some instances subjected them to savage repressions. Since the whole point of the Soviet strategy had been to create an environment in which the local Communists could begin their advance to power, the strategy may be said to have failed in its essential purpose.

No less disappointing was the tenuous hold that Moscow's friends had been able to establish on political power. Some of its staunchest supporters in the Third World, such as Sukarno in Indonesia, Nkrumah in Ghana and Allende in Chile, were toppled and replaced by hostile or at best neutral figures. The political situation in the Third World proved to be much more volatile and less amenable to manipulation from the outside than Soviet strategists and the Soviet politicians who followed their advice had believed.

These disappointments and frustrations have stimulated a fresh strategic debate in Soviet circles. One school of thought adheres to the old scheme, arguing that nothing short of the Third World's severance of ties with the West and socialization of their economies will be of any benefit to the Soviet Union. Another school, strongly represented in the social science institutes, advocates a policy of compromises. Aware that the USSR lacks the economic means required to carry out the orthodox program, they propose that for an indefinite period their allies in the Third World content themselves with seizing political power and crushing the political opposition. In the economic sphere, however, they should not rush into socialism and forced industrialization, exploiting instead for their own purposes such economic assistance as native and foreign capital is able and willing to provide. Some go so far as to argue that capitalism ought to be harnessed in the service of building "socialism" in the Third World. One advocate of this revisionist strategy is Serge Mikoyan, the son of Stalin's henchman and an expert on Latin America. He has been strongly urging the Nicaraguan Sandinistas to take advantage of the resources and enterprise of the domestic and foreign "bourgeoisie" to build up their economy.[31] Fidel Castro, who apparently has been initiated into this line, told a group of American journalists with a straight face that he now regretted having quarreled with the United States and had advised the Sandinistas not to repeat his mistake. The Sandinistas have manfully tried to pursue this schizophrenic policy, only to find that left-wing dictatorship and free enterprise do not mix. The result of the attempt has been a vacillating course at home and abroad.

As one surveys the history of Soviet involvement in the Third World since Stalin's death, the inescapable conclusion is that it has not fulfilled its expectations. Western powers have nowhere been expelled; they continue to invest in, loan to and buy from the Third World, making it as dependent on the West as ever. The hope of a gradual transition of the Third World countries from "feudalism" to "socialism" by a route that bypassed "capitalism" has proven chimerical, because it rested on an unrealistic estimate of both their internal situations and the Soviet Union's capability to provide them with economic assistance. It was one thing to help when all that the Third World countries needed was weapons and political backing in their struggle for independence; it is quite another to sustain them after they have gained independence and need the means to feed their growing populations, finance ambitious plans of industrialization, and cope with backwardness.

Apparently, this negative estimate is shared by influential Soviet figures, because in recent years Soviet Third World policy has undergone a noticeable shift away from the long-term effort to build up a commonwealth of semisocialist countries toward direct political and military intervention. The purpose of the latter is to secure for the USSR strategic outposts and bases in the Third World. Rather than back popular "bourgeois-nationalist" leaders of the type of Sukarno, Nasser or Nkrumah, the USSR now prefers to place in power creatures of its own making. These are minor politicians, wholly dependent on Moscow—men like Mengistu in Ethiopia, dos Santos in Angola, and Bishop in Grenada. They like to surround these vassals with Praetorian Guards, staffed mainly by KGB and East German personnel, whose job it is to protect them both from internal rivals and from themselves: if they have to show the slightest inclination to pursue a more even-handed policy between East and West, they are gunned down. This fate has befallen pro-Marxist rulers of Afghanistan and South Yemen, and suspicions exist that there were other victims as well. In carrying out this policy, Moscow presently favors minor countries of major strategic importance, because they cost less and are easier to control than more populous ones. A few years ago, had it wanted to, Moscow probably could have taken over Jamaica, then headed by a pro-Marxist leader, but it let go of it because Jamaica, overpopulated and desperately poor, would have required massive economic assistance. Instead, it picked up minuscule Grenada, which promised at small expense to provide it with valuable airfield and intelligence-gathering facilities. In the Middle East, the USSR has heavily committed itself in South Yemen, an important strategic outpost that controls access to and from the Red Sea. When in 1967 the British Labour Party, in a moment of financial stress, irresponsibly evacuated South Yemen, the Soviet Union took over, and today this small country is to all practical purposes a full-fledged Soviet colony.

The shift from a political to a military strategy in the Third World manifested itself most starkly in the invasion of Afghanistan. In the 1960s and 1970s, Moscow lavished foreign aid on Afghanistan and secured a sphere of influence there that the West acknowledged and respected. When, however, Moscow attempted to interfere actively in Afghan internal affairs with the aim of installing there a regime of a "socialist-oriented" type, it ran into headstrong opposition from the Muslim inhabitants. The fear that the pro-Soviet government might be overwhelmed caused the USSR to meddle ever more directly in internal Afghan politics. In the end, it murdered the incumbent, installed in his place a Soviet Quisling and dispatched an invasion force of over 100,000 men to back him up and destroy the guerrillas. This was an act of desperation, an admission that the strategy of establishing friendly regimes by means of indigenous forces had failed. What apparently was expected to be a campaign lasting three to six months is presently in its fifth year, with victory as elusive as on the day of the invasion. The difficulty of coping with the guerrilla movement has led the Soviet Army to resort increasingly to terror tactics against the civilian population; on occasion this behavior resembles that of the Nazis in occupied Europe. Such activities, needless to stress, have nothing whatever in common with the elaborate plans prepared by the Central Committee in the 1960s.

Moscow thus has had to scale down severely its ambitious designs for the Third World: the vision of a Soviet commonwealth spanning the globe has had to yield to a more modest program of securing bases for the military and engaging in direct armed intervention. In practice if not in words, Moscow has conceded defeat. The most apparent and painful result of this failure has been the erosion of Soviet influence throughout the Third World. Overseas colonial conquests have proven in the late twentieth century an expensive and futile endeavor.

## D. COMMUNIST PARTIES

When in 1919 he founded the Third, or Communist, International, Lenin intended its member parties to be entirely subservient to the

Communist Party of Soviet Russia. The size of membership was to him a secondary consideration; what mattered was ideological purity as manifested in unquestioning obedience to instructions from Moscow. When foreign, especially German, Communists objected to having to execute blindly Moscow's orders, Lenin compelled them to subscribe to a twenty-one-point program that he had drawn up as condition of membership in the International. It left them little room for independent action. Then and afterward, the international Communist movement experienced much dissent and many defections, but the principle of compliance with Moscow's wishes was firmly established. Stalin further transformed foreign Communist parties into mindless executors of his will. When he was anti-Nazi, they were anti-Nazi; when he joined with Hitler, they abused the Western democracies for opposing Hitler; and when Hitler invaded Russia, they dutifully once again turned against him. This pattern recurred whatever the issue. The more despotic Stalin's regime became, the louder foreign Communists sang the praises of Soviet democracy; the USSR, isolated from foreign eyes, turned for them into an El Dorado. It was as if they were determined to prove the Russian proverb according to which beating one's own people earns the respect of others.

For indeed, as soon as Stalin had died and the beating stopped, the international reputation of the Soviet Union went into decline. Told by Khrushchev himself that the "genius of mankind" was a demented despot and the Moscow "trials" were travesties, foreign Communists fell into a state of shock. Opportunities to see the Soviet Union with their own eyes revealed what a desperately backward country it was. Disclosures by Soviet dissenters, as well as uprisings of Polish, East German and, above all, Hungarian workers disoriented and demoralized them further. A mood of uncertainty spread through the international Communist movement that would have been unthinkable as long as Stalin held it in his grip.

The main problem that foreign Communist parties have always faced and can never entirely avoid stems from their actual and perceived connections with Moscow. As long as they faithfully follow Moscow's dictates at every turn and twist, they can enforce internal discipline, but, at the same time, condemn themselves to the status of minority parties with little influence. During Stalin's rule, Communist parties everywhere in Western Europe were barred from participation in government, and in several countries (e.g., West Germany and Spain) they were outlawed. To acquire the kind of respectability that would allow them to broaden their electoral appeal and enter the political mainstream, they must give the appearance of being independent national parties, and this means avoiding overt subservience to Moscow. But the instant this happens, party discipline breaks down, giving way to dissent and factionalism. A Communist Party that to any extent acts on its own is afflicted by the same internal disputes over strategy, tactics and leadership as any other party. To attract the voter, foreign Communists must assert their independence, and to demonstrate their independence they must tolerate disunity and at least occasionally take issue with Moscow.

These political realities confront Moscow with a genuine dilemma. If it insists on tightly disciplined, blindly obedient Communist parties in the "capitalist" world, it condemns them to isolation and impotence. If, however, it encourages them to become mass parties with a voice in national politics, it grants them license to follow an independent course that sooner or later brings them into conflict with itself.

In the 1950s, in pursuit of a general strategy of bringing the USSR out of the state of isolation into which Stalin had driven it, his successors relaxed the reins on foreign Communist parties. For a few years, habits of obedience continued to produce reflexive responses; but in time, differences emerged. The 1970s saw in Europe the rise of what came to be known as Eurocommunism, a movement which, for all its theoretical vagueness, bore unmistakable political implications. The Eurocommunists sought to disassociate Communism from its connections with traditional Russian despotism and to infuse it with a humanitarian, democratic spirit that the Western electorate would find attractive. The movement marked a return to the traditions of Social Democracy—at any rate, in theory, because the Eurocommunists showed little inclination to practice democracy inside their own party organizations.

Enthusiasm for Eurocommunism has since abated, and in the 1980s it no longer represents a threat to the Soviet Union. Even so, the time when Moscow could count on the automatic support of foreign Communist parties seems gone beyond recall. Its foreign affiliates take it for granted that they can assume an independent stand on issues to the point of openly criticizing Soviet actions, as many of them have done after the invasions of Czechoslovakia and Afghanistan. The Communist Party of Italy (PCI) is particularly outspoken. When martial law was imposed on Poland, its leaders publicly denounced this action and its perpetrator, the Soviet Union, in language much stronger than the heads of European democracies ever permitted themselves to use. At this time, the PCI came close to breaking relations with its Soviet counterpart, as China had done in the 1960s. The suppression of Solidarity caused the leaders of the PCI to reject Moscow's claim that it was the vanguard of the world's "progressive" forces. The First Secretary of the PCI, Enrico Berlinguer, declared that events in Poland had demonstrated that the October Revolution, "the greatest revolutionary event of our time," had become a spent force, because it had lost the capacity for creative renewal. This assessment was incorporated into a formal resolution of the PCI's Central Committee, adopted on December 29, 1981:

> We must take note that this phase of development of socialism which began with the October Revolution, has exhausted its propulsive force . . . The dramatic events of recent days convince us of the necessity of finding and pursuing completely new ways of restoring impetus to the struggle for democracy and socialism in the world.[32]

A month later Berlinguer announced that the PCI would no longer respond to events in accord with the wishes of Moscow, but would judge each case on its own merits.[33] True to its word, the PCI has parted ways with Moscow on a number of issues to which the latter attaches great importance: for instance, it has come out in favor of Italy's continuing membership in NATO and the installation on Italian soil of American cruise missiles. The Spanish Communist Party has adopted a similarly independent attitude; and voices of criticism and disapproval resound from other Communist parties around the world.

The importance of the stance that the PCI has adopted and urged on the other Communist organizations, derives from the fact that it is the largest Communist Party in Europe outside the Soviet Bloc. Experience thus confirms time and again that the smaller a foreign Communist party the more compulsively it clutches to Moscow's apron strings, and the larger, the more likely it is to follow an independent course. This means that Moscow can ensure its foreign allies of respectability and voter appeal only at the price of forfeiting control over them. It cannot have both: electoral success and obedience to its orders. The conclusion is clear: the more successful foreign Communists will be in gaining a following, the less will they submit to Moscow's demands.

Clashes between Moscow and its foreign affiliates must not obscure the fact that they do render each other all manner of useful services. A good part of the money that finances the operations of international Communist parties comes from the Soviet Union, in the form of subventions or kickbacks from East-West trade. It is difficult to see how most of these parties could survive, let alone aspire to be taken seriously, were they not affiliated with a world-wide movement, backed by a great power. In return, they perform services for Moscow. In countries where Communism has no mass following, they strive to take control of influential organizations and turn them in a direction favorable to Soviet interests. For example, in Great Britain, where the Communist Party has no significant following, its representatives have insinuated them-selves into positions of leadership in several major trade unions and use their influence to stage labor confrontations with Conser-vative governments. In Germany, an equally small Communist Party (legitimized in the course of détente) plays a major role in organizing forces clamoring for unilateral disarmament and in whipping up anti-American emotions. In countries where they enjoy large membership, such as Italy and France, Communist parties pressure governments to enter with the Soviet Union into commercial agreements; they have been known to threaten work stoppages and other actions against firms unwilling to cooperate with Moscow. The rank and file of these large parties have a siz-able Stalinist component, which applies the brakes on the leader-ship whenever, in the quest of political popularity, it flirts with social democracy or becomes too critical of the Soviet Union. For the sake of these benefits, Moscow tolerates insulting behavior and quarrels in Communist ranks. It certainly would prefer to reimpose tight discipline, but it realizes that any attempt to revert to Leninist and Stalinist practices would produce frightful rows in the international Communist movement and cause it to fall apart.

There still is an international Communist movement, and, its fractious character notwithstanding, it constitutes a Soviet asset. What no longer exists is a movement that serves Moscow at its beck and call to the neglect of its own wishes and needs. "In the future," says a German observer,

> it will no longer be possible for the leadership of the Communist Party of the Soviet Union to construe an identity of interest among all the Communist parties by appealing to the purported basic values and objectives of all Communists and, accordingly, to demand that the other parties proclaim their solidarity with Moscow's positions.[34]

This is a loss, from Moscow's point of view. Its inability for the past several years to convene an international conference of Com-munist parties for lack of agreement on an agenda and related issues underscores how tenuous its hold on its friends has become.*

## E. CHINA

No single event so shattered the *nomenklatura*'s self-confidence as the break with China, because none had aroused such high expectations in its ranks as had China's adherence to the Communist Bloc. The victory of Communist forces in China gained for the community one quarter of the world's population. Moscow expected the Chinese aggressively to promote the common cause in the Far East, using for this purpose Chinese colonies scattered throughout the region. The Soviet military looked forward to the day when, secure in the Far Eastern regions, which are remote and difficult to supply, they could concentrate all their attention on NATO. The disappointment of these hopes, therefore, had a traumatic effect on the Soviet elite, as anyone who had visited the USSR at that time can testify.

It was the West's turn now to attach exaggerated expectations to China. It came to believe that in the Far East things would go from bad to worse and that, as the Sino-Soviet conflict intensified, the USSR would have to shift its military forces eastward to meet the new danger, easing pressures on NATO. It further expected that, confronted with a threat in the East, Moscow would have to seek improved relations with the West. It was one of the assumptions of détente that the epicenter of international conflict had moved from Russia's western to its eastern frontier, with the result that good relations with NATO became for Moscow a matter of urgent self-interest.

These expectations too were disappointed. For a while Moscow threatened China with preemptive war, but it must have concluded that the Far East was a secondary front that did not merit

---

* There exist indications that Moscow has recently decided to follow Lenin's precept "better less but better" and support small, totally subservient Communist Parties, even at the cost of causing splits in the movement. In January 1984, in the presence of high-ranking Soviet functionaries, a new pro-Soviet Communist Party was formed in Spain to oppose the large, independently minded official Party. A Yugoslav journalist, Janez Stanic, writing in *Start* (Zagreb, Feb. 11, 1984), is of the opinion that "Moscow prefers small but disciplined parties that depend politically but also financially on Moscow. Large national parties are certainly difficult to lead and reconcile with current and future Soviet interests." (Radio Free Europe/Radio Liberty, *Soviet East European Report*, I, No. 12, March 15, 1984.)

deeper involvement. Instead of depleting its forces facing NATO to meet the Chinese threat, therefore, it created an entirely fresh Far Eastern force, sufficiently strong to repel any aggressive moves. China, for its part, refused to play the role of a pawn in East-West relations and, confronted with serious domestic problems, turned its attention inward. In the end, the Sino-Soviet split did not bring the West the benefits that it had hoped for. While the several initiatives on the part of Peking and Moscow to mend relations have failed to bear fruit so far, it is clear that the two former allies are determined to confine their disagreements to the verbal level—Moscow in order to be able the better to confront the West, China in order to deal with domestic matters.

Even though the worst had not happened, the experience with China was a bitter lesson for Moscow. It demonstrated that there is nothing irreversible about the spread of Communist power, and that a Communist regime not under Moscow's military and political control is an asset of dubious, if any, value. Especially troublesome was the cause of the Sino-Soviet split. The split occurred because China had demanded that the Soviet Union undertake certain foreign-policy steps—rendering China assistance in recovering the offshore islands, sharing with it atomic secrets, and abandoning the post-Stalin policy of peaceful coexistence with the West—that the USSR had refused to do. To retain China's friendship, Moscow was required, in effect, to give China a veto on its conduct of foreign relations. Such, then, were the bitter fruits of Communism's triumphant advance. In this respect, the dilemma was not unlike that which Moscow experienced in its relations with foreign Communist parties.

## 4 CAN THE SOVIET UNION REFORM?

Lenin may not have been an expert on all the subjects on which his authority is invoked in the Soviet Union, but there was one in which he had few peers, and that was the theory and practice of revolution. Having devoted his entire life to it, he had developed an uncanny instinct for the social and political situations that produce revolutions, and he had worked out strategies of action to ensure the outcome that he desired. One of the concepts that he employed in this connection was "revolutionary situation." This term meant to him a condition of stalemate between the ruling elite and the population at large: the former no longer could rule, and the latter no longer would be ruled in the old way. Once a society reached such a condition it was objectively ripe for a revo-

lutionary explosion. But for revolution to occur, a subjective element was needed as well, and that was the ability and will to act;
"the old government . . . never, not even in a period of crisis,
'falls,' if it is not toppled over." [35] When this subjective element is
absent, as it was, according to Lenin, in nineteenth-century Germany and Russia, then the "revolutionary situation" dissipates
without issue.

Were Lenin alive today, he would very likely conclude that conditions in his country and in its empire meet the criteria which he
had established for "revolutionary situations." Certainly, the Soviet Bloc experiences currently a much graver economic and political crisis than had either Russia or Germany in the nineteenth
century. What is lacking, however, is that subjective element, the
ability and the will that transform "revolutionary situations" into
revolutions. The ability to revolt is frustrated by the vast apparatus
of repression which Communist regimes have developed to a degree never before known, precisely because, having come to
power by revolution, they were determined to prevent being over-
thrown in the same way. But a way could be found around even
this obstacle, as events in Hungary, Czechoslovakia and Poland
have shown, if the revolutionary will were there. In Russia, at
least, this will is missing. Historical experience has caused Russians of every political orientation to dread the collapse of authority even more than despotism and to reject violence as an
instrument of change. Before 1917, the Russian intelligentsia had
unbounded faith in the innate goodness and democratic spirit of
its people. It was convinced that as soon as tsarist despotism fell,
democracy would emerge and triumph all along the line. These
Rousseauan illusions were shattered by the experiences of the
Revolution. The present generation of the educated in the Soviet
Union has been cured of all revolutionary romanticism. It believes
that if the Soviet government were to collapse, the result would be
a political vacuum that would only encourage the country's quarter of a billion inhabitants to settle old scores: village would move
against the city, Russian against Jew, Muslim against Russian,
Armenian against Muslim, in a murderous Hobbesian war of all
against all. But even the few who are prepared to pay this price if
it will rid the country of Communist tyranny, no longer believe
that it will purchase anything worthwhile. Having experienced
revolution in all its fury, Russians have learned not only its terrible
costs but also its futility; no matter how many eggs it breaks, it
somehow never produces an omelette. Thus, there is universal
disillusionment with political violence in the Soviet Union—at any
rate, no prominent dissident of either the democratic or the nation-

alist opposition is known to advocate it. The two camps are in agreement that if Russia is to emerge from its crisis it must do so by means of gradual and peaceful change; if this requires the Politbureau and the *nomenklatura* to stay in power, so be it—at any rate, for a time. The following passage from a recent *samizdat* tract, strongly anti-Communist in content, is typical in this respect:

> In its mass, the population of the USSR is far from ready for direct democracy. And we will assert that a new revolution in the USSR would be a genuine misfortune for the country. Solzhenitsyn believes that the moral level of the people today is even lower than it was in 1917. I do not know. Perhaps. In any event, it is entirely clear that without sufficiently prolonged experience of *consistent democratization of the existing sociopolitical order* one cannot take the risk of involving millions of politically uneducated people in the immensely complex task of sociopolitical transformation of the country. . . . The structural improvement of the country is preferable to its destruction. A reformed system has many advantages over one newly brought into being. The experience of Western democracies is for us a guarantee of this. Where the principle of continuity between the old and the new is strictly observed . . . there the result is a stable system of representative democracy of the English or Swedish type.[36]

Widespread political conservatism among the educated classes provides no assurance, of course, that a revolution will not break out on its own, uncalled for and unwanted, from a breakdown of authority. Lenin's insistence that if they are to fall governments must be pushed is too rigid, considering that the tsarist regime collapsed of its own weight when it proved unable to cope with the strains of war. Nevertheless, the likelihood of a revolutionary explosion in the Soviet Union is certainly much reduced by virtue of the fact that the *nomenklatura* has on this issue public opinion on its side. Essentially, its opposition does not want to topple it and take over, but hopes to circumscribe its authority by expanding the private sphere; this desire may be dangerous to a totalitarian regime, but it does not threaten it with uncontrollable violence.

If revolution is excluded, the Soviet regime faces three alternatives: reversion to Stalinism; intensified external aggression leading to a general war; and internal reform.

Among the *nomenklatura* and the less educated public there is much nostalgia for the days of Stalin—not, of course, for his genocidal savagery, but for an idealized regime of order and discipline, when everyone did his duty and corruption was unknown. Such glorified Stalinism seems to offer a way out of the difficulties that Soviet society faces, without resort to dangerous reforms. But this is an idle fantasy. Stalinism cannot be restored for any number of reasons, the most weighty of which is the impossibility of running the country's present-day sophisticated industrial plant and military establishment by brute force and in isolation from the rest of the world. Nor can the *nomenklatura* have forgotten how insecure and hard its life under Stalin was and how many of their people perished in his so-called purges. In any event, after thirty years of gradual dismantling and decay of Stalinism, it is senseless to speak of bringing it back; it would have to be recreated and reimposed anew. One suspects that those who speak so wistfully of it know this, and Stalinism is the last thing they want or would put up with if it really returned. The current nostalgia for Stalinism is very reminiscent of the longing of Russian bureaucratic and conservative circles during the "revolutionary situation" of the 1870s and 1880s for the "good old" days of Nicholas I (1825–1855), when the peasants were kept in their place by serfdom and the government tolerated no dissent whatever. Then, as now, this habit of looking backward is symptomatic of the unwillingness of the ruling apparatus to face up to changed realities and to decide on painful but unavoidable reforms.

In some ways the easiest if most dangerous way out of the crisis is to keep on raising the level of international tension. War scares, one of the major products of the Soviet propaganda industry since the 1920s, divert the masses' attention and make it possible to demand extraordinary sacrifices from labor as well as to silence the opposition in the name of patriotic duty. The constant harping on World War II and the linking of "Fascism" with American "imperialism" serve this purpose. But war scares are risky, because they have a way of getting out of hand; the logical outcome of war scares is war. The possibility of the *nomenklatura* taking a chance on war as a way of avoiding internal reforms cannot be precluded; in the opinion of some East European observers it is a risk the *nomenklatura* would take if it felt sufficiently endangered internally. The greater the probability of quick and cheap victory, the greater the temptation to use this avenue of escape from an intolerable internal predicament. Clearly, the more the West forecloses this option with its own military counterpreparations, the less viable will it appear.

If revolution is set aside because it lacks social support, a return to Stalinism because it is unrealistic, and recourse to war because of its uncertain outcome, reform looms as the only viable way out of the "revolutionary situation" that the Soviet Union faces. The vital question for Russia, its subjugated nations, and the rest of the world is whether the *nomenklatura* will come to see its predicament in this light, whether a dispassionate analysis of the facts will prevail over bluster and the "after us the deluge" mentality. The *nomenklatura* is not the first ruling elite to face the choice between holding on to all power and privilege at the risk of losing all of it, or surrendering some of both in the hope of holding on to the rest. History knows both outcomes. England has avoided revolution for three centuries because its monarchy, aristocracy and middle classes have always seen the inevitability of change and made timely concessions. In Imperial Russia, die-hard sentiment was much stronger, and so it is today in Latin America. The behavior of the Soviet *nomenklatura* under these circumstances is a subject on which expert opinion is divided.

A rather pessimistic assessment is provided by Milovan Djilas, the Yugoslav author of a pioneering study of the *nomenklatura* under the title *The New Class,* and someone who, as a close associate of Tito, has had the opportunity to learn at first hand how the Soviet elite thinks. "In my opinion," he writes,

> changes in the Soviet system are least likely. One reason is that this system is more than the other systems permeated, one might say, with imperialist class privileges. I believe that the Soviet system has no internal potential for change, just as Soviet imperialism cannot stop of its own will. In theory, the only possibility of change in the Soviet Union lies in the creation of some kind of enlightened absolutism which could initiate reforms, but even then bureaucratic repression can strangle the process of democratization. Even for such an enlightened autocrat to emerge, it is imperative that there be some sort of a *national crisis:* a military crisis or a revolutionary crisis, or both at the same time. Such a perspective, it must be noted, is in accord with Russian history.[37]

Djilas's conviction that nothing short of a catastrophe will induce the apparatus to undertake reforms is shared by many dissenters as well as loyal but apprehensive Communists.

Others maintain that the *nomenklatura* will soon have no choice in the matter, that life will push it onto the path of reform whether it likes it or not. An articulate spokesman for the more optimistic school of thought is Valerii Chalidze, a pioneer fighter for human rights in the USSR.

> Russia is filled with the sharpest contradictions. They are so numerous that sometimes it seems as if this were done on purpose, so that one contradiction would eclipse all the others. But should all these contradictions speak up, then the government will not be able to confine itself to promises and repressions, as it is doing now, because the entire

people will be pulled into this mass of internal contradictions. The government will have to disentangle these contradictions: it will have to busy itself improving internal conditions and organizing economic as well as social relations. And then, for a time, all the imperial dreams will fade, compared with the importance of internal problems.

One may object that the authorities will not bother to improve social relations, and instead resort to mass repressions. I think this will not happen. The country is ruled by a class of professionals who are interested in the Empire's stability and grandeur. Any outburst of dissatisfaction can be suppressed by force: no need to consider the morality of the rulers. But the growing social tension in the whole country, the sharpening of the many contradictions will cause these professionals to react in a manner that endangers neither the stability of their position nor that of the empire; this will compel them to carry out social reforms, and these reforms will mark a piecemeal, gradual transition to a more democratic system of government. The authorities are ready for such reforms as long as they do not threaten stability: being gradual, they will not.[38]

The difference between the two schools of thought, the one more optimistic, the other less so, is one of degree: Mr. Chalidze believes the conditions for an acute crisis to be much closer at hand than does Mr. Djilas. They agree, however—and this is of essential importance to Western policy—that reforms are conceivable only as a result of major internal and external setbacks, that they will come about only when the *nomenklatura* concludes that they are the price it must pay for its survival.

The intimate link between crises and reforms to which Mr. Djilas refers is corroborated by the entire record of Russian history. Russia is an extremely conservative country, so much so that even its socialism has acquired a thoroughly reactionary character. It is so vast and complex and so loosely held together that its leaders have always feared and rarely volunteered changes. They have consented to make changes only under duress caused either by humiliations abroad or upheavals at home. This was the case with the reforms of Peter the Great, Alexander II and Nicholas II. Even Lenin had to veer sharply toward more liberal practices when in 1921 social unrest and the near collapse of the economy placed his regime in jeopardy. The record of Russian history thus strongly suggests, and informed Russian opinion corroborates, that such changes for the better that one can expect in the nature of the Soviet government and in its conduct of foreign relations *will come about only from failures, instabilities, and fears of collapse and not from growing confidence and sense of security*. This assessment is antithetical to the one that lay behind détente and still continues to dominate thinking in the foreign services and liberal circles in Europe and the United States—that the more confident and secure the Soviet elite feels, the more restrained its conduct. The latter thesis cannot be supported by any evidence from the past and can only derive from ignorance of the mentality of the Soviet elite and the record of Russian history. Clearly, it makes a profound difference for United States foreign policy which of these two interpretations is correct.

Assuming that the crisis-reform thesis is correct and that the "revolutionary situation" will have ripened to the point where something must be done, what kind of reform can one reasonably expect from the Soviet leadership?

Speaking very generally, the trouble with the Soviet system as presently constituted is that it has the worst of both worlds: it suffers from all the drawbacks of a regime based on the command principle, but it no longer enjoys many of the benefits that this principle has to offer. Man can be motivated either by fear or by hope, either by threats or by inducements. Communists have always preferred to rely on the first of these methods. This practice has not given them the stability and productivity of democratic and free-market societies, but it has enabled them to concentrate their limited resources on whatever goals they decided to assign high priority. What they lacked in quantity, quality, and diversity of resources, they made up with the ability to mobilize them for specific tasks. This ability has been eroding for some time. In a sense, the current crisis of Communism is due to its vegetating in a kind of no man's land between compulsion and freedom, unable to profit from either. The all-pervasive fear that Stalin's regime had instilled in the people is gone beyond recall, and one can no longer rely on the faint memory it evokes to exact hard work and unthinking obedience; for any Communist Bloc citizen under forty —that is, the majority—Stalinism is ancient history. But fear has not been replaced with hope and inducements. As a result, the creative energies of the people living under regimes of the Soviet type are directed into private and oppositional channels that not only bring those regimes no benefit but in many ways positively injure them. The normal and healthy spirit of economic entrepreneurship, deprived of legitimate channels, seeks expression in semilegal or illegal activity connected with the "second economy," bribery and the black market. Citizens concerned with public affairs take to overt or concealed dissent, which the regime is unable to wipe out and can only try to keep within safe bounds. In other words, everything dynamic and creative, whether in the field of economic or of intellectual activity, is driven by the system into criminal channels; forces which should strengthen the regime are compelled to undermine it. This, in a nutshell, is the problem that post-Stalinist regimes have had to face and which sooner or later they must come to terms with. A way has to be found of reconciling the interests of the state and its ruling elite with the creative energies of the people. This cannot be accomplished unless the elite is prepared to sacrifice some of its authority and bring society into partnership, if only of a limited kind.

There is no need to spell out possible reform programs for the Soviet Union and its colonies. It is more useful to indicate the principles that such reforms must embody if they are to be of any benefit. The basic task is to harness the creative forces of the country in public service, to bridge the gap between the pursuit of private goals—presently the sole objective of the vast majority of citizens in Communist countries, their leaders included—and the interests of the whole. To this end, three reforms appear essential.

One is legality. The citizen of a Communist society need not necessarily participate in the making of laws—this is a right which the *nomenklatura* would never concede of its own will—but he must be assured that those laws that are on the books are binding on all, representatives of state authority included. For the citizen to know what he can and cannot do is a *sine qua non* of a properly functioning society. This requirement entails, among other things, strict judiciary control over the Party and state bureaucracy—that is, an end to the tradition inherited from tsarism that servants of the government are a law unto themselves. Since legality is compatible with authoritarian methods of government, this innovation should not prove unacceptable, once reforms are decided upon.

The other is wider scope for private enterprise. The first economy, controlled by the regime, must link up with the second economy, and draw on its dynamism. This probably calls for the decentralization of industrial decision making, the dismantling of collective farms, the adoption in industry and agriculture of the contractual principle as the rule rather than the exception, and the turning over of a good part of the consumer and service sectors to private enterprise. The consequence of such reforms would be a mixed economy, in which the state and its Party establishment would continue to wield immense power but would no longer stifle productive forces. That which the *nomenklatura* would give up in managerial authority it would gain many times over in increased productivity.

The third is administrative decentralization of the USSR. The *nomenklatura* will have to acknowledge that the days of colonialism are over, that it will never succeed in creating a synthetic "Soviet" nation by having the ethnic minorities dissolve tracelessly among the Russians. There is no likelihood that the Soviet government will voluntarily dissolve the Soviet Union into its constituent republics, but genuine federalism of some sort, with broad self-rule for the minorities, is not inconceivable; it only calls for making constitutional fiction constitutional reality. Such a step would go a long way toward reducing the ethnic tensions that now exist.

Viewed superficially, the fate of reforms in Communist societies may appear to hold merely academic interest for citizens of other societies. After all, it is not for them to tell Russians how to manage their lives; what matters is that the Soviet Union respect international standards of conduct and cease aggression. But as has been pointed out throughout this book, Soviet militarism and imperialism are imbedded in internal Soviet conditions; they are a byproduct of the system. This being the case, the fate of Soviet citizens must be of direct and personal interest to the rest of the world. As long as the *nomenklatura* remains what it is, as long as the Soviet Union lives in a state of lawlessness, as long as the energies of its peoples are not allowed to express themselves creatively, so long there can be no security for anyone else in the world.

A Soviet Union that will turn its energies inward will of necessity become less militaristic and expansionist. It is a precondition of all Soviet reforms that the *nomenklatura* surrender some of its authority to the people over whom it rules, that it restrain the arbitrary powers of its members, that it let law and contractual relations replace bureaucratic whim. Anything that occurs in this direction has to act as a brake on the regime's hitherto unbridled appetite for conquests because, much as they may be flattered by the might of Russia, its citizens have other concerns, closer to home. The immense task of internal reconstruction that confronts Russia cannot be undertaken as long as military expenditures remain at their present levels. Cutbacks in military budgets, however, demand a more pacific foreign policy. In other words, the greater the pressures on these regimes to deal with genuine crises at home instead of artificially created crises abroad, the greater their dependence on their citizens, and the greater, in consequence, the ability of these citizens to deflect their governments from foreign adventures. This point was made by Friedrich Engels nearly a century ago:

> This entire danger of a world war will vanish on the day when a change of affairs in Russia will permit the Russian people to put an end to its tsars' traditional policy of conquest and attend to its own vital domestic interests—interests which are endangered in the extreme—instead of to fantasies of world conquest.[39]

Anyone who doubts this prospect has only to consider the evolution of China since Mao's death. As long as Mao ruled China, that country conducted an exceedingly truculent foreign policy, threatening to set the Third World afire with campaigns of "national liberation" and even making light of nuclear war. Washington took these threats so much to heart that it sent hundreds of thousands of men halfway around the world to prove its ability to cope with them. Mao's successors, however, decided that their first priority had to be economic modernization; once this decision had fallen, aggressive actions and words miraculously ceased. Economic modernization entailed a series of reforms, including decentralization of decision-making, the gradual dismantling of the collective-farm system, and greater freedom to the private sector. Concurrently, attempts have been made to introduce greater legality into relations between state and citizenry. The entrenched bureaucracy has been sabotaging these reform measures in its own quiet way, but even so their effect on foreign policy has been startling. Realizing that better relations with the West were essential to the modernization program, China has cautiously moved toward closer economic, political and military relations with it. Thus, it was not success, but failure, that has caused Communist China to turn from a mortal enemy of the "capitalist" countries into their quasi partner: not promises of assistance from the West, but the desperate need for such assistance. And even after due allowance is made for the fact that Russia is not China, it is difficult to see why the experience of the one Stalinist state is not of immediate relevance to the other.

# WHAT CAN WE DO?

For we are here as on a darkling plain
Swept with confused alarms of struggle
and flight
—MATTHEW ARNOLD "Dover Beach"

Sun Tzu, the Chinese military thinker who in the fourth century before Christ had formulated some fundamental principles of strategy, wrote that winning battles was not the ultimate test of a great commander: "To win one hundred victories in one hundred battles is not the acme of skill. To subdue the enemy without fighting is the acme of skill . . . what is of supreme importance in war is to attack the enemy's strategy."[1] Although the conflict between East and West is a political not a military contest, the principle applies. The paramount objective of Western policy ought to be frustrating Soviet Grand Strategy: to prevent it from attaining its objectives and to do so without allowing the conflict to degenerate into a clash of arms. This is an extremely difficult task for democratic societies whose citizens tend to alternate between complacency and panic, a disposition their leaders humor by resorting now to appeasement, now to belligerence.

Nothing is easier than to draft a Western "counterstrategy" to frustrate Soviet plans as long as no allowance is made for the political limitations under which democratic statesmen must labor. But it is a fact of life that these statesmen are responsible to legislatures and are followed at every step by the press. They also have to run in elections, which they sometimes lose to persons with very different views. This signifies that democratic governments have at their disposal neither the spectrum of means nor the time needed to develop a full-fledged Grand Strategy. These realities need not, however, mean that the only option available to them is drifting with the tide of events. The craft of statesmanship always demands a reconciliation of the desirable with the possible, of general objectives with the opportunities that life brings forth. Tocqueville, who had the benefit of experience of both historical scholarship and practical politics, made an interesting observation on this subject:

> In my life I have come across literary men who wrote histories without taking part in public affairs, and politicians whose only concern was to control events without a thought of describing them. And I have invariably noticed that the former see general causes everywhere, whereas the latter, spending their lives amid the disconnected events of each day, freely attribute everything to particular incidents and think that all the little strings their hands are busy pulling daily are those that control the world's destiny. Probably, both of them are mistaken.[2]

Experience indicates that a compromise between the two approaches is possible, that distant purpose, rooted in "general causes," and accommodation to "particular incidents" can and indeed must be achieved by statesmen who confront serious tasks. To prove this contention one only has to study the manner in which Bismarck built the German Empire or the Zionists went about creating a Jewish state.

Americans, being an impatient and active people, are skeptical when told that there are occasions when thinking is as important as doing—that, indeed, thought is a form of action. The poor record of American policy vis-à-vis the Soviet Union stems not from insufficient appreciation of the threat or inadequate effort to cope with it, but from insufficient reflection on its nature. More than a third of a century has elapsed since the United States acknowledged that the Soviet Union is a hostile power, bent on causing harm to its interests and imposing on the world a system that in all important respects negates its own. To avert this threat, over one hundred thousand Americans have given their lives; trillions of dollars have been spent on defense; and an immense amount of public attention has been expended on the subject. And yet in all this stupendous endeavor little serious attention has been paid to the central questions: Why the threat? What sort of threat is it? How can it be permanently neutralized? This evasion of deeper analysis is a fatal flaw of United States foreign policy, for which it has had to pay a dear price. The United States saw no need for a chair of Vietnamese studies at a single American university when it sent into this unfamiliar land half a million men to fight an unknown enemy.

The policy suggestions in this chapter are intended neither as specific recommendations to those in office, nor as a "model" of United States-Soviet relations for the purpose of academic discussions. Their purpose is to make clearer what should be done and what should be avoided in coping with the threat discussed in the preceding chapters. They are mainly about ways of thinking; once this matter has been settled, the course of action follows with a certain inexorable logic.

# 1 PAST PATTERNS OF UNITED STATES-SOVIET RELATIONS

On the surface, the history of United States relations with the Soviet Union since 1917 is a succession of pendular swings between the extremes of hostility and accommodation. Foreigners are fond of telling Americans that they vacillate in their attitudes toward the Soviet Union to such an extent and with such unpredictability that they are unable to follow their leadership in this matter. While one cannot deny a record of vacillation, it is certainly not unique to the United States. In the nineteenth century, when of all the great powers it was the one most directly concerned with Russia, Great Britain displayed a similar pattern of alternation between hostility and friendliness. In 1827, British naval forces jointly with Russian ships fought and sank a Turkish navy; a quarter of a century later, Britain, in defense of the same Turkey, went to war with Russia; in the 1880s the two countries nearly came to blows over Afghanistan, only to sign a treaty of understanding in 1907 and to fight as allies in World War I. If there is any consistency in this record it is not readily apparent. The history of Germany's relations with Russia shows even wilder swings. Such patterns are caused by the very nature of Russia's position in international politics: Russia is the only country in the world that is in Europe and yet not of Europe, a giant who exerts pressure on unstable areas in three continents from its virtually impregnable homeland. Confronted with this unusual power, the others forever try to tame it, sometimes by accommodation, sometimes by force.

Notwithstanding these alternatives, underneath America's policies toward the USSR one can observe a certain continuity of attitude, which persists regardless of whether actual relations between the two countries happen to be friendly or hostile. A brief survey of United States-Soviet relations should bring out this fact.

The creation of the Soviet state in October 1917 at first provoked no strong response from the United States, because the Bolsheviks were then an unknown quantity and there was hope that despite their public declarations to the contrary, they would stay in the war to fight the Germans. For half a year the Allies chose to ignore Lenin and Trotsky's abuse of "capitalist" countries, their exhortations to European soldiers to stop fighting each other and turn their guns against the "bourgeois" governments, their renunciations of foreign debts and confiscations of foreign properties, all in order to keep the Eastern front alive. This tolerant attitude ended only in March 1918, when the Brest-Litovsk treaty between Moscow and Berlin turned the Soviet republic into a silent accomplice of the Central Powers. Allied attempts at intervention in Soviet Russia in 1918 were motivated by short-term military considerations: the Allies dreaded the possibility that the Germans, with their hands freed in the East, would mass sufficient troops in the West to break through Allied lines before the Americans arrived and would win the war. They sent small expeditionary units to Russia, in part to divert German forces, in part to prevent the large stocks of weapons and ammunition accumulated in Russian ports of entry from falling into enemy hands. For a year after the Armistice was signed, the British supported, with mainly vocal assistance from France, anti-Bolshevik Russian forces in the hope that, if they succeeded in capturing power, they would compensate them and their citizens for the financial losses suffered at Bolshevik hands. The United States, which had lost little in Lenin's defaults and expropriations, was loath to join in this undertaking. It eventually yielded to Allied entreaties and contributed a small expeditionary force; its troops, however, never came near the fronts of the civil war, never exchanged fire with the Red Army, and never had it as their mission to overthrow the Communist regime.

Through the 1920s and early 1930s the United States ignored the USSR diplomatically, which did not prevent American businessmen from vigorously exploring Soviet markets and doing their bit in the first Five Year Plan. In 1933, Washington extended diplomatic recognition to the USSR, partly in recognition of political reality, partly in the hope of encouraging more extensive economic relations. The Nazi-Soviet pact of 1939 and the Soviet invasion of Finland cast a dark shadow on the new relationship, but all was forgiven two years later when the Soviet Union itself came under Nazi attack, which it resisted and repelled with extraordinary heroism.

In conducting relations with Stalin during the war, President Roosevelt acted on the premise—instinctively arrived at rather than thought out—that Soviet secrecy, isolationism and aggressiveness resulted from a long record of insecurity and suffering. He was prepared to go far to assuage what he believed to be Russian anxieties. To lure the USSR out of its seclusion and bring it into the community of nations, he offered Moscow generous buffer zones, including the Eastern half of Europe. The Yalta agreements, which many observers now view as a shameful betrayal of Western ideals, the American delegation to Yalta saw as a triumph of farsighted statesmanship; the concessions to Stalin seemed to have purchased at a relatively modest cost Soviet cooperation in the building of a peaceful postwar world. Harry Hopkins, President Roosevelt's chief foreign-policy adviser, later spoke of the enthusiastic mood of the United States delegation as it returned from the Yalta conference:

> We really believed in our hearts that this was the dawn of the new day we had all been praying for and talking about for so many years. We were absolutely certain that we had won the first great victory of the peace—and, by "we," I mean *all* of us, the whole civilized human race. The Russians had proved that they could be reasonable and farseeing and there wasn't any doubt in the minds of the President or any of us that we could live with them and get along with them peacefully for as far into the future as any of us could imagine.[3]

However, even before Yalta, as the tide of war turned in his favor, Stalin's desire for accommodation with the West visibly cooled: in the words of Herbert Feis, the tone of his letters to Roosevelt and Churchill changed from "amiability to reserve, to bluntness, to bold rudeness." Roosevelt continued to the end to believe in the possibility of cooperation with the Soviet Union and in the good will of Stalin (the only worry in the United States delegation, according to Hopkins, was "what the results would be if anything should happen" to the "reasonable and sensible and understanding" Stalin), but these illusions did not long survive him. Boldly exploiting the vacuum that the defeat of Germany and Japan had left behind, Stalin moved against Western Europe and East Asia, apparently eager to make himself master of both regions. His aggressive actions violated the spirit of interallied agreements that were arrived at during the war and postulated mutual respect for the spheres of influence allotted to East and West.

The United States responded to these aggressive actions with great vigor in the hope of preventing a repetition of the events of the 1930s, when Allied weakness had emboldened Hitler and precipitated war. To help strengthen its social fabric, Washington extended economic assistance to Western Europe. It constituted NATO as an alliance that committed the United States to come to Europe's defense. The order of the day was "containment," which, in the words of George Kennan, its principal theorist, called for confronting the Russians "with unalterable counter-force at every point where they show signs of encroaching upon the interests of a peaceful and stable world."[4] What Mr. Kennan and his supporters meant by "unalterable counter-force" has been a subject of debate ever since. But, as best one can tell, it seems to have entailed a combination of political and military initiatives with resort to armed force whenever the situation so demanded.*

Containment must be judged to have been a success to the ex-

---

* Mr. Kennan insists that his recommendations had been misunderstood and accepts some of the blame for what he concedes to have been "careless and indiscriminate language," in his celebrated essay (*Memoirs, 1925–1950*, Boston, 1967, 358–60). It is, nevertheless, difficult to accept the retroactive interpretation that he gives of his views. "When I mentioned the containment of Soviet power," he writes in the *Memoirs*, "[it] was not the containment by military means of a military threat, but the political containment of a political threat." This claim has been shown to be at odds with the documentary evidence. Mr. Eduard Mark (in *Foreign Affairs*, January 1978, pp. 430–41) has demonstrated on the basis of archival sources that at that time Mr. Kennan unmistakably had military power in mind, as, for instance, when he contemplated recommending the dispatch of United States troops to Greece and Italy to prevent a possible Communist takeover. Nor does Mr. Kennan's second objection—that he did not mean the United States to contain the Soviet Union "everywhere," but only in areas "vital" to United States security—stand up, since his statement quoted above unequivocally recommends containment being applied at "every point" where the Russians threatened the "peaceful and stable world."

At the same time, one must sympathize with Mr. Kennan's disclaimer that his 1947 essay be held responsible for United States policies of the 1960s and 1970s, of which he strongly disapproves.

tent that it discouraged some aggressive moves and helped to isolate the Soviet Union. Its effectiveness was confirmed by Stalin's successors when they radically altered their international strategy and tactics. Beginning with the middle 1950s, they proceeded to knock down the main psychological prop from under containment, which was widespread fear of a secretive Soviet Union and its aggressive intentions. By initiating friendly contacts with the West and the Third World, renouncing the desirability—indeed, the possibility—of exporting revolution, and expeditiously settling with NATO a few outstanding issues, Moscow neutralized with remarkable ease the resolve that had made containment an effective policy. Differences of opinion now developed among the Allies, as Western Europe responded more positively than the United States to the new doctrine of "peaceful coexistence" unveiled in Moscow in the middle 1950s with spurious references to Lenin. First France and then Germany moved to normalize relations with Moscow. The United States finally joined in under President Nixon. A series of bilateral agreements covering virtually every area of their relationship was to ensure friendship and peace between Washington and Moscow.

As it had done in the 1940s, Moscow immediately proceeded to violate both the letter and the spirit of its accords with the West. The political and military aid that it extended to the Arab countries that attacked Israel in 1973; similar assistance to North Vietnam in its decisive military assault on South Vietnam; expeditions of Soviet and Cuban forces to strategic locations in Asia and Africa; and, perhaps most troublesome of all, the uninterrupted stockpiling of all types of weapons at a time when the United States was curtailing its own defense expenditures—all these actions perplexed American opinion and cooled its ardor for improved relations with the Communist Bloc. Disenchantment was greater in this country than in Europe because the United States had entered the new relationship in a spirit of romantic idealism that was absent in Europe, where détente was treated as a marriage of convenience. The invasion of Afghanistan shattered what was still left of the spirit of United States–Soviet détente, inaugurating yet another era of tension.

In this history that spans two thirds of a century, one can discern, underneath the flux of events, at least two constants.

The first is that, almost without exception, it was the Soviet Union that has acted and the United States that has reacted. Soviet policies toward the West in general and the United States in particular were and are determined in part by internal conditions and in part by Moscow's perception of the international "correlation of forces." Admittedly, a close scrutiny of the record of United States–Soviet relations will reveal instances when the United States took the initiative, sometimes aggressively so, occasionally even to an excess. "Revisionist" history thrives on evidence of this kind and constructs its case upon it, but this can be done only by tearing individual events out of their historical context. Why the Soviet Union should be the active partner in this bilateral relationship can best be explained by the greater role that foreign policy plays in Communist ideology and interests. If there were no Soviet Union, the United States would be able substantially to cut back its defense expenditures, but, in all other respects, its position in the world at large and its situation at home would remain what they are. If, however, the United States did not exist, for the Soviet Union everything would change. Hence the obsession with the United States, and hence the ceaseless efforts to outmaneuver it and drive it against the wall. If one seeks a historical parallel, the relationship is not unlike that which had prevailed at the turn of the century between Germany and Great Britain: Germany was then for Britain *a* problem, primarily military in character, whereas Britain was for Germany *the* problem, the main obstacle in its quest for status as the world's leading power.

The second recurrent theme is that in responding to Soviet initiatives, the United States resorts to what can best be described as didactic diplomacy. That is to say, it fashions its every response in such a manner as to teach Moscow a lesson: if Moscow behaves well (acts with "restraint" or "moderation") it is lavished with appropriate rewards; if it does not (if it acts "disruptively" or in the "spirit of adventurism") rewards give way to punishments. The theme of reward and punishment recurs in the speeches of United States Presidents and Secretaries of State of different administrations, Republican and Democratic, hawkish and dovish alike. It was succinctly expressed in President Carter's address to the Naval Academy in 1978: "Our long-term objective must be to convince the Soviet Union of the advantages of cooperation and of the costs of disruptive behavior." [5] But it has also resounded in the remarks of spokesmen for President Reagan, whose attitude toward the Soviet Union is much harsher and founded on a philosophical hostility to Communism. Secretary of State Haig put the matter as follows:

> During this sensitive and dangerous period of changing super-power relationships, the United States must make clear to the Soviet Union that there are penalties for aggression and incentives for restraint. We cannot conduct business as usual in the face of Soviet adventurism in

Afghanistan or Soviet-instigated repression in Poland . . . [But] we are prepared to show Soviet leaders that international moderation can help them face painful domestic dilemmas through broader relations with the United States and other western countries.[6]

The notion of manipulating Soviet behavior by a carefully adjusted mixture of punishments and rewards is rooted neither in historical experience nor in the practices of diplomacy. Its principal source seems to be American psychological theory, and more precisely the behaviorist psychology of John B. Watson. Watson, who was active early in this century, attempted to base psychology on uncompromisingly scientific methods, which meant banishing from it every concept that could not be observed and measured, among them mind, soul, and consciousness. The basic elements of psychology reduced themselves to stimulus and response. To elicit from a subject the desired response, one merely added or subtracted the appropriate stimuli. A correct dosage of such stimuli, according to Watson, produced results that were as predictable as those obtained by experiments in a laboratory. Armed with this knowledge, one could manipulate human beings at will. Human actions, individually and, by implication, collectively, had always identifiable causes, and these had to lie outside them, in the stimuli supplied by external agents. From these premises it implicitly followed that, just as individual human beings had no consciousness or will of their own, neither did societies.

There is something engaging about the self-assurance and simplemindedness of Watsonian psychology which sweeps aside thousands of years of accumulated religious, philosophical and historical wisdom as if it were so much refuse. What naïve confidence one must have in science to treat man as a purely passive subject without a mind and will of his own, a compliant tool in the hands of his master, the psychologist. (The psychologist, Watson wrote, feels that "he makes progress only to the extent that he can manipulate or control" human behavior.) Watson's theories have been applied with some success in the fields of psychotherapy and advertising. Their application to the field of foreign relations, however, has brought nothing but disaster. Its psychological-manipulative approach sets the United States apart from other nations and lends some of its policies an air of unpredictability as stimuli are switched back and forth from positive to negative, depending on the subject's observed behavior at any given time. Furthermore, it exonerates United States foreign-policy specialists from the need to learn the history, culture, ideology, and even the language of the societies with which it is their responsibility to deal.

A high proportion of American "experts" on the Soviet Union, including advisers to the Secretary of State and ambassadors to Moscow are individuals trained to deal with foreign-policy issues in the abstract rather than in the concrete. They feel no need to know what history and the system under which it lives have made of the Soviet Union, because they refuse to admit significant differences among nations and their conduct. Such expertise as they possess is in the field of stimulus application: their primary concern is with Soviet actions and their task is mainly to find out, through negotiations and "dialogues," what the opponent's mood happens to be at a given moment and which stimuli will most effectively steer him in the desired direction. It is a relatively simple matter, of course, for the other side, once it knows what symptoms American diplomats are looking for, to give appropriate responses, much as primitive people quickly learn what it is that visiting anthropologists want to hear.

The behaviorist approach explains the thinking that lay behind both the policy of containment and that of détente, the one of which resorts mainly to negative, the other to positive stimuli.

## A. CONTAINMENT

Containment is an offspring of the notion of international equilibrium or balance of power first formally introduced in the Treaty of Westphalia (1648). This concept dominated Continental politics during the eighteenth and nineteenth centuries. Its foremost practitioner was Great Britain, a country that had worldwide commercial interests but lacked adequate armies to protect them. Britain acted on the principle that no one power should be allowed to gain sufficient military strength to be able to threaten Britain's global interests. Whenever Continental states acquired the capability to do so—they were, successively, France in the eighteenth century, Russia in the nineteenth, and Germany in the twentieth —Britain resorted to diplomacy and financial subsidies to put together coalitions that, by their superior combined strength, could contain the actual or potential aggressor. The United States adopted this practice from Great Britain after World War II; but perhaps because its interests were less specific, it did so in a much grander, more ambitious and didactic manner. Although Britain had practiced containment for centuries, no British prime minister has ever committed his country to the kind of responsibilities that President Kennedy assumed for the United States in a famous passage of his Inaugural Address: "Let every nation know, whether it wish us well or ill, that we shall pay any price, bear any burden, meet any hardship, support any friend, oppose any foe, in order to assure the survival and success of liberty. This much we pledge and more." To fulfill the promise contained in these finely cadenced phrases, the United States constructed a chain of alliances along the Soviet frontier. These alliances were backed with the might of America's nuclear arsenal. When the situation called for it, the United States did not hesitate also to dispatch its own troops to bar their way, as it did in Korea and Vietnam. The whole purpose of the enterprise was to teach the Russians and their allies that aggression would never go unpunished.

The success of containment depended on two conditions: United States nuclear monopoly and a Soviet strategy of direct military assault. A decade after the adoption of containment as United States declaratory policy, neither condition prevailed. In the 1950s, the Soviet Union broke America's monopoly on nuclear weapons and its near-monopoly on delivery vehicles; by the end of the 1960s, with the acquiescence of Washington, it attained nuclear parity; and in the 1970s, it gained a nuclear edge. Once this shift in the balance of nuclear forces had occurred, the United States could no longer hope to contain Soviet expansion by means of a nuclear threat. Henceforth, it had to be prepared to field ground forces to any number of fronts where the Soviet Union, with its great superiority in conventional forces and no mean geopolitical advantages, chose to encroach on the interests of a "stable and peaceful world." This simply was not feasible, as the war in Vietnam demonstrated.

The other factor that rendered containment impracticable was a radical shift in Soviet Grand Strategy. Stalin, mistrusting anything that he could not control, had avoided close links with countries and movements which, even though anti-Western, were not subject to his commands. The ultimate result of the policy based on the principle "who is not with us, is against us" was the isolation of the Soviet Union. Its ability to expand power and influence was limited to military intervention with proxy forces in regions close to the USSR. Stalin's successors adopted a more flexible policy, whose guiding principle held that "who is not against us is with us." Employing in its foreign policy, in addition to military devices, also political and economic ones, the Soviet Union quickly broke out of its isolation. One by one the alliances with which the United States had surrounded the USSR either weakened or fell apart.

Thus, the post-Stalin Soviet leadership, acting in the spirit of Sun Tzu's maxim, attacked and nullified the United States strategy of containment without committing to combat a single soldier of its own. Containment had postulated the existence of a territorially definable Communist Bloc, but the lines which in the 1940s and 1950s had separated the Communist realm from the rest of the world subsequently dissolved. Today, Soviet and Soviet-supported forces are scattered in all parts of the globe. Moscow has client states in Asia, the Middle East, Africa and Central America. There is no longer any line to hold, even if the military capability to do so were available, which it is not. The United States can at best engage in what has been called "selective containment"— that is, the defense of a few areas of particular strategic interest to it, which obviously would include Western Europe, Central America and the Persian Gulf. But containment of this kind has nothing in common with its namesake, which assumed the globe to be divided into permanently fixed geographic spheres of influence.

## B. DÉTENTE

The term *détente* as currently used originated with General de Gaulle. In the 1950s, the French President spoke of East-West relations being normalized in stages that would begin with a relaxation of tensions (détente), go on to friendship *(entente)*, and culminate in full cooperation. De Gaulle's interest in détente stemmed from a desire to find in the East a counterweight to the dominant influence exercised in Europe by the two "Anglo-Saxon" countries, the United States and Great Britain, and in this manner to restore to France its traditional role as the foremost power on the Continent. The dissolution of the two military blocs, NATO and the Warsaw Pact, was a precondition for the success of this policy. In the late 1960s, Germany, for its own national reasons, took the same path. In its case, the principal motives were the desire to open channels to the eastern half of the country, occupied by the Soviet Union, and to reactivate the commercial ties that Germany had for many centuries maintained with Eastern Europe.

The United States was the last of the great powers to embrace détente. National and party interests played here—as in the case of the European powers—a certain role: the desire to heal the wounds of the Vietnam War; the need to keep in step with the Allies; and the wish to cast the Republican Party in the image of a party of peace. But in the American case much grander ideas were involved as well. Appealing to the instinctive isolationism of the American people and the related faith in the possibility of eternal peace (the advent of which would absolve the United States from having to have a foreign policy at all), the architects of détente in

Washington promised nothing less than comprehensive and permanent friendship with the Soviet Union. In the "Basic Principles of Relations," which President Nixon and Brezhnev signed in May 1972 in Moscow, the two powers pledged themselves to "do their utmost to avoid military confrontations," always to "exercise restraint in their mutual relations," and to be prepared "to negotiate and settle differences by peaceful means." They further confirmed that "efforts to obtain unilateral advantage at the expense of the other, directly or indirectly"—that is, the pursuit of their national interest—would be inconsistent with these objectives. This incredible document has probably only one analogy in the history of international relations, and that is the Holy Alliance, agreed upon by the European powers in 1815, to placate a Russian tsar in the grip of mystic fervor with the pledge henceforth to base relations among themselves on Christian principles. Metternich thought the whole idea "loud-sounding nothing," while Castlereagh dismissed it as a "piece of sublime mysticism and nonsense." But in democratic societies, such promises tend to be taken seriously by the electorate, yielding to bewilderment and anger when they are broken.

The American doctrine of détente was never given the kind of theoretical underpinning that George Kennan had provided for the strategy of containment. Inquiries among highly placed officials involved in its formulation indicate that there exists no official document from that time that spells out the assumptions and objectives of détente. In practice, the doctrine of détente, as adopted in Washington, turned out to be nothing more than a patchwork of commonsensical opinions, loosely stitched together and never subjected to the test of critical analysis. No well-managed business firm would consider launching a new product without doing more thorough homework.

The main commonsensical premise behind détente held that if one lavished enough economic benefits on the Soviet Union it would develop so powerful an interest in good relations with the West that it would be bound to reciprocate with restraint in foreign policy. Positive stimuli, in the form of commercial rewards, were to influence behavior in the direction of accommodation. Just how credits and technology would affect Soviet political behavior was a question never addressed; no one took the trouble to identify the mechanism by means of which Western generosity would translate into Eastern restraint. Nor did anyone concern himself with the reasons for Soviet aggressiveness that détente was intended to assuage, apart from some trite ideas about Russian paranoia; there was the conviction that Soviet behavior could and should be manipulated, but no explanation why it needed to be manipulated in the first place. Ultimately, the whole détente doctrine rested on nothing more substantial than the faith that if one was nice to people they repaid in kind. In respect to its theoretical foundations, therefore, détente could stand no comparison with containment. In his public writings and internal memoranda, Mr. Kennan vacillated as to the causes of Soviet aggressiveness, sometimes attributing them to historical experience and at other times to Marxism-Leninism, but at least he did feel the need to look for causes. As it turned out, he was too optimistic in expecting that the Soviet Union, bottled up by Western action within its borders, would in a finite period of time—from five to fifteen years was his estimate—"mellow" and perhaps even collapse in revolution. He never spelled out how containment would accomplish these things. But of all the American officials involved in formulating a policy toward the USSR, he alone made an effort to link Soviet actions abroad to Soviet internal conditions, and both to Western responses.

Proponents of détente American style can, with some justice, argue that their theory was never given a chance to prove itself. Détente presupposed massive credits to the Soviet Union, but these were precluded by the terms of the Stevenson and Jackson-Vanik amendments, the latter of which made them conditional on formal Soviet commitment to large-scale emigration—a commitment the USSR refused to make. The argument is unconvincing, however, in view of the fact that West European countries did freely extend such credits to the Soviet Union and Eastern Europe without inducing Soviet restraint. In the United States, official circles no longer entertain the expectation that one can purchase Soviet good will with economic generosity. Secretary Shultz goes even further: he believes that economic transfers actually had the opposite of the desired result—"The economic relationship," he stated in June 1983 in testimony before the Senate Foreign Relations Committee, "may have eased some of the domestic Soviet economic restraints that might have at least marginally inhibited Moscow's behavior."

## 2 STRATEGIC OPPORTUNITIES FOR THE UNITED STATES

Ideally, one Grand Strategy should be matched by another. In reality, under peacetime conditions, a democracy cannot develop a Grand Strategy. This term defines a foreign policy of very broad scope that employs, in addition to diplomacy, also a variety of military instrumentalities (such as proxy forces and guerrillas), the entire national economy, and the media. Totalitarian regimes, by their very structure, find it easy, almost natural, to conduct a foreign policy of this sort. In democracies, however, the authority of governments is constrained in all spheres by constitutions and representative bodies; normally, it does not extend over economic resources and the organs of opinion. Their ability to make use of military force is also subject to stringent limitations. In the light of these facts, it would be unrealistic to urge the United States to develop a full-fledged Grand Strategy with which to neutralize the Soviet one.

This point conceded, it does not follow that democracies must operate with a conception of foreign policy that is narrower than even democratic conditions allow. The view that prevails in the United States holds foreign policy to be synonymous with diplomacy, in the sense that the purpose of both is to promote the peaceful resolution of international conflicts. In this conception, military force or any other form of pressure (such as economic sanctions), violates the spirit of foreign policy. Only when foreign policy (diplomacy) has patently failed is it proper to have recourse to force.

The following example, insignificant as it is in itself, will illustrate this contention. In 1983, in an effort to forestall further Communist encroachments in Central America, President Reagan sent to this region a diplomatic mission to learn the facts and present him with recommendations for a peaceful resolution of the conflicts there. At the same time, he ordered to the waters of Central America units of the U.S. Navy. The coincidence of the two actions, one diplomatic, the other military, seems to have caused confusion. Reporting on these events a national newspaper wrote: "Some officials worry that American policies now appear more contradictory than ever. They note that the military moves come at precisely the same time that the U.S. has made new diplomatic overtures to defuse tensions in the region."[7] Of course, there is nothing contradictory in the willingness to negotiate with parties that rely on force to gain their objectives and applying military pressure to bring them to the negotiating table. Unfortunately, it is the contrary attitude that prevails in the United States. One of its many undesirable consequences is that, just as the United States tends to shy away from resorting to military force to strengthen the hand of its diplomats, so, once it has given up on negotiating and decided to fight, it tends to forget the political purpose of the conflict in a single-minded pursuit of military victory. One need not adopt a full-fledged Grand Strategy to recognize that there is a great deal more to foreign policy than diplomacy and negotiation, that the interests of national security can be served by various means at a society's disposal.

In conducting a strategy of any kind, one presumably wants to exploit the opponent's weaknesses and neutralize his advantages. The principal sources of Soviet weakness at the present time have been surveyed in Chapters Three and Four. They are, in most summary form, a slowing economy that is progressively less able to meet the increased demands made on it by expanding military and imperial commitments, and a ruling elite that is out of touch with the population and under assault, at home and in its imperial possessions, from democratic and nationalist oppositions of all kinds. The Soviet Bloc is in crisis and ready for substantial systemic changes. Its principal assets reside in its ability to interfere in Western affairs while keeping itself immune from reciprocal action, and in its successful resort to nuclear terror for the purpose of paralyzing resistance to its aggressive acts.

In the discussion that follows, these subjects will be taken up in this order: (1) neutralizing the Soviet military threat, especially its exploitation, for political purposes, of nuclear anxieties; (2) restricting the Soviet ability to interfere in Western politics; (3) using economic interdiction as a means of promoting economic reforms in the Soviet Union and its Bloc.

## 3 THE MILITARY ASPECT

The mission of the military forces of NATO is and has always been a defensive one, namely, preventing Soviet military encroachments on the territories of Western Europe. There is nothing that the countries of the Soviet Bloc possess that could conceivably tempt the Western alliance to commit aggression against them: neither natural resources (these can be gotten cheaper elsewhere), nor industrial or other forms of man-made wealth (poor and primitive by Western standards), nor markets for their goods (insignificant for lack of hard currency). It would produce an economic disaster of the first magnitude were the West to conquer the Eastern Bloc and assume responsibility for administering and feeding the area—the Marshall Plan would look by comparison like a grant-in-aid. The West would be well advised to decline the Communist Bloc if offered it free of charge; it certainly cannot have the slightest interest in going to war to seize it by force. Nor do Communist ideology and life style exert such attraction for their people as to threaten Western societies with internal subversion. All these considerations explain why the contingency plans of NATO have always been defensive. Whatever they say in public—and totalitarian regimes have a habit of ascribing to others their own intentions so as to disguise their aggressive designs as defensive reactions—the Soviet leaders are well aware of these facts. This is demonstrated by their willingness to maintain most of their military forces, nuclear ones included, on low levels of alert, something they would hardly risk if they feared coming under sudden attack.

Most succinctly defined, Western conventional forces have the task of containing the potential enemy, and Western nuclear forces that of deterring him. The relationship between the two types of force, however, is not well thought out in Western strategic doctrine, which may create some uncertainty in the mind of the Soviet General Staff, but is certain to cause chaos and confusion in Western ranks should hostilities ever break out.

Advocates of nuclear disarmament usually balance their calls for unilateral Western cutbacks or declarations of "no first use" with demands for improvements in conventional forces. Their argument rests on the twin assumptions that the shift from nuclear to conventional deterrence would diminish the risks of nuclear war and, at the same time, permit reductions in defense budgets. The first of these propositions is doubtful because it assumes that the decision to employ nuclear weapons is one for the West to make and depends on the ability of its conventional forces to stop the advance of the Warsaw Pact. Given the central role assigned to nuclear weapons in Soviet strategy, such an assumption seems unrealistic. As will be pointed out later, it is far more likely that recourse to nuclear weapons will be initiated by Moscow. The second proposition is demonstrably wrong. Nuclear weapons are relatively cheap: they absorb between 10 and 15 percent of the military budgets of the United States and the USSR. It is conventional forces that eat up defense allocations in both countries. Reductions of nuclear arsenals may bring all kinds of desirable results, but if they are accompanied by increases in conventional forces, such measures certainly will not reduce defense outlays, at any rate, in the West. Furthermore, in any competition restricted to conventional forces, the Soviet side has a marked advantage in that it pays its troops such low salaries that it can devote a much larger proportion of the defense budget to weapons and equipment—by some estimates, between two and three times as much as the United States.*

Setting aside the issue of the most efficient use of defense funds, the amount of money allocated for this purpose must clearly be measured against the military threat with which it is meant to cope and not against domestic needs, however urgent these may be. It is illogical to urge cuts in defense appropriations on the ground that there are higher "priorities" in education or medical services. The cartoon reproduced below engages in crude demagoguery when it depicts spending money on defense as gambling with money stolen from emaciated children. One may legitimately question whether the United States needs the MX or Britain the Trident submarine, but the argument has to be decided on military, not on social, criteria. Since defense expenditures, both in general and in particular, are designed to meet concrete threats posed by foreign powers—that is, powers outside the reach of our will—they cannot be treated as if they were wholly discretionary.

Nor is it sensible to question defense appropriations on the specious grounds that America's strength lies in other than military fields—that "the biggest deterrent to the Russians is a healthy economy in America," as the head of the National Association of Manufacturers recently put it.[8] Quite apart from the fact that a healthy American economy is precisely what whets the appetite of the Russians, the statement is absurd; if it were correct, then a healthy body would be the best deterrent against rape or murder, which is not quite what experience teaches. Economies do not stop armies any more than do schools or hospitals—only armies stop armies. It has been correctly pointed out that since every country has an army on its soil, the only choice citizens can exercise in the matter is to decide whether this army will be their own or someone else's.

It should be self-evident that the size and structure of military forces are determined by their mission, and that their mission, in turn, is, or at least ought to be, dictated by the size and structure of the forces at the disposal of the potential enemy. For a variety of reasons, however, this is not always the case. Military strategists are inclined to regard their discipline as something of a sci-

---

* A Soviet soldier is paid four rubles a month, which at the official exchange rate amounts to slightly over five dollars, but at black-market rates comes to less than one dollar. Since this is as much as no pay, the bulk of the Soviet Army may be said to consist of temporarily bonded serfs. The United States private, for comparison, receives nearly $600 a month.

## "BARGAINING CHIPS"

©1983 HERBLOCK

Reprinted with permission from *The Washington Post*

ence, and hence of universal validity. They are disinclined to take seriously other strategic doctrines, especially if such doctrines deviate significantly from their own. This phenomenon almost always bodes disaster for the party that is on the defensive; one need only recall the tragic consequences of the Allied attempt in 1940 to wage a stationary war against an enemy who was making open preparations for a campaign of rapid movement. Something similar seems to be recurring today. Western strategists have no difficulty confronting the threat posed by the conventional forces of the Warsaw Pact, since it is of a familiar kind, but they do not show the same receptivity to the innovative Soviet nuclear strategies. To be sure, the concept of escalation from a conventional to a nuclear defense has formed the backbone of NATO's "flexible response" doctrine since the 1960s. But the United States seems not to have thought through the uses to which nuclear weapons would be put, should circumstance require that the nuclear threshold be crossed. It is altogether difficult to know how seriously to take this doctrine now that Mr. Robert McNamara, who served as Secretary of Defense when "flexible response" was adopted, has gone on record that in his time the first use of nuclear weapons was not even seriously contemplated: "In long private conversations with successive presidents—Kennedy and Johnson," he has recently revealed, "I recommended, without qualification, that they never initiate, under any circumstances, the use of nuclear weapons. I believe they accepted my recommendation."[9] This authoritative statement constitutes an admission that the centerpiece of NATO's whole strategy has been a bluff since its inception and that the civilian leaders have been misleading their citizens for over twenty years in a matter of the greatest national importance.

This underscores the confusion and emotionalism that surround the entire issue of nuclear weapons in the mind of both military personnel and the public at large. Hardly anyone lacking in professional competence dares to intrude on the discussion of NATO's conventional forces and their strategy; this is a matter gladly left to the experts. But nuclear weapons have become everyone's business; indeed, any citizen who would claim incompetence on such issues as the MX or START would risk being accused of social irresponsibility. Some circles in the United States committed to unilateral nuclear disarmament are not averse to involving in the debate even children, apparently in the belief that the more important a subject is the less one needs to know about it. People who would not dream of advising a chef on preparing hollandaise sauce dispense advice freely when the topic is the immensely complicated one of nuclear weapons and strategy.

In the West, it is well-nigh axiomatic that nuclear weapons, "in the ultimate analysis," can serve only one function, and that is to deter or to serve as a kind of monstrous scarecrow, and that as long as this deterrent makes a sufficiently frightening impression, it will never have to be resorted to. Axioms being self-evident, the consequences of the deterrent's failure to deter have not been seriously considered. From what is known of Soviet doctrine, one must conclude that there exists by now an ominous discrepancy between Allied defensive and Soviet offensive plans—whereas the one party (the West) draws a sharp distinction between conventional and nuclear weapons, the other treats the two as different wavelengths on a single and continuous spectrum of the instruments of war. It is almost certain that should war ever break out, the Allies would find themselves thoroughly confused by the enemy's offensive moves and have to improvise their defenses in desperate haste—that is, if they will be given time to do so.

Considering the close correlation between Soviet theoretical writings and deployments, one might think that Western opinion would come to acknowledge that Moscow does look at nuclear weapons differently and assigns them different missions. Yet this is not the case; indeed, any attempt to call attention to the discrepancy in the two views arouses public anger as if some taboo were being broken.

The role that Western scientists have played in developing this immunity to evidence has been noted previously (pp. 92–94). But there are still profounder causes that explain the unwillingness of people to face the implications of Soviet nuclear strategy, and these have to do with collective anxieties rooted in the deepest recesses of the human psyche.

In the view of much of humanity, nuclear weapons are not weapons in the ordinary meaning of the word but instruments of cosmic destruction, the expectation of which forms part of what Karl Jung called mankind's "collective unconscious." It is an unsettling, but by no means unusual, experience in the 1980s to attend professional symposia at which so-called conventional war, which in 1939–45 had claimed 50 million lives, is calmly discussed as an acceptable alternative to nuclear war. Such discussions serve to confirm that nuclear weapons are in a category of their own and not only because of their destructiveness.

As a rule, religions that posit the existence of God or gods believe that the world had come into being from a deliberate act of divine will. A corollary of this belief is the expectation that the world and life are transient since whatever had a beginning must also have an end. In widely dispersed regions of the globe, long before the Christian era, legends circulated about the coming doomsday. Some religions envisaged it as taking the form of floods and earthquakes, others as inundations by molten metal flowing out of mountains. But the most prevalent doomsday vision was that of a cosmic holocaust—that is, the annihilation of the earth and life by an all-consuming fire. It is a theme that occurs in the epics of ancient Babylon, in the Indian Vedas, and in the Mithraic tales of Iran. It can be found also in the legends of classical Greece (e.g., the story of Phaëton whose theft of a chariot belonging to his father, Helios, nearly caused the universe to be destroyed by fire), in the epics of the Indo-Germanic peoples, and in Nordic tales. The Jews seem to have come under the spell of these images as well; in the Bible, the vision of the Last Judgment is closely linked to that of a fiery holocaust:

> Neither their silver nor their gold
> shall be able to deliver them
> on the day of the wrath of the Lord.
> *In the fire of his jealous wrath,*
> *all the earth shall be consumed;*
> *for a full, yea, sudden end*
> *he will make of all the inhabitants*
> *of the earth . . .*
> —ZEPHANIAH, 1:18 (SEVENTH CEN-
> TURY B.C.)

> Blow the trumpet in Zion;
> sound the alarm on my holy mountain!
> Let all the inhabitants of the land tremble,
> for the day of the Lord is coming, it is near,
> *a day of darkness and gloom,*
> *a day of clouds and thick darkness . . .*
>
> *Fire devours before them,*
> *and behind them a flame burns. . . .*
> —JOEL, 2:1–3 (FOURTH CENTURY B.C.)

The author of the two books of Peter in the Christian Bible wrote in this tradition, when he prophesied that "the day of the Lord will come like a thief, and then the heavens will pass away with a loud noise, *and the elements will be dissolved with fire, and the earth and the works that are upon it will be burned up.*" (II PETER 3:10)

Because it is so ancient and almost universal, so frequently re-iterated in religious works that until recent times have been the main source of human knowledge and wisdom, the expectation of an inevitable final holocaust has imbedded itself deeply in the human psyche; it is a classic archetype with which argument is powerless to contend. Once it had made its appearance, "the bomb" filled a role that had awaited casting for thousands of years. One can find surprising anticipations of this weapon in literary works unrelated to religion and religious visions. Thus, in Montesquieu's *Persian Letters,* published in 1721, in Letter 105 there occurs out of the blue the following passage: "I am always afraid that they will eventually succeed in discovering some secret which will provide a quicker way of making men die, and exterminate whole countries and nations." How did this thought cross Montesquieu's mind? Since in his time there were no scientific grounds for such a supposition, one must assume he was echoing fears whose sources lie in mythology. It is known that so-called Unidentified Flying Objects have been reported at least as early as the 1550s, because there exist published accounts and illustrations to this effect dating from that time.[10] Hence it is not fanciful to interpret the atomic mushroom which the "peace movement" likes to use for its logogram, as a modern version of the "flaming torch" of the Prophet Zechariah and the "high flame that reaches to the sky" of the Nordic epic.

The instantaneous pulverization of two Japanese cities by weapons that the public neither anticipated nor understood set off mass anxieties absent in the case of other calamities, of comparable if not greater destructiveness. Mankind apparently can tolerate the death, by starvation, in the man-made famine of the 1930s, of nine million Ukrainians and Russians, the annihilation by poison gas and bullet of six million Jews, the massacre by Communist forces of between one and two million Cambodians. These calamities, being man-made, are "natural." Nuclear weapons, however, though manufactured by man, are treated as supernatural, for they come from the sky, destroying by invisible rays. The dread of this magic power has even affected its peaceful uses. It touches on the rawest nerve in man's collective psyche.

The hundreds of thousands who march to protest nuclear war are not giving expression to their political convictions, since no one clamors in favor of such a war. Rather (when they are not being manipulated), they take part in pseudo-religious rituals meant to propitiate, by tokens of awe and fear, the evil spirits whose abode is neutrons and protons. Anyone who disparages such emotional displays and calls for a dispassionate analysis of the issues or, worse yet, for defenses against nuclear weapons, violates powerful taboos and is appropriately punished by the multitude. This helps to explain why so many proponents of the "freeze" and other forms of unilateral disarmament show no interest in the facts of the case, such as Soviet nuclear doctrine and Soviet nuclear deployments, and their combined effect on Western security. Mr. Kennan, whose record shows him to be an eminently well-informed and sober analyst of international relations, as soon as he approaches nuclear issues abandons his customary detachment and even scholarly curiosity. The facts, such as the numbers of missiles and warheads in the Soviet and United States arsenals, he dismisses as irrelevant—"I have no patience with 'worst-case' estimates of Soviet military strength"; "I have no confidence in sweeping quantitative figures"; "I have no confidence in statistics"; "I must totally reject . . . ," none of such *obiter dicta* supported with any evidence.[11] What Mr. Kennan does is castigate man for his wickedness and predict his imminent destruction, more in religious than in political or military terms. The same applies to Mr. Jonathan Schell, whose *Fate of the Earth* has been praised as a major contribution to the national debate. Actually, it is nothing of the kind. It is, instead, a long-winded jeremiad on the familiar horrors of nuclear war. It never even raises the questions that would really matter in a debate: Do Soviet generals think in the same way? If so, why are they piling missile upon missile long after crossing the line of "overkill"? And if not, what should our response be?

The tragedy of people who approach nuclear matters in archetypal religious terms is that in the genuine Jewish and Christian religious vision (as contrasted with its secular travesty), the holocaust was followed by the Last Judgment, which set the just apart from the wicked and restored Eden; from their heavenly abode the virtuous were to observe the eternal torments of the condemned. But following the general decline of belief in God and afterlife, man is left with the appalling prospect that his fate has passed into human hands; the unleashing of the holocaust, once the prerogative of God or gods, is now the prerogative of a few mortals with fingers on the "button." In a man-made holocaust, the virtuous will not be saved but will perish along with the sinners. Thus, agnosticism intensifies manifold an anxiety that has its origins in religious belief, leaving the horror but robbing it of hope. It produces an overpowering sense of helplessness that the unscrupulous exploit for their own political ends.

If man has become master of his fate, then he also is responsible for preventing that ultimate disaster, a holocaust unaccompanied by final judgment. Since nuclear weapons cannot be undone, a large part of the population has come to attach an exaggerated, almost manic importance to arms control. In the United States, nearly three fourths of those polled express faith in arms control as an effective means of reducing the risks of war. In Western Europe, their proportion is even higher; for many Europeans, arms control has become a surrogate for defense. Paraphrasing Churchill, one might say that never in history have so many attached so much importance to so little.

No reasonable person can deny that, all other things being equal, the fewer weapons abroad the better and that, should the antagonistic camps feel secure at lower levels of armaments, everyone will benefit. This can be said in principle, even though the historic record gives no grounds for confidence that treaties restricting weapon deployments are able significantly to restrain military preparations, let alone forestall war. Arms-control agreements concluded in the early decades of this century, mostly to regulate naval construction, have not made much difference and in one case (the British-German Naval Treaty of 1935) were used by the future aggressor to secure political and military advantages.

SALT and other arms-control accords are treaties and, as such, diplomatic and not military acts, for which reason they cannot serve as a substitute for maintaining the military balance. Nor can they be isolated or "decoupled" from the whole complex of international relations unrelated to the nuclear competition. Surely, any sensible individual about to sign a contract would want to learn all there is about the other party, especially its record of keeping contracts; he would not likely yield to arguments that a particular agreement is so critical that background investigations can be dispensed with. In the field of nuclear arms limitations, however, different rules prevail. Here it is not uncommon to be told that these accords are of such moment that all else the Soviet Union does or has done must be ignored. Logically, the more important a contract, the more reason to look at it in the broadest context possible rather than in isolation. It seems improbable that a regime that habitually violates law, especially at home, where it can act with impunity, and readily resorts to force to settle disputes in its favor, will show scrupulous respect for arms-control treaties and rely on peaceful procedures to resolve its differences with other nations. Respect for law and contract is a habit that one either acquires or does not. Indeed, because it assigns nuclear weapons the central role in modern warfare, the Soviet Union is more likely to honor treaties affecting ordinary matters than those limiting nuclear weapons.

The emotionalism that surrounds this whole issue transforms the process of nuclear-arms negotiation from what it ought to be

—namely, matter-of-fact bargaining—into a quasi-religious ritual, whose success is measured not by the results obtained but by the "sincerity" with which it is approached. In the 1970s, Western planners could not even decide on deploying a modest force of intermediate-range missiles to partly offset Soviet SS-20s, without coupling such deployment to arms negotiations with the Soviet Union. This double-track policy, hailed as the acme of political sophistication, has had the effect of giving Moscow a seat in NATO's councils. Whenever the USSR commissions, tests and deploys new missiles, which happens routinely, it never seems to occur to its leaders to make such actions dependent on Western approval. Feelings on this subject, however, run so high that democratic politicians have no choice but to yield to public clamor. President Reagan, who on assuming office had intended to proceed in this matter more deliberately than his predecessors, soon found himself swept by the emotional tide and compelled first to initiate arms-control talks before he was ready for them and, secondly, to shift them from the periphery of his foreign policy, where they properly belong, to its very center.

Soviet leaders, who are free of such domestic pressures, attach little importance to arms-control negotiations, except as they help to restrain *Western* advances in technology and to divide *Western* opinion. In internal Soviet literature on security issues, the subject is hardly ever mentioned. The USSR has not bothered even to establish a counterpart to the U.S. Arms Control and Disarmament Agency. Soviet personnel involved in these negotiations is dominated by the military, who, insofar as can be determined, are accountable to the General Staff, an institution not normally associated with disarmament. Evidence from SALT I, SALT II, and START negotiation suggests that the Soviet side first determines what weapons it requires to meet its strategic objectives and then concentrates on constraining, through negotiation, America's ability to respond. In the words of the French General Pierre Gallois, "[The Soviets] do what they want and negotiate about what you're going to do." [12]

Because its driving force is emotional, the arms-control movement is riddled with intellectual contradictions. The most glaring of these involves two incompatible notions, "overkill" and nuclear freeze, which most proponents of arms control manage to accommodate in their heads side by side without visible discomfort. The point is that if, indeed, the so-called superpowers possess already enough weapons to destroy each other many times over, then it follows that a freeze on their existing arsenals would accomplish nothing whatever; nor would reductions, as long as they fell short of the level of mutual destruction. And if it is true, as some of them (advocates of so-called "minimum deterrence") maintain, that a single submarine can annihilate an entire country, then even one submarine is too much; certainly anything above that level is redundant and does not materially affect anything. Yet no arms proposal is ever radical enough to take account of "overkill." The proponents of this concept can have only one logically consistent position, and that is that the deployment of weapons above present levels is a waste of money; they cannot hold that it increases the danger of universal destruction, since by their own premise that is already more than assured by the existing arsenals.

The American experts who in 1972 concluded SALT I with the USSR did not believe in the military utility of nuclear weapons on either the strategic or the theater level. To them, an arms agreement was primarily a political device, the second pillar of détente (the other being credits and trade). As one European specialist put it at the time, "There's a lot of eyewash in these agreements, but their significance lies in the extent to which they reflect the mutual recognition of the need to cooperate in the nuclear-disarmament field."[13] In other words, the terms did not matter as much as did the political atmospherics. From the beginning it was indeed the political process, cynically manipulated for its public-relations effect, rather than the deadly reality of the nuclear balance that the United States and its allies regarded as the foremost priority. As a result of this attitude, the United States has allowed some very disadvantageous features to intrude into these accords, of which the public at large is blissfully ignorant.

&#9633; The Soviet side has from the outset refused to furnish comprehensive data on its strategic systems—in itself, a most extraordinary procedure. Since, however, negotiation on limiting numbers could not very well proceed without agreement on what these numbers were, Moscow has consented (without prejudice) to accept the data for its side furnished by the United States. The United States could only account for those Soviet systems of which it had solid evidence from its intelligence-gathering sources, not those that were beyond their scope. Although the Soviet Union subsequently agreed to furnish random data on its nuclear forces, the information at the disposal of the United States is certain only to reflect the minimum dimension of the Soviet nuclear arsenal; the precise dimensions of this arsenal were not and are not known. It would certainly be difficult to find a businessman prepared to enter into relations with a company that refused to provide him with complete information on its assets and debts; in the field of national security, unfortunately, different standards prevail.

□ Because the United States has been compelled all along to rely on its "national means of verification" (mainly satellites and electronic intelligence) to verify Soviet compliance with the limits established by SALT, it had to choose a unit of measurement that lent itself to observation by these means. The choice, by mutual consent, fell on "launchers." In the case of Intercontinental Ballistic Missiles (ICBMs), a launcher is a hole in the ground called a silo. A silo can be seen from the air, whereas a missile can be concealed. Unfortunately, however, it is not silos but missiles that fly and their warheads that inflict damage. Knowledge of only launchers (silos, submarine tubes, and bombers) furnishes an inadequate idea of the other side's destructive capacity. The United States, therefore, cannot be said to dispose of accurate information on the number of missiles and warheads in the Soviet arsenal; the figures used in SALT and START postulate that each launcher holds a corresponding number of missiles, and that no missiles are unaccounted for. This is almost certainly an incorrect assumption. In the case of Soviet ICBMs, the number of stockpiled missiles must exceed that of known launchers (silos), because the USSR has been observed experimenting with "cold launch" techniques that allow the missile to fire its boosters after leaving the silo so as to leave the latter intact for the insertion of a second missile. This practice presupposes a strategic-missile reserve the size of which is not known. The SS-20 intermediate-range mobile missile is believed to be equipped with two missiles per launcher, although in the publicly released balance-of-forces statistics only one is assumed and counted. More disturbing still is the realization that the USSR need not emplace its ICBMs in silos at all; the more accurate American missiles become, the less reason does Moscow have to place its main strategic force (ICBMs account for three quarters of Soviet launchers) in static silos, where they are vulnerable. On these grounds, some American experts question whether the silos that satellites are busily observing and counting are not either decoys or expendable goods, while the bulk of Soviet ICBMs intended for use is concealed, to be launched in wartime from soft pads, such as sheds and other places of storage, beyond the range of United States observation.

□ In its insularity, the United States has consented in SALT and START to define a missile as "strategic" if it is capable of striking the continental United States from the Soviet Union and vice versa. Since the nearest distance between these two countries (across the Bering Strait) is a few miles, the range was arbitrarily set to be equal to the distance separating the northeastern United States from the northwestern USSR, that is, 5,500 kilometers. Only weapons capable of this or greater ranges come within the purview of SALT limits. Such a definition would perhaps make sense in a narrow "Fortress America" context, under which the United States would have neither forces overseas nor overseas allies whom it was committed to defend. It makes little sense in the context of global strategy. The rules to which the United States has agreed have given the Soviet Union, which controls the center of the Eurasian land mass, the license to deploy unlimited quantities of nuclear launchers with ranges just below the "intercontinental" threshold yet capable of striking targets in all the areas adjacent to its immense frontier in Europe, the Middle East, North Africa and East Asia. The Soviet Union accepted this definition of *strategic* only for the purpose of negotiating with the United States; in structuring its own nuclear forces, it has never adopted such a standard, since all its missiles with ranges exceeding one thousand kilometers come under the command of the Strategic Rocket Forces—a procedure that inadvertently throws light on Soviet thinking about the uses of nuclear weapons. So it has happened that quite lawfully, within the terms of SALT I and SALT II, free of any numerical constraints, the USSR has been able to deploy since the 1970s a massive force of modern, mostly mobile, intermediate-range nuclear systems. When NATO awoke to this reality and decided to counter it by deploying some intermediate-range, land-based missiles below the 5,500-kilometer range but capable of striking Soviet territory from Western Europe, the USSR charged that they fell within the definition of "strategic." Thus, the West's lack of attention and foresight has already caused it no end of trouble. Even with the Pershing IIs and cruise missiles in place, the USSR will still enjoy an immense advantage in substrategic systems.

□ The United States assiduously collects data on Soviet compliance with the provisions of SALT I and SALT II, the latter of which, although not ratified by Washington, is, by mutual consent, treated as though it were. Such investigations have revealed a consistent pattern of violations of the spirit, and even the letter, of these agreements. The information, however, has not been given much publicity, because committed advocates of arms control, afraid lest it undercut public support for the process, intimidate those who wish to bring it into the open. The fanaticism of some of these people goes to such lengths that instead of blaming the Soviet Union for violation of arms-control agreements, they accuse the United States of ill will for calling attention to them.

When President Reagan, in one of his speeches, referred to the poor Soviet record of compliance, he came under attack from some legislators and journalists for his alleged "insincerity" about arms negotiation. This is a dangerous variant of a theory popular in contemporary liberal circles that the victim of a crime is as guilty as, if not more than, its perpetrator.

Quite apart from its inequities and inconsistencies, the arms-control process has so far failed to achieve its principal stated objective, which is to stop the growth of nuclear arsenals. In 1970, when SALT I was being negotiated, the Soviet Union had approximately 1,400 strategic warheads; in 1977, as SALT II talks neared completion, its arsenal had grown to nearly five thousand warheads; in 1983–84, during START talks, this arsenal had risen further to 7,900 warheads. This growth was nearly a sixfold increase. During this same time, the United States, mainly by MIRVing its missiles to match the Soviet buildup, had more than tripled the number of warheads in its arsenal (from 2,200 to 7,400). If this is arms control, it might be interesting to experiment for a while with an honest arms race.

In dealing with nuclear weapons nothing is more important than demystifying them—that is, severing the psychic bonds that connect them, in our conscious and subconscious, with ancient religious myths. These are man-made weapons. The Soviet nuclear arsenal is at the disposal neither of gods nor of evil spirits but of ordinary men, many of them overweight and overworked, scared of losing what they have, observed to suffer from dandruff and bad breath. Our main purpose should be to convince these men that they cannot intimidate us. Fear of nuclear weapons, especially in its overt and hysterical forms, does not contribute to peace; on the contrary, it serves to encourage those in the Soviet Union who want to use them to terrorize and blackmail foreign powers and their citizens. It should also be made eminently clear to these people that if they should ever dare to carry out their strategic plans and fire nuclear missiles in anger, they and their families will perish. It is only when the magic and the taboos that surround it are removed, that one can deal with this real danger realistically. The analogy with cancer comes to mind. Not so long ago the very name of this dreaded disease could not be pronounced for fear of inviting it. Today, cancer is openly discussed, even by its victims, and it is this honest acknowledgment that has made it possible to deal with it more effectively. Nuclear weapons, which are a kind of cancer of the international body politic, should be looked upon with the same dispassion. The beginning of morality, Pascal has taught, is clear thinking.

It is essential for anyone concerned with nuclear weapons,

whether in a professional capacity or as a layman, to familiarize himself with Soviet nuclear doctrine and programs. They are the reality against which United States strategies and programs must be matched. In all deliberations on the matter at the public level, the issue should not be the settling of scores between American liberals and conservatives, nor the undisputed horrors of nuclear war, nor America's social and other domestic needs, but solely the nature and extent of the Soviet threat. Any statement on the subject of nuclear weapons and strategy that fails to address itself to this central subject ought to be dismissed as irrelevant.

United States strategic forces should be designed not simply to deter aggression and to punish it after it has been committed, but to prevent threats of subsequent damage. This means, among other things, that it was appropriate for the United States to renounce the policy—as barbaric as it was futile—of retaliatory strikes aimed at the civilian population. The target, indeed, should be the true culprits of such aggression, the *nomenklatura* and its armed forces. Specialists estimate that there are in the Soviet Union between 10,000 and 20,000 objectives of political and military significance. If that assessment is correct, then the United States needs that many accurate warheads left *after absorbing a first Soviet strike*; this capability alone will provide a deterrent credible to Moscow. It makes little sense to measure existing United States strategic forces against those available to the Soviet Strategic Rocket Forces command (even assuming that it is known precisely what these are), because the United States has no first-strike doctrine or capability whereas the Soviet side has both. The only force that counts, therefore, is the one left following a Soviet first strike. While the present survivable force could indubitably inflict grueling punishment on the USSR's civilian population, it could not destroy its political or military organization and the nuclear forces at their disposal.

Improving NATO's conventional forces is certainly desirable, but it is unlikely of itself to prevent a war from turning nuclear. The assumption that underlies Western strategy—that the decision whether to resort to nuclear weapons will be for the West to make—may have made sense when first devised, but it seems unrealistic today in the light of what is known of Soviet plans and capabilities in this regard. A military command that has built its armed forces around a nuclear core is unlikely to defer use of it until the enemy has given it an excuse to do so. The USSR is not in a position, either politically or economically, to engage in a military war of attrition. Such a war would exacerbate all its latent problems and unleash an internal crisis under the worst possible circumstances. Should it decide that war has become unavoidable,

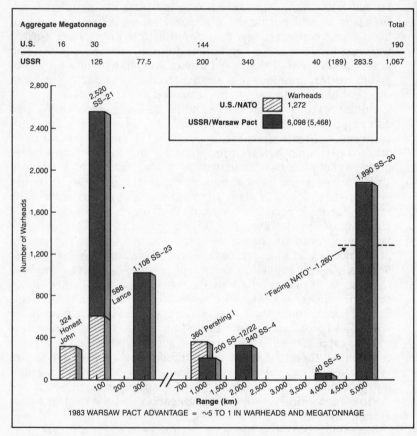

COMPARISON OF NATO/WARSAW PACT LAND-BASED
SURFACE-TO-SURFACE NUCLEAR FORCES IN EUROPE
(As of 1983) *

| Aggregate Megatonnage | | | | | | | | Total |
|---|---|---|---|---|---|---|---|---|
| **U.S.** | 16 | 30 | | 144 | | | | 190 |
| **USSR** | | 126 | 77.5 | 200 | 340 | 40 (189) | 283.5 | 1,067 |

therefore, it will almost certainly have prompt recourse to nuclear
weapons, since they alone offer it a chance of gaining a rapid and
decisive victory. Tactical nuclear weapons are fully integrated into
Soviet land forces, down to the divisional level, each commander
disposing of rockets systems of a range appropriate to his mission,
which suggests that they are meant to be fired in the first hours of
combat:

* Table based on D. Cotter et al., *The Nuclear "Balance" in Europe: Status, Trends, Implications* (Washington, D.C., 1983). Reproduced with permission of the United States Strategic Institute.

Soviet theater nuclear weapons are not simply "there," as a "reaction" to NATO nuclear capabilities or even in some vague back-up role for Soviet conventional operations. Rather, they were developed, produced and deployed in response to *specific requirements within a concept of offensive operations;* they are assigned specific missions within that concept; and they thus form an integral part of the Soviet–Warsaw Pact posture in Europe.[14]

The scenario for the use of these forces has been depicted by General Gallois as follows:

It is a fact that the Kremlin leaders know that they may only engage their armed forces in a victorious war. Therefore they would have recourse to the strategy, tactics, and weapons of success. With their ballistic arsenal, utilizable with the advantage of total surprise, they now have possession of such weapons in quantity . . . [By] the way it today deploys its conventional contingents, NATO obligingly offers up for destruction some 400 to 500 crucial targets that, when neutralized, will leave all resistance completely paralyzed. And these targets are planes in their air fields, the antennae of fixed radars, munition and tank depots, military headquarters, among others. Precision ballistic weapons carrying nuclear warheads, all the more powerful the greater their precision, could destroy the majority of these targets without considerable damage. Thus, and only after having launched this initial salvo, the Warsaw Pact tanks and airborne units would occupy the previously disarmed and practically intact territories.[15]

These considerations suggest that it is as naïve to envision a potential East-West conflict being waged on the model of World War II —that is, with tanks and bombers—as it was to expect in the 1930s to fight another war with Germany in the trenches. Should World War III ever break out, the Soviet Union is likely swiftly to take the initiative with all the weapons at its disposal, including nuclear ones. It makes, therefore, little sense to concentrate one's attention on preventing nuclear war as such, as if conventional war were a viable alternative; one must strive to avoid war altogether, because any general war with the USSR probably will not remain in a conventional mode for any length of time, if at all.

The West would do well to emulate Soviet planners and pay greater attention to defensive measures. The Reagan administration has taken steps to improve the protection of United States command, control and communications networks, which is welcome news, since they are a declared prime target of Soviet strategic forces. Because an effective program of civil defense does not seem practical in a democracy as large and diverse as the United States, there is reason to devote greater effort to antiballistic-missile-defense programs. Those who dismiss the idea as science fiction might change their mind after taking a closer look at Soviet efforts in this direction. Moscow's deployment of an elaborate ABM system around Moscow suggests that it takes defenses against missiles seriously. There are so many other indicators of intense Soviet work on missile defenses, that some American military analysts fear a technical breakthrough followed by Soviet renunciation of the treaty limiting ABM deployments. Once its arsenals are overflowing with offensive weapons, it would make sense for Moscow to shift its attention in this field to defensive measures, which, in any event, have always played a major role in its strategic thinking. Should such a development take place, it would pose a serious threat to United States security. Opposition to nuclear defenses on the ground that they are "destabilizing" should go the way of the advocacy of Mutually Assured Destruction, whose ill-begotten child it is.

Efforts toward arms-control agreements certainly ought to be pursued, but much more modest expectations are in order. Accords on arms cannot be expected to pave the way for political agreements; they have to follow them. It is only when the USSR will have adopted established norms of international conduct and reconciled itself to a world composed of a community of sovereign nations, that diplomacy will be in a position to devise procedures for resolving East-West differences comparable to those it now has for settling West-West differences; then and only then will resort to violence become unnecessary, and the instruments of violence will become redundant. No one in the United States loses sleep over the British and French nuclear arsenals, which have a combined force of 300 warheads (with more to come), even though they are capable of obliterating every American city with 50,000 or more inhabitants, or some seventy million people. The threat derives not from these lifeless objects, but from human animosities that cause them to be manufactured, stockpiled and readied for use in the first place. If and when the Soviet Union alters its system, ideology and policies to the point where it will desire a genuine *rapprochement* with the rest of the world, then and only then will meaningful arms-control agreements become possible. Until such time, they are best looked upon as modest efforts, most likely to succeed in dealing with those weapons or practices that both parties have an interest in eliminating, such as, for example, nuclear proliferation.

Should political conditions make meaningful agreements possible, at least three cardinal requirements ought to be met. The most important of those is on-site verification, because the existing "national means," marvels of technological ingenuity that they are, do not provide the requisite certainty. The second is agreement on a sensible unit of measurement, which, once verification on the ground has been agreed upon, will assuredly be something other than launchers. The third calls for the adoption by the United States of a definition of "strategic weapons" that corresponds to the Soviet one; this measure will eliminate the possibility of the USSR being free to construct a panoply of nuclear weapons that, unable though they are to reach the continental United States, can very well reach and destroy its allies. Arms-control agreements concluded under different circumstances and on other terms are either pointless or deceptive or both.

The rearmament program inaugurated by President Reagan, when completed, should allow the United States to match Soviet military capabilities. This effort is commendable but not sufficient. The true military balance lies not in equality of military forces alone but in the combination of force and strategy. The history of warfare knows many examples of superior strategic skill defeating larger armies. Napoleon routinely beat armies that on paper were stronger than his own, only to be crushed, in turn, by the Russian army which, too weak to give him battle, retreated and in retreating chanced upon a strategy that rendered him helpless. In 1940, the Allied force in France was larger and in many respects better equipped than the German, but it was burdened with a strategy that looked backward. Arming oneself, therefore, is not enough; an even greater threat than being outgunned is being outsmarted.

As it has not thought through how to meet the Soviet nuclear challenge, so the United States has not given adequate attention to proxy and other forms of indirect warfare, which are likely to pose to it ever greater dangers.

Given its desire to reduce the United States without resort to general war, it is natural for the Soviet Union to rely heavily on the regular and irregular forces of third parties. Except for Afghanistan, the Red Army has engaged itself in combat only in countries that lie inside Moscow's imperial borders, where its right to do so is tacitly acknowledged by the international community. Elsewhere, Moscow has preferred to use colonial troops, guerrillas and terrorists. As it experiences increasing difficulties in extending its influence in the Third World, it is likely to be tempted to resort ever more to such indirect forms of warfare. It is imprudent, therefore, for the United States military to persist in treating proxy warfare as a sort of nuisance; it promises to be much more than that.

Proxy warfare assumes three forms: (1) expansion by means of the armed forces of other Communist countries, such as Cuba and Vietnam, which are politically and economically dependent on the Soviet Union, and on occasion, of non-Communist countries (e.g., Libya) that, for reasons of their own, make common cause with Moscow; (2) guerrilla movements in the Third World, operating with Soviet support and often under close Soviet supervision (e.g., Philippines, El Salvador); (3) terrorist groups of all kinds, whom Soviet secret services help train and equip in order to eliminate or to intimidate unfriendly forces (e.g., American troops in Germany and Lebanon or Israel) or else to sow chaos in countries that Moscow has an interest in destabilizing (e.g., Turkey).

One of the main difficulties which the West encounters in coping with all three forms of indirect warfare is of a legal nature:

> The Western states, throughout their history, have adhered to the concept of direct responsibility of government for their conduct. Indeed, this is one of the central tenets of that international law which is a product of Western culture. The nation-states of the West, when they have gone to war, have usually done so only after fastening, to their own satisfaction, the precise legal blame upon the culprit government directly responsible for violating international legal rights. Therefore, the Communists take pains to present their challenges indirectly or by proxy.[16]

This particular legal tradition makes it difficult to call to account the country that stands behind proxy forces and supplies them with weapons, logistics and intelligence, since the security services involved in such operations rarely leave behind fingerprints. In coping with this danger, it will be necessary to devise legal formulas that will make it possible to pin the responsibility where it belongs. The principles of international law developed within the Western community, whose members do not normally engage in such activities, can hardly be maintained in regard to countries that act on entirely different rules.

The Soviet Union uses proxy forces in a deliberate manner to avoid potential humiliations of its forces and a confrontation with the United States. Once this strategy is understood, it makes little sense for the United States to respond to indirect Soviet provocations with the direct intervention of its own forces. Except where overwhelming military preponderance assures such intervention of quick and decisive results, as was the case with the liberation of Grenada, the involvement of United States forces in combat with Soviet proxies is in every respect counterproductive. One of its worst consequences is to encourage isolationist sentiments in the United States and thereby to make it more difficult for the administration to secure public support for dealing with Soviet aggression in regions remote from the continental United States. It is preferable by far to meet Soviet indirect aggression with an indirect response of one's own, relying on proxy forces sympathetic to the United States and resorting to other forms of indirect warfare, such as quarantines and blockades. The inability of a majority of United States legislators to grasp the need for such countermeasures against Soviet and Cuban aggression in Central America indicates a disturbing incomprehension of Soviet strategy.

Guerrilla movements present an almost insurmountable problem for any government. Experience indicates that a well-led and motivated guerrilla force, assisted from the outside, is virtually immune to suppression. Western media, by emphasizing and often gloating over the failure of non-Communist regimes to cope with revolutionary movements, give the impression that these movements succeed because they enjoy popular support, whereas the legitimate governments do not. Such a conclusion can be reached only by ignoring the record of anti-Communist guerrilla movements. In fact, democracies and totalitarian states have suffered identical difficulties in trying to cope with partisan warfare. While Communist guerrillas have succeeded in seizing power in Cuba and Nicaragua, at the same time, notwithstanding their overwhelming military superiority, Communist and Communist-supported regimes have proven unable to crush hostile guerrillas in Afghanistan, Angola and Mozambique. After four years of battling Afghan partisans, the Soviet Army still controls only 10–20 percent of the territory of Afghanistan, and much of that tenuously.

The task of devising strategies and tactics of dealing with the military aspect of irregular warfare is best left to military experts. But warfare of this type poses not only a military challenge; it also has a political dimension. All successful antiguerrilla campaigns (such as the Soviet suppression of the Basmachis in Central Asia in the 1920s and British successes against Communist guerrillas in Malaysia after World War II) augmented military operations with political initiatives designed to isolate the partisans from the population at large, divide them within, and seal off their sources of external support. The historical record indicates that any antiguerrilla effort that ignores the political dimension is almost certain to fail. This suggests that responsibility for this matter cannot be left entirely in the hands of conventional military commands but requires novel political-military formations, especially trained for such combat and operating in close collaboration with political personnel.

As concerns organized terrorism, which is a form of hit-and-run, small-scale guerrilla warfare, its links with Soviet security organs should be apparent even if the evidence is of necessity circumstantial. It cannot be an accident that Soviet personnel or interests are almost never the target of terrorist action either inside or outside the Communist Bloc. This holds true even of the Middle East, where one might expect some Muslim terrorist bands to strike at Soviet citizens in retaliation for Afghanistan and the suppression of Islam in the USSR. It is known that numerous terrorist movements, some of them with no ideological affinities for Communism, receive training in Communist Bloc countries; Israeli intelligence, for instance, has been able to identify numerous training facilities for the PLO in the USSR and Eastern Europe. Terrorist gangs operating in diverse parts of the world have formed under the aegis of the KGB something like an international network whose members shift from country to country, as opportunities for their bloody work present themselves. Whatever the personal objectives of its individual members (and these are sometimes no more than murder for money) they serve Moscow's interests by helping it to unsettle countries that it has an interest in taking over. The possibility of systematic, large-scale terrorism within the United States, controlled by Moscow, cannot be excluded.

The military threat that the Soviet Union poses to the West is as visible as it is serious; and to say that it is not the principal danger confronting the West is not to minimize it. For the USSR, military power is only one arrow in the quiver of its Grand Strategy. It would be a tragic mistake, therefore, to confine the West's response to the Soviet threat exclusively to the production of weapons. It can be taken for granted that should Moscow find that its military power no longer brought the desired political results, it would avail itself of the other tools in its arsenal to pursue the assault. Hence it is of utmost importance for the democracies to make fullest use of such nonmilitary capabilities as they have to neutralize Soviet imperialism and to weaken it at its source.

## 4  THE POLITICAL ASPECT

It was stated earlier in this book that the chief instrument of Soviet Grand Strategy is political attrition, which, in practice, means exploiting the open character of democratic societies for the purpose of inciting internal divisions among different social groups and between their citizens and their elected governments, as well as sowing discord among the allies. This strategy cannot be completely neutralized if only because democracies will not remain democracies once they disallow conflicts of interests and differences of opinion. But its pernicious effects can be significantly reduced when it is realized what it is and how it functions.

## A. PARTY POLITICS

Ideally, political parties in democratic countries should seek to pursue in regard to the Soviet Union a strictly bipartisan policy. That such a policy is possible was demonstrated in the late 1940s and early 1950s in both the United States and West Germany. The breakdown of bipartisanship which has occurred subsequently as a result of the Soviet shift to "peaceful coexistence" provides Moscow with excellent opportunities to play on internal political rivalries in democratic countries by encouraging parties that are not in the least degree pro-Soviet or pro-Communist to assume, for narrow partisan interests, the positions it favors. It is a sorry spectacle to see the candidates for the Democratic Presidential nomination in the United States trying to outbid each other with pledges of being the first to fly to Moscow to "settle" with its leader United States-Soviet differences. In several countries (e.g., Great Britain and Germany) socialist parties, in the quest for support from the neutralist segment of the electorate, have taken positions that come dangerously close to unilateral disarmament—positions which they would inevitably abandon if elected to office, but that they can irresponsibly exploit as long as responsibility for defense lies on the other party, the party in office. Such pressures from the opposition, in turn, compel heads of state to seek a *rapprochement* with Moscow at any price, for they cannot afford to find themselves in the exposed and dangerous position of being the "party of war." If the democracies persist in allowing intraparty rivalries to overshadow the fundamental interest all their citizens have in maintaining their way of life, the day may come when they will lose the right to engage in party politics altogether.

It is essential for the West not to allow Moscow to insinuate itself into its domestic politics and not to give it any opportunity for exploiting the "rifts" in the enemy camp which Lenin regarded as the prime objective of his political strategy. Not that there must be no disagreements in the Western camp, but rather that the West should instantly close ranks whenever the Soviet Union attempts to take sides in them. Instead of giving Moscow such an opening, the West would do well to strike back and challenge the Soviet effort to seal off its domain from any outside interference. Through radio broadcasts (and, in the future, possibly television transmissions as well), through speeches of its statesmen, and through symbolic acts, it should be possible to raise in the minds of the citizens of Communist countries doubts about the omnipotence of their regimes. To allow the Soviet Union to meddle in Western affairs but to desist from meddling in its affairs is to play into the hands of Soviet strategists.

## B. THE ALLIANCE

The Soviet Union is even more successful in exploiting divisions in the Western alliance, whose cohesion, were it realizable, would constitute a most formidable obstacle to Soviet global ambitions.

It requires no elaborate proof to demonstrate that the alliance binding the United States to the countries of NATO, and, once removed, Japan, is of immense value to its members. The industrial democracies linked by this alliance enjoy vast technological and industrial superiority over the Communist Bloc. Their combined Gross National Product is at the lowest reckoning three to four times that of the Soviet Bloc and probably considerably in excess of that; the GNP of Western Europe alone is nearly double that of the USSR and its colonies. Were the Soviet Union to succeed in establishing hegemony over Western Europe and Japan, its industrial capacity would in a short time double or treble, enabling it in one fell swoop to overcome all the economic difficulties that presently constrain its imperial ambitions. Should this occur, the United States would be left alone to confront the Soviet threat; under these conditions, the survival of free institutions in the United States would become most problematic. This is why the United States stands prepared to defend Western Europe as if it were its own territory, and why the Soviet Union, on its part, regards Western Europe as a prime objective of its Grand Strategy.

The defensive ties binding the United States to Europe were, from the outset, territorially restricted to Europe, North America and the Atlantic Ocean north of the Tropic of Cancer. This arrangement created serious problems because Soviet Grand Strategy is not regional but global in scope. The result was that all the areas outside the North Atlantic community came within the purview of other regional alliances tied to the United States but not to NATO: among them, the Baghdad Pact, SEATO and the Rio Treaty. Inasmuch, however, as all regional defensive treaties except NATO proved to be paper compacts, the United States has had to assume responsibility on its own behalf as well as that of its European allies for the security of most of the non-Western world outside the North Atlantic region.

Such an arrangement made sense in 1949, when NATO came into being, because at that time Europe was still incapable of ensuring its own security, let alone the defense of distant regions. Today it is difficult to justify on grounds of either equity or military expediency, for it imposes on the United States excessive burdens of protecting the approaches to Europe as well as coping with Soviet expansionism in the Third World. The defense of the Middle East, without whose oil Europe could hardly carry on, is entrusted to the United States, as is that of the mineral resources of Africa, not to speak of the strategic areas in East Asia and Central America. Whenever Communist forces commit acts of aggression in these outlying areas, Europe assumes the stance of a neutral observer. The detachment with which its leaders react to such events sometimes conveys the impression that they are not unhappy to have Russia dissipate its aggressive energies far away from the European continent.* There seems little awareness in European thinking (a few honorable exceptions apart) that the Soviet Union pursues a global and not a continental strategy, that the invasion of Afghanistan has some bearing on the security of Europe's oil supplies, that a series of successful Communist revolutions in Central America may have the consequence of diverting American attention away from NATO. These matters, which do not happen to impinge on Europe's territorial interests but affect its security in every other respect, are left to the care of the United States and such smaller non-European countries as Washington can persuade, bribe or cajole into rendering it assistance.

An alliance kept in place long after the circumstances that shaped it have either profoundly changed or disappeared, is a monument to the shortsightedness of American diplomacy. NATO really is not so much an alliance as an insurance policy, extended by the United States to Western Europe at low expense to the insured but at an immense cost and risk to the insurer. As such, it offers Moscow superb opportunities for driving wedges between the United States and Western Europe. Moscow can, and does, deliberately exacerbate its differences with the United States, while offering "security" to Western Europe, so as to reduce artificially the East-West conflict to one that involves only the two "superpowers," which allegedly does not affect Europe's interests

---

* This is nothing new: Napoleon and Hitler had encouraged Russia to expand in the direction of India, while Kaiser Wilhelm II incited it to move against China and Japan. In all three cases the motive was to keep Russia so busy elsewhere that it could not meddle in the affairs of Europe.

and from which it best keep out. It heightens this effect by maintaining stable the East-West border in Europe, and committing acts of aggression exclusively in regions outside the confines of NATO, where it runs into American but not European resistance. In this manner, Moscow succeeds in implementing the *divide et impera* principle which lies at the heart of its political strategy.

The unwillingness of a fully reconstructed and prosperous Europe to join the United States in a policy of global defense, its political and military parochialism, have been the principal cause of the discords troubling the alliance during the past twenty years. True, the United States is also annoyed that its allies, although equally affluent, contribute proportionately less to the common defense, but it is not defense budgets that American participants in an NBC poll of 1982 had on their mind when four out of five of them responded negatively to the question whether the Allies were "providing the right amount of support for American foreign policies."[17] They meant that the United States was too often left in the lurch to confront Soviet and Soviet-sponsored aggression while the Allies looked the other way, as had happened in Korea, Vietnam, Afghanistan, El Salvador, and throughout the Middle East.

Europe's disinclination to stand by its protector of the ultimate resort anywhere outside the heavily fortified West Europe-North Atlantic bastion is not confined to military matters. It also affects the politics of the Alliance. The Allies frequently vote against the United States or abstain when serious questions involving the United States come up before the United Nations. Their delegations there routinely caucus without United States participation to decide on how to cast their votes. Their eagerness to disassociate themselves from United States positions sometimes assumes very odious forms, as the following example will illustrate. Early in 1983, labor disturbances broke out in Cuba; rumors had it that some striking Cuban workers had called for the formation of a Solidarity-type trade union, and that for making this demand they were sentenced to death. On receipt of this information, the United States Interest Section in Havana convened a meeting of a dozen Allied ambassadors, at which it asked them to join the United States in a diplomatic *démarche* to the Cuban government. The press reported the latter's reaction as follows:

> No one agreed to join in, according to the participants, and no one thought it was a good idea for the United States to go ahead alone. One European ambassador reportedly walked out before the meeting

was over, eager to disassociate his government from the whole idea. Others complained that Cuban officials might conclude from the cars gathered around the U.S. building that European allies already were part of the American plan. "Join with the United States for a démarche, here?" said a European diplomat. "It was madness, a stupidity." [18]

The American public takes a very sober, even cynical, view of domestic politics. Its attitude toward foreign policy, however, is a different matter. Essentially insular, Americans see no reason to involve themselves in foreign ventures unless it is to promote some ethical ideal, to make the world better, safer or more democratic. *Realpolitik* in foreign policy makes no sense to them, since realism tells them to stay home and mind their own business. Given this attitude, it should cause no surprise that the American public takes a very dim view of Allied behavior. In the late 1940s, it had let itself be persuaded to abandon strongly held, traditional objections to "entangling alliances," and committed the country to the defense of the "Free World," understanding this to mean literally the *Free World* and not a military "forward base" for the protection of the continental United States. Rightly or wrongly, the American public sees no connection between the security of Western Europe and that of the United States. It believes that it is acting selflessly in placing troops in Europe and subjecting the continental United States to the risk of a Soviet nuclear attack. Consequently, it is bewildered and angered by Europe's lack of cooperation in other regions of the world, by its unconcealed contempt for the moral element that Americans always inject into their foreign policy and lacking which they cannot be drawn out of their insularity, and by Europe's reluctance to accept nuclear weapons mutually agreed upon as essential for the continent's defense.

This mood carries the risk that some day public support in the United States for NATO will erode to the point where its chief executive will no longer be able to call for the sacrifices that the Alliance demands. Some European politicians, in private conversation, profess to be untroubled by this prospect, on the grounds that the United States needs Europe more than Europe needs the United States, and hence has no choice but to accommodate itself to Europe's actions and inactions. This argument is wholly irresponsible. For one, *need* is a subjective concept; the objective reality is that the average American simply is not aware that he needs Europe to defend his country. Nor is the military premise of such thinking sound: for, while Europe indeed serves as America's first line of defense, it happens to be Europe's last. [19]

Of all the Allied powers, it is the Federal Republic of Germany that makes the greatest contribution to NATO and causes the greatest problems within it. Germany occupies a location of unique importance, in that any military conflict on the continent is certain to begin on its territory and there to find its decision. Germany has the largest economy in Europe and provides NATO with the largest contingent of troops. The Soviet leadership, aware of these facts, concentrates its political offensive in Europe on West Germany. It knows that should it succeed in neutralizing Germany, NATO would fall apart and the continent would become indefensible.

To all appearances, the West German population is fully committed to the Alliance. Public-opinion polls indicate that most Germans approve of NATO—78 percent desire to remain in NATO, and 63 percent regard it as essential to their security.[20] Although anti-Americanism is not uncommon in Germany (it has become for some Europeans a psychological surrogate for anti-Semitism), its sporadic manifestations do not reflect the feelings of the population at large. The personal popularity of Americans is relatively high and if anything it is increasing: in 1957, only 37 percent of Germans responded affirmatively to the question, "Do you like Americans?" whereas in 1981 the proportion of such respondents rose to 56 percent.[21] Fifty-three percent of Germans consider "good relations with the United States" essential for the security of the West, which happens to be a higher proportion than in any other nation of NATO. (By comparison, only one quarter of British citizens hold this opinion.)[22] The Germans, who are among the most heavily polled people in the world, give such answers consistently no matter how the questions are phrased, which indicates a solid majority in favor of the Alliance and collaboration with the United States.

But this holds true only as long as the Soviet Union is excluded from the equation and the choice reduces itself to a simple alternative: with NATO and the United States, or without them? The instant the USSR is introduced as a factor, the picture turns murky. A good part of the German public wants close association with the NATO allies but only on condition that this relationship not irritate or appear to menace the Soviet Union. It is as if many Germans wanted the Alliance to confine itself to political formalities, largely devoid of military or economic substance; such an alliance would serve Germany as a guarantee that it will not be left alone to face the giant who borders it in the east, that it will have friends to fall back on in the event of trouble, but not that it needs to commit itself to anything faintly anti-Soviet, even if only in a defensive sense. Thus, 40 percent of West Germans unconditionally oppose the stationing of United States nuclear missiles on their soil, regardless of how many such missiles the Soviet Union deploys and targets on Germany. Nearly the same proportion rejects resort to nuclear weapons, even in retaliation for Soviet nuclear strikes.[23] These results indicate that fully two fifths of German citizens are prepared to surrender, once it becomes certain that the Alliance cannot defend itself conventionally against either a conventional or a nuclear Soviet assault. Asked whether Germany should cooperate more closely with the United States or the Soviet Union, 56 percent express a preference for the first option, and only 1 percent for the second, but an important bloc (32 percent) want "an even-handed" policy toward both Washington and Moscow.[24] Thus, there exists in Germany a sizable body of committed neutralists—between one third and two fifths of the population—who have psychologically opted out of the Alliance and regard it either as altogether undesirable or at best as a symbolic bond that imposes no serious obligations on their country. Sociological inquiries indicate that a high proportion of these neutralists consists of mass-educated young people—teachers, students, and functionaries—products of the ambitious higher education programs of postwar Germany, who live in a cultural no man's land and whose prospects for securing jobs commensurate with what they consider their skills and abilities are so low as to breed in them a permanent state of discontent.

The mood of its electorate obliges every German administration, regardless of its own preferences, to conduct an ambivalent foreign policy in which professions of undying loyalty to the Western Alliance are coupled with assurances to the Soviet Union that it can count on Germany being a reliable "partner," and an "intermediary" between East and West. ("Our national interest does not allow us to stand between East and West," Chancellor Brandt pronounced cryptically in 1970. "Our country needs cooperation and harmony with the West and agreement with the East.")[25] German governments are indubitably committed to the defense of the central front, which, after all, cuts across their own territory. They are also willing discreetly to provide money and political support to nations threatened by the Communists: this they have done with excellent results in Portugal and Turkey. But they are emphatically not prepared either to withhold economic and technical aid from the Soviet Bloc or to participate in any effort to cope with Soviet military expansion outside the confines of NATO.

In some measure this ambivalence can be explained by geography and history. Germany—Communist and democratic alike—is the focal point of East-West confrontations and the battlefield of any potential war between NATO and the Warsaw Pact. This location makes Germans particularly sensitive to any worsening of relations between the two blocs. Another factor is the memory of Nazism, which has the effect of discrediting both militarism and anti-Communism; for many Germans, the notion of an anti-Communist alliance evokes sordid associations with the Axis. But probably the most important consideration influencing German attitudes toward the East-West conflict is the division of Germany: Germany is the only politically bifurcated country in Europe, one fifth of whose population and nearly one third of whose territory is under foreign occupation.

Germans have never reconciled themselves to the status of a truncated nation, and the desire for reunification is a powerful force in their politics. Theoretically, there are two ways by which reunification can be accomplished: by force or by conciliation. Force is not a realistic option under any conceivable circumstances; even if Germany decided to resort to war to recover its eastern marches, it could not do so alone, and not a single ally would support it. It is the alternative, conciliation, that appears feasible and attractive. Since the 1960s, German policies toward the USSR have been strongly affected by the hope that *Ostpolitik*, the German variant of détente, will increase contacts between the two Germanies to the point where somehow, in the end, reunification will occur. The expectation is almost certainly misplaced: there is not the remotest chance that the Soviet Union will ever allow East Germany—its military and political springboard against Western Europe—to join with West Germany except on terms that would amount to the Federal Republic being detached from its allies and transformed into a Soviet client state. Nevertheless, the hope persists and affects policy in many ways.

Extensive commercial relations with Moscow are one price that Bonn must pay and is not averse to paying for access to East Germany. In the 1960s, West Germany tried to make direct contact with its Communist half, but that endeavor was thwarted. It discovered eventually that the road to East Berlin required a detour through Moscow. Moscow closely monitors relations between the two halves of Germany and exacts a price for its friendly services —when Bonn is accommodating, it facilitates contacts; when not, it blocks them. Should West Germany ever dare to join the United States in a program of embargoes and boycotts, it would promptly find its lines of communication with East Germany—a very important matter to the millions of Germans who have relatives there— reduced or even cut. West Germany is for the Soviet Union the most important trading partner in NATO, and since East-West trade generally calls for Western credits and subsidies, it is also the recipient of generous German economic aid.

This economic aid is extended to the Soviet Union and its East European colonies not only directly, but also indirectly, by way of East Germany. The founders of the European Economic Community, which came into being in 1957, in a special protocol attached to the Treaty of Rome, decided to treat Germany as a single political entity. This little-known provision has made Communist East Germany a *de facto* member of the EEC, able to enjoy its bounties but exempt from its obligations. The critical factor is that trade between the two halves of Germany is regarded as internal trade, which means that West German firms can import goods from East Germany without having to pay the duties imposed on the other members of the EEC whenever they import from non-members. Through this loophole, East Germany can unload its merchandise in the EEC duty-free. The protocol is so strictly enforced that the exact dimensions of the intra-German trade cannot be determined because Bonn treats it as an internal matter and refuses to share the information with its allies. The arrangement brings no mean profits to the West German economy as well. It is common practice, for instance, for West German firms, eager to profit from lower labor costs there, to subcontract to East Germany; as long as the contractor is West German, the manufactured goods (they are said to include uniforms for the West German army!) are admitted duty-free.[26]

Nor does Bonn's assistance to Communist Germany stop at trade. It has lent generously to it vast sums of money (at latest reckoning, East Germany's debts amount to $13 billion, most of it owed to West Germany). When in 1983, East Germany could not meet its interest payments and teetered on the brink of insolvency, Franz Josef Strauss, Germany's leading right-wing politician, came to its rescue by arranging a one-billion-deutschmark ($400 million) loan to East Germany, without political strings attached and without the usual stipulation that the money be used to purchase West German products. West German subsidies to the East German economy assume also some highly exotic forms. It is estimated, for example, that in the past twenty years, Bonn has ransomed from East German jails 20,000 political prisoners at an average price of 50,000 DM ($20,000) per head, which amounts to the transfer of nearly half a billion dollars.[27] In 1983, West Germany completed the construction of a superhighway connecting Berlin with

Hamburg. Its ostensible purpose is to ease the economic isolation of West Berlin, but it might just conceivably someday also help solve the transportation problems of Soviet armored units stationed in East Germany in their race to the North Sea.

When confronted with this evidence and criticized for it, Germans are prone to respond that geographic proximity and age-old contacts have made them uniquely qualified to understand the Russians and to deal with them. One would feel more encouraged by this self-confidence were it not for the historical record. After all, it was the Germans who in World War I made it possible for the Bolsheviks to come to power in Russia and to hold on to it when in 1918 they were near collapse. In World War II, it was they who brought Russia to the eastern half of Europe. Many of them pride themselves today on conducting a highly sophisticated policy toward the Soviet Union, a policy that someday will pay rich dividends. But one wonders whether they are not once again deceiving themselves, and instead of doing the manipulating are not themselves the victims of manipulation, who will end up fatally weakening the Western Alliance without obtaining from Moscow anything in return.


In the United States, NATO is decidedly unpopular. Public opinion has it that the NATO allies show neither adequate cooperation nor appreciation of America's contribution. The military complain that the United States is so heavily committed to the defense of Europe that it lacks adequate forces to meet obligations elsewhere. Some argue that the conciliatory policies of the Allies make it impossible for the United States to behave as a true superpower, because any sign of assertiveness on its part disrupts the Alliance. Knowledgeable observers in Congress believe that if the Mansfield Amendment, which calls for the withdrawal of United States troops from Europe, were put up for a vote today, it would pass with a comfortable majority. These rumblings ought to concern the Western European allies more than they apparently do, because they have to be interpreted against the background of a partnership whose only *raison d'être* is the Soviet threat and the common willingness to stand up to it.

The thing that is wrong with the Alliance, however, is not the United States commitment to defend Europe but the inequitable distribution of responsibilities within it. Economically, Europe and Japan have long been capable of ensuring their own defense in all but nuclear weapons. Hence, there is no justification for the United States expending over 6 percent of its GNP each year on defense (overwhelmingly for the defense of Europe) while the European countries spend at most 3 percent and Japan less than 1 percent. This budgetary disparity means that the United States has been subsidizing to a large extent the defenses of its allies and encouraging them to devote ever greater sums to "social programs." In 1981, the countries of the European Community allocated 26 percent of their combined GNP on such programs, compared to 10 percent that the United States committed to this purpose. The ratio of social allocations to defense allocations is thus less than 2–1 in the United States.and nearly 9–1 in Western Europe. Social expenditures are known to give rise to powerful constituencies among both the dispensers and the recipients of public largesse, who share an interest in reducing defense outlays; and since the margin of electoral victory in most European countries is very narrow, few politicians dare to risk tampering with funds assigned for this purpose.

The United States has contributed to these financial inequities by its willingness to bear disproportionate burdens long after this has ceased to be necessary. As a result, the Allies have the best of both worlds: they maintain their military establishments at a minimum level acceptable to their senior partner, restrict their defense obligations to the European continent and adjoining waters, deposit the money thus saved in the pot for distribution among the voters, and rely on the United States to rescue them should Russia attack Europe.

Such a situation cannot go on forever, because the American electorate will not forever tolerate it. The spread of Communist power in areas nearer home is likely in time to require a diversion of United States military forces from Europe; one can hardly expect the United States to concentrate on the defense of Europe while Central America and Mexico are threatened with Communist domination. The great commercial interest that the United States has developed in the Pacific basin will, very likely, also call for greater military commitments to that region. With four out of five Americans convinced that the Allies are not doing their share in supporting the foreign policy of the United States, the ground is psychologically prepared for a reevaluation of the Alliance. The Allies are frequently heard to complain that the United States is not sufficiently sensitive to their concerns—for some reason, no one asks them to show any sensitivity to the concerns of the United States.

These strains and inequities call for a reassessment of an alliance that no longer meets the needs of the time. However the matter is worked out in practice, if NATO is to remain viable, changes seem unavoidable. One alternative is for NATO to expand its responsibilities beyond its present confines, to include at least some areas contiguous to Europe, particularly the Middle East. Since, however, it is the unanimous opinion of well-informed persons that European parliaments would never approve such a revision of the terms of the Alliance, one may have to look for another solution, namely, creating a separate alliance with selected members of NATO to assume this responsibility. An alternative arrangement would be for the Allies to take upon themselves a greater share of the burden of self-defense while the United States withdrew the bulk of its forces from Europe to be better able to fulfill its global responsibilities. It is difficult to see how the United States can continue to meet the global Soviet threat when the overwhelming bulk of its forces is allocated to the defense of Europe and the forces of its European allies are exclusively committed to this end.

Whatever the best solution, clearly something must be done about a treaty that is more than a third of a century old, that was conceived before the USSR had missiles and an oceangoing navy and Western Europe had a GNP greater than that of the United States.

In objection to such proposals, it is said that, should the United States withdraw its troop contingents, Europe would turn neutral and arrive at an accommodation with the Soviet Union. To this argument there are two rejoinders. If, indeed, all that prevents Western Europe from Finlandizing itself is the presence of United States troops, then it becomes questionable whether it can or should be defended; the function of NATO, after all, is to safeguard Europe from the Soviet Union, not from itself. Secondly, the threat need not be taken very seriously. Western Europe desperately does not want to become dependent on the Soviet Union, let alone share the fate of Europe's eastern half. Under the present arrangement, it can avoid either fate, because it has United States guarantees, purchased at rather low cost. Having persuaded themselves and the United States that NATO serves primarily the interests of United States security, not their own, America's allies are in the comfortable position of being able to eat the cake (conduct a militarily limited and politically semineutralist policy) and have it too (enjoy United States military protection if this policy fails). One cannot blame them for taking advantage of such an opportunity; NATO represents probably a singular instance in history of an alliance in which the senior partner asks too little rather than too much of his allies.

For these reasons one need not worry that a gradual shift of responsibility for the defense of Western Europe to the Europeans would lead to a disintegration of the Alliance and the loss of the Continent. Mr. Michel Tatu, a prominent French journalist, has argued this point very convincingly:

> Every government and every society seeks security not in order to become part of one or another system and thus as an end in itself, but because security will permit the government or the society to maintain its identity and its values. Just as a shipwrecked person who has lost one plank will not let himself drown but will look for another plank, so there is no reason to suppose that the European governments, not abandoned by America but simply invited to take charge progressively of their own defense, will immediately give up the values in whose name they [have] so long attached themselves to America. . . .
>
> Must one believe that the European attachment to liberalism and democracy is valid only so long as the United States is willing to guarantee these values? Or is it rather the contrary, that the alliance with America springs from the Europeans' own attachment to these values? The argument that Europe would turn herself into another Finland lacks dignity as well as cogency.[28]

Should Western Europe confront the prospect of Finlandization or still worse, it is certain to galvanize its resources; but this can happen only if and when the United States extricates itself from the psychological dependence on the Alliance, which allows many Europeans to pretend they are doing the United States a favor in allowing themselves to be defended.

## 5 THE ECONOMIC ASPECT

In the West it is widely believed that the Soviet economy is self-sufficient and that, for Moscow, commercial relations with it are an option that it is at liberty to exercise or to reject. This assumption makes it possible to argue that there is no point in resorting to sanctions and embargoes to withhold from Communist states equipment and technology; the only effect such measures have is to push the Soviet Union toward autarky, to deprive Western firms of business, and to worsen the climate of international relations.

For all its popularity, this argument rests on a fallacious premise. Solid evidence that no one so far has been able to refute shows that the Soviet economy has never been self-sufficient and today is less so than ever. From 1921 onward, almost without interruption, the USSR has been importing from the West significant quantities of materiel and know-how to modernize existing industries and to introduce new technology. In the words of Antony Sutton, the author of the most comprehensive survey on the subject, "from 1930 to 1945 Soviet technology was in effect Western technology converted to the metric system." [29] The debt of the Soviet Union to Western assistance is not widely known, because neither of the parties involved wishes to advertise it—the Soviet Union wants to avoid the embarrassment of conceding that it is more or less permanently dependent on the "capitalist camp," while Western firms are coy about doing business with a power that most Westerners view as hostile and spend great sums to arm themselves against. (To this day, the U.S. Department of Commerce will not release lists of industrial corporations granted export licenses to the Soviet Union, although such business is perfectly legitimate.)

Western assistance to the Soviet economy began as early as 1921, with the inauguration of Lenin's New Economic Policy. At that time, the not inconsiderable industrial plant that the Bolsheviks had inherited from the tsarist regime lay in shambles; Russian industry, for all practical purposes, had ceased to function. The first foreigners invited to help with industrial reconstruction came from Germany, with which Moscow had signed a trade agreement that year. Their assistance helped Soviet industry to attain by 1927 prewar production levels. In the late 1920s, the USSR switched most of its business to the United States, whose corporations became a major factor in the implementation of the first Five-Year Plan. At this time, Ford Motors constructed in Soviet Russia a huge integrated plant at Gorkii to build Model A cars, trucks and buses. General Electric helped with the development of Soviet electrical industry, while DuPont contributed to the chemical and RCA to the communications industry. Mr. Sutton estimates that during this critical phase of Soviet industrial development, at least 95 percent of Soviet industries benefited from Western assistance.

This cooperation continued during the 1930s. The McKee Corporation of Cleveland designed the famous Magnitogorsk steel mill, a copy of U. S. Steel's plant at Gary, Indiana, then the largest integrated iron and steel plant in the world. All the refineries in Russia's principal oil-producing area at Baku were constructed by United States firms, which also furnished them with the bulk of their drilling and pumping equipment. Most of the plants built during the third Five Year Plan (1936–40), with the exception of those working exclusively for the military, were planned and in many cases constructed by Western companies, including (for a while) even those from Nazi Germany. Later on, during the war, U.S. Lend Lease provided the USSR not only with expendable military materiel but also with advanced equipment, which is estimated to have increased Soviet industrial potential by one third.

The point is that Western involvement was at no point marginal and therefore a matter of choice; it was all along essential to the entire Soviet industrialization drive. "During the period from 1930 to 1945, Soviet technology was almost completely a transfer from Western countries . . ." Mr. Sutton concludes, "No major technology or major plant under construction between 1930 and 1945 has been identified as a purely Soviet effort."[30]

So much for the vaunted Soviet self-sufficiency under Stalin. In the decade that immediately followed World War II, the USSR imported little from the West, because it needed time to absorb its Lend Lease equipment and the immense quantities of war booty that it had seized in Germany and Eastern Europe. The purchase of Western equipment and know-how resumed in the late 1950s, this time on a grander scale than ever before. The critical factor which made such an expansion of industrial imports possible, was a change in the attitude of Western governments; whereas before they had been rather neutral toward trade with Moscow, they now began actively to encourage it. It is difficult to tell whether in this case economic interest was the driving force and the expectation of political benefits a rationalization, or the other way around; the consequences were the same. Since the late 1950s, Western governments have cooperated with their banks and business corporations to promote exports of industrial equipment and technology to the USSR and Eastern Europe, as well as to enhance the latter's ability to earn hard currency with which to pay for these goods. Since the USSR is relatively poor in cash and usually suffers an unfavorable balance of trade with the industrial countries, no significant expansion of East-West trade could take place without Western credits, and no credits would flow without government participation. The latter assumes two forms: Western governments lend directly to Communist countries to enable them to pay for purchases from their business firms, or else they guarantee repayment of the loans extended to the exporting firms by private banks. By availing themselves of this credit, Warsaw Pact countries have run up a debt of over $80 billion, most of it in the decade of the 1970s. The USSR likes to insist on paying for its loans interest rates that are substantially below (as much as 5 percent) those prevailing on international markets. The purpose of this practice, with which Western governments and banks connive, is to help the Soviet Union maintain the reputation for unique creditworthiness and, in this manner, to enhance its international prestige. As a rule, the USSR discreetly compensates its creditors for their losses on interest by paying premiums for the goods and services purchased with the borrowed money. An interesting variant in East-West trade practices are the so-called "compensation" deals under which the USSR repays its loans not in cash but in the product that the loans had made possible. This method has been employed in financing the Siberian pipeline, the costs of which are to be recovered in future deliveries of natural gas.* For a while the Soviet leadership believed that it had found in "compensation" arrangements a kind of financial perpetual-motion machine: Western firms would develop Soviet industrial capacities and natural resources at little or no cost to Moscow, receive payment in the product, reinvest the proceeds, and so on, in perpetuity. Unfortunately, it soon dawned on their European partners that by so doing they were competing against themselves and as a result compensation deals became much less popular than expected.

Western economic involvement in the Soviet Union and Eastern Europe since the 1960s has been deep and consequential. Once again, as happened in the 1890s and 1930s, the USSR has received from the West essential help modernizing those industries that advances in technology had rendered obsolete and familiarizing it with technologies that it has not been able to master on its own.

A survey of the technology acquired by the USSR in the past quarter century from the West shows the following:

□ Motor vehicles: Italy has built for the Soviet Union at Togliatti a giant automobile plant (equipped mainly, it may be noted, with United States machinery) to turn out copies of Fiat passenger cars, while Pullman-Swindell of Pittsburgh, a subsidiary of the M. W. Kellogg Co., has constructed for Moscow on the Kama River the world's largest truck plant. The two establishments account for the production of one half of Soviet passenger cars and heavy trucks, respectively.

□ Oil industry: the equipment purchased by the USSR from the West has enabled it to raise substantially its oil production, by some estimates as much as two million barrels a day, which at 1984 prices brings in (or saves) $21 billion a year: in effect, this

---

* After these costs have been repaid, the income generated by gas sales is expected to be used by Moscow to buy imports from Germany and the other countries in Western Europe. It was obviously the desire to place cash in Soviet hands for such purchases rather than the alleged need to diversify energy supplies that motivated the German government, financial institutions and corporations to promote the Siberian pipeline with such single-minded determination, even at the risk of conflict with the United States.

imported technology subsidizes Soviet energy exports to Eastern Europe.

□ Chemical industry: the USSR has carried out an ambitious program of importing chemical plants from the West. These have largely freed it from the necessity of buying chemicals abroad.

□ Electronic industry: the Soviet Union has made abroad significant purchases of integrated-circuit technology.

□ Steel: Moscow has purchased abroad the equipment to produce high-grade specialized steel; currently, the French company Creusot-Loire is constructing in the USSR a mill capable of turning out seven million tons of such steel annually.

□ Ammonia: Western equipment has enabled the USSR to become the world's leading exporter of industrial ammonia.

□ Natural gas: the story of the Yamal Pipeline, built with the assistance of critical Western technology (large-diameter pipes and compressors) and capital is well known. At present, negotiations are quietly underway to continue such development beyond the existing line. In addition, the German company Mannesmann is negotiating for contracts to build in the Soviet Union synthetic liquid fuel plants estimated to be worth as much as $16.5 billion.

□ The bulk of the Soviet merchant navy—the largest in the world—consists of vessels built by foreign shipyards.

Unusual reticence accompanies these and other industrial endeavors, as if the parties had entered into a gentleman's agreement to keep the information privileged.

The industrial assistance given to the Soviet Union helps its military effort directly and indirectly—directly, by providing so-called "dual use" technology which can be used for the production of both military and nonmilitary equipment; and indirectly, by strengthening the Soviet wartime mobilization base. The development of Soviet energy resources has the effect of providing the USSR with hard currency which its own economy cannot generate; normally, most of it is spent on acquiring abroad equipment of some military application.

The so-called "dual-use" technology, lavishly sold to the USSR in the 1960s and especially 1970s, has had a most impressive effect in enhancing Soviet military power. While basic Soviet military equipment is of native manufacture, the West and Japan have supplied Soviet war industry with specialized and advanced technology which Soviet engineers integrate into their output—it makes all the difference between equipment of adequate and superior quality. A plant built by a United States corporation to manufacture rock-drill bits to explore for oil can be and very likely is used to turn out antitank ammunition. Specialized steel sold to the USSR has a variety of applications in tank armor and submarine hulls. Integrated circuits, knowledge of which was acquired in the West, have critical applications in electronic warfare. And it takes no great imagination to realize that the heavy trucks that the Kama River truck plant turns out are either shipped to the Red Army or earmarked for it in the event of hostilities. The same applies to the merchant marine, which in peacetime catches fish and transports cargoes, but forms an integral part of the Soviet Navy and operates under its command.

The most shocking instance of the contribution that Western technology has made to Soviet military capabilities was the sale by the United States in the early 1970s of equipment to manufacture miniature ball bearings. As noted above (p. 98) the Soviet leadership decided in 1959–60 to proceed with the mass-production of nuclear weapons. German technology, acquired after World War II, combined with native science and industry, provided nearly all the components required. Among the equipment that could not be produced domestically, however, was machinery to manufacture large quantities of miniature ball bearings for missile-guidance systems. At the time Soviet representatives approached the only firm that made such machinery, the Bryant Chucking Grinder Company, of Springfield, Vermont. In 1961, with Soviet orders pending, Bryant applied for a license to sell this equipment to the Soviet Union, but Defense Department objections moved President Kennedy to deny the application. In 1972, in the more favorable climate of détente, Bryant applied once again for a license to ship to the USSR its Centalign grinders. This time, permission came through.[31] The bearings produced by this United States equipment are almost certainly integrated into the guidance system of Soviet missiles. In the opinion of some experts, they have materially contributed to the enhancement of accuracies of Soviet missiles, to the extent of putting at risk the United States force of Minuteman ICBMs and requiring the development of a new land-based missile, the MX.

NATO long ago recognized the need to withhold from the USSR, and from countries likely to pass on to the USSR, equipment with indisputable and direct military applications. In practice, enforcement of this principle has been hopelessly lax, especially since the inauguration of détente. The agency charged with monitoring technology transfer to the East is known by the acronym COCOM. Formed by NATO countries in 1949 with headquarters in Paris, and joined a few years later by Japan, COCOM maintains lists of embargoed technology, agreed upon by the Allies. Alas, COCOM is virtually powerless to carry out its mandate. It is assigned an absurdly small budget (under $500,000 a year) with a correspondingly minuscule staff and can only recommend but not enforce its recommendations. In practice, it routinely processes and approves requests for the sale of equipment and technology to the Soviet Bloc; and on the infrequent occasions when it turns down a request, it has no means of ensuring that its decisions are implemented, because it has neither the necessary authority nor the personnel. After President Nixon assumed office, the United States relaxed significantly its more stringent national rules on exports to Communist countries, which in turn caused a further watering down of COCOM. If one adds that the neutral countries of Europe—Switzerland, Sweden and Austria—do not even receive COCOM recommendations and both sell embargoed materiel and provide transit for it, it becomes evident that few effective restrictions exist on the transfer to the Communist Bloc of advanced technology with direct military application. The West, notably the Federal Republic of Germany, France and Japan, which together account for nearly two thirds of the technology sold to the USSR (1979) constitutes a giant supermarket of military know-how where the USSR shops (often with borrowed money) for goods to integrate into its arsenal of destruction. The United States alone seems to be aware of the danger of such sales and makes an earnest effort to control them. But Washington has difficulty maintaining its resolve in the face of unremitting pressure from both the Allies and domestic commercial interests, usually backed by the Departments of State and Commerce, which argue that such restrictions serve only to divert Soviet business elsewhere. In his first eighteen months in office, President Reagan had tried to enforce industrial controls, but his resolve weakened as the Allies refused to cooperate and United States business firms loudly complained. By the end of 1983, he seemed to have given up trying. The sad reality is that while there are powerful vested interests lobbying for exports, no one has a vested interest in restricting the flow of technology to the potential enemy. Private enterprise does not seem especially concerned who buys its product, as if oblivious of any connection between technology and military power; and governments lack the will to impose on it considerations higher than immediate profit. So it happens that while the West busily arms itself, it also helps arm its opponent.

The transfer of military technology, however, is not the only problem; another major Western contribution to the Soviet military effort lies in assistance extended to its mobilization base. As pointed out above (Chapter Three), in the Soviet Union the line separating the military and civilian economies is so indistinct as to be almost meaningless, inasmuch as the leadership views the entire national economy as either actually or potentially destined for military ends: we are dealing here with a war economy operating on a moderate level of mobilization. It has been noted that Soviet military personnel participate closely in economic planning and carry a strong, probably decisive voice in decisions on allocations for the civilian sector of the economy. The central planning agency, Gosplan, makes no major investments unless the generals on its staff are satisfied that they meet the needs of wartime mobilization. Furthermore, each major industrial establishment has a military office that supervises those departments that work for the armed forces. On the eve of World War II, the German High Command compiled a list of Soviet war industries: this list turned out to have been virtually identical with a list of Soviet industrial establishments.[32] Nothing suggests that matters have changed in this respect. Since the Soviet leadership views all industries in the light of their contribution to the war effort, it must view industrial imports in the same manner; from which it follows that *any* contribution to the Soviet industrial potential is at the same time a contribution to its war-making potential. Help extended to the Soviet Union to construct plants for the manufacture of goods which ostensibly serve peaceful purposes, such as automobiles and trucks, tractors, or specialized steel, serve in fact a double purpose, partly civilian, partly military, with the military one always paramount.

The other objection to technology and equipment transfer has to do with its effect on the Stalinist system. Foreign technology and foreign credits help prop up an economic regime which shows every sign of having lost its vitality; they also enable Moscow to allocate its capital and resources in a manner that continues to favor the military sector. It is in the interest of the West that the USSR reform its labor policies, raising productivity by greater incentives and decentralized decision making. This would represent a step toward weakening the economic and political power of the *nomenklatura*. To the extent that it helps to make the system more efficient, Western technology makes it easier to avoid such reforms. If one can imagine a Soviet economy that would be one hundred percent automated and able to dispense with human labor altogether, such an economy would be entirely freed from the need to take the human factor into account: it would make people redundant altogether. Of course, such an economy is not possible; but everything that contributes to the automation of Soviet production, that supplies it with what the Stalinist system cannot provide, serves to solidify the despotic arrangement.

Were it not for vested interests, that is, for individuals and firms profiting from such business, it would not be difficult to make an unanswerable argument against sales to the Soviet Union and its dependencies of any equipment or technology with likely military applications. The matter turns more contentious, however, as soon as one comes to materiel that has no obvious military application, the development of Soviet natural resources, and the extension of credits. In this sphere, one runs also into convictions about the value of international trade as a bridge among nations and a force for peace.

Commerce among nations is indubitably an instrument capable of bringing them closer together because it weaves a tissue of private bonds independent of and more durable than the volatile political relations that link sovereign states. It has been almost axiomatic in Western thought since the early eighteenth century that everyone profits from trade to the extent that one is able to buy abroad commodities more cheaply than it costs to produce them at home; it has an additional bonus in that it brings nations into peaceful intercourse. Indeed, international relations may be friendly or they may be hostile, but international trade can only be friendly. It is difficult even to conceive what "hostile trade relations" could be; the concept seems a contradiction in terms. (Tariff wars, embargoes and the like can be set aside for the purposes of this discussion since they are forms not of trade but of political interference with it.) It has been the consensus of Western liberal literature for over two centuries that trade spells peace, and restrictions on trade mean war. Roosevelt's Secretary of State, Cordell Hull, was merely restating a commonplace when he wrote of himself:

> toward 1916 I embraced the philosophy I carried throughout my twelve years as Secretary of State. . . . From then on, to me, unhampered trade dovetailed with peace; high tariffs, trade barriers, and unfair economic competition, with war. Though realizing that many other factors were involved, I reasoned that, if we could get a freer flow of trade—freer in the sense of fewer discriminations and obstruction—so that one country would not be deadly jealous of another and the living standards of all countries might rise, thereby eliminating the economic dissatisfaction that breeds war, we might have a reasonable chance for lasting peace.[33]

Economic benefits may accrue under any arrangement of international trade; but the political benefits expected of it are in fact confined to commerce between private parties. Trade between governments is indistinguishable from state-to-state relations, being subordinated to them and just as volatile; the same rule applies when one party is private and the other public.

Now, trade with the Soviet Union and the other Communist countries falls entirely into the last-named category. Western private firms negotiate contracts with appropriate Communist ministries (usually in close cooperation with their own governments), without ever coming into contact with the population at large; the process brings together corporate officials of the one party with public officials of the other. The population remains uninvolved and largely uninformed. It is possible that if the inhabitants of the Soviet Union knew that the bulk of their automobiles are produced with "capitalist" machinery or that much of their meat comes from livestock raised on imported fodder, they would develop friendly attitudes toward the foreign supplier. But most of them do not know this; the facts are deliberately concealed from them and hence cannot serve as blocks for building "bridges" between West and East.

A further argument made in favor of East-West trade as a political instrument holds that as the East expands its trade relations with the West it becomes dependent on it and therefore is constrained from engaging in "adventures." This was the celebrated doctrine of the "web of interest," which argued that the ties created by commerce would gradually bind the USSR to its political rival in other ways as well. To the extent that détente had a theory, it rested on the notion, formulated by Mr. Kissinger, that the transfer to the East of credits, machinery and food would in time translate into political gains. The implausibility of this occurring should have been evident to anyone with a modicum of historical recall. In the 1920s and 1930s, when the USSR relied heavily on Western know-how and equipment to industrialize, it pursued a rigidly Stalinist course at home and abroad. Even after World War II, when its economy lay in ruins, Moscow refused the proffered Marshall Plan aid, and ordered its clients to follow suit, because it objected to the political strings that it believed attached to it. If Marxism means anything, it means the dependence of politics on economics, a principle of which not even the most obtuse member of the *nomenklatura* can be unaware. It is therefore not in the least surprising that the expectations of the 1970s were cruelly disappointed. Upon entering into the détente relationship Moscow took extreme care that the economic assistance which it solicited not place it in conditions of dependence or constrain its freedom of movement. Its preference for buying samples of equipment to copy, and for so-called "turnkey factories," which, once made operational by foreign specialists, passed fully under Soviet management, are manifestations of this awareness.

Characteristically, even Communist Poland, which, following a less cautious policy, had made itself heavily dependent on Western suppliers and bankers, did not allow economic considerations to affect its conduct once the decision had been taken to crush Solidarity. Notwithstanding Western threats of embargoes and credit denials, it proceeded methodically to dismantle the free institutions that endangered its authority. This nonchalance must have been influenced at least in part by the knowledge that European governments and banks, which had lent it some $25 billion, had a high stake in raising Poland's productivity, since exports were the only way it could obtain the hard currency with which to honor its debts. Economic generosity has thus not yielded political leverage; the "web of interest" proved to be spun of gossamer. A chastened Henry Kissinger conceded that much a decade later, when he described as "fallacious" the theory of the "automatic mellowing effect of trade":

> Soviet behavior in recent years has given the lie to the argument that trade and credits by themselves will bring about a benign evolution of the Soviet system. Soviet-Cuban intervention in Angola, in Ethiopia, and in South Yemen; the invasion of Afghanistan; the suppression of Solidarity in Poland; and the use of toxic chemical and biological warfare in Afghanistan and Southeast Asia have all occurred in precisely the period of expanded East-West economic cooperation.[34]

Speaking realistically, the only justification for East-West trade for Western firms is to make money, and for Communist countries to acquire advanced technology. Every other excuse involves either self-deception or hypocrisy. The alleged "fall-out" from trade in the form of good will and political leverage has proved to be too elusive to deserve serious consideration.

"Money answereth all things," says the author of Ecclesiastes, but the question is: Does it make sense for society to let itself be heavily taxed to pay for its defenses and, at the same time, for private enterprise to make profit by helping the potential enemy improve his military capabilities? Do the few millions earned by this or that corporation—as often as not one that has lost its economic viability anyway and can be kept alive only by subsidized exports to the East—justify the much larger sums that have to be spent by taxpayers to match the improvements in the Soviet arsenal that these profits make possible? These questions answer themselves.

To stop the flow of technology to the Soviet Union it is necessary to resort to a variety of constraints on trade, and in this connection the question arises: How effective are such constraints? The response depends on the circumstances in which they are applied as well as on one's definition of "effectiveness." A recent survey of nearly one hundred sanctions applied in the course of the twentieth century indicates that in a surprising number of cases—more than two out of five—they have indeed "worked" in the sense that they have contributed to making the countries to which they had been applied comply with the stated political demands of the country that had put them into effect. However, success was obtained mainly in cases involving a large power against a small one. Where two great powers were involved, the results were much less clearcut.[35]

As a rule, a great power invokes sanctions against another great power in response to actions that it sees as a gross violation of accepted norms of international behavior or as an immediate threat to its security. Because of this cause-and-effect relationship —outrage followed by sanction—the public views punitive measures as intended to compel the other party to recant. If they do not do so, sanctions are judged a failure. For instance, in 1935, in response to Mussolini's invasion of Ethiopia, the League of Nations voted sanctions against Italy. Italy, however, not only refused to withdraw its troops but carried the campaign to a successful conclusion and then annexed Ethiopia. In 1979, Soviet armies invaded Afghanistan: this time the United States took the initiative in imposing against the aggressor sanctions, which some Allies ignored and others half-heartedly imitated. Five years later, the Soviet Army was still ravaging Afghanistan, whereas the sanctions were being quietly lifted. Observing such experiences, one may well conclude that it is useless for one great power to impose sanctions on another, because no power of the first rank will tolerate having its actions controlled by another power.

The matter acquires a different complexion when one separates the event that has led to sanctions from the purpose of the sanctions—that is, when one ceases to insist that as long as event X had been the reason for the punitive measures, then the aim of these measures must be nothing short of reversion to the state of things before X had taken place—Italy out of Ethiopia, Russia out of Afghanistan. It is doubtful whether any statesman in invoking sanctions had ever expected such a result. This is not the purpose of international punitive measures. Their purpose is to communicate to one's own public and to the aggressor the sense of outrage; it is a demonstration of great value quite independently of its immediate and practical results.

One only has to consider what happens when aggression is not followed by some kind of punitive measures: not to react in such instances is silently to condone them. Because in 1968 the Soviet invasion of Czechoslovakia had not been followed by sanctions, Moscow was free to attribute to the West the view that Eastern Europe was its preserve where it could behave as it pleased. This consideration may have contributed to the Soviet decision in 1979 to invade Afghanistan, for, although Afghanistan was not in Eastern Europe, it had been for many years tacitly acknowledged to lie in the Soviet sphere of influence. This time sanctions were imposed. The Soviet Union did not react by withdrawing from Afghanistan, nor was it expected to do so. But the strong response from the United States in 1979 may well have influenced the Soviet Union not to send its troops into Poland a year later. We do not know this for certain and will not know until the archives of the Politbureau have been opened for inspection. But it is not unreasonable to assume that the penalties, more or less openly discussed by NATO in the event of Warsaw Pact's armed aggression against Poland (they included the likelihood of a cancellation of the Siberian pipeline) weighed heavily on the scales when the decision fell in favor of internal repression. The relative mildness of martial law in Poland and the efforts of the Polish government to give the appearance of moderation are almost certainly related to its desire to have the United States lift its sanctions, which it admits to having cost it many billions of dollars.

If economic sanctions were eliminated as an instrument of foreign policy, then the West would be left with no responses to aggression other than military action or acquiescence. Since military action against the USSR is in practice out of the question, failure to resort to sanctions is inevitably interpreted by Moscow and the public at large as acquiescence. Thus, the effectiveness of sanctions must be measured by another yardstick than the customary one—their purpose is not so much to compel the aggressor to repent and recant as to give expression to moral indignation, to send a message, and to raise the costs of aggression. It is a political measure, first and foremost, the effectiveness of which can only be judged when set against the costs of inaction.

Curiously, opponents of sanctions against the Communist Bloc have no difficulty understanding their utility when the intended object is South Africa or some other "right-wing" regime. In such cases, *The New York Times* and liberal legislators loudly demand sanctions, while academics call for their universities to "divest" themselves of stocks in companies doing business in South Africa as a way of expressing outrage with apartheid. *The New York Times* thinks it also a fine idea to prevent Colonel Qaddafi from buying technology in the United States as punishment for invading Chad —this, it says, will cause the aggressor "frustration" and "show him our contempt."[36] For some reason, however, where the Soviet Union or some other Communist country, such as Poland, is concerned, moral considerations recede, and sanctions are declared "empty" gestures.

In the case of the Soviet Union, a coordinated Allied policy of economic denial would have the most profound effects on both the nature of the Soviet system and its military capabilities.

Nothing that the West could do—certainly no arms-control agreements—would contribute more to restraining Soviet military capabilities than a well-formulated and strictly enforced interallied embargo on both military and "dual-use" equipment and technology. As we have pointed out, materiel imported from the West since the late 1920s has greatly contributed to modernizing Soviet industry and thereby also the Soviet military, which enjoys with Soviet industry a symbiotic relationship—he who feeds the one fattens the other. A COCOM that would work from comprehensive lists of embargoed goods, that would have the authority and the personnel to enforce its recommendations, would make an immense contribution to Western security. If a fraction of the emotion invested in arms-control agreements went into keeping technology out of Soviet hands, the world would be a much safer place.

But beyond withholding equipment and know-how, the West should also refrain from making it possible for the *nomenklatura* effortlessly to earn foreign currency. The development, with Western capital and equipment of Soviet export industries, notably energy, enables Moscow to keep intact its lopsided priorities, which are heavily tilted in favor of military expenditures. The contribution that Western aid in these fields makes to the preservation of the *status quo* in the USSR seems more evident to some Soviet commentators than to the Western proponents of détente. Thus, the authors of an article in *Pravda* on the Siberian pipeline explained to their readers that the moneys earned abroad from this undertaking made it possible for the country to preserve its patterns of investments: "The construction of the . . . pipeline using commercial credits on a compensatory basis frees us of the necessity of diverting budgetary resources from other economic programs."[37] What these other "economic programs" are the authors did not spell out, but they obviously include military ones.

Another step which could usefully be taken would involve abolishing state guarantees of loans and credits extended to the Communist Bloc, which would force firms and banks to assume all the risks and treat business with the East as a strictly commercial proposition.

The purpose of the West in its commercial dealings with the Communist Bloc should be twofold: first, to keep out of its hands anything able to contribute directly or indirectly, now or in the event of war, to its military potential; and, second, to enable internal pressures generated by the failures of the Stalinist economy to build up to the point where they compel a diversion of resources from military production and give further impetus to economic reform.

## 6 WHO SHOULD BE IN CHARGE OF POLICY TOWARD THE USSR?

The Department of State is widely thought of as the proper agency to conduct the foreign policy of the United States; an arrogation of this responsibility by another agency of the government is seen as a violation of both the constitutional division of powers and of good political practices. This view is incorrect on two counts. The constitution, in effect, charges the President with the conduct of foreign affairs, so no matter how much authority the President may decide to delegate to his Secretary of State, the ultimate responsibility is his. This means that the State Department cannot be the prime mover of foreign policy: constitutionally it is the agency that implements the President's will.

This holds true also for reasons of practical politics. The belief that the State Department is the proper instrument of foreign policy derives from the fallacious view that foreign policy is synonymous with diplomacy—which, as has been pointed out, is not the case. The Department of State is the branch of government specifically responsible for diplomacy in all its aspects, and this involves, first and foremost, the peaceful resolution of disagreements and conflicts with other sovereign states. This task has a great deal in common with law. And indeed, on closer acquaintance, the Department gives the impression of a giant law firm. Its staff of Foreign Service officers, many of them highly competent in the area of their responsibility, are professionally trained to reach agreements—a successful diplomat is by definition one who knows how to negotiate an agreement favorable to his country. Diplomats have an instinctive aversion to violence and an insurmountable suspicion of ideology; the one is to them evidence of professional failure, the other, a hindrance to accords. Foreign Service officers have as much taste for ideas and political strategies as trial lawyers have for the philosophy of law. They squirm at the very mention of the words *good* and *evil*, which in their professional capacity they regard as meaningless. Since ideas lead to ideology, they scorn ideas, contrasting them with "pragmatism," which in practice means muddling through from case to case, from crisis to crisis, without the need even to consider long-term objectives. They are capable of drafting meticulously crafted position papers setting out policy recommendations or options, without ever asking themselves what the ultimate purpose of these policies is to be. Their attitude toward the representative of even the most hostile power is somewhat like that of one attorney to another: they never allow anger, indignation or any other emotion to enter into their relationship, seeking instead to base it on mutual professional respect, safe in the knowledge that crises come and crises go, but lawyers stay on.

This sort of mentality serves diplomats well when the issues in dispute are specific and therefore negotiable—that is, when the parties quarrel not over the principles of law or the jurisdiction of the court, but over the facts of the case and their interpretation. Essentially, diplomacy is a device for settling disputes out of court, the court, in the case of international conflicts, being the battlefield. It is an irreplaceable method for resolving controversies over such issues as treaties, rescheduling of debts, fishing and water rights, and the myriad other issues among states that life constantly brings forth. But these issues embrace only a part, and not even necessarily the most important part, of international relations as practiced in the twentieth century; the latter include also military power, ideology, and a host of other matters that are implicit in Grand Strategy and do not lend themselves to resolution by diplomatic means. As soon as international conflict is shifted to this ground, diplomacy is powerless. The natural reaction of diplomats under these circumstances is to minimize the phenomena they are incompetent to deal with, so as to reduce everything to manageable—that is, negotiable—terms, where their particular skills can come into play.

Because totalitarian regimes do not operate within a narrowly defined concept of foreign policy, the collective record of the world's foreign services in dealing with them has been most unimpressive. By virtue of their professional upbringing, diplomats could never take seriously the ravings of a Lenin, a Hitler or a Mao, and so they dismissed them as rhetoric behind which had to lie concealed the dictator's "real" demands, and concentrated on discovering what those alleged "real" demands were, in order to bring them to the negotiating table. Appeasement, whether of Hitler or of Stalin, so rampant in the foreign offices in their day, was due neither to stupidity nor to treason, but to a *déformation professionelle* of foreign offices. It is astonishing to read, for instance, in what cavalier manner British and American diplomats during World War II dismissed the flow of reports that the Nazis were engaged in a systematic program of exterminating Jews, on the grounds that such things could not be.* One may expand this point and say that most of totalitarian politics, with its ideology, Grand Strategy, psychological warfare, and programmed brutality, is outside the intellectual ken and therefore beyond the professional reach of diplomacy. It is, therefore, no service to the Department of State or the profession of diplomacy to charge them with responsibility for problems that they were never meant to cope with.

Thus, for both constitutional reasons and reasons connected with the peculiarities of totalitarian politics, the State Department is not the proper agency to formulate and execute foreign policy toward the Soviet Union or any other totalitarian state. These states play by different rules and must be dealt with accordingly. Since they employ Grand Strategy, to the extent that democracies are capable of coordinated foreign policies, these must be undertaken by the chief executive. In the United States, the natural locus for such coordination is the office of the President and his staff, the National Security Council. At the time of its founding in 1949, the NSC was formally and specifically charged with responsibility for advising the President "with respect to the integration of domestic, foreign and military policies relating to national security" —which is precisely what Grand Strategy is supposed to accomplish. The National Security Council alone is sufficiently close to the President to know his thoughts and political interests. Because it is not a Department, with a large bureaucracy or an influential outside constituency, it is best qualified to coordinate the various branches of administration, which tend to advance contradictory interests and demands. And because it combines in miniature all the skills that go into a Grand Strategy—politics, economics, the military and intelligence—it possesses a unique capability of for-

---

* See, for example, a report that the U.S. Department of State rejected information of this nature received from the representative of the World Jewish Congress in Geneva, who in turn had obtained it from a well-informed German industrialist, as "fantastic" and "unsubstantiated." (*The Washington Post*, Sept. 28, 1983, A2.)

mulating the kind of foreign policy that the professional diplomat abhors but the current situation requires. The transfer,
under President Reagan (on Secretary Haig's insistence) of the
main foreign-policy coordinating bodies (interagency committees)
from the NSC to State has had a very detrimental influence
on the administration's ability to translate the President's approach to East-West relations into concrete policy. At every occasion, State Department staff sought to water down attempts at
developing a United States strategy. Its preference has been and
continues to be for traditional "dialogues" with Moscow, even
though in the first three years of the Reagan Administration such
exchanges have yielded virtually no results. It has an abiding faith
that agreements on small issues lead to accords on major ones,
although the entire history of Soviet foreign policy shows this faith
to be misplaced. Whenever the NSC sought to assert what clearly
were the President's wishes, the alarmed Department of State
would intercede, provoking political and jurisdictional disputes.
This, of course, is nothing new; rivalry between NSC and State is
imbedded in the system. Every President seeks to resolve it, usually by making the Secretary of State responsible for foreign policy.
It is an unworkable solution as long as there are in the world
countries not heirs to that Western diplomatic tradition of which
the Secretary of State is the American custodian—and this is likely
to be for some time to come.

Soviet policy is conducted globally from the International Department of the Central Committee. This being the case, it would
be desirable for the United States to create a counterpart institution
to monitor Soviet activities globally. As of now, no such body
exists: neither at the National Security Council, nor at the Department of State, nor at the Central Intelligence Agency is there a
group of experts who follow from day to day the plans and activities of the International Department. The situation in the Department of State in this respect is remarkably antiquated, dating in
conception to the nineteenth century. The principal political desks
at State are organized on the geographic principle: the Soviet
Union comes within the purview of the Assistant Secretary for
European Affairs, who is also responsible for all of Western and
Eastern Europe, and, as if this were not enough, Canada as well.
An official responsible for this vast area, where are located most
of the allies of the United States, must of necessity devote his
attention mainly to relations with friendly states. He thus has
neither the time nor the personnel to deal adequately with the
central problem of United States foreign policy, which is the Soviet
Bloc.

To make matters still worse, because of the regional nature of the political desks, no one office at State is responsible for tracking the international Communist movement as such: the Latin American desk follows Soviet activities in Cuba and Nicaragua, the African desk those in Angola, the Middle Eastern desk gathers information on Soviet activities in Syria and Lebanon. There is no overview and therefore no sense of Soviet Grand Strategy or of the fluctuating Soviet "line" in regard to broader issues, which are not primarily regional. The present arrangement ensures that the whole picture of Soviet global policy is broken down into disjointed fragments which the regional desks cannot properly interpret because they are not aware of the broader context into which they fit.

One way to remedy this shortcoming would be to appoint a State Department official, at the rank of Undersecretary or Counselor, to assume responsibility for monitoring East-West relations and Soviet strategy in their broadest sense in all the fields and in all the regions where they manifest themselves. Only in such a manner will the government feel the pulse of Soviet global activities and the Secretary of State be in a position to advise the President on an intelligent response to them. For this to happen, of course, the Secretary of State must first persuade himself that unlike the United States, the Soviet Union has a Grand Strategy that is not only pragmatic but also ideological, and not only regional but also global in scope.

# 7 CONCLUDING REMARKS

This book has approached East-West relations in a manner different from that customary in Western literature. It has proceeded on the assumption, in the first place, that the issue at stake is not settling scores between contending bodies of Western opinion over the shape of Western society, for whom the USSR serves as a pretext for disagreement, but the Soviet threat to that society. Secondly, it viewed Soviet aggressiveness as rooted in the Soviet system and argued that it will not diminish until and unless that system has undergone substantial change. Thirdly, it has presented evidence that the Soviet system is afflicted by serious economic and political crises which push the country toward reform. It has concluded with advocacy of a policy designed to assist from the outside the forces that make for change internally.

The real issue is peaceful intentions, with peace being understood in a sense broader and profounder than the mere absence of overt hostilities. If absence of overt hostilities were the criterion, then any society terrorized by a superior power could be said to enjoy peace. But pacification is not peace: the latter is a state of accord which makes coercion unnecessary. It is rooted in law and justice, for which reason it is absurd to urge that in the age of nuclear weapons freedom and morality be subordinated to the cause of "peace." The elimination of overt violence, when enforced by coercion, is by its very nature transient, because it can last only as long as the coercing party enjoys superior strength. Such "peace" is really only institutionalized violence. Hence the overriding importance of conditions inside Communist regimes, and in particular the adoption by these regimes of legal norms and procedures capable of producing a state of civil accord at home. To put it in different words: the Soviet Union will be a partner in peace only if and when it makes peace with its own people. Only then will the danger of nuclear war recede. Arms-control agreements, summit meetings and other forms of negotiation, commercial and cultural relations, are entirely subordinate to this overriding objective.

The main thesis of this book runs counter to the arguments of both the "dovish" and the "hawkish" schools of thought. The former rests its case on the argument that nuclear weapons have allegedly made East and West equally interested in peaceful relations and that indulgence and friendly gestures on the part of the United States will gradually eliminate frictions between them. This point of view ignores the expansionist, aggressive elements built into the Communist system, trivializes the concept of peace, and places too heavy a burden on unilateral United States initiatives. The "hawks," for their part, are overly obsessed with the strictly military aspects of the relationship, despite the historical record, which shows that no amount of United States military superiority can prevent Soviet expansion. Neither school sees the relevance of internal conditions in the Communist Bloc to United States national security and neither addresses itself to the dangers posed by Soviet Grand Strategy. The policy of détente, advocated by the "doves," may be feasible, but it has proven undesirable, whereas containment, urged by the "hawks," may work up to a point, but it has ceased to be feasible. Hence some other way must be found.

It has been a tacit premise of this book that Soviet society and its political culture are significantly different from those familiar to Westerners. This proposition may appear entirely trite, but it has been the experience of the author as a scholar and government official that nothing is more difficult to convey to an American audience. Americans feel uncomfortable when told that other peoples are "different," in part because this word often serves as a euphemism for inferior, and in part because it is a basic premise of American culture, derivative and multinational as it is, that people are everywhere the same and only conditions under which they happen to live differ. This belief in the identity of human nature and human interests, and the view of conflict as rooted in ignorance, prejudice, or misunderstanding, is the source of the widespread conviction that, if the American and Soviet leaders only got together, they could solve all the problems dividing their countries. The same conviction underlies the abiding faith in the efficacy of negotiation, arms-control agreements, or cultural and "people-to-people exchanges." Now it is true in one sense that at bottom all human beings—indeed, all living creatures, from the highest to the lowest—are the same and want the same, that is to survive and to procreate. But it is no less true that in so doing they must both make use of such means as nature has endowed them with and adapt themselves to the conditions in which it has placed them. This can produce wildly different results. No amount of "mutual understanding" can undo the fact that the various species and genera, and, for that matter, nations, meet their common biological and other needs in idiosyncratic ways. Sheep and wolves may want the same, but sheep happen to satisfy their needs by eating grass, and wolves by eating sheep. Political and social structures, fortunately, are not as rigidly determined as biological ones and can undergo change; but change they must if they are to behave differently.

The key to peace lies in an internal transformation of the Soviet system in the direction of economic decentralization, greater scope for contractual work and free enterprise, national self-determination, human rights and legality. The obstacles to such reforms are formidable. The *nomenklatura* will resist changes as long as it can, and that means, in effect, as long as it is able to compensate for internal failures with triumphs abroad. It will always find the pursuit of an aggressive foreign policy preferable to coping with internal problems, because in the former case it can buy time with tactical maneuvers of all sorts, whereas internal problems call for structural changes which are far more difficult to undo. The point is that the majority of inhabitants of any country, the USSR included, are not deeply concerned with foreign policy. They may be disgusted with their country's humiliations and elated by its triumphs, but they feel the effects of such events only indirectly. What happens at home, however, is to them of immediate and direct relevance; here, every citizen is an expert. Competing against democracies, which only want to be left in peace to pursue their commercial interests, a government like the Soviet one can always stay on the offensive. At home, by contrast, it is forever waging a defensive battle against its own people, who are ready to pounce at every opportunity, every sign of weakness to arrogate for themselves more economic and political rights. Once they have seized a position, they are difficult to dislodge.

This conceded, it is nevertheless true that the Stalinist system now prevailing in the Soviet Union has outlived its usefulness and that the forces making for change are becoming well-nigh irresistible. The West can promote these forces by a combination of active resistance to Soviet expansion and political-military blackmail and the denial of economic and other forms of aid.

To save itself from having to make concessions certain to reduce its power and privilege, the *nomenklatura* relies heavily on terror. At home, it threatens those who dare stand in its way with imprisonment and exile; abroad, it brandishes the threat of nuclear holocaust. Its principal effort is directed toward that which Clausewitz called "the killing of courage." To frustrate it, the West must learn from dissidents in Communist countries who have demonstrated how powerless the system is when confronted with imperviousness to terror. "The essence of the struggle"—in the words of Vladimir Bukovskii, a Russian dissenter of proven record—"is the struggle against fear." It is the same advice that Karl Marx gave the Western powers in the middle of the nineteenth century, "There is only one way to deal with a power like Russia," he wrote in December 1853 in *The New York Tribune*, "and that is the fearless way."

It is difficult to tell whether democracies, constrained as they are by vested interests, public opinion and political rivalries, are capable of sustaining an indirect, long-range policy which requires the courage of quiet firmness and patience. Unquestionably it is much easier to evoke a response from a democratic electorate with either calls to arms or promises of eternal peace. What can be said with confidence is that as long as the present system prevails in the Soviet Union, war will remain an ever-present danger which neither rearmament nor accommodation can entirely avert.

It is these tasks, not sheer physical survival, that confront the West. Survival in itself cannot be a proper objective for nations any more than it is for individual citizens. To view escape from danger as the supreme good is to give license to those who habitually rely on violence as a means of suasion, and thereby help tear apart the fabric of national as well as international communities. As everyone seeks to safeguard his life and abandons all else to its own fate, societies become atomized, making it possible for forces which place a lower value on life to gain their ends. Once this happens, war ceases to be a threat and turns into a permanent condition.

# NOTES

## CHAPTER I

[1] Charles Howard McIlwain, *The Growth of Political Thought in the West* (New York, 1932), 394.

[2] Lev Trotsky, *Stalinskaia shkola falsifikatsii [The Stalinist School of Falsification]* (Berlin, 1932), 124.

[3] Boris Pilniak, "Golyi god" ["The Naked Year"] in *Izbrannye proizvedeniia [Selected Works]* (Moscow, 1976), 83.

[4] Leon Trotsky, *Our Revolution* (New York, 1918), 136–37.

[5] V. I. Lenin, *Collected Works*, Vol. 32 (London, 1965), 480.

[6] T. H. Rigby, *Lenin's Government: Sovnarkom, 1917–1922* (Cambridge, 1979), 51.

[7] The civil-service statistics are from "K voprosu o slome burzhuaznoi gosudarstvennoi mashiny v Rossii" ["On the question of the breakup of the bourgeois state machinery in Russia"], by M. P. Iroshnikov in *Problemy gosudarstvennogo stroitel'stva v pervye gody sovetskoi vlasti [Problems of Government Construction in the Early Years of Soviet Authority]* (Leningrad, 1973), 54; those on the Red Army, from S. A. Fediukin, *Velikii Oktiabr' i intelligentsiia [The Great October Revolution and the Intelligentsia]* (Moscow, 1972), 123, 142.

[8] V. I. Lenin, "How we Should Reorganize the Workers' and Peasants' Inspection," *Collected Works* (London, 1966), XXXIII, 481.

[9] M. Bakunin, "Gosudarstvennost' i anarkhiia" ["The State and Anarchy"] *Archives Bakounine*, ed. Arthur Lehning, III (Leiden, 1967), 150.

[10] Lenin, *Collected Works*, XXVII (London, 1965), 90–91.

[11] On this subject, see Paul Craig Roberts, "War Communism—Product of Marxian Ideas" in *Alienation and the Soviet Economy* (University of New Mexico Press, 1971), 20–47.

[12] Iu. S. Novopashin in *Voprosy filosofii*, No. 8 (1982), 9.

[13] B. Gorev, ed., *Voina i voennoe iskusstvo v svete istoricheskogo materializma [War and the Art of War in the Light of Historical Materialism]* (Moscow-Leningrad, 1927), 126–27.

[14] John Erickson, *The Soviet High Command* (London, 1962), 326; Max Werner, *The Military Strength of the Powers* (London, 1939), 40.

[15] N. N. Sukhotin, *Voina v istorii russkogo mira [War in the History of the Russian World]* (St. Petersburg, 1898), 13–14.

[16] On this subject, see Colin Gray, *The Geopolitics of the Nuclear Era: Heartland, Rimlands, and the Technological Revolution* (New York, 1977).

[17] *Dagens Nyheter* (Stockholm), June 9, 1983, 12.

[18] Friedrich Engels, "Die auswärtige Politik des russischen Zarenthums" ["The Foreign Policy of Russian Tsarism"] *Die Neue Zeit*, VIII (1890), 146.

[19] M. Iu. Lermontov, "Izmail bey," in his *Izbrannye proizvedeniia v dvukh tomakh [Selected Works in Two Volumes]*, Vol. I (Moscow/Leningrad, 1938), 271.

[20] Michael Voslenskii, "Die sowjetische Aussenpolitik; Verteidigung oder Aggression?" ["Soviet Foreign Policy: Defense or Aggression?"] in Daniel Frei, ed., *Konflikte unserer Zeit—Konflikte der Zukunft [Conflicts of our Time—Conflicts of the Future]* (Zurich, 1981), 53.

[21] Michael S. Voslenskii, *Nomenklatura: Die herrschende Klasse der Sowjetunion [Nomenklatura: The Ruling Class of the Soviet Union]* (Vienna, 1980), 161–63.

# CHAPTER II

[1] N. N. Maslov in *Voprosy Istorii KPSS*, No. 3, March 1983, p. 38. On this subject, consult Elliot Goodman, *Soviet Design for a World State* (New York, 1960).

[2] O. V. Kuusinen, et al. *Osnovy Marksizma-Leninizma: Uchebnoe posobie [The Fundamentals of Marxism-Leninism: A Textbook]* 2nd ed. (Moscow, 1962), 360.

[3] Edward R. Stettinius, *Roosevelt and the Russians: The Yalta Conference* (New York, 1949), p. 309.

[4] Letter to Secretary of State Rogers, cited in Henry A. Kissinger, *White House Years* (Boston, 1979), 135.

[5] State of the Union Address, in *The New York Times*, Jan. 24, 1980, 12.

[6] *The Cambridge History of the British Empire*, I (Cambridge, 1929), 207. The passage refers to the origins of British imperial policy in the seventeenth century.

[7] V. I. Lenin, *Sochineniia [Works]*, 3rd ed. (Moscow-Leningrad, 1935), XXVI, 604, 605.

[8] Jan H. Meijer, ed., *The Trotsky Papers, 1917–1922*, I (London, 1964), 623–25.

[9] Andrei V. Sakharov, *My Country and the World* (New York, 1975), 81.

[10] Published in Moscow, 1973; the citation is from p. 101.

11 *Ibid.*, 99.
12 As cited on p. 57.
13 *"Left-Wing" Communism, an Infantile Disorder,* in *Collected Works* (Moscow, 1966), XXXI, 70–71.
14 *The Campaign of 1812 in Russia* (London, 1843), 184.
15 Hans-Adolf Jacobsen, *Der Zweite Weltkrieg [The Second World War]* (Frankfurt a/M, 1965), 57, 59.
16 With Victor C. Johnson, *Foreign Affairs,* Spring, 1979, 919. Emphasis added.
17 "Abschreckung-nur eine Atempause?" ["Deterrence: Only a Breathing Space?"] *Die Zeit,* No. 13 (March 26, 1982), 19. Emphasis added.
18 *Die Angst in der Politik [Anxiety in Politics]* (Düsseldorf and Vienna, 1967), 61–62.
19 XXIV S'ezd KPSS: *Stenograficheskii otchet* [24th Congress of the CPSU: *Stenographic Record*] (Moscow, 1971), I, 482.
20 *Boston Globe,* June 24, 1983, and *The New York Times,* June 23, 1983.
21 "Diary," *London Review of Books,* Feb. 17–March 2, 1983, 21.
22 On the relations of U.S. businessmen with the Soviet government, see Joseph Finder, *Red Carpet* (New York, 1983).
23 U.S. Department of Agriculture, Economic Research Service, *USSR: Review of Agriculture in 1981 and Outlook for 1982* (Washington, D.C., May, 1982), 13.
24 *The New Criterion,* No. 10 (June 1983), 3.
25 This survey, conducted by a Columbia University research institute and directed by S. Robert Lichter and Stanley Rothman, is reproduced in the *Congressional Record* of March 23, 1982, S2619-2622.
26 *Epoche,* May 1982, 7.
27 Survey conducted by Lichter and Rothman, summarized in *The Wall Street Journal,* July 21, 1983, under the rubric "Asides," 26.
28 Joe Sobran in the *Dartmouth Review,* III, No. 23 (May 16, 1983).
29 *Szkice [Sketches]* (Cracow, 1981), 13.
30 Ladislas Bod, "Langage et pouvoir politique: réflexions sur le Stalinisme" ["Language and Political Power: Reflections on Stalinism"], *Études* (Feb., 1975), 178.
31 "Politics and the English Language," *Selected Essays* (London, 1958), 77, 82.
32 Veljko Mičunović, *Moscow Diary* (London, 1980), 30.
33 Ambassador Jeane J. Kirkpatrick, interview with George Urban, Radio Free Europe, Munich, Germany, July, 1983, 104.
34 V. I. Lenin, *Collected Works* (London, 1964), VIII, 268; XXI, 299; XXX, 224; XIII, 80; XXVII, 106.
35 *Collected Works,* XXIX, 153.
36 *Literaturnaia gazeta,* Nov. 5, 1972.
37 *Sovetskaia voennaia entsiklopediia [Soviet Military Encyclopedia]* VI (Moscow, 1978), 252–53. Emphasis supplied.
38 *Ibid.,* II (Moscow, 1976), 184.
39 "Mezhdu Khelsinki i Venoi" ["Between Helsinki and Vienna"], *SShA,* No. 1 (Jan. 1970), 62–63.

[40] *Pravda*, May 9, 1983.
[41] F. A. Hayek, *The Counter-Revolution of Science: Studies of the Abuse of Reason*, 2nd ed. (Indianapolis, Ind., 1979), 37. Emphasis supplied.
[42] Dispatch of Sept. 30, 1945: *Foreign Relations of the United States: Diplomatic Papers, 1945*, V, Europe (Washington, D.C.: Government Printing Office, 1967), 885.
[43] Cited by E. Mark, *Foreign Affairs*, Jan. 1978, 433.
[44] William W. Kaufmann, *The McNamara Strategy* (New York, 1964), 97.
[45] Albert Wohlstetter in *Foreign Policy*, XV (Summer, 1974), 3–21; XVI (Fall, 1974), 48–81; XX (Fall, 1975), 170–98.
[46] See, for example, S. L. Kozlov and others, *O sovetskoi voennoi nauke [On Soviet Military Science]* 2nd ed. (Moscow, 1964), 232–33.
[47] *V. I. Lenin i sovetskie vooruzhonnye sily [V. I. Lenin and the Soviet Armed Forces]* 2nd ed. (Moscow, Military Publishing House of the Ministry of Defense of the USSR, 1969), 229, 230–31, 233. Emphasis supplied.
[48] *The New York Times*, Oct. 5, 1981, A21.
[49] B. Drummond Ayres, Jr., in *The New York Times*, July 26, 1983, B16.
[50] J. M. Mackintosh, *The Strategy and Tactics of Soviet Foreign Policy* (London, 1962), 272.
[51] *Ibid.*, 273.
[52] Mohammed Heikal, *Sphinx and Commissar* (London, 1978), 30.
[53] Resolutions of the II Congress of the Communist International, 19 July–6 Aug., 1920, in V. I. Lenin, *Sochineniia [Works]*, 2nd ed. (Moscow, 1935), XXV, 573.
[54] *Kommunist*, No. 8 (May 1961), 42.
[55] Wolfgang Leonhard, "Soviet Foreign Policy: Interests, Motives and Objectives," paper presented at a United States Information Agency conference in Washington, D.C., in February, 1983. This point is also made in M. Voslensky's *Nomenklatura: die herrschende Klasse der Sowjetunion* (Vienna, 1980), 452.
[56] David J. Dallin, *Soviet Foreign Policy after Stalin* (Philadelphia, 1961), 104.
[57] W. C. J. van Rensburg and D. A. Pretorius, *South Africa's Strategic Minerals* (Johannesburg, 1977), *passim*.
[58] A. Aleksin in *Kommunist*, No. 10 (July, 1970), 93.

## CHAPTER III

[1] *Marksizm-Leninizm o voine i armii [Marxism-Leninism on War and Army]* (Moscow-Leningrad, 1965), 88.
[2] Frane Barbieri in *La Stampa* (Turin), Feb. 22, 1981.
[3] *Pravda*, Dec. 22, 1972, 5; translated in *Current Digest of the Soviet Press*, XXIV/51 (Jan. 17, 1973), 16.
[4] A. G. Aganbegian, cited in *SSSR-Vnutrennie protivorechiia* (New York, No. 6 [1982]), 173.
[5] *Sovetskaia Rossiia*, July 22, 1981, 2.
[6] *Pravda*, June 16, 1983.

[7] E.g. Igor Birman in *Crossroads* (Jerusalem), (Winter-Spring, 1981), 121–22. Mr. Birman estimates the Soviet GNP to be one fourth, rather than one half, of the American one, as the CIA believes.

[8] These examples come from Aron Katzenelinboigen in *SSSR-Vnutrennie protivorechiia* (New York, No. 4 [1982]), 26–42; and William Odom in *Russia* (New York, No. 2 [1981]), 54–55.

[9] A. G. Aganbegian, cited in *SSSR-Vnutrennie protivorechiia* (New York, No. 6 [1982]), 171; Odom, *loc. cit.*, 54.

[10] On this topic, see David Mitrany, *Marx Against the Peasant* (University of North Carolina Press, 1951).

[11] Alec Nove, *An Economic History of the U.S.S.R.* (Penguin Books, 1972), 242–43.

[12] Even in the early 1980s, only one village household in three in the U.S.S.R. had running water and sewage: see the U.S. Department of Agriculture, Economic Research Service, *USSR: Review of Agriculture in 1981 and Outlook for 1982* (Washington, D.C., 1982), 17.

[13] *Ibid.*, 16–17.

[14] V. V. Tikhonov in *Sotsialisticheskaia industriia*, April 9, 1982.

[15] Marshall Goldman, *USSR in Crisis* (New York, 1983), 76, citing David M. Schoonover.

[16] Gertrude E. Schroeder in Congress of the United States, Joint Economic Committee, *Soviet Economy in the 1980's: Problems and Prospects*, Part 2 (Washington, D.C., 1982), 368–69.

[17] Radio Free Europe/Radio Liberty, "Food Supply in the USSR: a Worsening Trend, First Semester, 1982," AR No. 10-82 (November, 1982), 6.

[18] Robert A. Lewis, Richard H. Rowland and Ralph C. Clem, *Nationality and Population Change in Russia and the USSR* (New York, 1976), 272–73.

[19] Vladimir Treml in *The Wall Street Journal*, Nov. 10, 1981. The author says that such mortality from acute alcohol poisoning is "completely outside the range of human experience."

[20] Murray Feshbach, in *Problems of Communism*, January-February, 1982, 31.

[21] Nick Eberstadt, "The Health Crisis in the USSR," *New York Review of Books*, Feb. 19, 1981, 23.

[22] Quoted in *The New Republic*, Feb. 17, 1982, 14.

[23] Dusko Doder in *The Washington Post*, Aug. 3, 1983.

[24] Thomas H. Naylor in *The New York Times*, Oct. 16, 1982, 27; P. Ignatovskii in *Kommunist*, No. 12 (Aug. 1983), 60ff.

[25] *Sovetskaia Rossiia*, July 19, 22 and 24, 1981.

[26] *Kommunist*, No. 10 (July, 1982), 16.

[27] F. Chernetskii in *Izvestiia*, March 23, 1982.

[28] Vladlen Kuznetsov in *New Times*, No. 14 (April 1978), 21–22.

[29] D. E. Tagunov in *Sovetskoe gosudarstvo i pravo*, VII (1981), 130.

[30] Boris Rumer, "The 'Second' Agriculture in the USSR," *Soviet Studies*, No. 4 (Oct. 1981), 565.

[31] P. Samylkin in *Izvestiia*, Jan. 12, 1980.

[32] Rumer, *loc. cit.*, 567–68. Emphasis added.

[33] Iu. S. Novopashin in *Voprosy filosofii*, No. 8 (1982), 9.

# CHAPTER IV

[1] S. Tsvigun in *Kommunist*, No. 14 (Sept. 1981), 96.

[2] Ilia Zemtsov, *Partiia ili Mafiia? Razvorovannaia Respublika [A Party or a Mafia? The Plundered Republic]* (Paris, 1976), 26, 33–35. This book has been translated into French under the title *La corruption en Union Soviétique* (Paris, 1976).

[3] *Literaturnaia gazeta*, Nov. 18, 1981.

[4] *Frankfurter Allgemeine Zeitung*, July 7, 1981, citing the *Daily Telegraph;* see further *Keesing's Contemporary Archives*, Oct. 2, 1981, p. 31,108.

[5] *Literaturnaia gazeta*, Nov. 18, 1981.

[6] *Kultura* (Warsaw), June 21, 1981, 2.

[7] Konstantin M. Simis, *U.S.S.R.—The Corrupt Society* (New York, 1982), 121.

[8] *Ibid.*, 299.

[9] A. I. Herzen, "Du développement des idées révolutionnaires en Russie" ["On the Development of Revolutionary Ideas in Russia"] *Sobranie sochinenii v tridtsati tomakh [Collected Works in Thirty Volumes]* (Moscow, 1956), VII, 74.

[10] Oskar Köhler cited by Manfred Fuhrmann in *Frankfurter Allgemeine Zeitung*, June 4, 1983.

[11] Harold J. Berman, ed., *Soviet Criminal Law and Procedure: The RSFSR Codes*, 2nd ed. (Cambridge, Mass., 1972), 49–57, 126.

[12] *The New York Times Magazine*, June 8, 1980, 110.

[13] A good account of Soviet industrial strikes can be found in Karl Schlögel's *Opposition sowjetischer Arbeiter heute [The Opposition of Soviet Workers Today]* Berichte des Bundesinstituts für ostwissenschaftliche und internationale Studien (Cologne, 1981).

[14] See Aleksandr I. Solzhenitsyn, *The Gulag Archipelago, 1918–1956*, Part V–VII (New York, 1978), 506–13, and Victor Haynes and Olga Semyonova, *Workers Against the Gulag* (London, 1979), 73–79.

[15] F. Nesterov, *Sviaz' vremen [The Bond of Ages]* (Moscow, 1980), 40–41; A. N. Sakharov, *Diplomatiia drevnei Rusi [The Diplomacy of Ancient Rus']* (Moscow, 1980), 300.

[16] On this subject see the essay by Michael Agursky, "Contemporary Russian Nationalism: History Revisited," Hebrew University of Jerusalem, Soviet and East European Research Centre, Research Paper No. 45, Jan., 1982.

[17] Vadim Kozhinov in *Nash Sovremennik*, No. 11 (1981), 154.

[18] Dusko Doder in *The Washington Post*, June 30, 1983.

[19] D. Tiktina (Shturman) in *Antisemitizm v Sovetskom Soiuze: ego korni i posledstviia [Antisemitism in the Soviet Union: Its Roots and Consequences]* (Jerusalem, 1979), 86. See also William Korey, "Anti-Semitism and the Soviet Military," *Freedom at Issue*, March-April, 1983, 13–15.

[20] Cited in Joshua Rubenstein, *Soviet Dissidents* (Boston, 1980), 204. Emphasis added.

[21] *The Kenyon Review*, New Series, I, No. 4 (Fall, 1979), 4.

[22] Andrei Sakharov, *O pis'me Aleksandra Solzhenitsyna "Vozhdiam Sovetskogo Soiuza" [On the Letter of Alexander Solzhenitsyn "To the Leaders of the Soviet*

*Union"]* (New York, 1974), 6, 10, 13. This essay was translated into English in the *New York Review of Books,* June 13, 1974.

23 *Notes of a Revolutionary* (New York, 1982), 26.

24 Alain Besançon, *Présent soviétique et passé russe [The Soviet Present and the Russian Past]* (Paris, 1980), 221–22.

25 Richard Portes in *Deficits and Détente* (The Twentieth Century Fund, New York, 1983), 25.

26 V. I. Lenin, *Sochineniia [Works],* 3rd ed. XXV, 624.

27 *Afrika—problemy sotsialisticheskoi orientatsii [Africa—Problems of Socialist Orientation]* (Moscow, 1976), 11.

28 *The New York Times,* Jan. 4, 1984, A4.

29 *Afrika,* 11.

30 Iu. S. Novopashin in *Voprosy filosofii* No. 8 (1982), 13.

31 S. A. Mikoyan in *Latinskaia Amerika,* No. 3 (March 1980), 43–44.

32 *The New York Times,* Dec. 19 and 30, 1981.

33 *L'Unità,* Jan. 24, 1982.

34 Heinz Timmermann, *Aktuelle Tendenzen im Kommunistischen Parteiensystem [Current Tendencies in the Communist Party System],* Berichte des Bundesinstituts für ostwissenschaftliche und internationale Studien, No. 7 (Cologne, 1983), 26.

35 "The Collapse of the Second International," *Collected Works,* XXI (London, 1963), 214.

36 "Iu. K. Petrov," "Metamorfozy russkogo liberalizma" ["Metamorphoses of Russian Liberalism"], 109–10. Manuscript in the author's possession.

37 *Sintaksis* (Paris), No. 6 (1980), 112–13.

38 "O politicheskom prosveshchenii naseleniia Sovetskogo Soiuza" ["On the Political Enlightenment of the Population of the Soviet Union"], *Problemy Vostochnoi Evropy,* 2 (1981), 133–34.

39 Friedrich Engels, "Die auswärtige Politik des Russischen Zarenthums" ["The Foreign Policy of Russian Tsarism"], *Die Neue Zeit* VIII (1890), 202.

# CHAPTER V

1 Sun Tzu, *The Art of War* (Oxford, 1963), 77.

2 *Recollections,* edited by J. P. Mayer and A. P. Kerr (London, 1970), 61–62.

3 Robert E. Sherwood, *Roosevelt and Hopkins* (New York, 1948), 870.

4 "X" [George F. Kennan] in *Foreign Affairs,* July 1947, 581.

5 Public Papers of the Presidents of the United States, *Jimmy Carter, 1978,* I (Washington, D.C., 1979), 1053.

6 "American Power and American Purpose," Address delivered before the U.S. Chamber of Commerce on April 27, 1982, U.S. Department of State, Bureau of Public Affairs, Current Policy No. 388.

7 Gerald F. Seib and Walter S. Mossberg in *The Wall Street Journal,* July 26, 1983.

8 Bernard J. O'Keefe cited in *The New York Times,* Aug. 12, 1983, IV, 2.

9 "The Military Role of Nuclear Weapons: Perceptions and Misperceptions," *Foreign Affairs*, Fall 1983, 79.

10 C. Jung, *Flying Saucers: A Modern Myth of Things Seen in the Skies* (London, 1959).

11 *Encounters with Kennan* (London, 1979), 161–62.

12 *The Wall Street Journal*, Sept. 28, 1983.

13 *Newsweek*, May 29, 1972, 43.

14 Donald R. Cotter et al., *The Nuclear "Balance" in Europe: Status, Trends, Implications* (Washington, D.C., United States Strategic Institute, 1983), 8; emphasis added.

15 *Orbis*, Fall 1981, 655.

16 Robert Strausz-Hupé et al., *Protracted Conflict* (New York, 1959), 57.

17 Ben J. Wattenberg in *The Wall Street Journal*, June 3, 1982.

18 *The Washington Post*, June 5, 1983.

19 Walter Hahn in *Strategic Review*, IX:2 (Spring 1981), 8.

20 U.S. International Communication Agency, Office of Research, Foreign Opinion Note, N-8/7/81.

21 *Frankfurter Allgemeine Zeitung*, Oct. 30, 1981.

22 *Frankfurter Allgemeine Zeitung*, Oct. 27, 1982.

23 U.S. International Communication Agency, Office of Research, Briefing Paper, B-12/23/81.

24 U.S. International Communication Agency, Office of Research, Foreign Opinion Note, N-8/7/81.

25 Bundeskanzler Brandt, *Reden und Interviews [Speeches and Interviews]* (Hamburg, 1971), 203.

26 Diane L. Coutu in *The Wall Street Journal*, April 18, 1983.

27 *The New York Times*, Aug. 13, 1983.

28 Michel Tatu, "The Devolution of Power: A Dream?," *Foreign Affairs*, July 1975, 680.

29 Antony Sutton, *Western Technology and Soviet Economic Development, 1930 to 1945* (Stanford, California, Hoover Institution, 1971), 329. In his three-volume detailed account of Soviet purchases of Western equipment and technology, of which this is the second volume, Sutton comes to conclusions that are uncomfortable for many businessmen and economists. For this reason his work tends to be either dismissed out of hand as "extreme" or, more often, simply ignored.

30 Sutton, *loc. cit.*, 329, 346.

31 Sutton, *Western Technology . . . 1945–1965* (Stanford, 1973), 312–14; *The New York Times*, March 3, 1961, A6; *Congressional Record*, November 13, 1979, S-32059.

32 Sutton, *Western Technology . . . 1930 to 1945*, 344.

33 *The Memoirs of Cordell Hull* (New York, 1948), I, 81.

34 *The New Republic*, June 2, 1982, 15.

35 Gary C. Hufbauer and Jeffrey J. Schott, *Economic Sanctions in Support of Foreign Policy* (Washington, D. C., Institute for International Economics, 1983).

36 *The New York Times*, May 5 and Aug. 26, 1983.

37 S. Klepikov and V. Linnik in *Pravda*, June 28, 1982, 6.

# INDEX

*Absolute Weapon, The* (Yale University Press), 92
Academic community, 72–74
Adelman, Kenneth, 70–71
Administrative decentralization, 206–7
Afghanistan, 39–40, 58, 69, 76, 82, 90, 104, 183, 192, 193, 195, 243, 246
  anti-Communist guerrillas in, 245
  cost of operations in, 187*n*
  Imperial Russia and, 211
  Middle East strategy and, 108
  NATO and, 249
  U.S. sanctions and, 270, 271
AFL-CIO, 75*n*
Africa, 103, 277
  sub-Saharan, 108
Agriculture:
  capital investments in, 124–25
  collectivization of, 122–23
  cooperative "links," 138–39
  in Poland, 115
  private, 126
  second economy in, 143–45
  urbanization and, 126
Agriculture Department, U.S., 125

Albania, 112
Alcoholism, 130–31
Alexander II, Tsar, 204
Alexander the Great, 51, 102, 135
Algeria, 182, 185
Aliev, Gaidar, 155, 156
Allende, Salvador, 191
Amalrik, Andrei, 177
American Relief Administration, 122
Ammonia industry, 263
Andropov, Yurii, 45, 117, 151
Angola, 69, 90, 106, 192, 245, 277
Anti-anti-Communism, 77–80
Antiballistic missiles (ABMs), 243
Anti-Semitism, 172, 173, 177, 252
Arbatov, Georgi, 79–80, 82
Armenia, 182–85
Arms control, 233–38
Arms Control and Disarmament Agency, U.S., 70–71, 260
Arnold, Matthew, 209
*Artel* (cooperatives), 137–38
Attrition, political, 53, 246
Austria, 265
Azerbaijan, 154–55
Azeris, 183

Babylon, ancient, 230
Backfire bomber, 100
Baghdad Pact, 58, 248
Bakunin, Michael, 28–29
Balearic Islands, 56
Baltic Republics, 182, 184
"Basic Principles of Relations"
    (Nixon–Brezhnev agreement),
    221
Basmachis, 245
Behaviorist psychology, 217–18
Belgium, 189
Belorussia, 54, 183
Bennett, Arnold, 77
Berlinguer, Enrico, 196
Besançon, Alain, 80, 178
Bible, 230
Bingham, Jonathan, 67
Birth rate, 129, 130
Bishop, Maurice, 192
Bismarck, Otto von, 210
Bolsheviks, 22–26, 30, 33–35, 80–
    81, 104–5, 114, 149–50, 181,
    256, 260
  agriculture and, 121
  antinationalism of, 170
  United States response to, 212
Bonapartism, 87
Brandt, Willy, 253
Brest-Litovsk treaty, 212
Brezhnev, Leonid, 112–13, 119,
    139, 221
  corruption under, 151, 156
Brezhnev Doctrine, 69, 70, 179, 188
Bribe taking, 154–57
Britain, Battle of, 55
British–German Naval Treaty, 233
Brodie, Bernard, 92, 95
Bryant Chucking Grinder
    Company, 264
Bulgaria, 63, 186
  economic reform in, 141
Bukovskii, Vladimir, 280
Business community, 74–77
  technology transfer and, 260,
    261, 266
Business contracts, 61–62

Cambodia, 109, 231
Carter, Jimmy, 55, 216

Castro, Fidel, 70, 78, 191
Censorship, 80–81
Central America, 109–10, 257
  Cuban aggression in, 245
  NATO and, 249
  U.S. strategy in, 222
Central Committee, 30, 31
  agriculture and, 122
  International Department of,
    106, 276
  military police and, 87
  Third World strategy and, 193
  Trotsky's 1919 letter to, 57–58
Central Executive Committee of
    the Soviets, 24
Central Intelligence Agency (CIA),
    95, 112, 117
Centralized planning, 114–17
Chad, 272
Chalidze, Valerii, 203–4
Chamberlain, Neville, 55
Chemical industry, 260, 263
Chernenko, Konstantin, 151
Chiang Kai-shek, 105
Chicherin, G. V., 84–85
Chief Political Directorate, 87
Chile, 191
China, 33, 63, 84, 95, 249$n$
  anticolonial movements in, 105
  break with, 195, 198–99
  *divide et impera* tactics and, 103
  Imperial Russia and, 56
  *rapprochement* with U.S., 82
  reforms in, 208
  Southeast Asia strategy and, 109
  Yalta accords and, 54
*Chronicle of Human Events,* 164
Churchill, Winston, 46, 213, 233
*Class Essence of Zionism, The*
    (Korneev), 172–73
Class warfare, 53–54, 65
Clausewitz, Karl von, 61
COCOM, 265, 272
Cold War, 54–55, 132
"Collective unconscious," 229
Collectives, agricultural, 122–26
Colonies, Soviet, 186–88
Command principle, 205
Commerce Department, U.S., 260,
    265

Communist Bloc Economic
  Community, 190
Communist International, 104, 193–
  195
  Second Congress of, 57, 60, 104
Communist Party:
  Central Committee of, see
    Central Committee
  control of armed forces by, 86–
    87
  corruption in, 149–58
  economic reforms and, 136, 139
  Grand Strategy of, 51–60
  growth in membership of, 27–28
  left opposition to, 165–66
  1934 Congress of, 30
  nomenklatura and, 29, 30
  nuclear weapons and, 98–99
  reform and, 206
  subordination of state to, 181
Congress, U.S., 256
Construction brigades, 146
Containment, 214–15, 218–20, 278
  détente compared with, 221, 222
Cooperatives, 137–39
Correlation of forces, 51, 52, 86,
  216
Corrupt Society (Simis), 157
Corruption, 149–58
Cotter, Donald, 240n
Creusot-Loire Co., 263
Criminal Codes, 163–65
Cruise missiles, 237
Cuba, 90, 109, 277
  armed forces of, 244
  Central America and, 245
  labor disputes in, 250
  Soviet position on defense of,
    188
Czechoslovakia, 33, 42, 142, 186,
  187, 200
  dissent in, 167
  economic reform in, 136, 141
  invasion of, 161, 195, 271

Dam, Kenneth, 71
Daniel, Iurii, 164
Decentralization, 136–37, 206–7
Defense allocations, 225–26
Defense Department, U.S., 92, 264

Defense Council, 87
de Gaulle, Charles, 220
Delta submarine, 100
Democratic opposition in U.S.S.R.,
  162–69
Democratic Party in U.S., 78, 247
Dependencies, 188–93
"De-Stalinization," 30
Détente, 55, 69–70, 75, 76, 86, 197,
  198, 204, 215, 220–22, 278
  arms control and, 235
  behaviorist psychology and, 218
  German, 254
  technology transfer and, 264
  trade and, 132, 133, 135, 268, 273
Deterrence, doctrine of, 91–93, 96,
  99–100
Dissent, see Intellectual dissent
Divide et impera policy, 60–63, 250
Djilas, Milovan, 203, 204
dos Santos, José Eduardo, 192
Dostoevsky, Feodor, 21, 172, 174
Dulles, John Foster, 58
DuPont Corporation, 260


East Germany, 142, 186, 194, 254,
  255
  economic reform in, 141
Economic crisis, 110–47
  agriculture and, 120–27
  attempts at reform and, 136–42
  centralization and, 114–17
  foreign debts and, 132–35
  lack of incentives and, 116–17
  living standards and, 127–28
  military spending and, 117–20
  political impact of, 113–14
  population trends and, 128–31
  productivity and, 112–13
  second economy and, 142–46
  U.S. response to, 259–73
Economic modernization, 208
Economic policy, 33–37
Egypt, 58, 108
Eisenhower, Dwight D., 93
El Salvador, 69, 244, 250
Electrical industry, 260
Electronic industry, 263
Engels, Friedrich, 41, 207

Epishev, General A. A., 87
Estonia, 183, 184
Ethiopia, 90, 106, 108, 192
  Italian invasion of, 270
Ethnic minorities, 179–85
  reform and, 207–8
Eumenes, 135
Eurocommunism, 195
European Economic Community
    (EEC), 255, 257
Expansionism, 37–44
  of Imperial Russia, 56
  military policy and, 89–91
  objective of, 49–50
  in Third World, 103–4
  after Yalta accords, 55


Fascists, 88–89, 149–50
*Fate of the Earth* (Schell), 232
Federal Republic of Germany, *see*
    West Germany
Feis, Herbert, 213
Finland, 213
Five Year Plans, 116
  first, 36, 90, 122, 213, 260
  military spending and, 119
  third, 260
"Flexible response," 66, 228
Food, availability of, 127–28
*Forbes* magazine, 72
Ford Motors, 260
Foreign debts, 132–35
France, 21, 29, 181
  anti-Bolsheviks supported by,
    212
  anti-Communism in, 77*n*
  colonies of, 182, 185
  Communist Party of, 197
  Communist trade unions in, 62
  détente and, 220
  foreign policy of, 62
  nuclear arsenal of, 242
  peaceful coexistence and, 215
  per capita consumption in, 127
  technology acquired from, 265
  in World War II, 63*n*, 89, 96, 243
*Frankfurter Allgemeine Zeitung*, 134*n*
Freemasons, 171
Frunze, M. V., 88

Gallois, General Pierre, 234, 241
General Electric, 260
General Staff academies, 88
Georgia, Republic of, 146, 182–84
  corruption in, 155
Germany, 21, 260
  Britain and, 216
  history of relations of Russia
    and, 211–12
  imperial, 56, 210
  nineteenth-century, 200
  in World War I, 34, 35, 212, 241,
    243, 256
  in World War II, 53, 63, 89–90,
    102, 214, 256, 260, 261, 266
  *See also* East Germany; West
    Germany
Ghana, 191
Gibraltar, 56
Gierek, Eduard, 156
Giscard d'Estaing, Valéry, 62
Gorbachev, Mikhail Sergeevich,
    139
Gorkii automobile plant, 260
Gosplan (State Planning
    Commission), 35, 116, 266
  Military-Economic Department
    of, 90
Gramsci, Antonio, 80
Grand Strategy, 51–60, 110, 274–
    278
  applied to given historic
    circumstances, 64
  post-Stalin shift in, 219
  Western policy toward, 209–10
  U.S. response to, 222–24
  *See also* Military strategy;
    Political strategy; Third World
    strategy
Great Britain, 181, 226
  anti-anti-Communism in, 77
  anti-Bolsheviks supported by,
    212
  antiguerrilla campaign in
    Malaysia by, 245
  avoidance of revolution in, 203
  Communist Party of, 197
  containment policy of, 218
  France and, 220
  Germany and, 216

imperialism of, 53, 55–56, 105, 182
  nuclear arsenal of, 242
  party politics in, 247
  relations of Imperial Russia and, 211
  in World War II, 63n, 89, 96, 108
Greece, 127, 214n
  ancient, 50, 95, 230
  Italian invasion of, 55
Grenada, 192, 244
Gromyko, Andrei, 69
Gross National Product (GNP):
  of EEC, 257
  of industrial democracies, 248
  military expenditures as percentage of, 117–18
  Soviet, 111–12, 115
Guerrilla movements, 244, 245
Gulag Archipelago (Solzhenitsyn), 175

Haig, Alexander, 216–17, 276
Hart, Gary, 101
Hayek, Frederick, 93
Health problems, 130–31
Hegel, G. W. F., 158
Hegemony, 50–51, 102, 111, 248
Helsinki accords, 62, 164
Herling, John, 75n
Herzen, Alexander, 159
Hitler, Adolf, 55, 88n, 107–8, 161n, 214, 249n, 275
  nonaggression pact with Stalin, 63, 108, 184, 194
Hobson, John, 104
Holmes, Oliver Wendell, 80
Holocaust, 173
Holy Alliance, 221
Honecker, Erich, 142
Hoover, Herbert, 122
Hopkins, Harry, 213
Hull, Cordell, 267
Hungary, 33, 57, 142, 186, 194, 200
  dissent in, 167
  economic reforms in, 116, 140–141
  treatment of scholars in, 73–74
Husak, Gustav, 142

"Ideological warfare," 65, 70
Imperial Russia, 56, 179–80, 203
  British policy toward, 211
  constitutional rights in possessions of, 141
  corruption in, 152, 155n
  Department of Police of, 151
  population trends in, 129
Imperialism, 37–44
  British, 53, 55–56, 104, 182
  as final stage of capitalism, 103
  goal of, 49–50
  nationalist opposition to, 175
  political crisis and, 178–99
  reform and, 207
  resources drained by, 111
  war of political attrition and, 53
Imperialism (Hobson), 104
Imperialism, the Highest Stage of Capitalism (Lenin), 104
Import-Export Bank, 75
Incentives, economic, 137–39
  lack of, 116–18
India, 57–58, 104, 230, 249n
  British in, 182
  famines in, 123
Indonesia, 191
Industrialization:
  agriculture and, 122–23
  in Third World, 190, 192
  Western aid in, 260–61
Infant mortality, 131
Inflation, 132
Institute for Concrete Sociological Research, 151–52
Institute for Policy Studies, 80
Intellectual dissent, 158–78
  nationalist, 169–78
  Westernizing, 163–69
Intelligentsia, 22, 158, 200
  nationalist loathing of, 169
  persecuted by Stalin, 163
Intercontinental Ballistic Missiles (ICBMs), 236
Investment policies, 118–20
  agriculture and, 124–25
Iran, 91, 183, 230
Israel, 70, 109, 215
  terrorism in, 244, 246

Italy, 214n, 262
Communist Party of (PCI), 195–
196
Communist trade unions in, 62
invasion of Ethiopia by, 270
Ivan the Terrible, 179–80

Jamaica, 192
Japan, 109, 249n
defense spending in, 257
imperialism of, 39
mineral imports of, 108
oil supplies of, 108
technology supplied by, 263,
265
U.S. defense commitments to,
103, 248
war with (1904–1905), 20, 56
in World War II, 53, 54, 214
Jews, 168
doomsday visions of, 230
émigrés, 62
excluded from nomenklatura, 32
in Middle East, 109
nationalist antagonism toward,
171–73
Stalin and, 170
Joel (prophet), 230
Johnson, Lyndon Baines, 228
Judicial system:
corruption in, 157
reforms in, 163–64
Jung, Karl, 229
Just and Unjust Wars in Our Time
(Scheler and Kiessling), 85n

Kaluga Turbine Works, 138
Kama River truck plant, 262, 264
Kennan, George, 94, 214, 221, 222,
232
Kennedy, John F., 109, 218–19,
228, 264
KGB, 31, 87, 151, 155
dissent and, 165, 168–69
minority nationalism and, 184
terrorists and, 245
Third Department of, 87
Third World and, 192

Khrushchev, Nikita, 30, 108, 163,
194
Kiev Motorcycle Works, 167
Kissinger, Henry, 133, 268, 269
Kommunist (journal), 137
Korea, 91, 219, 250
Korneev, Lev, 172
Kramer, Hilton, 77
"Kremlin Canteen," 32
Kulaks, 123
Kuomintang, 105

Labor shortage, 129, 131
Labour Party, British, 193
Laos, 109
Last Judgment, 230, 232
Latin America, 103, 191, 203, 277
See also Central America
Latvia, 183, 184
League of Nations, 270
Lebanon, 244, 277
Legality, 206
Lend Lease, 260–61
Lenin, V. I., 22–29, 34–35, 42, 43,
49, 72, 159–60, 165, 198n, 204,
215
Allies and, 212
business interests and, 74–75
colonies and, 187
Communist International
founded by, 193–94
concept of revolutionary party
of, 149–50
economic policies of, 141, 260
ethnic minorities and, 180–81
on imperialism, 104
nationalists and, 170
peasants and, 121, 122
political strategy of, 60–61, 63,
64, 247
"revolutionary situation"
concept of, 199–200
on war and peace, 84–85
Lermontov, Mikhail, 41
Lewis, Anthony, 101
Libya, 244
Life expectancy, 131
Links, 138–39
Literature, dissent in, 163
Lithuania, 183

Living standards, 127–28
  in Baltic countries, 184
  rural, 125
Lycurgus, 156

M. W. Kellogg Company, 262
McCarthy, Joseph, 77
McGovern, George, 78
McIlwain, Charles, 19
McKee Corporation, 260
McNamara, Robert, 93, 94, 228
Madrid Conference, 165
Magnitogorsk steel mill, 260
Maine, Sir Henry, 147
Malacca, Straits of, 109
Malaysia, 245
Mannesmann Company, 263
Mansfield Amendment, 256
Mao Tse-tung, 208
Mark, Eduard, 214n
Marshall Plan, 224, 268
Marx, Karl, 28, 29, 41, 42, 84, 121,
    159, 280
Marxism, 20, 22, 43, 80, 114, 149,
    268
  prerequisites for social
    revolution in, 105–6
  proletariat and, 64
  view of war in, 83–85
Marxism-Leninism, 17, 21, 22, 104,
    151, 159, 160, 222
  dissenting view of, 165–66
  militancy of, 83–84
Mason, Timothy W., 161n
Massive retaliation, doctrine of, 93
Mathias, Charles, 71
Medvedev, Roy, 166
Mengistu, 192
Merchant navy, 263
Mexico, 257
Michnik, Adam, 80
Middle Ages, 17–18, 160
  nationalist idealization of, 171
Middle East, 58, 103, 107, 250, 277
  NATO and, 258
  terrorism in, 246
Mikoyan, Anastas, 75n
Mikoyan, Serge, 191
Militarization of politics, 53–54

Military expenditures, 117–20
Military strategy, 83–102
  control of, 86–87
  economic impact of, 88–89
  expansionism and, 90
  nuclear weapons in, 91–102
  political ends served by, 84–86
  propaganda and, 88–90
  reform and, 207
  U.S. response to, 224–46
  Western technology and, 263–67
Milshtein, General Mikhail A., 97n
Ministry of Defense, Soviet, 85, 98
Ministry of Interior, Soviet, 87
Minuteman missile, 101, 264
Mithraic tales, 230
Molotov, V. M., 63n
Monarchists, 172
Monarchy, Russian:
  fall of, 23
  premodern, 18, 19
  Westernization of, 20
Mongolia, 186
Mongols, 38
Monroe Doctrine, 56, 109
Montesquieu, Charles, 231
Moral Majority, 77
Motor-vehicle industry, 260,
    262
Mozambique, 106, 190, 245
Multinational corporations, 64
Munich pact, 55
Muslims, 182–84, 246
Mussolini, Benito, 55, 63, 149–50,
    270
MX missile, 71, 101, 226, 228, 264

Namibia, 64, 70
Napoleon, 38, 51, 91, 243, 249n
Nasser, Gamal Abdel, 103, 192
National Association of
    Manufacturers, 75, 226
National Democracy, 106–7
"National liberation, wars of," 65
National Security Council, 275–76
Nationalism, 169–78
  of ethnic minorities, 179–85
Nationalization, 34
  of agricultural land, 122

NATO, 59, 88, 89, 95, 103, 215, 220
  arms control and, 234, 237
  business community and, 76
  Communist Parties in countries
    of, 71
  defensive mission of, 224–25
  "flexible response" theory of, 66
  formation of, 214
  nuclear policy of, 228, 239, 241
  PCI and, 196
  political strategy toward, 61–62
  sanctions and, 270–71
  technology transfer and, 264–65
  United States and, 248–59
Natural gas, 262, 263
Nazis, 38, 63, 88n, 185, 213, 254,
  260
NBC poll, 250
Neocolonialism, 105–6
Nesterov, F., 171
*New Class, The* (Djilas), 203
New Economic Policy (NEP), 35,
  122, 141, 165, 260
New Economic Mechanism, 140–
  143
*New Leader*, 75n
*New York Times*, 75n, 80, 97n, 101,
  272
*New York Tribune*, 280
Nicaragua, 69, 90, 191, 245, 277
Nicholas I, Tsar, 202
Nicholas II, Tsar, 23, 204
Nixon, Richard, 55, 62, 215, 265
Nkrumah, Kwame, 191, 192
*Nomenklatura*, 29–33, 272, 279, 280
  academics and, 73
  agricultural policy of, 124
  business community and, 76
  challenges to authority of, 148–
    149
  China and, 198
  colonies and, 186–88
  conservatism of, 74
  corruption and, 150, 151, 154
  dissent and, 164–66
  economic crisis and, 110–16
  economic reforms of, 136
  ethnic minorities and, 183–84
  foreign debts and, 133
  Hungarian, 141

imperialism and, 39, 42–44, 50
  military policy and, 86–87, 89–
    90, 91–92, 96
  nationalism and, 173–74
  peace theme and, 65
  population trends and, 129
  pragmatism of, 55
  psychology of, 44–48
  reform and, 201–4, 206, 207
  second economy and, 146
  Stalin and, 163
  technology transfer and, 266
  trade and, 268
  U.S. nuclear strategy and, 239
North Atlantic Treaty
    Organization, *see* NATO
Nuclear weapons, 278
  arms-control movement and, 231–
    238
  containment and, 219
  costs of, 225–26
  deterrence through, 225, 229
  military strategy and, 90–101
  NATO and, 228
  political strategy and, 65–71
  technology needed for, 264

October Revolution, 23, 170, 196
Ogarkov, Marshal N. V., 97n
Oil industry, 262–64
  *See also* Petroleum exports
Okhrana, 151
Oltmans, Willem, 79
OPEC, 132
Orthodox Christianity, 18, 172
  among ethnic minorities, 182–83
  tolerated by Stalin, 176–77
Orwell, George, 81
Ottoman Empire, 107
*Our Contemporary* (journal), 171,
  172, 177
"Overkill," 234–35
Overpopulation, 36
*Oxford English Dictionary*, 95

Pacifism, 84–85
Palestine Liberation Organization
    (PLO), 246

Palestinians, 64
Panama Canal, 109
*Party or a Mafia?, A* (Zemtsov), 154
Party politics, 247–49
Pascal, Blaise, 238
Peace theme, 65–66
"Peaceful coexistence," 132, 215
Peasants, 121–23
  influx into cities of, 125–26
  legality and, 166
  mutinies of, 167–68
  in rural collectives, 139
  in second economy, 143–44
People's Will, 22
Pershing II missile, 237
Persian Gulf, 107
Peter the Great, 20, 31, 158, 159, 204
Petroleum exports, 132–33, 186–87
Philippines, 244
Pilniak, Boris, 24
*Pioneer Truth* (journal), 171
Plutarch, 135
Poland, 33, 42, 84, 142, 160, 186, 187, 194, 200
  agriculture in, 115
  corruption in, 156
  erosion of Party authority in, 149
  foreign debts of, 134, 135
  Hungary and, 141
  Imperial Russia and, 56
  intellectual dissent and, 166–67
  martial law in, 195, 196
  trade policy of, 269
  U.S. sanctions against, 271, 272
Politbureau, 45, 55, 87, 155, 168, 201
Political attrition, 53, 246
Political crisis, 148–208
  China and, 198–99
  colonies and, 186–88
  corruption and, 149–58
  dependencies and, 188–93
  ethnic minorities and, 179–85
  foreign Communist Parties and, 193–98
  imperialism and, 178–79
  intellectual dissent and, 158–78
  possibility of reform and, 199–208

Political strategy, 60–83
  *divide et impera* policy in, 60–63
  of divisiveness, 71–78
  "general line" and, 63–65
  linguistic manipulation in, 80–83
  nuclear weapons and, 66–69
  peace theme in, 65–66
  "rules of the game" in, 69–71
  U.S. response to, 246–59
Ponomarev, Boris, 106
Population trends, 128–31
Portugal, 127, 190, 253
Pragmatism, 54, 55
  of business executives, 76–77
*Pravda,* 272
Presidium, 58
Proletariat, 64
Productivity, 112–13, 117
  agricultural, 125, 139
  industrial, 145
  in Third World, 190
*Protocols of the Elders of Zion,* 173
Proxy warfare, 243–45
Pullman-Swindell Company, 262
Purges, 30
  population loss in, 130

Qaddafi, Muammar, 272

Radio Liberty, 127
Rand Corporation, 187*n*
RCA, 260
Reagan, Ronald, 68, 70, 78, 90, 216, 223, 234, 265, 276
  military expenditures under, 117
  nuclear weapons and, 238–39, 241, 243
Red Army, 27, 91, 212, 264
  in Afghanistan, 243, 245
  anti-Semitism and, 173
  colonies and, 186, 187
  economic policy and, 36–37
  Grand Strategy and, 57
  peasant rebellions suppressed by, 123
Republican Party, 220
"Revolutionary situations," 199–200, 202, 205
Rio Treaty, 248
Roman jurisprudence, 166

Rome, Treaty of, 255
Roosevelt, Franklin Delano, 54, 55, 213, 267
Ross, Alan, 77
Rumania, 186
Russian Revolution, 23–26, 28, 34, 36
  expropriation of landed estates in, 121
  nationalistic view of, 171, 173–75
  *See also* October Revolution
Russification, 180–82
Russophile movement, 169–70

Sakharov, Andrei, 58, 69, 118, 165
  Solzhenitsyn criticized by, 176–177
Sakharov, A. N., 171
SALT, 233–38
Sanctions, 264–73
Sandinistas, 191–92
Schell, Jonathan, 232
Schwarz, Urs, 68–69
SEATO, 248
Second economy, 126, 128n, 142–146
  reform and, 206
Secretariat, Soviet, 30
Seeley, John, 56
Senate Foreign Relations Committee, 70–71, 222
*Shabashniki*, 146
Shcharanskii, Anatolii, 161
Shchekino Chemical Combine, 138
Shiite Muslims, 183
Shultz, George, 222
Siberian pipeline, 186, 262, 271, 272–73
Simis, Konstantin, 157
Siniavskii, Andrei, 164
Social Darwinism, 84
Social Democratic Party, German, 62, 67
Social Democrats, 22, 121, 195
  antinationalism of, 170
Social indicators, 77
Socialism:
  "in one country," 24, 27, 36
  origins of, 21

  *See also* Marxism; Marxism-Leninism
Sokolovskii, Marshal V. D., 94–95
Solidarity, 33, 80, 156, 160
  intellectual dissent and, 167
  suppression of, 195, 269
Solzhenitsyn, Alexander, 21, 174–177
Somalia, 108
Sophists, 95
South Africa, 70
  mineral production of, 108
  Mozambique and, 190
  sanctions against, 271–72
South Yemen, 90, 106, 192–93
Southeast Asia, 103
  *See also* Vietnam
Soviet Academy of Sciences, 151
*Soviet Viewpoint, The* (Arbatov), 79
Spain, 56, 194
  Communist Party of, 196, 198n
Sparta, 156
Special Boards, 163
SS-17, SS-18, SS-19 missiles, 71, 100
SS-20 missile, 100, 236
Stalin, Josef, 116, 165, 191, 261, 275
  anticolonial movements and, 105
  central planning under, 137
  collectivization under, 143
  colonies and, 186, 187
  economic policy of, 35–37
  exports under, 132
  forced industrialization program of, 122, 123
  foreign Communist Parties and, 194, 195
  Georgians and, 184
  Grand Strategy under, 219
  military policy under, 90–91, 96
  nationalism and, 170
  *nomenklatura* and, 29–30, 150
  nonaggression pact with Hitler, 55, 63, 107–8, 184, 194
  official language introduced by, 81–83
  persecution of intelligentsia by, 163
  religion tolerated by, 177

during World War II, 213–14
Yalta accords and, 55
Stalinism, 44, 205
  economic crisis and, 111, 140
  nostalgia for, 201–2
  technology transfer and, 266
START, 228, 234, 236
*Start* (journal), 198n
*State and Revolution* (Lenin), 25
State Department, U.S., 92, 265,
  273–77
Standard of living, *see* Living
  standards
Stanic, Janez, 198n
Steel industry, 260, 263
Stoic philosophy, 166
Strategic Rocket Forces, 98, 99, 239
*Strategy in the Missile Age* (Brodie),
  95
Strauss, Franz Josef, 255
Strikes, 167–68
Subsidiary farming, 145
Sukarno, 191, 192
Sun Tzu, 209, 219
Sunni Muslims, 183
Supreme Council of National
  Economy, 34
Sushko, General Major N. Ia., 97n
Suslov, Mikhail, 151
Sutton, Antony, 259–60
Sweden, 20, 265
  Baltic possessions of, 56
Swiss Creditanstalt, 134
Switzerland, 265
Syria, 90, 108, 277

Tajiks, 183
Tatar kingdoms, 179–80
Tatu, Michel, 259
Taylor, A. J. P., 73–74
Technology, transfer of, 259–67
  embargo on, 272
Terrorism, 62, 244, 246
Third World strategy, 102–9
  in Central America, 109
  costs of, 187n
  in Middle East, 108, 109
  of "National Democracy," 106–7
  political crisis and, 188–93
  proxy wars in, 243, 244

in Southeast Asia, 109
in sub-Saharan Africa, 108
Tiushkevich, Colonel S. A., 97n
Tocqueville, Alexis de, 210
Togliatti automobile plant, 262
Trade, 75–76, 259–63, 267–70
  constraints on, 270–73
  foreign debts and, 132–33, 261
Trade unions:
  American, 75
  Communist, in Western Europe,
    62
Trident submarine, 100, 226
Trinidad and Tobago, 76
Trotsky, Leon, 24, 25, 30, 64, 104,
  170
  Allies and, 212
  letter to Central Committee, 57–
    58
Tukhachevskii, Marshal Mikhail
  Nikolaevich, 36
Turgenev, Ivan, 92
Turkey, 20, 63, 184, 253
  Britain and, 211
  Imperial Russia and, 211
  terrorism in, 244

Ukraine, 54, 183
  peasantry of, 122, 123
Unidentified Flying Objects, 231
United Nations, 250
  General Assembly of, 54
  Human Rights Charter, 164
United States, 46, 50, 68, 109, 113,
  205
  agriculture in, 125
  anti-anti-Communism in, 77–78
  arms control and, 233–38
  Britain and, 55–56, 64
  containment policy of, 214–15,
    218–20
  defense allocations in, 225–26
  defense commitments of, 103–4
  détente with, *see* Détente
  ethnic minorities in, 182
  evasion of analysis in foreign
    policy of, 210–11
  forces for accommodation in, 74–
    76
  foreign aid expenditures of, 189

United States (*cont.*)
  Grand Strategy and, 52, 53
  hate campaigns against, 70
  history of relations with Soviet
    Union, 211–18
  Jewish émigrés and, 62
  mineral production in, 108
  NATO and, 90, 248–59
  "nuclear freeze" rejected by, 71
  nuclear strategy of, 92–102, 228,
    239–43
  party politics in, 247
  per capita consumption in, 127
  proxy wars and, 243–45
  *rapprochement* with China, 82
  responsibility for foreign policy
    of, 273–77
  sanctions imposed by, 270–72
  strategic opportunities for, 222–
    224
  technology acquired from, 260–
    261, 264–65
  trade with, 75–76
  in World War II, 89
  Yalta accords with, 54–55
U.S. Chamber of Commerce, 75
U.S. Steel Corporation, 260
Urbanization, 126
  birth rates and, 130
Ustinov, Marshal Dmitri
  Fedorovich, 89
Uzbek Republic, 139

Vedas, 230
Vietnam, 90, 109, 250
  armed forces of, 244
  French in, 182
  Soviet assistance to, 215
  U.S. involvement in, 219, 220
Voroshilov, K. E., 88
Voslensky, Michael S., 31

*Wall Street Journal*, 187*n*
War Communism, 34
War of political attrition, 53
War scares, 202
Warsaw Pact, 186, 220, 225, 228,
  254, 261, 271
Watson, John B., 217

Weizsäcker, Carl–Friedrich von, 67–
  68
West Bank, 70
West Germany, 194
  American troops in, 244
  business contracts with, 61–62
  Communist Party of, 197
  détente with, 220
  journalists in, 78
  NATO and, 252–56
  neo-Nazis in, 173
  party politics in, 247
  peaceful coexistence and, 215
  per capita consumption in, 127
  technology acquired from, 265
  trade with, 262*n*
  workers in, 64
Westphalia, Treaty of, 218
White Armies, 170
Wilde, Oscar, 102
Wilhelm II, 249*n*
Witte, Serge, 56
Wolf, Charles, Jr., 187*n*
Wolfers, Arnold, 92, 94
*World Communist Movement, The:*
  *Outline of Strategy and Tactics*
  (Zagladin), 59
World Jewish Congress, 275*n*
World War I, 34, 56, 110, 114, 211,
  212, 256
World War II, 64, 88, 110, 202, 241,
  256, 261, 266
  Allied strategy in, 228, 243
  population loss in, 130
  U.S.–Soviet relations during,
    213

Yalta accords, 54–55, 188, 213
Yamal Pipeline, 263
Yemen, People's Republic of, *see*
  South Yemen
*Young Guard* (journal), 171, 177
Yugoslavia, 33, 186

Zagladin, V. V., 58, 103
Zemtsov, Ilia, 154
Zephaniah (prophet), 230
Zionists, 210
*Zveno* (rural cooperatives), 138–39